ORACLE®   *Oracle Press*™

Oracle Database Cloud Cookbook with Oracle Enterprise Manager Cloud Control 13c

About the Author

Porus Homi Havewala works as the Strategic Program Advisor in the Enterprise Architecture office (ASEAN) at Oracle Corporation Singapore and is a regional Subject Matter Expert (SME) on Oracle Enterprise Manager Technology, specifically concentrating on private database cloud capabilities on Oracle systems. He is a double Oracle Certified Master (OCM) in 10*g* and 11*g*, as well as the first Oracle employee ACE in Singapore. He was awarded the prestigious Oracle ACE Director title in 2008. There are less than 200 Oracle ACE Directors in the entire world and Porus was the very first Oracle ACE and ACE Director in Singapore—recognition of his outstanding achievements in the Oracle world.

Porus has had extensive experience in Oracle technology since 1994; this includes work as a Senior Production DBA, Principal Database Consultant, Database Architect, E-Business Technical DBA, Development DBA, and Database Designer and Modeler (using Oracle Designer). He has published 13 technical articles and 3 white papers on Oracle Enterprise Manager on OTN, and his work has been featured on the most popular OTN article list. The OTN is the world's largest community of developers, DBAs, and architects.

Porus created http://enterprise-manager.blogspot.com, one of the world's first blogs dedicated to Enterprise Manager. He is also the creator and manager of the Oracle Senior DBA group on LinkedIn.com, with more than 58,000 members.

Porus is the sole author of the 2010 book *Oracle Enterprise Manager Grid Control* (Rampant TechPress). He is also the sole author of the 2012 book *Oracle Enterprise Manager Cloud Control 12c: Managing Data Center Chaos* (PACKT Publishing).

He started in the IT industry in the mid-1980s as a Turbo-C programmer in India and then as a dBase/FoxPro Developer in Australia. In 1994 he wrote a book on Microsoft FoxPro 2.5/2.6, which was his first published technical work, from Wordware Publishing. He entered the heady world of Oracle technology in 1994 as an Oracle DBA/developer (using Oracle Forms, Oracle Reports, and Oracle Designer) in multiple-client companies.

In the largest telecommunications company in Australia, Porus was the Senior Database Consultant in the central DBA team for a number of years and was responsible for database standards, database architecture, and the architecture, setup, and management of the first production Enterprise Manager Grid Control 10*g* site in the world. He next worked in Oracle

Advanced Customer Services (ACS) India (Mumbai), and then with an Oracle Platinum Partner, S&I Systems in Singapore, before rejoining Oracle Corporation in the same city.

Porus is an enthusiast for Oracle technology, especially Oracle Enterprise Manager, on which he has conducted popular seminars and webinars for large multinational corporations, and has implemented this powerful enterprise toolset. Because Enterprise Manager is the backbone of the Oracle Database Cloud, it was a natural progression for him to work on and write on the myriad Database as a Service capabilities of Oracle technology. He enjoys the power of Oracle technology.

About the Technical Editors

Richard Ridge has more than 15 years of experience in the IT industry, including working in both Australia and the United Kingdom, predominantly for global financial, telecommunications and retail companies. His technical background is as a Senior DBA with specialist knowledge of SQL Server and Oracle software and management of DB2 platforms. Richard's management experience includes running large multifunctional teams (20–30 staff) with a combination of onshore and offshore resources. He and Porus worked together in the early 2000s.

Kamran Aghayev A. is an Oracle ACE Director and Oracle Certified Master DBA with seven years of experience managing UNIX-based Oracle Databases. Currently he is working at AzerCell Telecom as an Expert DBA and also serves as a lecturer teaching Oracle Database Administration at Qafqaz University.

Kamran is an author of the book *Oracle Backup & Recovery: Expert Secrets for Using RMAN and Data Pump* and also publishes a popular blog at http://kamranagayev.com.

He has also presented at Oracle Open World conference twice (2010/2011) at San Francisco, Thailand Oracle User Group (OUGTH), and Turkish Oracle User Group (TROUG) events.

ORACLE®

Oracle Press™

Oracle Database Cloud Cookbook with Oracle Enterprise Manager Cloud Control 13c

Porus Homi Havewala

New York   Chicago   San Francisco
Athens   London   Madrid   Mexico City
Milan   New Delhi   Singapore   Sydney   Toronto

Cataloging-in-Publication Data is on file with the Library of Congress

McGraw-Hill Education books are available at special quantity discounts to use as premiums and sales promotions, or for use in corporate training programs. To contact a representative, please visit the Contact Us pages at www.mhprofessional.com.

Oracle Database Cloud Cookbook with Oracle Enterprise Manager Cloud Control 13c

1 2 3 4 5 6 7 8 9   DOC   21 20 19 18 17 16

ISBN   978-0-07-183353-0
MHID   0-07-183353-6

Sponsoring Editor	**Copy Editor**	**Composition**
Wendy Rinaldi	Lisa Theobald	Cenveo Publisher Services
Editorial Supervisor	**Proofreader**	**Illustration**
Janet Walden	Claire Splan	Cenveo Publisher Services
Project Manager	**Indexer**	**Art Director, Cover**
Rinki Kaur,	Claire Splan	Jeff Weeks
Cenveo® Publisher Services	**Production Supervisor**	
Technical Editors	Pamela Pelton	
Richard Ridge and		
Kamran Aghayev A.		

At the start, I would like to dedicate this book to Lord Shri Ganesha, the lovable elephant-headed deity of my motherland India where I was born. Shri Ganesha is the Lord of Beginnings (every start is dedicated to Him) and the remover of obstacles.

I dedicate this book to my dear departed father, Homi Maneckji Havewala, who was a great unpublished writer of the English language and who imparted his love of English, as well as all things spiritual, to me as his only son. I dedicate this book to my dear departed mother, Gospi Homi Havewala, who was a most loving and dedicated mother, and who has now joined her lifelong husband in heaven. May they be together in the seventh and highest heaven Garothman Behest forever and ever, in the company of Dadar Ahura Mazda (the name of God in the Zoroastrian faith). I pray for the blessings of my beloved parents on this work of mine; may it be a success.

I dedicate this book to the mighty spiritual mountain Demavand Koh that stands majestically in the ancient land of Iran. The great mountain is the spiritual storehouse of our Zoroastrian religion and has protected our religion and people for thousands of years, inspiring us continually. The mountain touches the heavens in an amazing manner, as can be seen here, and as such is the ideal first image for a cloud-based book. I pray for Demavand Koh's blessings on this work of mine; may it be a success.

Contents at a Glance

Contents

Acknowledgments

First and foremost, and most importantly, I would like to thank Havovi, my beloved wife, who has helped and supported me throughout the writing of this book. The book was possible because of her support.

I would like to thank my ex-manager, David Russell, who lives and works in Australia. I was the Lead Database Architect for Enterprise Manager under his corporate Database Technologies team for many years, and it is there that I started working with Enterprise Manager Grid Control 10g. Our company, Telstra, was the first production site for this version of Enterprise Manager, and we never looked back.

I would like to thank my technical reviewers, Richard Ridge and Kamran Aghayev, for agreeing to review the chapters of the book. Richard is my former colleague at Telstra, and Kamran is a fellow Oracle ACE Director (although I had to give up the title when I joined Oracle). Both are great chaps.

I would like to thank all the editorial staff at Oracle Press, especially Wendy, Janet, Paul, Amanda, and Rinki from Cenveo for helping out with the publication and editing of this book through all the versions and chapters. They have been most kind, polite, and considerate, and the most respectful and patient editors I have ever seen.

I would like to thank my readers who have made my Enterprise Manager articles on the Oracle Technical Network popular over the years, and who have consistently liked reading my books. I write for my readers.

Of course, the views and opinions expressed in this book are entirely my own and do not represent the views and position of Oracle Corporation.

Introduction

I would like to extend a warm welcome to my readers, once again. Thank you all for choosing to read what I write. I normally write in easy-to-understand English, unlike many technical documents and even the official documentation from Oracle.

This is my third book on Oracle's fantastic enterprise management product, Oracle Enterprise Manager, and it concentrates on the Oracle Private Database Cloud.

In this new book, *Oracle Database Cloud Cookbook with Oracle Enterprise Manager Cloud Control 13c,* I provide a solid introduction to creating and managing an on-premise private database cloud computing infrastructure built around the Oracle Database (11*g* and 12*c*), and the latest 13*c* version of Oracle Enterprise Manager Cloud Control.

You will learn about Enterprise Manager's Consolidation Planner and its use in the initial planning of your cloud infrastructure. I will demonstrate how to create and configure diverse Oracle technology-based cloud services such as Database as a Service (DBaaS), Schema as a Service (SCHaaS), and Pluggable Database as a Service (PDBaaS). We will also look at Snap Clone databases and will start using the CloneDB technology on dNFS to create snap clones of your own. You will learn how to build and manage all these different clouds using Oracle Enterprise Manager Cloud Control. And then we will look at using the RESTful API to access the cloud services—to query, request to create, monitor the creation, and request to destroy each of these.

As part of configuring these varied cloud types, you will learn how to set up self-service provisioning—how to let your clients do your work for you. We will closely examine the topics of metering and chargeback. These feature sets are critical to cloud computing because they enable you to allocate costs properly to your cloud clients, and IT suddenly becomes more valuable.

We will also look at setting up hybrid cloud agents, so that an on-premise Enterprise Manager can monitor and manage Oracle public cloud databases, compare configurations and enforce compliance on both on-premise and the cloud, and clone full PDBs from on-premise to the cloud and vice versa.

You will learn about setting up and managing Oracle RMAN database backups with Enterprise Manager, and setting up and managing Oracle Data Guard database standbys. Controlling and managing these essential DBA activities from Enterprise Manager is essential in cloud-based environments. Some of this work can be done by self-service users, but some still needs to be done by the cloud administrators (DBAs responsible for the private database cloud).

I have based the chapters of the book on an existing Enterprise Manager Cloud Control installation. If you would like to follow the same steps, install Enterprise Manager using the installation guide or download an Oracle VBOX image with Enterprise Manager preinstalled. Oracle provides these under the OTN license agreement. The download page is

www.oracle.com/technetwork/oem/enterprise-manager/downloads/oem-templates-2767917.html

JSON Files to Download

As a companion to Chapter 6 "Using the Cloud REST API," you can download the zip file 353_06_ServicesCollectionsJSON.zip, which contains a number of JSON files that can be used to create multiple collections for the services in Postman in Google Chrome.

You can download the zip file from the McGraw-Hill Professional website at www.mhprofessional.com. Simply enter the book's title or ISBN in the search box and then click the Downloads & Resources tab on the book's home page.

Further explanation for the files is provided in the section "Importing Postman Collections from JSON Files (Optional)" in Chapter 6.

CHAPTER
1

Consolidation Planning for the Cloud

A new era has dawned in computing. It is the age of self-service, when office workers can create and configure their own accounts on the Internet, enter their own service requests, and perform other computer-related activities that were once the domain of back-end specialized staff.

Similarly, project managers and development staff have also wanted self-service capabilities for provisioning servers, databases, and applications. Traditionally, this work was done by the System Administrators and the Database Administrators (DBAs)—every new server that was required by a project or a customer was provisioned manually by the System Administrators, and every new database was created and configured by the DBA team. The requesting project manager or customer was informed only after the successful completion of the task, and access to the new system was handed over at that time.

Introducing Oracle Cloud Computing

But what if the project team or the customer could go to a self-service page and request a new server or database, as per a preexisting quota that has been allocated? That would be preferable for sure. The system itself would automatically take care of the provisioning and start calculating the metering and chargeback without any human administrator intervention (except when things go wrong). The project team or customer would get the results they want in the shortest possible time, thus ensuring full quality of service.

This is the promise of the Cloud, and Oracle provides this functionality in a number of different ways, such as Infrastructure as a Service (IaaS), Database as a Service (DBaaS), Schema as a Service (SCHaaS), Pluggable Database as a Service (PDBaaS), or Middleware as a Service (MWaaS). Each of these ways represents a different type of cloud.

IaaS is the basic infrastructure cloud, whereas the other services are also called Plaftorm as a Service (PaaS) because they supply a made-to-order platform that can be used by the developer or implementor. In the case of IaaS, a pool of Oracle Virtual Machine (VM) Servers is used to provision new Guest Virtual Machines via the self-service portal. In DBaaS, a pool of Oracle Database servers with Oracle Homes preinstalled is used to provision new databases on the fly. MWaaS, on the other hand, uses WebLogic Server pools to provision Java applications via self-service.

These different types of cloud require either the Oracle Enterprise Manager Cloud Management Pack for Database or Cloud Management Pack for Fusion Middleware to be licensed. These packs, in turn, require the prerequisite license and foundation capabilities of the Database Lifecycle Management (DBLM) Pack and WebLogic Management Pack, respectively. For example, you cannot offer a database

in self-service mode without using the provisioning capabilities of the Database
Lifecycle Management Pack.

In all, Oracle technology provides the broadest range of cloud services, and
Oracle Enterprise Manager Cloud Control is used throughout the cloud lifecycle—
from planning to setup, followed by the build, testing, and deployment. When the
cloud is functional and in production, Oracle Enterprise Manager helps to monitor,
manage, and optimize the cloud, and, finally, to meter and charge the end-user
project or customer.

Consolidating to Physical Servers

Suppose that your company has decided that existing servers and databases will
be moved to a new cloud infrastructure. This infrastructure must be properly
sized according to the systems to be moved, the intended workload, and future
scale factors.

Therefore, the first phase of setting up the cloud infrastructure is consolidation
planning. One of the main goals of this phase is to identify underused servers and
include them in a host consolidation plan, thereby enabling the enterprise to free up
as many servers as possible while continuing to maintain or exceed service levels.
To achieve this, the configuration, computing capabilities, and usage of the existing
systems must be clearly understood by the IT department before they can decide on
the target systems to be used for the cloud consolidation.

To aid in such planning, Enterprise Manager Cloud Control offers the twin
capabilities of the Host Consolidation Planner and the Database Consolidation
Workbench. The latter capability is new in Enterprise Manager Cloud Control 13c.
Let's take a look at both.

Running the Host Consolidation Planner

The Host Consolidation Planner uses historical metric data (CPU, memory, and
storage) from the source servers that is stored by Enterprise Manager in the repository,
and allows you to specify the target servers, whether actual or planned, in the form of
a consolidation project with multiple scenarios.

You can identify various business and technical constraints to help guide the
consolidation process, such as a constraint that specifies that two Real Application
Cluster (RAC) instances should not be consolidated to the same target node, or that a
development database should not be placed with a production database on the same
consolidated server. The planner then performs mathematical calculations to decide
which servers are suitable for the consolidation and offers its recommendations.

To start the Host Consolidation Planner, select Enterprise | Consolidation | Host Consolidation Planner from the Cloud Control menu. Figure 1-1 shows the opening screen.

FIGURE 1-1. *Host Consolidation Planner opening screen*

We can see that there are no projects currently defined. To start a new consolidation project, click Create Project. Figure 1-2 shows the project being created.

FIGURE 1-2. *Create a new consolidation project.*

Specify the appropriate Project Name and Description.

Next, indicate the Consolidation Type from the two choices: From Physical Servers To Oracle Virtual Servers (P2V) or from Physical Servers To Physical Servers (P2P). The correct choice depends on the consolidation strategy adopted by your enterprise. In this example, select From Physical Servers To Physical Servers (P2P). This means we are planning to consolidate to actual physical target servers and not to virtual machines in this project. Click Next.

Next, click the Add Servers button (Figure 1-3) to select the servers to be involved in the consolidation. These servers are called "managed targets" in the Enterprise Manager system—that is, the Enterprise Manager Agent has been previously promoted to these servers and they are being monitored and managed in Enterprise Manager.

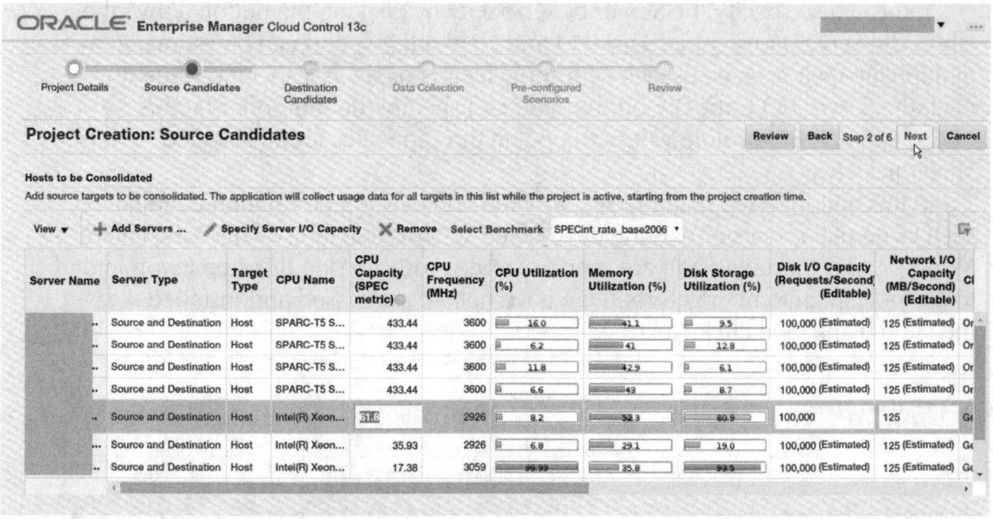

FIGURE 1-3.   *Specify the source server candidates.*

When the servers have been added, the resource and usage data for each server is displayed on the screen, such as CPU Utilization, Memory Utilization, Disk Storage Utilization, and so on. Notice that certain fields in the list are editable, such as CPU Capacity, Disk I/O Capacity, and Network I/O Capacity, so you can add your own figures as needed.

The CPU capacity is based on the SPECint, a benchmark specification for the CPU processing power. The SPECint_base_rate2006 benchmark is used by Consolidation Planner for database or application hosts, or hosts with a mixed workload. The SPECjbb2005 benchmark is used for middleware platforms.

The Consolidation Planner relies on the SPECint library from SPEC.org, which covers the majority of CPUs in the market. If a particular CPU's SPEC rate is available in the SPECint library, that rate will be used. If a particular CPU is not available in the library, the CPU specifications may not have been published by the manufacturer or a benchmark is not available for it (if it is a very old CPU or a brand new CPU). In this case, the Planner estimates the CPU's spec rate based on the CPU configuration details Enterprise Manager has collected. In this case, "(Estimated)" will be displayed in the CPU Capacity (SPEC metric) column.

In this case, it is the normal practice to use the estimated rate. However, based on your experience, or if you have compared this particular CPU to other systems and believe there is a better rate than the estimated rate, you can change the rate in the Planner.

You can also specify the Server I/O Capacity by clicking the button above the table. The Server I/O signifies Disk I/O and Network I/O, and can be estimated by multiplying their average usages with some factors or set as a specific value. If you click the Server I/O Capacity button, you can specify the multiplier factors (defaulted to 3) or absolute values to update the capacities for all selected servers. Then click Next.

In this optional step (Figure 1-4), you can add existing destination candidates such as normal servers or existing engineered systems that already have the Enterprise Manager Agent installed and are seen as targets. You can skip this step if you intend to use new (phantom) targets that you have not yet purchased and installed. Leave the table blank, and click Next.

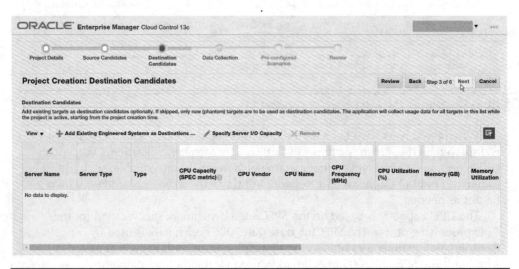

FIGURE 1-4. *Specify the destination candidates.*

At this point you can specify the minimum and maximum days for data collection for all the targets, as shown in Figure 1-5. The defaults are 21 and 90 days, respectively. If you specify 0 for the minimum days, the collection results will be available immediately (for fast results, such as during a test); otherwise, Enterprise Manager will wait until it has collected data for the specified minimum days before making it available.

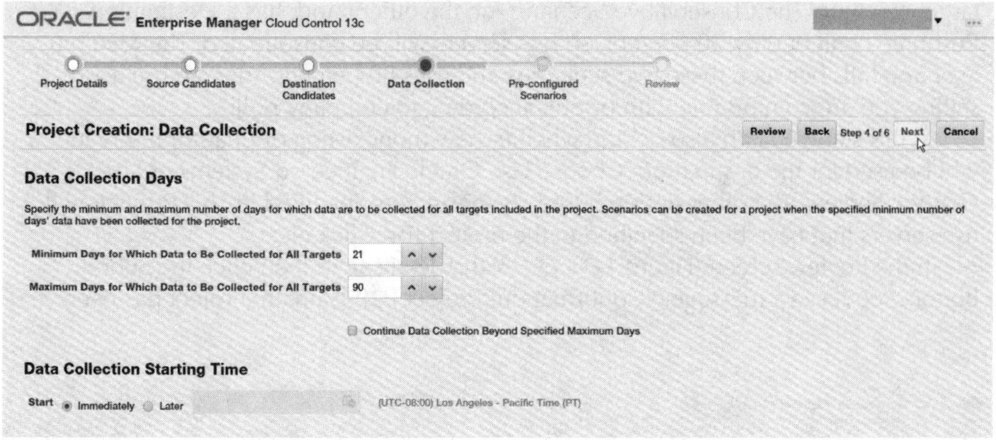

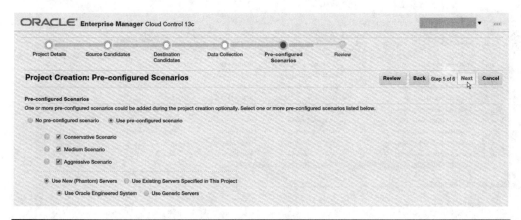

FIGURE 1-5.   *Data collection days details*

To test data collection, change the minimum days to 0. Specify the Data Collection Starting Time as Immediately, or use a later date and time. Then click Next.

Three preconfigured scenarios, Conservative, Medium, or Aggressive, are available for selection (Figure 1-6), or later on in the process you can use your own custom scenario.

FIGURE 1-6.   *Addition of Preconfigured scenarios*

In the Aggressive Scenario, the Destination Resource Limit can be as high as 90 percent, which means that more servers will be consolidated on to the target machine. The Conservative Scenario, on the other hand, has a Destination Resource Limit of only 70 percent, so less servers will be consolidated. The Medium Scenario falls between these two scenarios and uses 80 percent. You can use a setting you are comfortable with or one according to company policy.

At this step you can also decide whether new (nonexisting or phantom) servers will be used for the destination: Choose Use Oracle Engineered Systems or Use Generic Servers. The other option, Use Existing Servers Specified In This Project, will use servers that have been specified in the project list. Click Next.

In the Review screen (Figure 1-7), check the details, and then click the Submit button. You'll see a message: "Confirmation: Project P2P_Sainath_Project has been

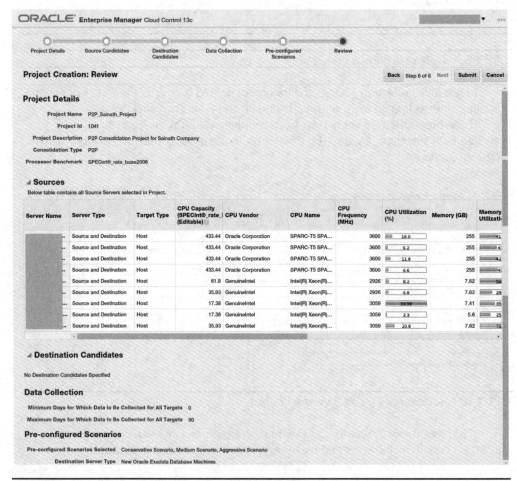

FIGURE 1-7. *Review the project before submitting.*

defined successfully. An EM job has been submitted to perform further operations. Refresh console to view the detailed results." Click the Refresh button.

The Status column on the Host Consolidation Planner screen initially displays the status of Scheduled. Keep refreshing the screen until the status changes to Collecting Over Minimum (Figure 1-8). In the General tab, the Data Collection status is shown: Data Collection Task In Progress.

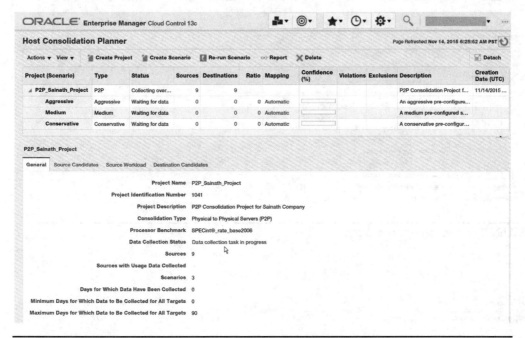

FIGURE 1-8. *Project status*

As shown in Figure 1-9, the job completes within a couple of minutes, because 0 days were specified (for test purposes) as the minimum number of days for collection. The data collection status now shows Collecting Data, Required Minimum Days Reached. The Status column for the three preconfigured scenarios displays Analysis Completed.

You can examine the project details on the General tab, and then move to the Source Candidates tab (Figure 1-10), which displays the Source Servers that were selected; the CPU SPEC metric that was used; CPU, Memory, and Disk Storage Utilization; and other resource and usage details that were collected for these servers.

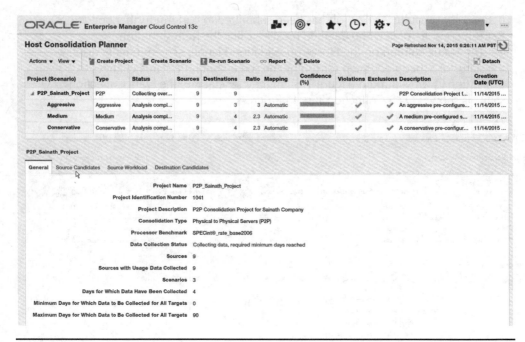

FIGURE 1-9.   *Analysis completed*

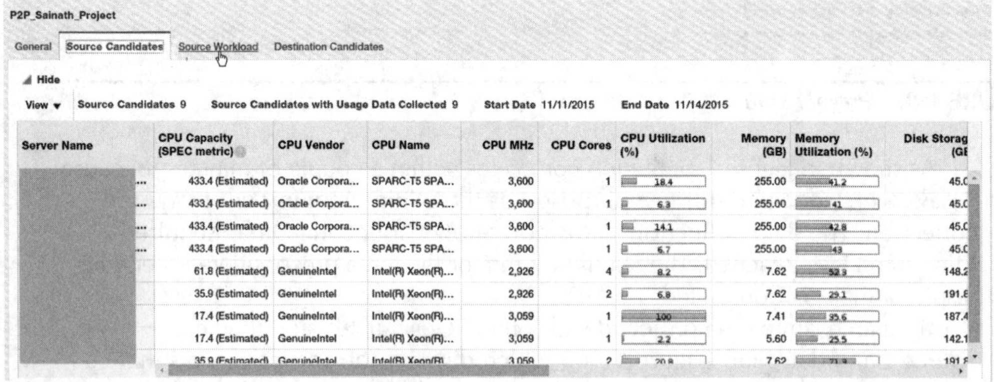

FIGURE 1-10.   *Source Candidates tab*

Move to the Source Workload tab, shown in Figure 1-11.

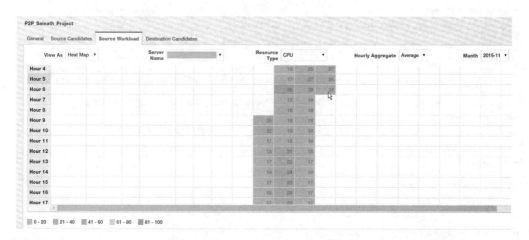

FIGURE 1-11. *Source Workload heat map with color coding*

This tab shows a graphical representation of the resource workload for each of the source candidates, mapped against days and hours. This is known as a heat map. By default, the resource type used is CPU. Color coding (explained at the bottom of Figure 1-11) is used to show at a glance which servers are heavily used. For example, the colors either show under-utilization (0–20 and 21–40 percent), higher utilization (41–60 and 61–80 percent), or the highest utilization (81–100 percent).

From the Server Name drop-down box, you can select a particular source server in your project list and examine the associated resource workload. The different Resource Types you can select from the drop-down menu are CPU, Memory, Disk Storage, and Network I/O Volume. The chart display changes accordingly. In Figure 1-11, you see the CPU resource type workload for this particular server displayed in the chart.

Now click the Aggressive preconfigured scenario row; this displays the scenario details shown in Figure 1-12.

The goal is to consolidate to the fewest destination servers. You can also see that in the preconfigured Aggressive scenario, an Exadata X5-2 full rack is used by default. Click the link for the Destination Server Type to see the full rack configuration details, shown in Figure 1-13.

There are eight compute nodes in this machine, and the configuration of one compute node is displayed. Click the OK button to continue. We are not interested in a full rack, so we will not explore this scenario further. We need to see if we can consolidate the source servers onto a smaller quarter rack or eighth rack. For that purpose, we need to create a custom scenario.

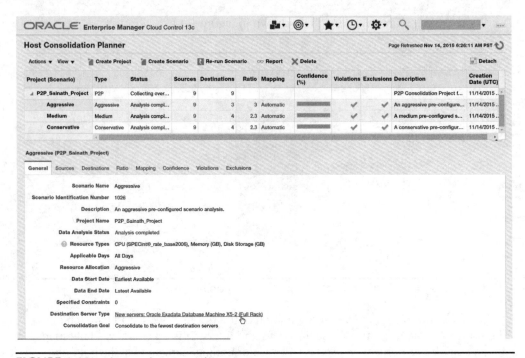

FIGURE 1-12. *Aggressive scenario*

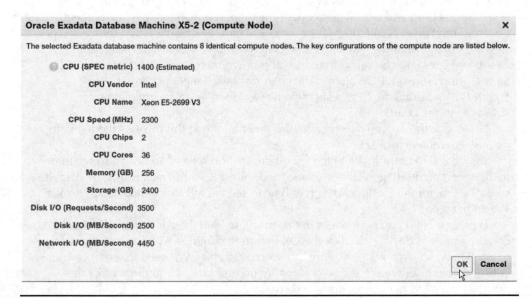

FIGURE 1-13. *Exadata full rack configuration*

Creating a Custom Consolidation Scenario for P2P

Using scenarios, you can explore different possibilities for the consolidation project. You can create separate scenarios that act like "what-if" situations to help you select the scenario that best suits your consolidation goals.

Select the existing project, and then click Create Scenario. Figure 1-14 shows the Create Scenario screen.

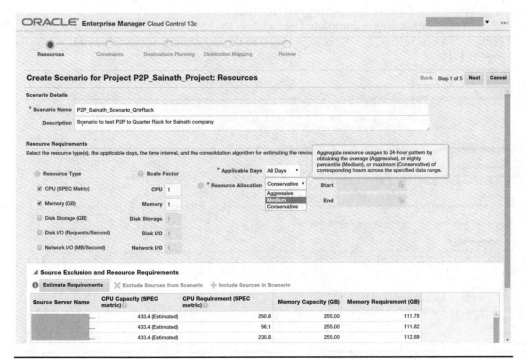

FIGURE 1-14.   *Entering details for a new scenario*

Let's look at an Exadata Quarter Rack scenario; name the scenario appropriately. To estimate the resource requirements, from the Resource Type list, select CPU and Memory. In the Scale Factor column, you can increase the scale factors for the resources you have chosen to accommodate expected future growth in the systems you are consolidating. Oracle will scale up the resource requirements according to what you specify.

Keep the Applicable Days set to the default value, which is All Days (other options are Weekdays or Weekends).

The consolidation algorithm is decided by the Resource Allocation that you select. If you select Conservative, the resource usage will be aggregated to a 24-hour pattern by gathering the maximum number of corresponding hours in the data range that has been specified. If you select Aggressive, an average number of corresponding hours is used; 80 percent is used if Medium is selected. The maximum number, average number, or 80 percent of the hours therefore decides how the consolidation algorithm is calculated.

You can also specify Start and End dates for the data that will be used for the estimation of the resource requirements, or you can leave this information blank.

Next, click the Estimate Requirements button to view the updated resource requirements, based on the options you selected.

After the estimation is completed, the details for each server are displayed at the bottom of the screen. Click Next to proceed to the Constraints screen shown in Figure 1-15.

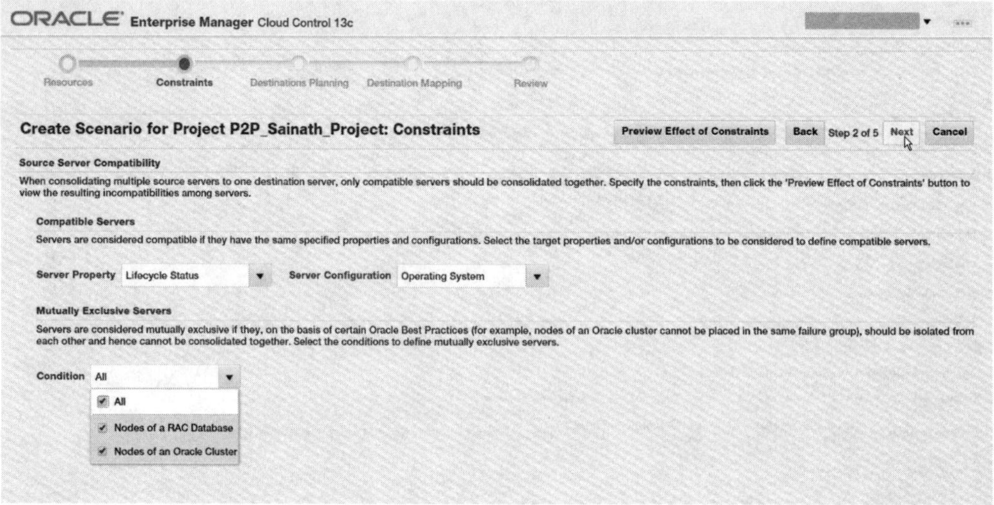

FIGURE 1-15. *Constraints for the scenario*

On this screen, you define the constraints that will control the consolidation of multiple source servers to one destination server. At this stage, you can decide that only compatible servers should be consolidated together.

Compatible servers can be defined as having the same server property or the same server configuration. For example, for Server Property, you can select Lifecycle Status, Department, or Location. You can also select a Server Configuration, such as System Vendor, System Configuration, CPU Vendor, CPU Name, Operating System, or Network Domain.

In this case, specify Lifecycle Status as the Server Property, and Operating System as the Server Configuration. With these selections, development servers will be consolidated separately from test or production servers, and Linux or Windows servers will also be consolidated separately.

In the Condition field, you can also define Mutually Exclusive Servers that should not be consolidated together, such as the Nodes of a RAC Database or the Nodes of an Oracle Cluster. These settings are according to Oracle best practices.

If you select any of the constraints on this screen, the Preview Effect Of Constraints button is activated and you can click it to view a list of incompatible servers. The reason for the incompatibility will also be shown.

Click Next to proceed. Figure 1-16 shows the Destinations Planning screen.

FIGURE 1-16.   *Destinations Planning screen*

For the nine selected source candidates, the Minimum Required CPU (SPEC Metric) rate is displayed as 517, and the Minimum Required Memory is 449GB.

In the Maximum Allowed Resource Utilization Destination Servers section, specify the CPU (%) as 75 and Memory (%) as 90. This means the consolidation will not allow any more servers to be included on the destination machine if the calculated resource utilization goes beyond these limits on that machine.

As the Destination Candidates, select Use New (Phantom) Servers. Select the Oracle Exadata Database Machine X5-2 with a quarter rack configuration from the Configuration list shown in Figure 1-17.

If required, Exalogic machine configurations are also available if you had selected Oracle Exalogic Elastic Cloud System as the Server Type.

Click Next to open the Destination Mapping screen (Figure 1-18).

Search and Select Exadata Database Machine Configuration ✕

◢ Search   Advanced

CPU Chips

CPU Cores

                                          Search   Reset

Configuration ▲ ▼	System Vendor
Oracle Exadata Database Machine X3-8	Oracle
Oracle Exadata Database Machine X4-2 (Eighth Rack)	Oracle
Oracle Exadata Database Machine X4-2 (Quarter Rack)	Oracle
Oracle Exadata Database Machine X4-2 (Half Rack)	Oracle
Oracle Exadata Database Machine X4-2 (Full Rack)	Oracle
Oracle Exadata Database Machine X4-8	Oracle
Oracle Exadata Database Machine X5-2 (Eighth Rack)	Oracle
Oracle Exadata Database Machine X5-2 (Quarter Rack)	Oracle
Oracle Exadata Database Machine X5-2 (Half Rack)	Oracle
Oracle Exadata Database Machine X2-2 (Half Rack)	Oracle

                                          OK   Cancel

FIGURE 1-17. *Exadata configuration choices*

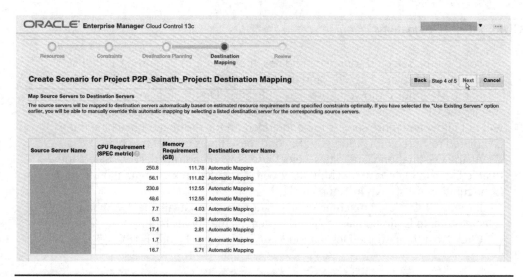

ORACLE Enterprise Manager Cloud Control 13c   ▼ •••

○——————○——————○——————●——————○
Resources   Constraints   Destinations Planning   Destination   Review
                                          Mapping

Create Scenario for Project P2P_Sainath_Project: Destination Mapping   Back Step 4 of 5 Next Cancel

Map Source Servers to Destination Servers

The source servers will be mapped to destination servers automatically based on estimated resource requirements and specified constraints optimally. If you have selected the "Use Existing Servers" option earlier, you will be able to manually override this automatic mapping by selecting a listed destination server for the corresponding source servers.

Source Server Name	CPU Requirement (SPEC metric)	Memory Requirement (GB)	Destination Server Name
	250.8	111.78	Automatic Mapping
	56.1	111.82	Automatic Mapping
	230.8	112.55	Automatic Mapping
	48.6	112.55	Automatic Mapping
	7.7	4.03	Automatic Mapping
	6.3	2.28	Automatic Mapping
	17.4	2.81	Automatic Mapping
	1.7	1.81	Automatic Mapping
	16.7	5.71	Automatic Mapping

FIGURE 1-18. *Destination Mapping screen*

On this screen, source servers are mapped to destination servers automatically. If existing servers were selected for the destination, you can override the destination server for each source server.

In this case, since we have selected a phantom Exadata database machine as the destination, no override is possible. Click Next to continue.

The Review screen for the scenario creation is displayed, as shown in Figure 1-19. You can save the scenario as a template so that it can be used again. Verify the details and click Submit.

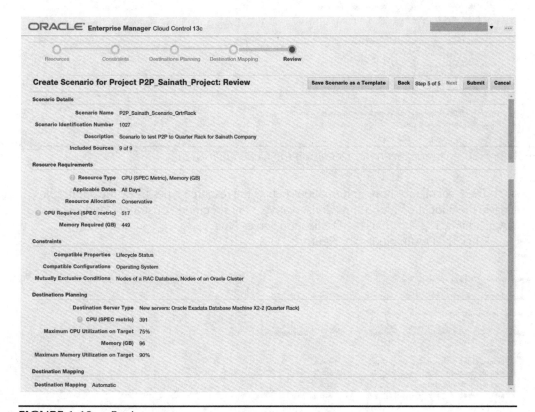

FIGURE 1-19.   *Review screen*

An Enterprise Manager job is submitted to perform further analysis. On the Consolidation Planner console, the status for the newly created custom scenario shows Analysis In Progress. Keep refreshing the console. In a few minutes, the status changes to Analysis Completed. The Confidence is shown as 100 percent.

Reviewing Scenario Analysis Results

Select the customized scenario to display the details in the lower half of the screen. A number of tabs are displayed, as shown in Figure 1-20.

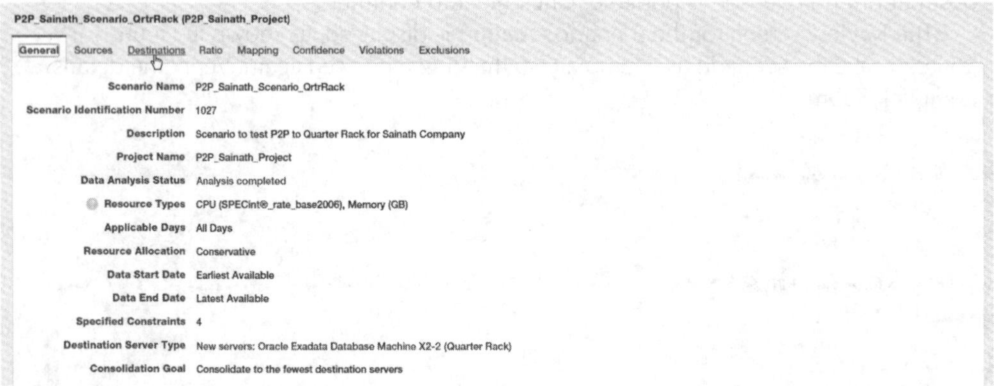

FIGURE 1-20. *Custom Scenario Details on the General tab*

The General tab shows information such as the resource types used, the applicable days, the allocation algorithm (Conservative), any specified constraints, and so on. A quarter rack is shown as the Destination Server Type.

Click the Destinations tab (Figure 1-21).

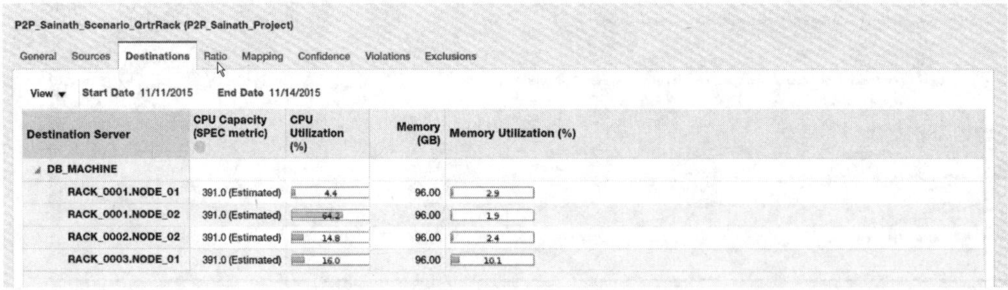

FIGURE 1-21. *Destinations tab*

In this tab, you see that the Destination Server is the phantom Exadata Database machine with four rack nodes (since it is a quarter rack). The CPU Capacity (SPEC Metric) rate is shown as 391.0 (Estimated) for each node. The CPU and memory utilizations that would result after the consolidation on the two nodes are also shown.

You can see that the one of the rack nodes would reach 64.2 percent of CPU utilization, which is more than the other nodes. Click the Ratio tab, displayed in Figure 1-22, to see that the Consolidation Ratio of Source servers to the Target servers is calculated as 1.3. This is because only five source servers have been consolidated to the four rack nodes of the database machine.

FIGURE 1-22. *Consolidation ratio*

Click the Mapping tab, shown in Figure 1-23.

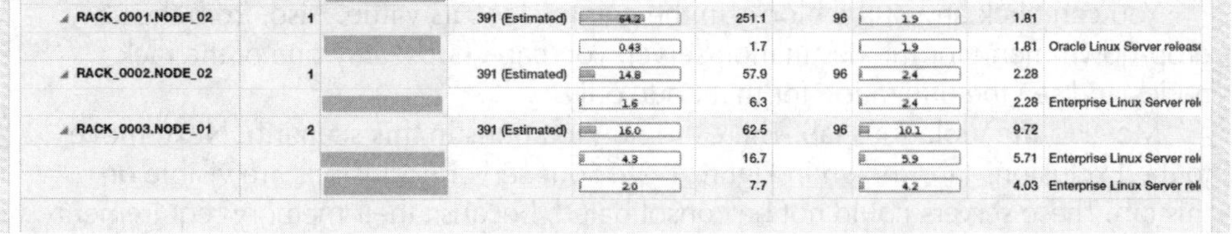

FIGURE 1-23. *Mapping tab*

On this tab, the destination and source servers are shown together along with their SPEC metric rates and the resource utilizations. This helps you get an idea of how the CPU and memory utilizations of the destination servers have been calculated. The Destination Mapping shows Automatic.

Click the Confidence tab shown in Figure 1-24. On this tab, the Confidence is 100 percent. Out of the data collected from the source servers, 199 total data points were evaluated and all of them met the requirements.

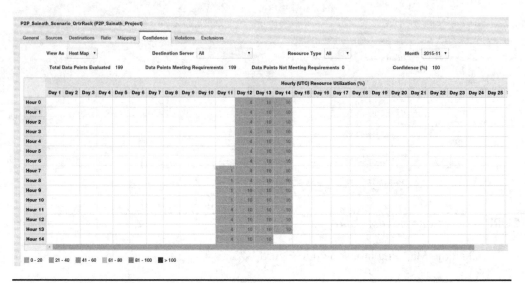

FIGURE 1-24. *Confidence tab*

The heat map graph on the Confidence tab shows the Hourly Resource Utilization of all resources (including CPU and Memory) for all destination servers; it is color-coded to show the hours and days when there is maximum and least resource utilization. In this particular scenario, shown in Figure 1-24, blue-colored blocks show 0–20 percent utilization on certain days and hours. This seems fine.

You can click any of the blocks in the graph to see its value. Also, from the drop-down menu for the destination server, you can choose any one of the rack nodes and see the utilization for that node only.

Move to the Violations tab. There are no Violations in this scenario. Next, move to the Exclusions tab, shown in Figure 1-25. Four server exclusions are visible on this tab. These servers could not be consolidated, because their memory requirement at a certain hour was higher than what was available. We obviously require a more powerful Exadata machine.

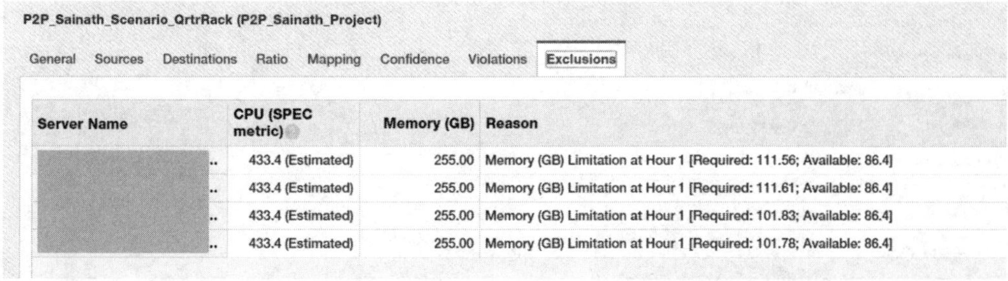

FIGURE 1-25. *Exclusions tab*

Go back to the Create Scenario screen (shown in Figure 1-14) and create a new "what-if" scenario. In this case, select X5-2 (Eighth Rack), a more powerful machine. Also remove the constraints. Figure 1-26 shows the completed scenario analysis.

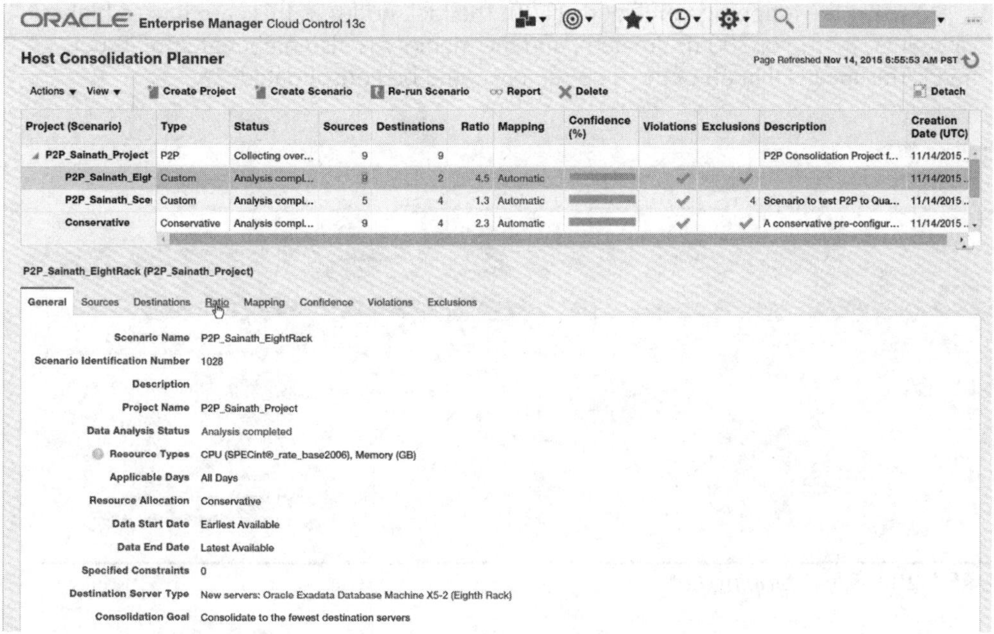

FIGURE 1-26. *The new custom scenario for an eighth rack*

Click the Ratio tab, and you'll see that all nine servers have been consolidated on the two nodes, three servers on the first node, and six servers on the second node (Figure 1-27).

P2P_Sainath_EightRack (P2P_Sainath_Project)

General   Sources   Destinations   **Ratio**   Mapping   Confidence   Violations   Exclusions

View ▼   Servers to be Consolidated 9   Target Servers 2   Consolidation Ratio 4.5

Destination Server	Source Servers	Source Server
◢ RACK_0001.NODE_01	3	
◢ RACK_0001.NODE_02	6	

FIGURE 1-27.   *The Ratio tab shows the consolidation ratios.*

Move to the Mapping tab (Figure 1-28). The rack nodes in this case have a higher CPU SPEC metric of 700 (Estimated), and the memory is also higher at 256GB per node. This means that all of the nine servers could be consolidated.

P2P_Sainath_EightRack (P2P_Sainath_Project)

General   Sources   Destinations   Ratio   **Mapping**   Confidence   Violations   Exclusions

View ▼   Start Date 11/11/2015   End Date 11/14/2015   Destination Mapping Automatic   Configuration New servers: Oracle Exadata Database Machine X5-2 (Eighth Rack)

Destination Server	Source Servers	Source Server	CPU (SPEC metric)	CPU Utilization (%)	CPU Usage (SPEC Metric)	Memory (GB)	Memory Utilization (%)	Memory Usage (GB)	Operating System
◢ DB_MACHINE									
◢ RACK_0001.NODE_01	3		700 (Estimated)	69.1	483.4	256	85.9	218.33	
		...		35.9	251.0		43.6	111.69	SunOS
		...		0.90	6.3		0.89	2.28	Enterprise Linux Server release 5.10 (Carthage)
		...		32.9	230.6		43.9	112.46	SunOS
◢ RACK_0001.NODE_02	6		700 (Estimated)	19.5	136.2	256	89.9	230.02	
		...		8.0	55.9		43.7	111.94	SunOS
		...		6.9	48.5		43.9	112.46	SunOS
		...		2.4	16.7		2.2	5.71	Enterprise Linux Server release 5.8 (Carthage)
		...		2.5	17.4		1.1	2.81	Oracle Linux Server release 6.2
		...		0.24	1.7		0.71	1.81	Oracle Linux Server release 6.4
		...		1.1	7.7		1.6	4.03	Enterprise Linux Server release 5.8 (Carthage)

FIGURE 1-28.   *The Mapping tab*

The Confidence tab also shows 100 percent confidence (Figure 1-29), although there are hot spots on some hours approaching 90 percent usage.

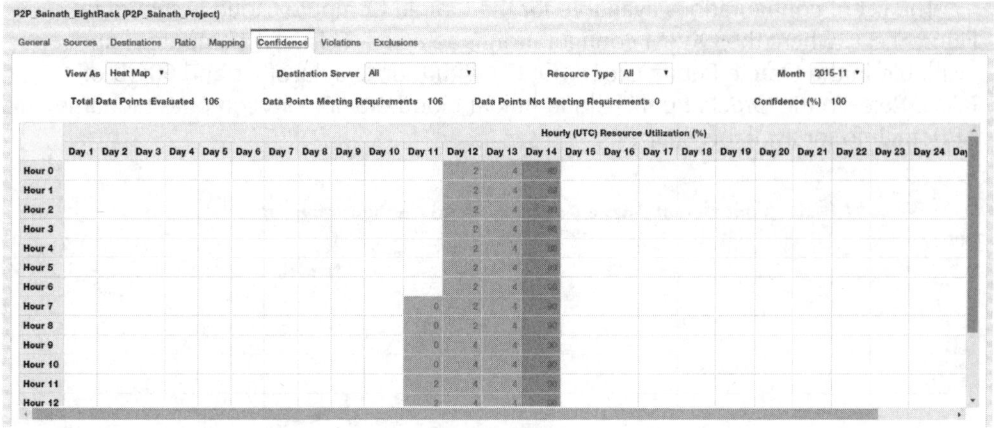

FIGURE 1-29. *The Confidence tab*

There are no violations and exceptions.

Now you have seen the first P2P project and scenario results, with their "what-if" scenarios.

Consolidating to Oracle Public Cloud Servers

The Enterprise Manager 13c Host Consolidation Planner also enables you to select the Oracle Compute Cloud as a phantom destination server. In Figure 1-30, you can see that the Oracle Compute Cloud has been selected as the destination server.

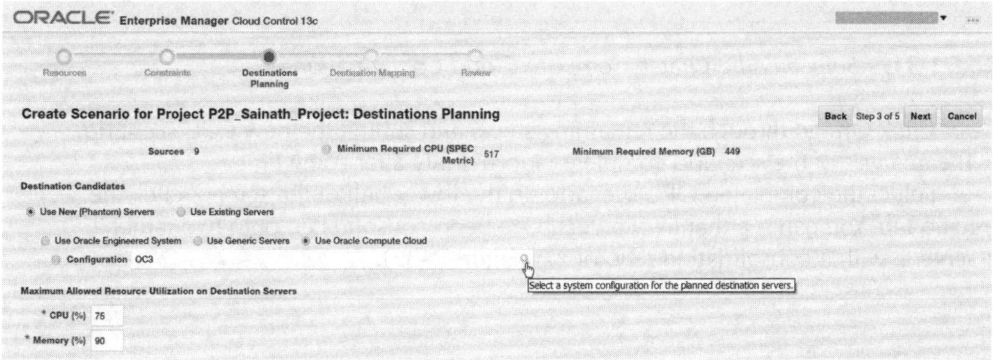

FIGURE 1-30. *Consolidating to the Oracle Compute Cloud*

The list of configurations available for the Oracle Compute Cloud is shown in Figure 1-31, where the OC3M configuration is selected. This is a "compute shape" available in the Oracle Public Cloud (OPC), with four Oracle CPUs and 60GB of RAM. Refer to the Oracle Public Cloud link at cloud.oracle.com/compute?tabname =PricingInfo for available shapes.

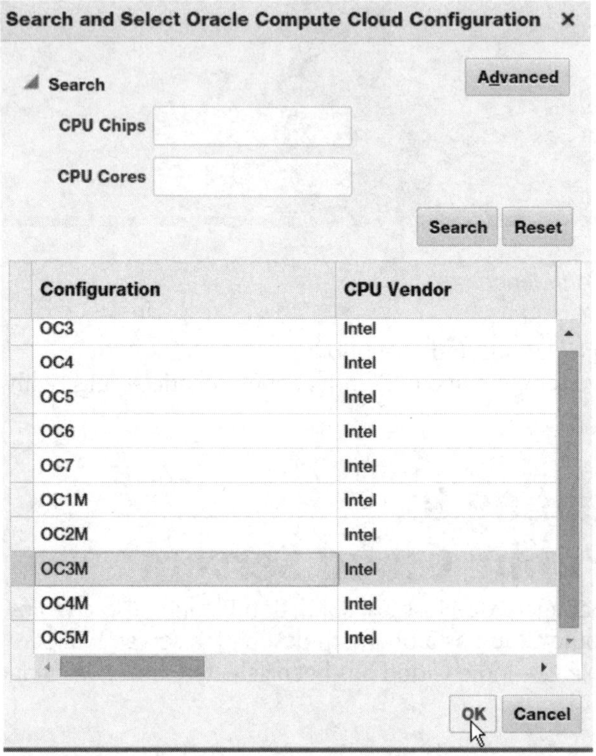

Search and Select Oracle Compute Cloud Configuration ✕

◢ Search   Advanced

CPU Chips _____

CPU Cores _____

                                          Search   Reset

Configuration	CPU Vendor
OC3	Intel
OC4	Intel
OC5	Intel
OC6	Intel
OC7	Intel
OC1M	Intel
OC2M	Intel
OC3M	Intel
OC4M	Intel
OC5M	Intel

                                          OK   Cancel

FIGURE 1-31. *Selecting the Oracle Compute Cloud Configuration*

Click OK, go through the remaining steps, and submit the new OPC scenario. The analysis of the scenario completes successfully after some time.

Select the completed OPC scenario. In the lower half of the screen, click the Ratio tab. You can see that five servers have been consolidated onto two target servers, with a consolidation ratio of 2.5 (Figure 1-32).

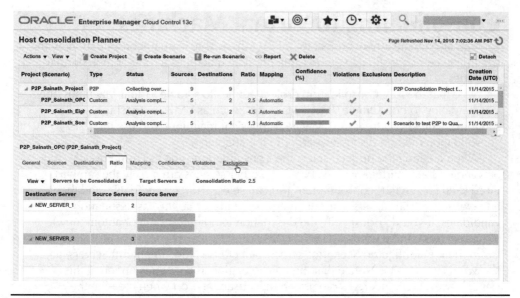

FIGURE 1-32. *Ratio tab of OPC scenario*

Move to the Exclusions tab (Figure 1-33), where you can see that four of the source servers have been excluded from the consolidation, along with reasons for their exclusion. For these servers, either the CPU requirements or the memory requirements at certain hours were more than could be handled by the two target servers, so they were excluded.

P2P_Sainath_OPC (P2P_Sainath_Project)

General   Sources   Destinations   Ratio   Mapping   Confidence   Violations   **Exclusions**

Server Name	CPU (SPEC metric)	Memory (GB)	Reason
	433.4 (Estimated)	255.00	CPU (SPECint®_rate_base2006) Limitation at Hour 23 [Required: 250.85; Available: 132]
	433.4 (Estimated)	255.00	Memory (GB) Limitation at Hour 1 [Required: 111.61; Available: 54]
	433.4 (Estimated)	255.00	CPU (SPECint®_rate_base2006) Limitation at Hour 23 [Required: 230.77; Available: 132]
	433.4 (Estimated)	255.00	Memory (GB) Limitation at Hour 1 [Required: 101.78; Available: 54]

FIGURE 1-33. *Exclusions tab of OPC scenario*

Consolidating to Virtual Machines

You can also create a new project for a P2V (physical-to-virtual) consolidation, with which you can consolidate your existing physical machines to one or more virtual machines.

Note that the P2V consolidation project applies to Oracle Virtual Machines only. Consolidating to non-Oracle Virtual Machines, such as VMware machines, is not supported unless you treat the VMware as physical machines and use the P2P consolidation method discussed earlier in the chapter.

When creating the project, select the Consolidation Type as From Physical Servers To Oracle Virtual Servers (P2V). The other screens are mostly the same as those used for the P2P consolidation. You can select source candidates, and then add existing virtual servers (current Enterprise Manager targets) as destination candidates. If you do not specify the destination candidates, only phantom (new) virtual servers will be used.

In the Pre-configured Scenarios screen, select Use New (Phantom) Servers, as shown in Figure 1-34. Notice that there is no engineered systems option at this stage; however, engineered systems can be chosen later on when creating the scenario.

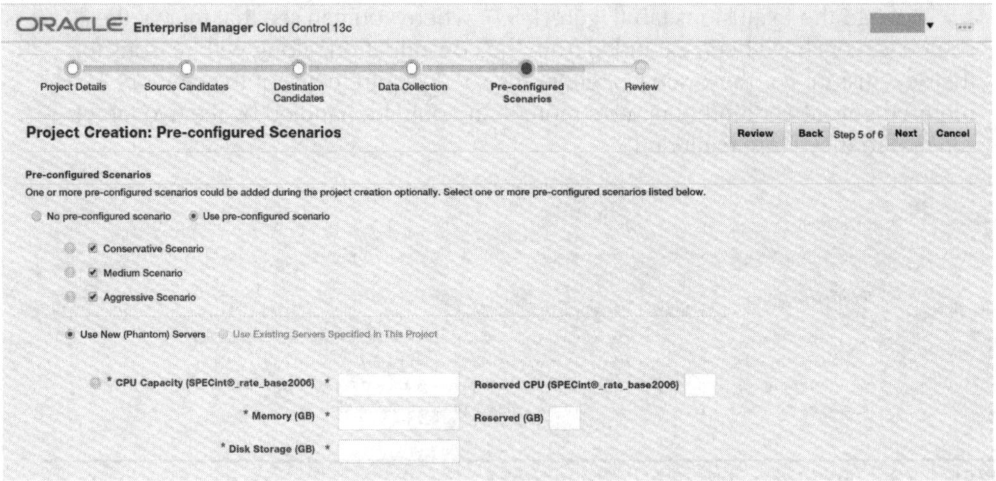

FIGURE 1-34. *Phantom servers for a P2V project*

If you do not intend to use engineered systems as the destination, you can manually specify the CPU Capacity, Memory, and Disk Storage of your phantom virtualized servers, along with optional selections for reserved CPU and memory. Finish creating and then submit the P2V project.

Once the project is ready, you can create a scenario. In the case of a P2V scenario, you can select an option from the list of Exalogic configurations that is provided. We have selected the Oracle Exalogic Elastic Cloud X5-2 (Eighth Rack), as shown in Figure 1-35.

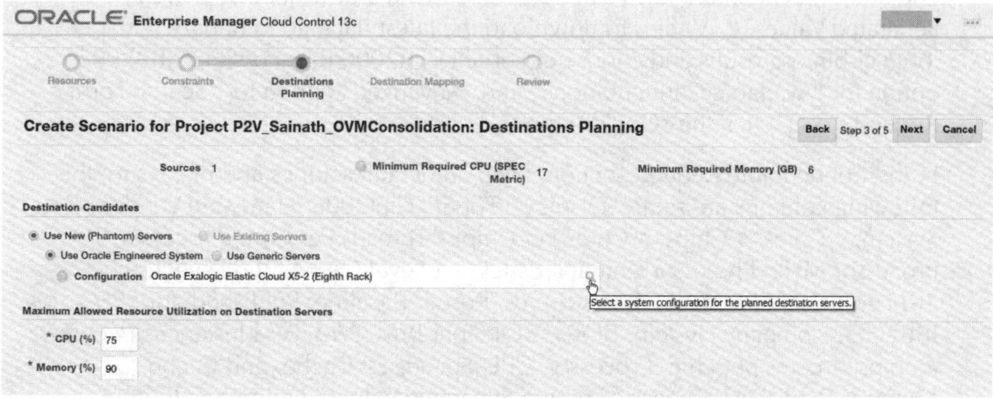

FIGURE 1-35.   *Selecting an Exalogic X5-2 (Eighth Rack) for the P2V scenario*

The rest of the scenario calculations and mapping work in a similar manner. Use the same steps as in the P2P scenario. The physical source servers are mapped to the destination phantom eighth rack.

As we have seen, the Consolidation Planner enables you to play a number of "what-if" scenarios for P2P or P2V consolidations on the basis of sound mathematical calculations. You can specify which metrics will be analyzed, and this results in the calculation of the resource requirements for every source server. Each resource is aggregated to a 24-hour pattern based on a different formula, depending on whether you selected Conservative, Medium, or Aggressive as the algorithm.

Constraints can also be specified as to which server workloads can coexist together, and which workloads should be placed on different target servers for business or technical reasons.

Updating the Benchmark Rates

The SPECint_base_rate2006 benchmark is used by the Consolidation Planner for database or application hosts, or for hosts with a mixed workload. The SPECjbb2005 benchmark is used for middleware platforms. These benchmarks represent the processing power of CPUs, including Intel Itanium, Intel Xeon, SPARC T3, SPARC64, AMD Opteron, and IBM Power Systems.

The SPEC rates in Enterprise Manager can also be updated by users in the following way.

Go to the Host Consolidation Planner home page by selecting Enterprise | Consolidation | Host Consolidation Planner. Then select Actions | View Data Collection. Look for the section Load Benchmark CSV File.

You'll see the following information:

The built-in benchmark rates can be updated with a downloaded Comma Separated Values (CSV) file. To download the latest data, go to http://www.spec .org/cgi-bin/osgresults and choose either SPECint2006 Rates or SPEC JBB2005 option for "Available Configurations" and "Advanced" option for "Search Form Request," then click the "Go!" button.

In the Configurable Request section, keep all default settings and make sure the following columns are set to "Display": For SPECint2006: Hardware Vendor, System, # Cores, # Chips, # Cores Per Chip, # Threads Per Core, Processor, Processor MHz, Processor Characteristics, 1st Level Cache, 2nd Level Cache, 3rd Level Cache, Memory, Base Copies, Result, Baseline, Published; for SPEC JBB2005: Company, System, BOPS, BOPS per JVM, JVM, JVM Instances, # cores, # chips, # cores per chip, Processor, CPU Speed, 1st Cache, 2nd Cache, Memory, Published. Choose "Comma Separated Values" option for "Output Format", then click "Fetch Results" button to show retrieved results in CSV format and save the content via the "Download" link in a CSV file, which can be loaded to update the built-in rates.

In this manner, you can download the latest spec rates from SPEC.org in the form of CSV files, and then upload them to the repository. You'll find the full list of all the SPEC rates being used in Enterprise Manager in the repository table EMCT_SPEC_ RATE_LIB (owned by the SYSMAN user in the repository database).

You can then review the host consolidation plan results and the consolidation ratio, mapping, target server utilization, and excluded servers.

The Host Consolidation Planner is essentially a server consolidation tool that is based on CPU, memory, and I/O metrics at the operating system level. These metrics are collected by Enterprise Manager for Linux, Solaris, HP-UX, AIX, and Windows; this means the Planner will operate on all these platforms.

Note that if a Phantom Exadata server is used as the destination candidate in a P2P project and scenario, the Host Consolidation Planner (which was the only consolidation planner available in the Enterprise Manager Cloud Control 12*c* version) does not *by itself* take into account Exadata features such as Smart Scan, which could potentially have a positive impact on performance by reducing the CPU utilization of the databases and allowing more servers to be consolidated on the Exadata server. However, in the new Enterprise Manager Cloud Control 13*c* version, a new Database Consolidation Workbench helps to cater for the effects of the Exadata features on consolidation. This is described in the next section.

Database Consolidation Workbench

Enterprise Manager Cloud Control 13c offers the new capability of a Database Consolidation Workbench. This is a feature of the Real Application Testing (RAT) database option, so it is mandatory that your enterprise holds the RAT license if you intend to use the Database Consolidation Workbench.

The Workbench is accessed by choosing Enterprise | Consolidation | Database Consolidation Workbench. This new comprehensive end-to-end solution is used to manage database consolidation. The analysis is based on historical workload data—database and host metrics, in combination with Automatic Workload Repository (AWR) data. The Workbench provides automation in all consolidation phases, from planning to deployment and validation. Using the Workbench helps eliminate guesswork and human errors in database consolidation.

Oracle Database versions 10.2 and later are supported, as is consolidation to the Oracle Private/Public Cloud or consolidation to Exadata. The Workbench also supports high-availability options for the implementation to minimize downtime, depending on the platform and version of Oracle Database at the source and destination.

Note that for the Database Consolidation Workbench, if you have the RAT option, you can run the SQL Performance Analyzer (SPA) Exadata simulation, which will help you assess the benefit for Exadata Smart Scans for phantom servers. SPA's Exadata simulation runs on existing hardware and uses the init.ora parameter `cell_simulation_enabled` to assess the benefit. You can perform the simulation by going to each database's home page, and selecting Performance | SQL | SQL Tuning Sets to create a SQL Tuning set. Then select Performance | SQL | SQL Performance Analyzer Home, and select Exadata Simulation on that page.

The Database Consolidation Workbench runs in three phases: planning, migration, and validation.

- In the planning phase, consolidation advice is provided by identifying candidate databases for the designated consolidation platform, and AWR data gathered from the databases is used for this phase. Because this uses AWR, the Diagnostics Pack license is required.

- In the migration phase, the consolidation plan is implemented by migrating the databases to the new consolidation platform using Enterprise Manager's provisioning features. The DBLM Pack for Oracle Database must be licensed, and if you use RAC or Active Data Guard in the migration phase, those database options need to be licensed as well.

- In the validation phase, the consolidation plan is validated with SPA (a component of the RAT option) by running test workloads on the consolidated databases. The RAT option license is required.

Conflicts are identified based on workload characteristics, and you are also notified if the workload is not suitable for Exadata consolidation. Storage/platform advice is made available—such as the impact of using compression on I/O and storage, and the impact of the I/O offloading and Flash Cache features of Exadata.

Let's take a look at creating some projects with the Database Consolidation Workbench.

Creating a D2S Project and Scenario

Start by creating a new database consolidation project. As the Consolidation Type, select From Databases To Servers (D2S), as shown in Figure 1-36, because you are consolidating existing databases to a new server (for example, Exadata consolidation). If the workload is found to be suitable, all the databases will be consolidated onto the new server.

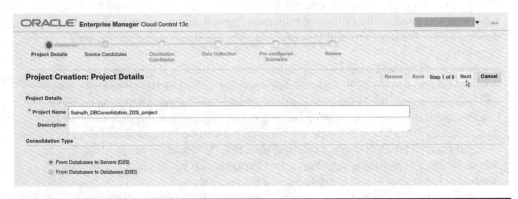

FIGURE 1-36. *Creating a D2S project*

If you choose the second option, From Databases To Databases (D2D), you will consolidate existing databases onto an Oracle 12*c* multitenant database. And a third possibility exists as well, consolidation onto the Oracle Public Cloud. This option is not available from the Project Creation screen, but it is available as a Phantom destination option when you are creating a scenario for a D2S or D2D project.

Click Next to open the Source Candidates screen (Figure 1-37).

In this screen, add the source targets to be consolidated. Usage data will be collected for all targets in this list. Because the value in the Estimated Compression Ratio column is Not Available, it signifies that compression estimates were not available for the target over the past 30 days. To estimate compressed storage requirements, you can submit the Deploy Database Consolidation Workbench Packages job with SYSDBA credentials on such targets to run compression advice and collect estimates before creating scenarios.

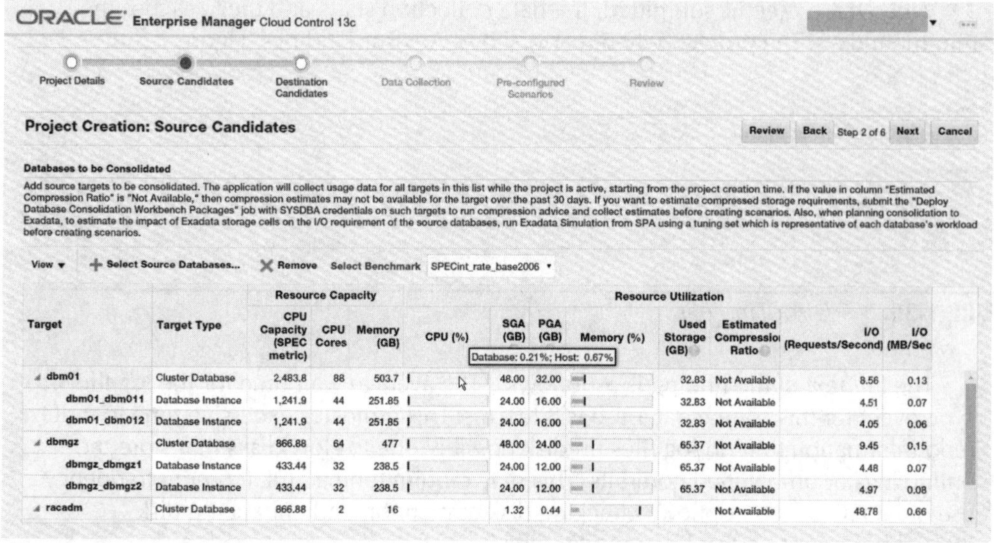

FIGURE 1-37. *Source Candidates screen*

In addition, when you're planning consolidation to Exadata, to estimate the impact of Exadata storage cells on the I/O requirement of the source databases, you can run Exadata Simulation from SPA using a tuning set that is representative of each database's workload, before creating scenarios.

In the next Pre-configured Scenarios screen (Figure 1-38), choose Use New (Phantom) Exadata Database Machines.

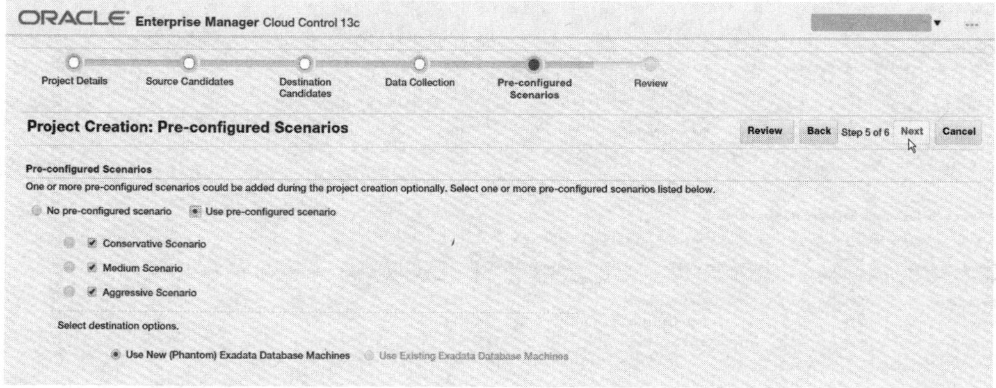

FIGURE 1-38. *Choose the new destination option in the Pre-configured Scenarios screen.*

When the project is submitted, the data collection starts and then reaches the minimum days. The project, when ready, shows Advisor Findings (Figure 1-39).

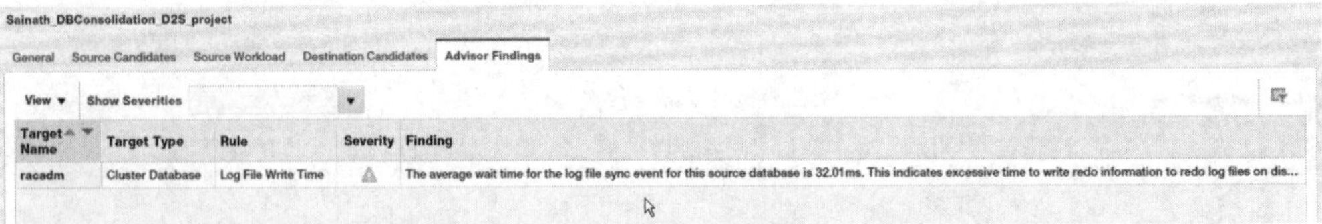

FIGURE 1-39. *Advisor Findings*

The full text of the finding is as follows: "The average wait time for the log file sync event for this source database is 32.01ms. This indicates excessive time to write redo information to redo log files on disk possibly due to slow disks that store the online logs or un-batched commits. This may require tuning SQL (commit frequency, use of NOLOGGING option), checking disk contention and enhancing disk throughput prior to consolidation planning."

As mentioned in the finding, tuning the source databases should be attempted and completed prior to proceeding further with consolidation planning.

Next, create a "what-if" scenario for the D2S project (Figure 1-40).

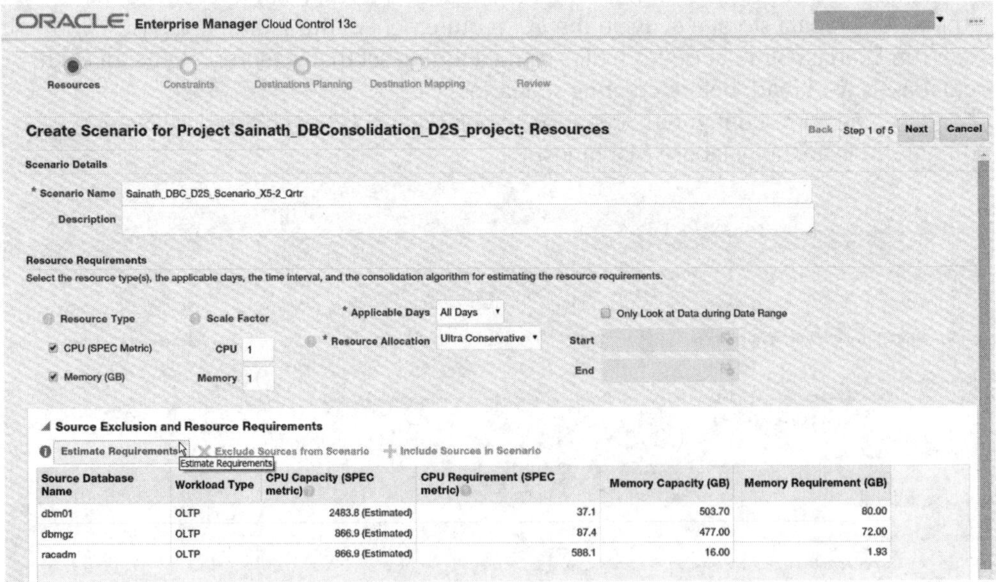

FIGURE 1-40. *Create a scenario for the D2S project.*

We will attempt consolidation onto an X5-2 quarter rack, so we have named the scenario accordingly. The Scale Factor in the Resource Requirements section indicates the type of load we are expecting in the future—if we input a scale factor of 5, for example, the consolidated load will be increasing by a factor of 5 in the future. A separate scale factor can be used for CPU and Memory. In this case, we have used a scale factor of 1 for both.

Estimate resource usages by obtaining the average (Aggressive), or 80 percentile (Medium), or maximum (Conservative) of average hourly usage across the specified data range. Specify Ultra Conservative to use the highest usage observed across the specified data range.

Click the Estimate Requirements button, and the estimate figures are shown for the CPU capacity. Click Next to open the Constraints screen (Figure 1-41).

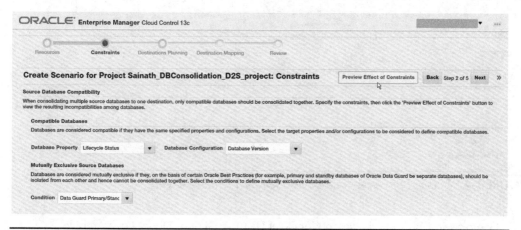

FIGURE 1-41. *Constraints screen*

We have chosen a few constraints for the databases on this screen. The available options for Database Property are Lifecycle Status, Department, and Location. You can set Database Configuration to Database Version, Database Edition, Operating System, or Network Domain. Under Mutually Exclusive Source Databases, the Condition can be Data Guard Primary/Standby Databases.

Click Preview Effect Of Constraints to see how these constraints will affect the consolidation scenario—the incompatibilities will be found and displayed.

Click Next to open the Destinations Planning screen (Figure 1-42). Here you can select the New (Phantom) server to be either Oracle Exadata, Oracle Compute Cloud, or a Generic Server.

In the Shared Storage Configuration section, we have selected the Exadata Storage Server. The ASM Redundancy can be set to Normal or High. The Table

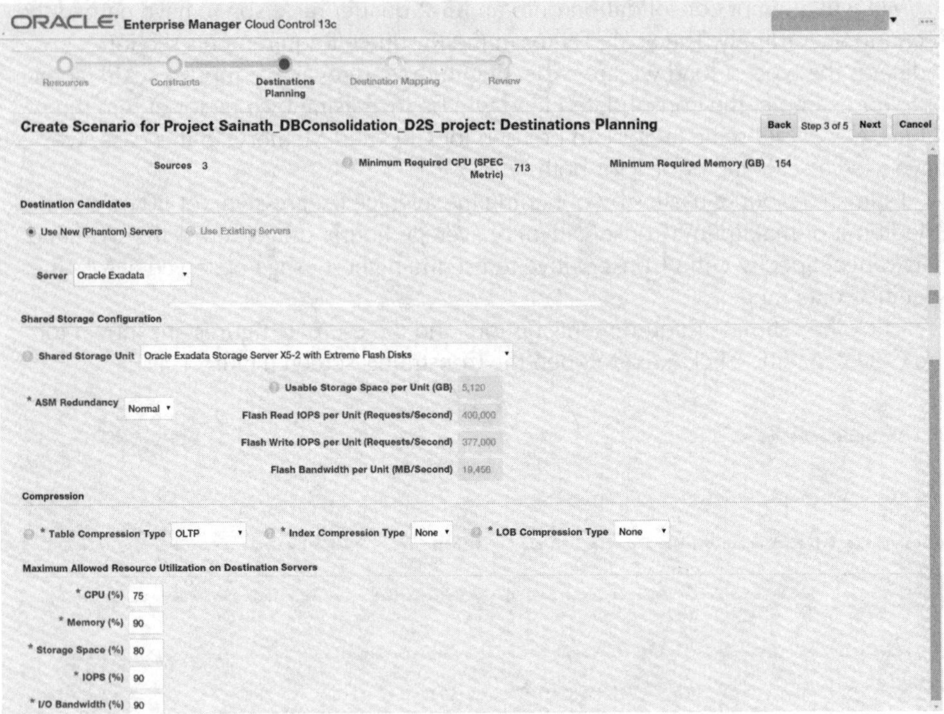

FIGURE 1-42. *Select the server in the Destinations Planning screen.*

Compression Type can be set to None, OLTP, Query High, Query Low, Archive High, or Archive Low. The Index Compression Type can be None, High, or Low; and the LOB Compression Type can be None, High, Medium, or Low.

Figure 1-43 shows the various options available for the Shared Storage Unit.

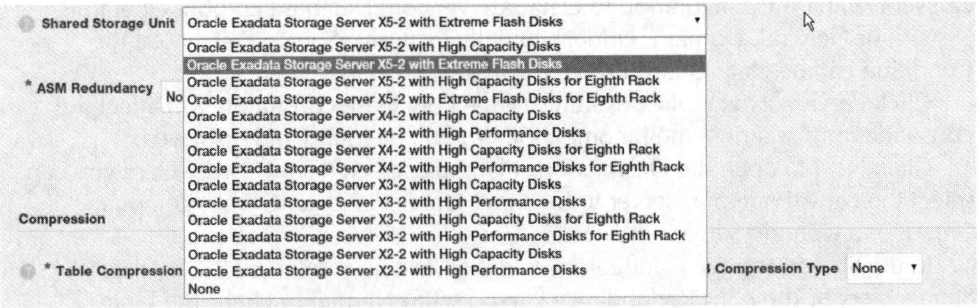

FIGURE 1-43. *Shared Storage Unit options*

In the next Destination Mapping screen (Figure 1-44), retain the default of Automatic Mapping.

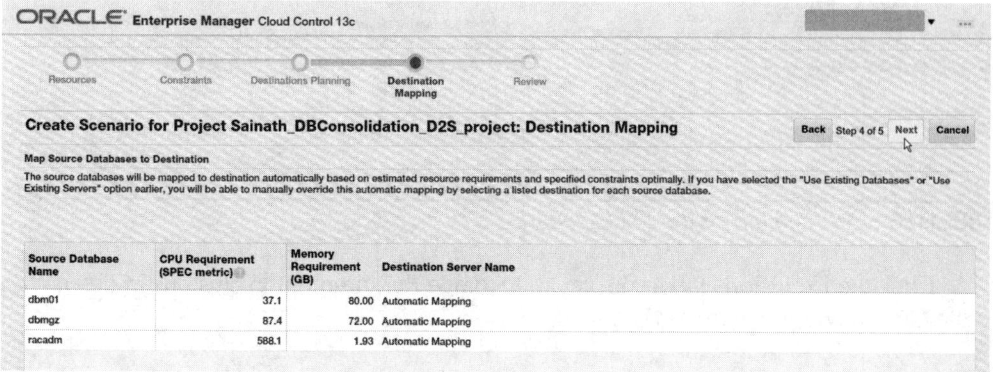

FIGURE 1-44.   *Destination Mapping*

When the scenario is finally submitted and complete, examine the Mapping tab of the scenario, as shown in Figure 1-45. You can see that the source databases have been distributed across the two nodes of the RAC database in the Exadata Database Machine. The utilization seems to be reasonable. (These are indicated in green on the Mapping tab.)

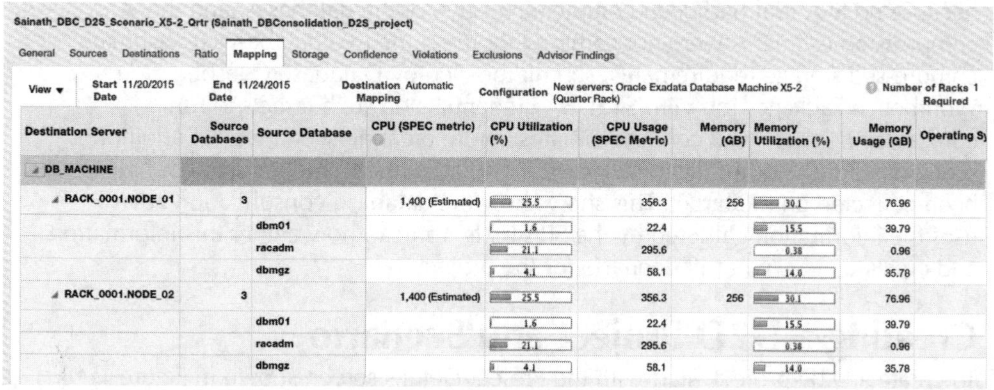

FIGURE 1-45.   *Mapping tab of the D2S scenario*

Moving to the Storage tab, you can see three storage requirement exclusions (Figure 1-46).

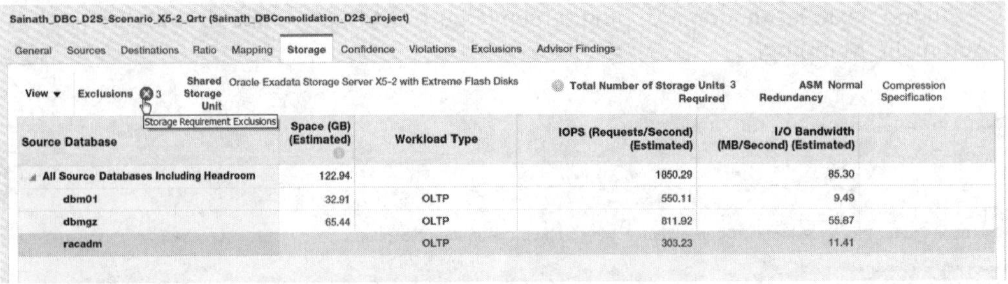

FIGURE 1-46. *Storage tab of the D2S scenario*

Click the Exclusions tab to display the Storage Requirement Exclusions in detail. They are shown in Figure 1-47.

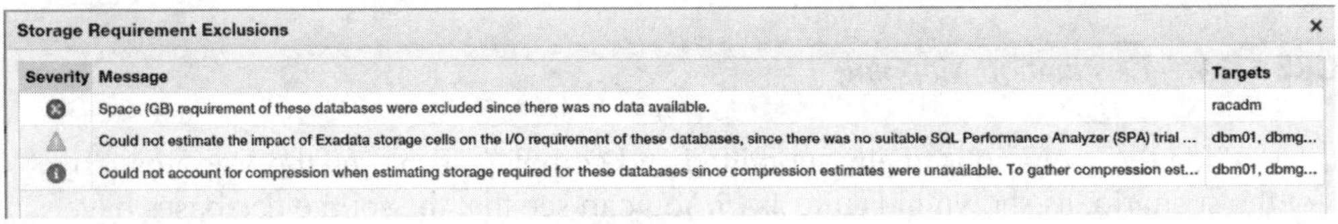

FIGURE 1-47. *Storage Requirement Exclusions*

Here, you can see that several of these exclusions have appeared. This is because no SPA trial had been completed for two of the databases, and the compression estimates were not gathered for the same two databases (to estimate compressed storage requirements, submit the Deploy Database Consolidation Workbench Packages job with SYSDBA credentials on such targets to run compression advice and collect estimates before creating scenarios). In addition, space data for the other database was not available due to metric data not having been collected on the target. This shows how the database consolidation advisor uses the information gathered by the SPA trials. You can now gather this information and create a new "what-if" scenario for the project.

Creating a D2D Project and Scenario

To create a D2D project, start with the Project Details screen shown in Figure 1-48.

Click Next. In the Source Candidates screen, select an 11*g* database and a 12*c* non-CDB (container database). As the destination, select a 12*c* CDB database. Our intention is to consolidate the former databases into the CDB. Do not select any preconfigured scenarios. Complete the project creation.

Next, create a scenario for the D2D project, as shown in Figure 1-49.

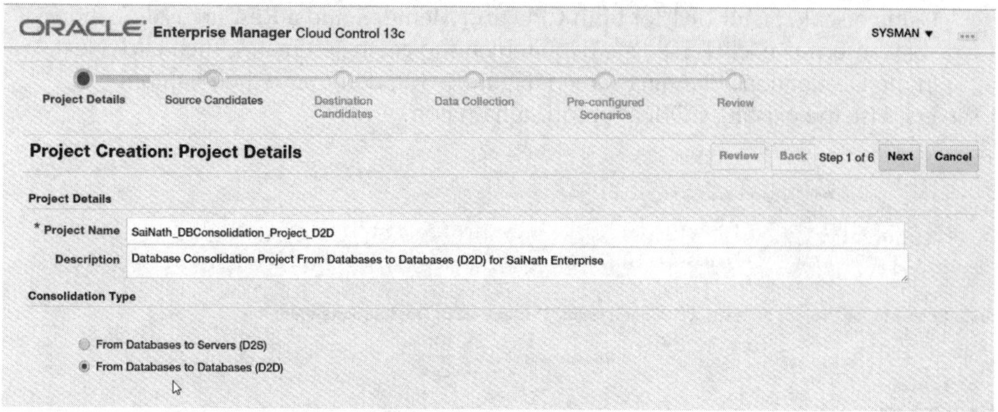

FIGURE 1-48.   *Creating a D2D project*

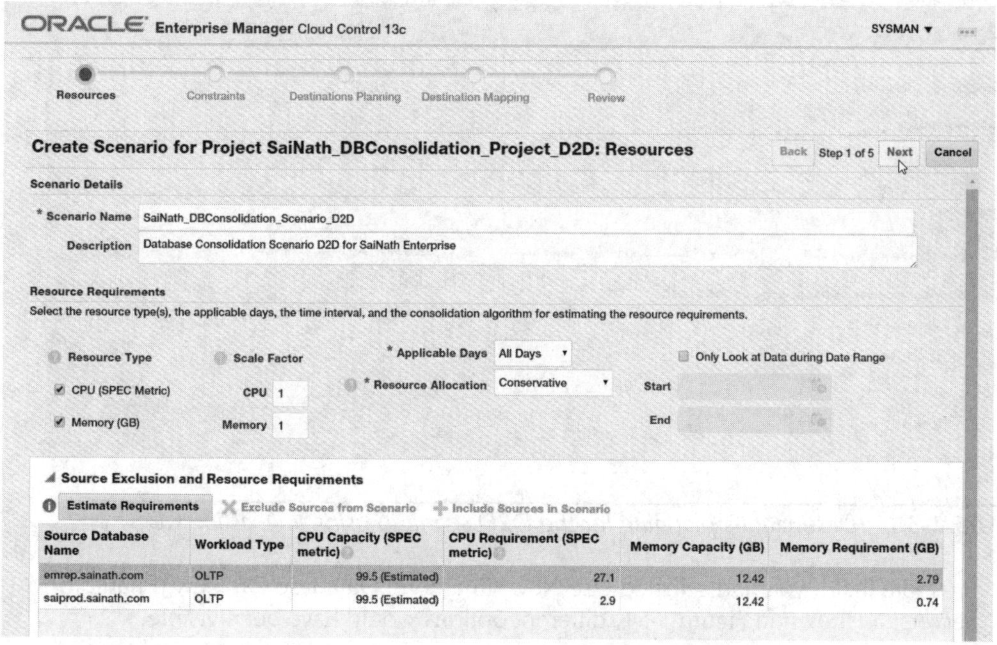

FIGURE 1-49.   *Creating a scenario for the D2D project*

Using a scale factor of 1 for both CPU and Memory, and a Resource Allocation type of Conservative, click Estimate Requirements to get the estimates. Then click Next. In the Destinations Planning screen (Figure 1-50), do not use the Phantom servers. Use the existing CDB, ahuprod.sainath.com.

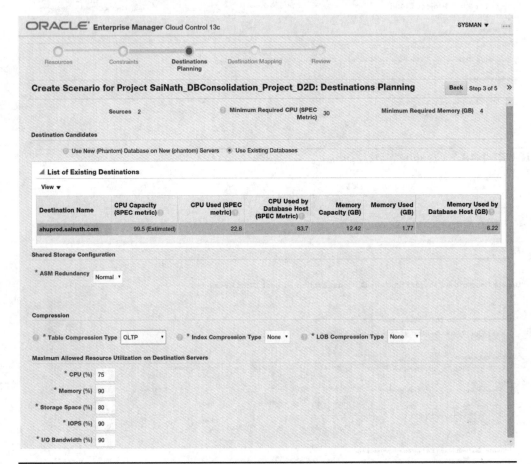

FIGURE 1-50. *Destinations planning for the D2D scenario using an existing CDB*

Note that if you had selected Use New (Phantom) Database On New (Phantom) Servers, as shown in Figure 1-51, different options would have been visible.

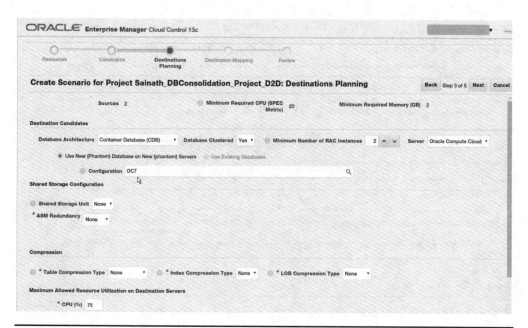

FIGURE 1-51. *Destinations planning for the D2D scenario using a phantom CDB*

You could have selected a CDB or non-CDB, a clustered database or single instance, the number of RAC instances, and whether the server was on Oracle Exadata, the Oracle Compute Cloud, or a Generic server. If you select the Oracle Compute Cloud, you can select the configuration of the server—in this case select an OC7 compute shape in the Configuration field.

Coming back to the existing CDB, we select OLTP compression, and move ahead to complete the scenario.

The scenario completes its analysis, and you can see the Confidence level is 100 percent (Figure 1-52). You can view the confidence as a heat map, with colors that also show the low levels of utilization.

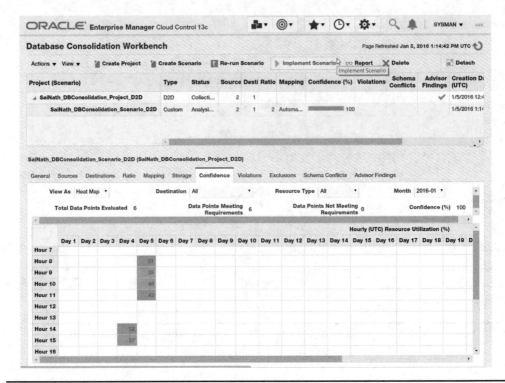

FIGURE 1-52. *Confidence level heat map for the D2D scenario*

Implementing the Consolidation

After consolidation of a successful scenario, you can implement the consolidation. Click the Implement Scenario button to open the Implement Scenario screen (Figure 1-53).

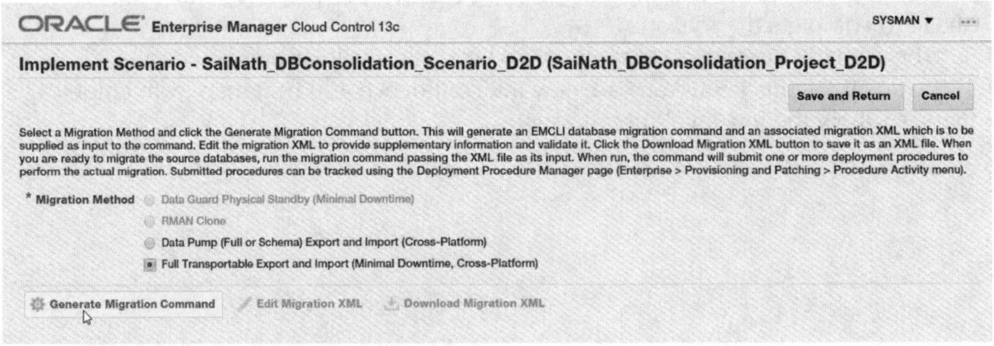

FIGURE 1-53. *Implement Scenario screen*

For the Migration Method, select Full Transportable Export And Import and click Generate Migration Command. A migration XML is generated along with the Enterprise Manager command line interface `emcli` migration command and instructions, as shown in Figure 1-54. You can save the generated command and the XML, and download the XML.

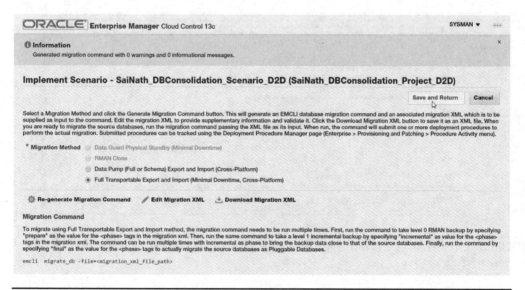

FIGURE 1-54. *Generated migration command/XML for full transportable method*

You need to edit the migration XML to provide supplementary information and validate it. When you are ready to migrate the source databases, run the migration command, passing the XML file as its input. The command will submit one or more Enterprise Manager deployment procedures to perform the actual migration. You can track submitted procedures from the Deployment Procedure Manager screen (Enterprise | Provisioning and Patching | Procedure Activity).

If you had selected the Data Pump migration method, a message would be displayed after generating the migration command, as shown in Figure 1-55.

Notice that various modes of migration of the source databases onto the target databases are supported, based on the source and target environments and also business needs.

For multitenant databases being moved to multitenant, an option is provided to unplug and plug-in the specific databases being consolidated. For databases on different platforms (endianness), the option is provided to migrate using Data Pump. For database environments requiring zero or minimal downtime, online migration is supported using DataGuard. This will provision the standby environment on the

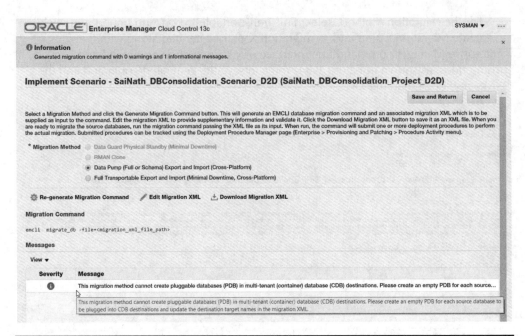

FIGURE 1-55. *A message is displayed when you choose the Data Pump migration method*

consolidation environment and then switch over to the standby as the primary, thus minimizing downtime.

Summary

In this chapter you saw the Host Consolidation Planner and Database Consolidation Workbench in action. These twin tools, available in Oracle Enterprise Manager Cloud Control 13*c*, are very useful for planning host and database consolidation into the cloud infrastructure.

In the Host Consolidation Planner you can select existing source servers and collect actual resource usage data from these servers over several days, and then use this information to map the source servers either to existing or planned (phantom), physical or virtual destination servers. The Database Consolidation Workbench, on the other hand, works with database metric data and AWR data to perform database-to-server or database-to-database consolidation. These tools enable you to create server and database consolidation scenarios that are useful for planning purposes.

The tools also help you to identify underutilized or overutilized servers, based on the resource usage data collected by Enterprise Manager. You can decide on appropriate candidates for host or database consolidation, satisfy business and technical constraints at the same time, maximize consolidation on the destination targets, and make sure performance on these targets is not degraded below a certain level—all controlled by the maximum resource usage limits you specified.

You have also seen the brand new consolidation implementation capabilities of the database consolidation process. Building on the consolidation scenarios and analysis performed on the Database Consolidation Workbench, the implementation capability enables the DBA to implement the consolidation plan generated by the database consolidation process.

The implementation aspect therefore saves DBAs the manual, error-prone efforts of consolidation, since the entire database consolidation implementation process is automated. The different methods of consolidation that are supported enable administrators to select a consolidation method that is specific to their business needs, so that the business does not suffer planned downtime—or possible unplanned downtime due to wrong choices made using the manual consolidation process. In addition, the ability to execute the consolidation process in parallel and in an automated fashion means that the business can realize consolidation savings faster and remove legacy hardware or software versions, enabling a quicker reduction of operating costs.

Note, too, that the RAT option also offers database replay capability, which enables you to capture a production database's concurrent workload and replay it on a test database system. You can then determine whether the SQL has improved in performance or has regressed. This option has been enhanced (since May 2012) to support consolidated database replay, so that two or more captured production database workloads from the same or different systems can be replayed concurrently on a single test database. This consolidated database replay functionality can be used to validate the consolidation strategy recommended by the twin consolidation tools in Enterprise Manager Cloud Control 13c.

In short, the Host Consolidation Planner and Database Consolidation Workbench are welcome and useful additions to the Enterprise Manager arsenal.

In the next chapter, we will examine Database as a Service (DBaaS) in detail, as set up and managed by Enterprise Manager Cloud Control 13c.

CHAPTER
2

Database as a Service

Oracle Enterprise Manager Cloud Control 13*c* offers many capabilities for Oracle's private database cloud services, including the Database as a Service (DBaaS) solution. Private database cloud services use Oracle homes, which are preinstalled on a pool of database servers, and it allows self-service users to request the creation of either single-instance databases or multiple-instance Real Application Cluster (RAC) databases on these homes quickly and easily. As part of the DBaaS solution, Oracle Snap Clone's CloneDB is a Direct NFS (dNFS) feature that enables users to make a smaller copy of an Oracle database using copy-on-write technology. Snap Clone databases are rapid and space-efficient thin clones of large databases and are normally used for functional testing, development, or data analysis purposes.

The base private database cloud infrastructure comprises zones, pools, quotas, database profiles, service templates, and request settings, along with a simple chargeback mechanism, which you will set up later in this chapter. In this chapter, you'll also learn about the self-service experience—how a self-service user can log in and request a new full-copy database or a Snap Clone database using CloneDB. In the remaining chapters, we will look into setting up Schema as a Service (SCHaaS), Pluggable Database as a Service (PDBaaS), the chargeback results, and the use of the Cloud REST API to talk to Enterprise Manager from an external orchestration engine.

DBaaS functionality is provided by the Enterprise Manager Cloud Management Pack for Oracle Database. The prerequisite for this pack is the Database Lifecycle Management (DBLM) Pack license, since the cloud self-service capability essentially uses the provisioning features of DBLM. Behind the scenes, the database provisioning procedures of DBLM serve as the foundation for the database cloud. The packs are simply a way of licensing different functionalities of Enterprise Manager.

In addition to serving as the foundation of the database cloud, the DBLM pack offers other capabilities such as database patching, configuration management, security compliance, and database change management. Because of these manifold capabilities of the DBLM and cloud management packs, Oracle Enterprise Manager Cloud Control 13*c* can achieve complete lifecycle management of the database cloud.

Database cloud administrators can create database pools of single-instance or RAC (clustered) database servers, set up roles to access these pools, create a service catalog with items that can be provisioned, and set up chargeback plans. Quotas can be set up to limit the number of databases created and the total memory and disk space consumed by the users.

Cloud users can then log in to the Self Service Portal and request that a database be provisioned on demand, rather than via the traditional method of going through a DBA team for the provisioning. Thus, quality of service can be increased substantially without incurring the additional cost of hiring short-term DBAs. For example, a project team would be able to request and automatically provision a new database on its own, in a much shorter time than if it were to go through the DBA team.

Such databases, once used for a certain period of time, can be automatically retired (deleted) or kept indefinitely. Fixed as well as usage costs for the Oracle Database Cloud Service can be defined by the cloud administrator and then automatically calculated and displayed in chargeback reports—thus leading to an understanding of the total charges involved in the use of the database cloud.

Configuring the Self Service Portal

Suppose existing database targets are being monitored and managed by your Enterprise Manager Cloud Control 13c system, either single-instance or RAC databases. These database servers have the Enterprise Manager Agent installed and are managed targets in your Enterprise Manager installation. You can decide to use a few of these servers for setting up a private database cloud in your enterprise using the DBaaS capabilities of Enterprise Manager.

Alternatively, you could set up a totally new set of servers and discover them in Enterprise Manager, or use engineered systems such as Exadata as the basis of your private database cloud. You decide on the Oracle Database versions to use, whether single-instance or clustered databases, and install the appropriate Oracle software on these servers in Oracle homes. You then install the Enterprise Manager Agent on these servers so that they appear as targets in Enterprise Manager.

The Self Service Portal is the main gateway that the Self Service Application (SSA) user will access to request new databases on these servers. Your first step in a private database cloud setup is to configure this portal.

The cloud administrator takes several steps to enable the use of the Self Service Portal for the SSA user. These include the setup of the Software Library, creation of user privileges, creation of roles that can access the pools of database servers, creation of the Platform as a Service (PaaS) Infrastructure Zones, specification of quotas for users, creation of service templates, and optionally, creation of chargeback plans.

Set Up the Software Library

You'll first configure the Software Library in Enterprise Manager Cloud Control 13c. This is where the database profiles and gold images are stored for the purpose of provisioning.

Start by specifying the storage location for the Software Library. As SYSMAN or another super administrator, click the Setup icon (the gear icon) and then choose Provisioning and Patching | Software Library to access the following screen (Figure 2-1).

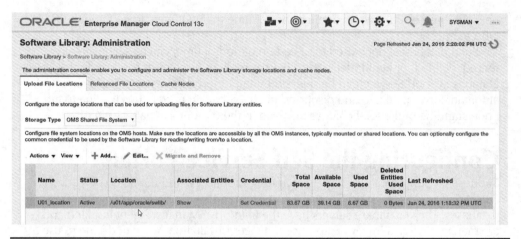

FIGURE 2-1. *Software Library Administration*

Select the Upload File Locations tab. Set the Storage Type as OMS Shared Filesystem, and click the Add button to create an Upload File Location of that type. In this scenario, a U01_location has been created with the directory path as shown in Figure 2-1.

You can use a local directory with a single Oracle Management Service (OMS) Enterprise Manager system, but for multi-OMS systems, a shared file system should be used, especially for high availability (HA) purposes. This can be set up by using the Oracle Cluster File System (OCFS2), Oracle Automatic Storage Management Cluster File System (ACFS), or even a network-attached storage (NAS) file system. The shared file system should be accessible by all the OMS instances, and highly available.

Optionally, click Set Credential (in the Credential column) to configure the common credential to be used by the Software Library for reading from or writing to a location.

If you select the other option for Storage Type, OMS Agent File System, you can configure file system locations on OMS hosts. These locations are then accessed by the Enterprise Manager 13*c* Agents monitoring the OMS hosts, primarily to read data from or write data to using the configured credentials.

For large files that you do not want to upload to the Software Library and that reside on non-OMS servers, you can move to the Referenced File Locations tab and add storage locations that are read-only for the Software Library. These locations will not be used for uploading files. The available storage types are HTTP, NFS, or Agent.

Note that in Enterprise Manager versions 12.1.0.4 and later, the Software Library is configured by the administrator who performs the installation of Enterprise Manager, so you may not need to configure it separately. But be sure to check the details of how it is set up, using the steps mentioned previously.

Set Up Self Update

The next step is to set up the Enterprise Manager Self Update system, whereby you can download the latest plug-ins from the external Enterprise Manager Store either online (recommended) or offline, depending on your company policy. Online mode is recommended for optimal usability. In online mode, Enterprise Manager connects to My Oracle Support to download patches, get the latest health checks, download self-updates, and so on. Note that this is a one-way connection; no outside services can connect to Enterprise Manager. Also, no customer data is sent from Enterprise Manager to Oracle.

If you are using online mode, the OMS server needs to be connected to the Internet, either directly or via a company proxy. To select the proxy, choose Settings | Proxy Settings | My Oracle Support. The screen shown in Figure 2-2 is displayed.

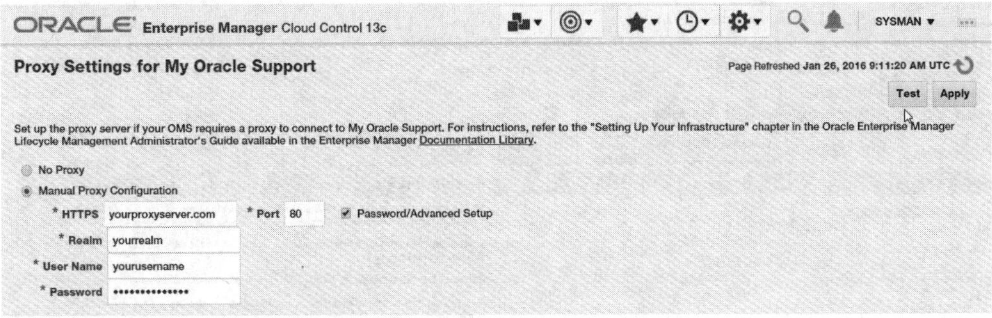

FIGURE 2-2. *Selecting proxy settings for My Oracle Support*

Click Test to test the settings, and then click Apply to apply them.

Next, set up the My Oracle Support credentials, which are required if you will be using online mode for the self-update of plug-ins. Do this as SYSMAN: Select Setup | My Oracle Support | Set Credentials (Figure 2-3).

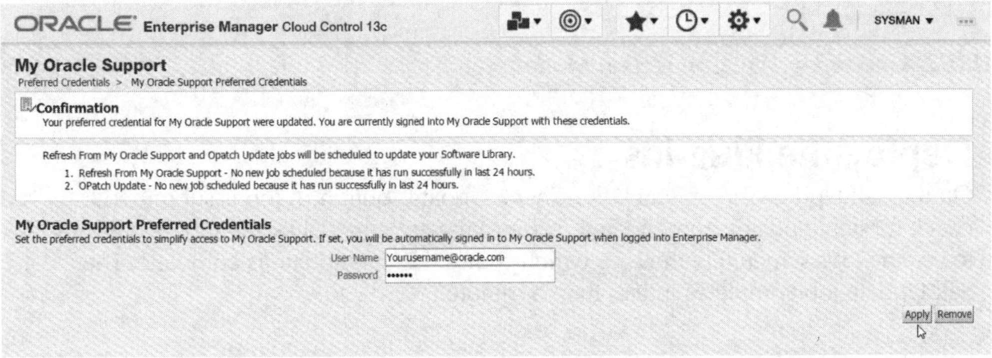

FIGURE 2-3. *Preferred credentials for My Oracle Support*

When you update the credentials and the credentials are correct, two Enterprise Manager jobs, Refresh From My Oracle Support and OPatch Update, will be scheduled to update the Software Library. However, if these jobs have run successfully in the last 24 hours, no new jobs will be scheduled.

Next, set up Enterprise Manager Self Update. Log in as SYSMAN or a super administrator and select Setup | Extensibility | Self Update. The Self Update screen is shown in Figure 2-4. Click Connection Mode to change from Online to Offline if required by company policy. Online is recommended, as mentioned.

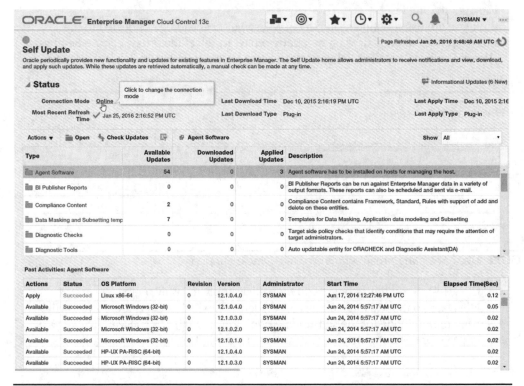

FIGURE 2-4. *Self Update: Connection Mode*

Deploy the Plug-ins

On the Self Update screen, click the Check Updates button. A job is submitted to check for new updates from the Enterprise Manager Store. Click the Job Details link to see the Jobs screen (Figure 2-5), which shows that the update is complete. The Self Update job completes in less than a minute.

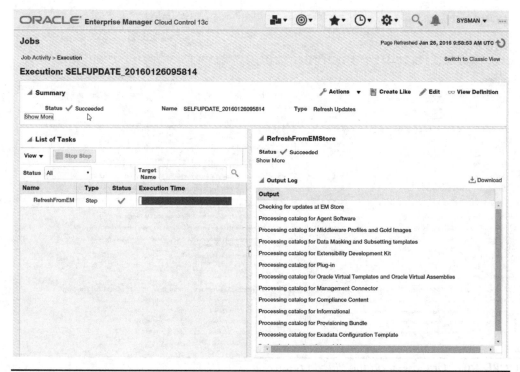

FIGURE 2-5.   *The completed update is displayed.*

Go back to the Self Update screen (Setup | Extensibility | Self Update). Under Type, scroll down to Plug-In, as shown in Figure 2-6, and click the link to drill down.

In the Plug-in Updates screen (Figure 2-7), click the Sort Ascending icon (the upright triangle) in the Plug-in Name column header, and scroll down.

The plug-ins required to enable DBaaS are listed here, with their names as they appear in Self Update. Check to see if any new versions of the following plug-ins are displayed on the screen with Status Available.

- Oracle Cloud Framework

- Oracle Database

- Oracle Fusion Middleware (mandatory even if not performing any Fusion Middleware or Middleware as a Service operations)

- Oracle Virtualization

- Oracle Cloud Application

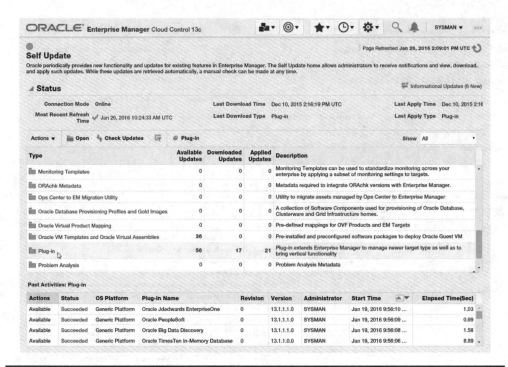

FIGURE 2-6. *Drill down on the Plug-In type*

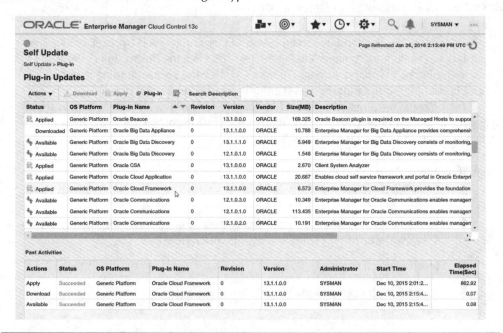

FIGURE 2-7. *Scrolling plug-in updates*

- Oracle Storage Management Framework

- Oracle Consolidation Planning and Chargeback

Starting from the first plug-in in the list, check each name to see if any row shows the Available status. If such a row exists, it means a new version of the plug-in is available. There may be multiple rows with multiple versions, so locate the most recent version of the plug-in. Select the corresponding row and click the Download button.

Once all the plug-ins in the list are downloaded, click Apply. At the Plug-ins Manager Console (Figure 2-8), you can deploy or undeploy plug-ins.

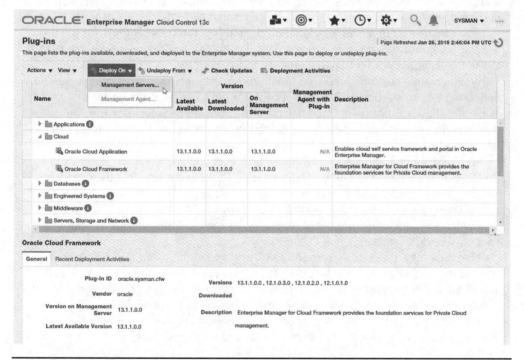

FIGURE 2-8. *Deploy or undeploy plug-ins from the console.*

In the console, find the plug-in you want to deploy, and check the version numbers under Latest Available, Latest Downloaded, and On Management Server. If the latest downloaded version is a higher version than the version under the On Management Server column, click the Deploy button.

Note that some plug-ins can be deployed only on the Management Server and others on both the Management Server and the Management Agent. For example, as shown in Figure 2-8, the Oracle Cloud Framework plug-in can be deployed only on the Management Server. Management Agent cannot be selected.

Remember to perform the deploy in the exact same order discussed previously—deploy the Cloud Framework plug-in before the Oracle Database plug-in, and so on.

Create the Portal Role and User

The next step is to create a global host named credential that is able to access the database servers you intend to use in the database pool.

Select Setup | Security | Named Credentials and create the new global credential. Specify Oracle as the Unix user, with the Run Privilege set to None. The user name and password need to be the same on all the servers, since you are using a global host credential. For this exercise, name the credential NC_DBZONE_ORACLE.

You can also set up a similar global credential NC_DBZONE_ROOT for the root user, or set up a user with sudo access. This is optional, but it is needed if you plan to use the database pool for Snap Clone database requests.

Next, create a custom cloud role in Enterprise Manager. Although predefined out-of-the-box roles such as EM_SSA_USER (for cloud self-service end users) are available, these cannot be granted to zones or service templates. Because the predefined roles will not appear in the selection list, only custom cloud roles can be selected.

As SYSMAN or another super administrator, select Setup | Security | Roles. Click Create. Name the new role SAINATH_SSA_USER_ROLE and assign to it the predefined role EM_SSA_USER. Click Finish. The new role is created.

You now need to create the cloud SSA user. This is an Enterprise Manager user who will be assigned this role. As SYSMAN or a super administrator, select Setup | Security | Administrators. Click Create.

Name the new cloud SSA user SAI_DAS, and assign the user the previously created role of SAINATH_SSA_USER_ROLE. However, remove the roles EM_USER and PUBLIC from the list of selected roles to ensure that the SSA user does not log in to the main Enterprise Manager console, but only to the SSA console.

For the remainder of the screens, accept the defaults until you come to the Review screen; then click the Finish button to create the new user.

Create the PaaS Infrastructure Zone

When you create a PaaS Infrastructure Zone, you are defining the infrastructure that will be used for PaaS, which may be for databases, middleware, or even service-oriented architecture (SOA) or Oracle Service Bus.

In this example, the zone you create will be used only for database-related provisioning. This includes single-instance or RAC databases, schemas, or pluggable databases created via self-service.

A PaaS Infrastructure Zone can contain a group of hosts; these need to be managed hosts in Enterprise Manager—that is, the Enterprise Manager Agent must have been previously installed on these hosts, and they must have been discovered as targets. Note that each zone can contain homogeneous resources of only one type, such as hosts with the same operating system (Linux) and the same platform (x86_64).

Log in as SYSMAN or a cloud administrator and select Enterprise | Cloud | Cloud Home. In the Cloud Home screen's Cloud Home menu, select Resource Providers. Click the Create button to bring up the Create Resource Provider screen (Figure 2-9).

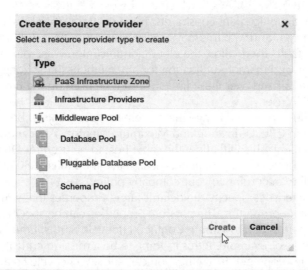

FIGURE 2-9. *Create Resource Provider screen*

Select PaaS Infrastructure Zone and click Create. The first step in the wizard to create the zone is displayed (Figure 2-10).

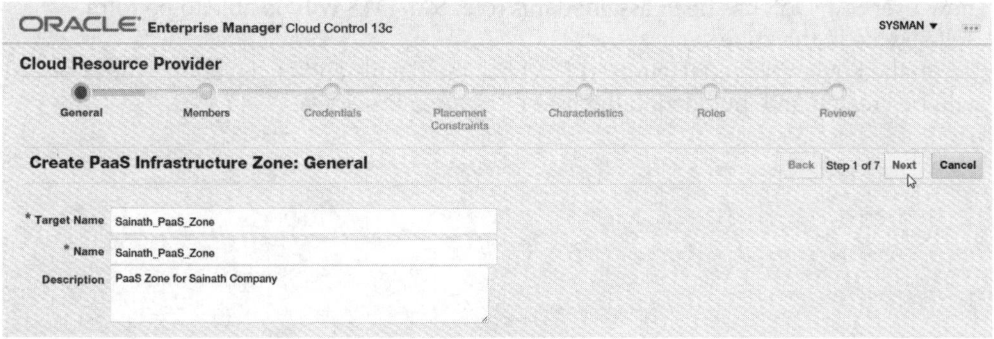

FIGURE 2-10. *Create PaaS Infrastructure Zone: first step*

Name the zone Sainath_PaaS_Zone and click Next. In the second step, add the Members (hosts) that will be part of the PaaS Infrastructure Zone. You can add a single or multiple hosts. Note that the hosts you select cannot be present in more than one PaaS Infrastructure Zone. If they have already been used in another zone, they will not appear in the selection list.

Move to the next step, and add the host credentials to be used for provisioning in this PaaS Infrastructure Zone. The credentials should be global—that is, valid across all the member hosts in the zone. We have already created a global host credential NC_DBZONE_ORACLE, which can be used at this stage.

Next, specify the placement constraints. Two constraints can be set—Maximum CPU Utilization (%), and Maximum Memory Allocation (%). Both are set to 80 percent by default. These allow the cloud administrator to set maximum limits of CPU utilization and memory utilization for any member in the zone. As a result, members that are utilized over these limits will not be used during creation of new services by the SSA user.

On a demo host, you can change the placement constraints to be 95 percent for both the Maximum CPU Utilization and Maximum Memory Allocation instead of the default 80 percent. This will allow the same host to be used for DBaaS even if there are less resources. On a production host, leave the limits at 80 percent, or reduce them further according to your company policy.

For the characteristics, specify the default Target Properties that will be applied to the zone as target properties. The possible properties can be specified: Contact, Cost Center, Department, Downtime Contact, Lifecycle Status, Line of Business, Location, and Site. For example, if this is going to be a mission critical or production or test zone, or development or staging, you can specify Lifecycle Status as one of these, and all databases created in this zone will have this property set to the value you have selected.

In the next step, you specify the roles that can access this zone. This enables you to restrict access to the zone to a set of users who have been granted these roles. You can assign the SAINATH_SSA_USER_ROLE to the zone. Because the new user SAI_DAS has been assigned this role, SAI_DAS will be able to perform self-service in the zone.

In the Review screen (Figure 2-11), check the details and click Submit. The zone will be created and included in the list of Resource Providers.

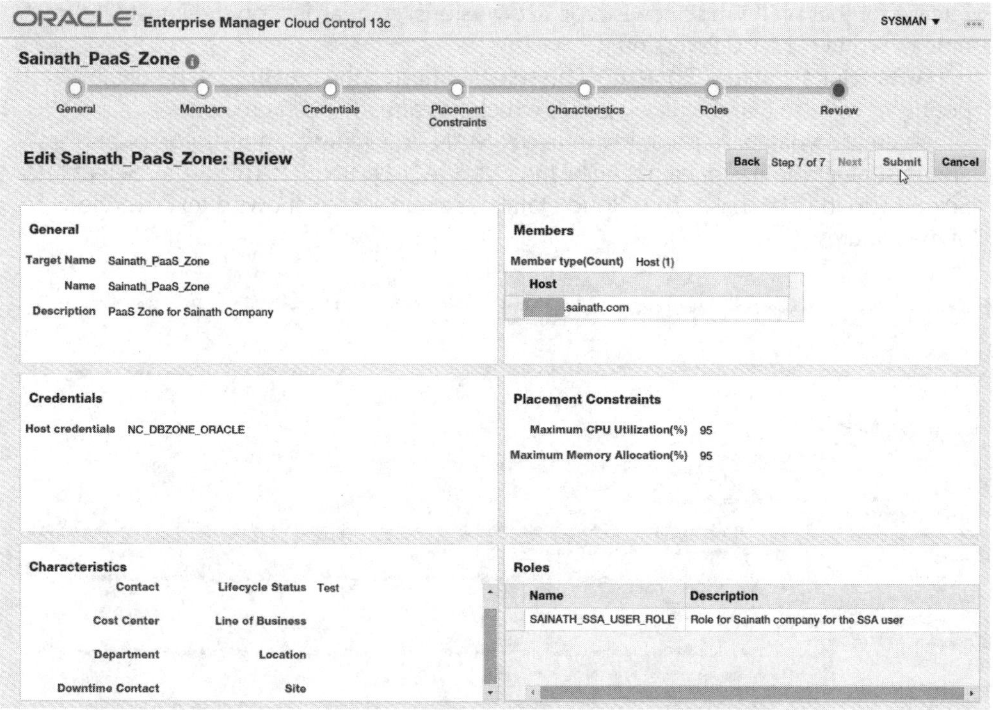

FIGURE 2-11. *Click Submit in the Review screen*

Create a Database Pool

A database pool is a group of database servers on which the database software has been preinstalled. These database servers can be stand-alone servers or clustered servers with the cluster infrastructure and Oracle clusterware already configured.

All the servers in a database pool must be of the same platform as well as the same database version. For example, you can create a pool of Oracle Database 11.2.0.3 servers on Linux x86 64-bit servers. There can be no other Oracle Database versions in the same pool, neither can there be any Linux x86 32-bit machines in the pool.

If you have a database home of a different version, say 11.1, on the same server, you must create a different database pool specifically for that version, and so on, for other versions. However, this is not recommended, since standardization is one of the key goals of creating the service catalog that will be used in the DBaaS project. If there are multiple 11*g* versions, standardize on one version, such as the terminal release for that platform. Likewise for 12*c* versions, standardize on the latest (at the time of writing) 12.1.0.2 version.

A PaaS Infrastructure Zone must be selected during the creation of the database pool. We will use Sainath_PaaS_Zone, which has already been created.

To create a database pool, log in as SYSMAN or a super administrator, or an administrator who has been assigned the EM_SSA_ADMINISTRATOR role. Select Setup | Cloud | Database. The Cloud Database setup screen shows a text overview of the features (Figure 2-12).

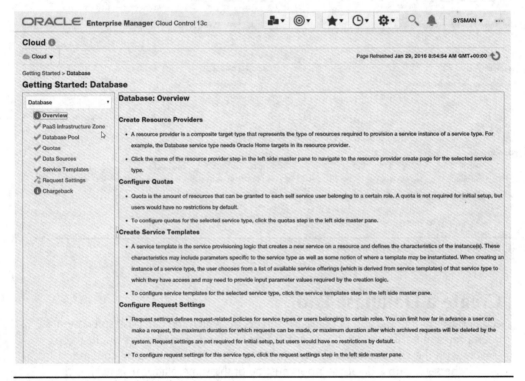

FIGURE 2-12.   *Cloud Database setup overview*

By default, Database is selected in the drop-down box above the leftmost pane. The other options are Pluggable Database and Schema, which you will see in the following chapters.

Click the PaaS Infrastructure Zone in the left pane. You'll see the zone that we set up initially in this chapter (Figure 2-13).

FIGURE 2-13. *Database: PaaS Infrastructure Zone*

Click Database Pool in the left pane. Then click the Create button to see the next screen (Figure 2-14).

Name the pool Sainath_Database11204_Pool and add a description. Also enter the host credentials that will be used for performing the database creation operations. We use the Global Host Named Credential that uses the Oracle UNIX user and password. Root credentials are also needed since we plan to use the pool for Snap Clone database requests.

Grid infrastructure and ASM credentials are needed only if you plan to use this pool for live cloning of a database using ASM. In our case, this is not required.

Select the PaaS Infrastructure Zone to be used and the Platform as Linux x86-64 from the drop-down list. The Database Configuration in this pool is of a Database Instance (single instance, as opposed to Cluster Database), and the Version is 11.2.0.4.0. This is what we want in the pool.

Next, add your Oracle home targets to the pool. Only those database homes and hosts will appear in the selection list that are the same as the platform, database configuration, and database version you have chosen. Note that each Oracle home target can belong only to a single database pool. If the Oracle home you want is already in another pool, you must first remove the home from there before you add it here.

If the Database Configuration selected was Cluster Database instead of Database Instance, you would need to select the Oracle home from each node in your cluster.

Remember that the PaaS Infrastructure Zone was made available to a role. The users that are assigned this role will now be able to use the database pool for their self-service provisioning.

In the Standby Pools section, you can also associate one or more separate database pools for provisioning a physical standby database(s). When you click Add, the list displays only the pools that are suitable for use, as per the Data Guard

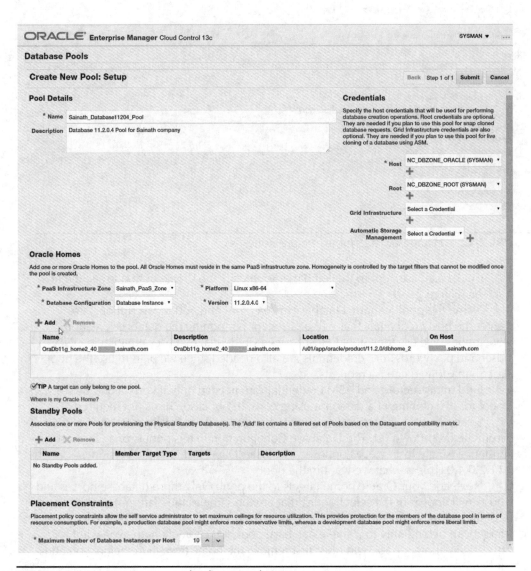

FIGURE 2-14. *Create a new database pool.*

compatibility matrix. You would have pre-created the standby pools before you could select them in this section.

This then would allow Enable Standby Database to be selected in the next step when you create the service template, and the self-service user would then be able to have a standby database automatically created along with the main requested database. In our case, we have decided not to use this option.

The Placement Policy Constraint on this screen is the Maximum Number Of Database Instances Per Host. This, combined with the Maximum CPU Utilization (%) and the Maximum Memory Allocation (%) defined in the PaaS Infrastructure Zone, are the maximum ceilings for any database server in the pool. These can be modified appropriately, with lower ceilings for production zones and higher for development or test zones.

In our case, we have used the ceilings of 95 percent for both CPU and memory in the PaaS Infrastructure Zone, and specified a maximum number of 10 instances on any of the servers in the pool. Because of these ceilings, when it is time for the database to be provisioned in the pool, the first database server that satisfies the placement constraints will be selected. In this way, overutilized servers in the pool will not be used for the new database.

Click Submit to create the database pool. You will return to the Database Cloud Setup screen (shown in Figure 2-12), where the newly created pool is listed.

Suppose you had made a mistake when naming the database pool and wrongly named it as Sainath_Database11203_Pool during creation, while the Oracle home inside the pool had been selected as 11.2.0.4. Since this is just the pool's text name, it has no effect on the rest of the setup, but it shows the importance of naming pools correctly to prevent confusion later on. Once named and created, the pool cannot be renamed—even if you use the Edit button. You will need to delete it and re-create it.

Enter Quotas

Now select Quotas from the left panel, and click Create. You can enter the quotas for the role you select (Figure 2-15).

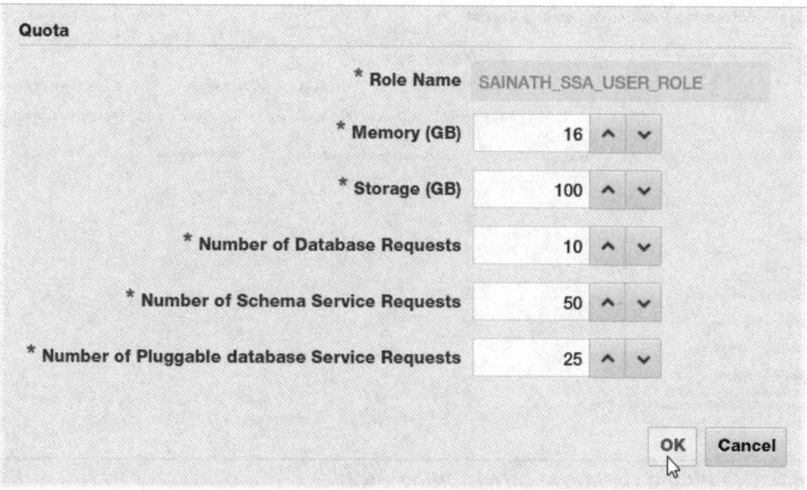

FIGURE 2-15. *Entering quota details*

In the Quota screen, the SSA administrator can configure the total amount of resources that are allocated to the self-service user via the role. Quotas are an important aspect of the cloud and are required in order to control the usage of the self-service aspect of the cloud. Otherwise, self-service users could possibly request an untenable amount of resources as a result of their direct ability to do so.

Select SAINATH_SSA_USER_ROLE from the Role Name list. This is the same role you created previously. Note that only custom roles that have the EM_SSA_USER predefined role assigned to them are visible in the list.

We have set a Memory quota of 16GB, a Storage quota of 100GB, the Number Of Database Requests at 10, the Number Of Schema Service Requests at 50, and the Number Of Pluggable Database Service Requests at 25. This is the total amount of resources that can be used by any SSA user to whom the custom role is assigned.

Click the OK button. The new quota for the custom role now appears in the quota list.

Create a Data Profile: Single-Instance Database

From the left panel of the Database Cloud setup screen, click Data Sources. On the next screen, click the Data Profiles tab. Click Create to make a new profile. The creation wizard starts, and the first step, the Reference Target screen, is shown in Figure 2-16.

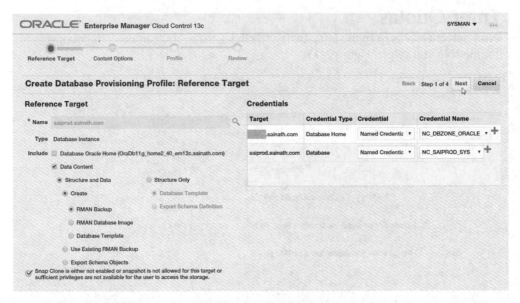

FIGURE 2-16. *Creating a database provisioning profile*

In the first step of the creation wizard, select the Reference Target database saiprod .sainath.com. This is the production database that will be used as the master source.

Choose the Data Content and Structure And Data options and choose to create an RMAN Backup from the source database. The other options enable you to create either an RMAN Database Image or a Database Template. You can also use an existing RMAN backup or export schema objects and create an export dump that can be used in self-service.

Alternatively, you can select Structure Only—in this case, only a database template or a schema export dump can be created. This will then be used in self-service to create an empty database with just the template structure or the schema structure.

Select the Credential for the database home (Oracle user at the UNIX level) and the database itself (SYS user at the database level). Click Next.

In the Content Options screen (Figure 2-17), you are asked to specify whether an online or offline RMAN backup is to be taken, the number of concurrent RMAN channels to use (to increase parallelism in the backup process), whether the backup files are to be compressed and/or encrypted, and the location where the new backup is to be stored—either the Fast Recovery Area or a totally separate location for backups that are to be used in DBaaS.

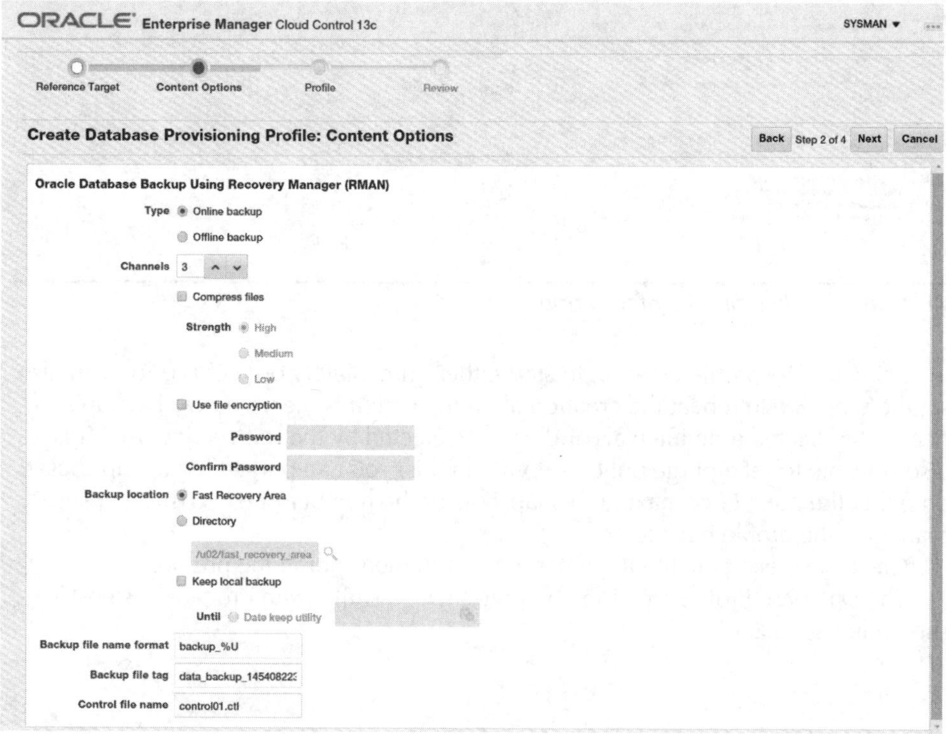

FIGURE 2-17. *Content Options*

If you select Keep Local Backup, this is a further safeguard. It will override the default retention policy only for the current backup. This means the DBaaS backup will be retained irrespective of the retention policy.

The Backup File Name Format, Backup File Tag, and Control File Name can also be changed, so that these backups can be distinguished from other normal database backups. We have kept all of these at the default for demonstration purposes. Channels have been increased to 3 instead of the default 2. Click Next.

In the Profile Information screen (Figure 2-18), you can change the profile location in the Software Library if you want or accept the suggested location. Name this profile Database saiprod.sainath.com Profile RMAN Full Backup. This will be used for the Database as a Service functionality.

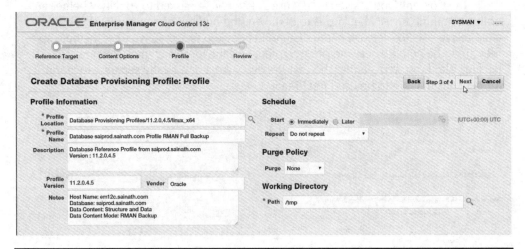

FIGURE 2-18. *Adding profile information*

Schedule the profile creation to start either immediately or later on. You can also set the schedule to repeat the creation at an interval; this means a new backup will occur at indicated time intervals and can be selected by the self-service user. It is also possible to set a purge policy—if you do this, you can purge the backups based on either the number of maximum snapshots or the number of days. This helps in managing the profile backups.

Click Next, examine the Review screen, and then submit the profile.

The Database Profile creation completes successfully, with procedure steps shown in Figure 2-19.

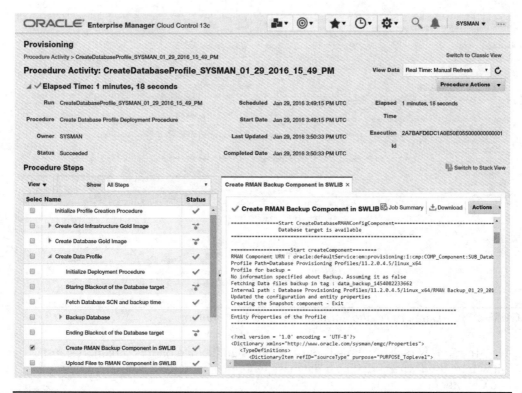

FIGURE 2-19. *Successful completion of profile creation*

The steps show that the RMAN database backup completed, after which the RMAN backup component was created in the Software Library, and configuration files were uploaded to that component. If you examine the upload files step in detail, you will see that the following two configuration files have been uploaded to the Software Library, and not the entire backup, which still resides in the backup location.

```
Init File name:initsaiprod.ora
User File name:dbusers.lst
```

Refresh the Data Profile

Now select Setup | Cloud | Database, and in the setup screen, select Data Sources in the left pane. In the Data Profiles tab, select the RMAN Full Backup Profile. When the profile is selected, the Contents section displays the actual RMAN backup that is a part of that profile (Figure 2-20).

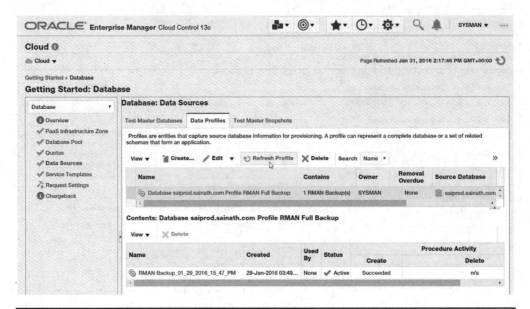

FIGURE 2-20. *Data Profile and corresponding RMAN content*

The RMAN backup name is of particular significance on this screen, because it will be used when creating a database with the Cloud REST API, explained in Chapter 6.

Now suppose a few days have gone by, and the data in the saiprod database has changed. For example, a new record has been added to the HR Employees table, since a new employee has joined the operation. As the cloud administrator, you would want the new data to be available to the self-service user for creating the copy of the saiprod database.

To achieve this purpose, you do not need to re-create the profile. Instead, you can simply click Refresh Profile. This creates a new RMAN full backup with the changed data. This new backup version can then be selected by the SSA user at the time of self-service of the single-instance database.

When you click the Refresh Profile button, you are asked the following question: "This action creates a new snapshot under this profile. Are you sure that you want to continue with the refresh of selected Profile?" Click Yes.

The refresh profile procedure is submitted successfully. You can check the steps at the link provided. After the procedure completes, move back to the Data Profiles tab. The new RMAN backup is displayed in the Contents section (Figure 2-21).

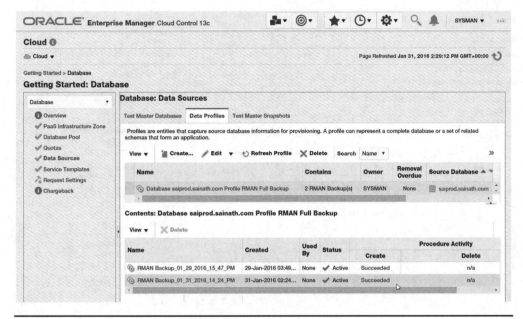

FIGURE 2-21. *New RMAN backup displayed*

Create a Data Profile: Snap Clone Database

Let's now create a new database profile to be used for the Snap Clone functionality. In the Data Profiles tab, click Create.

In the first step of the wizard, specify the Reference Target again as the saiprod database. Choose to include the Structure And Data by including an RMAN Database Image for this new profile, instead of an RMAN Backup. Select the credentials as you did for the single-instance database.

In the second step, where you specify the Content Options, select Online Backup as the RMAN Database Backup Type and the Fast Recovery Area (or a special directory) as the Backup Location.

This profile will be used for the Database as a Service solution using the Snap Clone functionality. So in the third step, name this profile Database saiprod.sainath .com RMAN Datafile Image Backup Profile. Schedule it to run immediately. As with the single-instance database example, you can optionally set a repeating schedule and a purge policy if required.

Submit the profile creation. The procedure performs the creation, and the new profile appears in the list of Data Profiles, as shown in Figure 2-22.

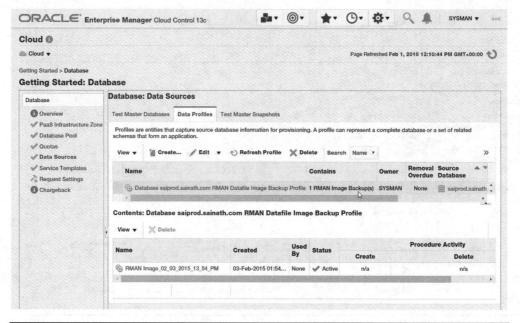

FIGURE 2-22. *RMAN image backup*

Note that RMAN Image Backup(s) is clearly shown in the Contains column, as opposed to RMAN Backup in the single-instance profile. The section in the lower half of the page shows the actual RMAN Datafile Image Backup that will be used by the profile.

If the production data has changed, the cloud administrator can click Refresh Profile at any time after the profile creation to create a new RMAN datafile image backup.

Create a Service Template: Single-Instance Database

The next step is to create service templates for the database cloud, which can then be used by the SSA user to provision databases in the pool. The profiles created in the previous section are like gold copies of an Oracle Database, and they are used by service templates.

The service template is offered to the SSA user and forms the basis of the functionality of the cloud. However, before a service template can be created, you need to set up multiple database sizes. These will be used to override the initialization parameter values in the service template once the database is associated with that template.

The `create_database_size` verb is explained in the "Oracle Enterprise Manager Command Line Interface" (EMCLI) documentation. This is used to specify multiple database sizes. Use EMCLI commands, as follows, to create the database sizes you want to use in your service templates. (Note that we have used conservative numbers to avoid overloading our demonstration host, which has limited memory. Note, too, that the OMS home directory may be different in your case, depending on where you have installed Enterprise Manager.)

```
cd /u01/app/oracle/middleware/oms/bin
./emcli login -username=sysman
Enter password
Login successful

./emcli create_database_size   -name=Small   -description="Small size
database"  -attributes="cpu:2;storage:2;memory:1;processes:350"

Database size 'Small' has been successfully created

./emcli create_database_size   -name=Medium -description="Medium size
database"  -attributes="cpu:3;storage:3;memory:1;processes:500"

Database size 'Medium' has been successfully created

./emcli create_database_size  -name=Large  -description="Large size
database"  -attributes="cpu:4;storage:4;memory:2;processes:700"

Database size 'Large' has been successfully created
```

List the database sizes using `emcli`:

```
./emcli list_database_sizes
```

```
Name:Large
Description:Large size database
CPU(cores):4
Memory(GB):2
Processes(COUNT):700
Storage(GB):4
```

```
Name:Medium
Description:Medium size database
CPU(cores):3
Memory(GB):1
Processes(COUNT):500
Storage(GB):3
```

```
Name:Small
Description:Small size database
CPU(cores):2
Memory(GB):1
Processes(COUNT):350
Storage(GB):2
```

Note that the Storage GB database size is not a hard limit, but serves only as a storage budget for the SSA administrator. It is used for setting threshold limits at the Enterprise Manager level, to display alerts if the thresholds have been crossed by increasing database size.

Now we can proceed with creating the service templates. Choose Setup | Cloud | Database and select Service Templates in the left pane. Click the Create button. The first step of the wizard is shown in Figure 2-23.

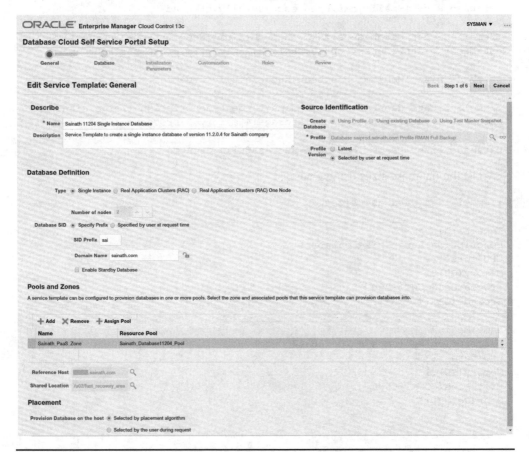

FIGURE 2-23. *Creating a service template*

Name the service template Sainath 11204 Single Instance Database. In the Source Identification section, select Using Profile for the Create Database option and then search for the profile. From the list of profiles, select the appropriate profile that was created with an RMAN full backup. This profile with its reference information is then associated with the service template you are creating. If the profile contains data, the data will also be copied when the service template is executed.

As the Profile Version, choose Selected By User At Request Time. This will allow the SSA user to select any of the available RMAN backups that have been created by refreshing the profile. If you instead selected Latest, only the latest backup will be available to the SSA user.

The other options for Create Database are Using Existing Database and Using Test Master Snapshot, a snapshot of an RMAN image backup from a production database. Test master snapshots are new in Enterprise Manager 13.1 and can be used to create Snap Clones. However, these require special storage hardware such as NetApp Storage Appliance, Sun ZFS Storage Appliance, EMC Storage Array, or even the Solaris File System (ZFS). Note that the dNFS file system and CloneDB cannot be used for test master snapshots.

Next, under Database Definition, select Single Instance. In our case, we specify the SID prefix as *sai* (up to six letters are allowed) and the domain name as sainath .com. This can be defined according to company standards, or you may allow the SSA user to specify the prefix at request time. The domain name can be kept unlocked (the default); or, by clicking the lock icon, you can prevent the SSA user from changing the domain name at request time.

You can also select Enable Standby Database for this service template, provided you have already set up the infrastructure for this and have a standby database pool of servers that you can select at this stage.

Under the section Pools and Zones, click Add, and select the previously created Sainath_PaaS_Zone. Then click Assign Pool and select Sainath_Database11204_Pool to be assigned to this zone. The self-service databases will be created in this pool. You can add multiple zones and pools in this way, but they must all have similar characteristics to the profile that you specified for the service template. For example, all the database pools you select must consist of 11.2.0.4 Oracle homes if your profile is using that version.

Note that the Reference Host field is populated after you select the zone and the pool. A shared location must also be specified—in this case, we have selected the fast recovery area.

In the Placement section, there are two possibilities. The provisioning of the database on the host can be selected by the Placement Algorithm or selected by the user during request. The placement algorithm is controlled by the placement constraints that have been configured in the PaaS Infrastructure Zone we have selected. The two constraints—Maximum CPU Utilization (%) and Maximum Memory Allocation (%)—have been set to 95 percent in our case.

The placement algorithm is also influenced by the placement policy constraint specified in the database pool—the Maximum Number Of Database Instances Per Host, which was specified as 10 in our case. The algorithm looks at all these factors and decides which member of the zone should be used for the creation of new services. In our case, there is only one host, but if the algorithm returns false for that host, no new service will be created.

If Selected By User During Request is chosen, the algorithm doesn't decide on the member, and instead the human user makes that decision. However, the constraints will still apply. If there are multiple hosts in the pool and the human user selects a host that is already overutilized, the creation of the new service will not work. So it is best to leave the selection to the placement algorithm, except in special service catalog offerings where a manual selection of a host is required. For example, there may be a few hosts in your pool with higher performance (more processors and memory available, or a faster storage subsystem), and you want a specially important database to be created on that specific host rather than other hosts with lower grade performance. Or perhaps you want certain databases to be created only on a particular host in the pool and other databases to be created on any of the hosts.

Note that database cloud requests can fail for certain reasons, such as placement logic failures. Placement logic uses a seven-day average for memory and CPU constraints when locating a suitable database server within the selected PaaS Infrastructure Zone where the new database can be created.

Click Next to go to the screen shown in Figure 2-24.

For both the Storage Type and Fast Recovery, select File System. Set the Fast Recovery Area Size (MB) to 6000. Check the Enable Archiving check box.

It is important that you configure the fast recovery area (FRA) and enable archiving, if you want the SSA user to schedule database backups and perform restores themselves. This puts the onus of power right in the hands of the SSA users—they need to use this power responsibly and wisely for the sake of their own databases.

For the Listener Port, enter the port number that should be associated with the new database. If you are provisioning a version 11.2 or later RAC database, you must specify the scan port number.

On the same screen, enter the passwords you want to use for the administrative users (SYS, SYSTEM, and DBSNMP) in a self-service–created database. Note that as the SSA administrator, you are currently creating the service catalog entry for the database, and once the SSA user has created a database using your service catalog, you can use these logins to manage the database. The SSA user will have no access to these passwords. Since this is a demonstration system, we select Use The Same Password; we would use different passwords for a production or test system.

You can also select users (schemas) in the copied database that you do not want to be accessible to the SSA user. If you select such users, you need to specify a password for those users. This password will not be available to the SSA users, effectively stopping them from accessing those schemas.

ORACLE Enterprise Manager Cloud Control 13c   SYSMAN ▼ ....

Database Cloud Self Service Portal Setup

○————————●————————○————————○————————○————————○
General   Database   Initialization   Customization   Roles   Review
                                Parameters

Edit Service Template: Database   Back Step 2 of 6 **Next** **Cancel**

Reference Host   **Administrator Credentials**

The reference host is used to select the necessary database content values like ASM disk group, data file location,   Specify passwords for the administrative users (SYS, SYSTEM and DBSNMP) in the new database. These users are used
listener port that are available on the reference host.   by the SSA Administrator to manage the database. The SSA User has no access to these users.

Zone Sainath_PaaS_Zone   Pool Sainath_Database11204_Pool   Host ▓▓▓▓.sainath.com   ◉ Use the same password

Storage type   * Password ••••••   * Confirm Password ••••••

○ Automatic Storage Management   ○ Use different passwords

Disk Group [   ]🔍 | User Name | Password | Confirm Password |
                                                              |-----------|----------|------------------|
◉ File System | SYS | ••••••• | ••••••• |
                                                              | SYSTEM | ••••••• | ••••••• |
* Location [/u02/oradata   ]🔍 | DBSNMP | ••••••• | ••••••• |

Fast Recovery   **Non Administrator Credentials**

Specify the location where recovery related files (archived redo logs, RMAN backups and other related files) will be   Select users that should not be accessible to the SSA User.
created.

☑ Enable Fast Recovery Area   Available Users   Selected Users

                    ○ Automatic Storage Management   OLAPSYS
                                                              SI_INFORMTN_SCHEMA
                    Disk Group [   ]🔍   OWBSYS
                                                              ORDPLUGINS   ⏵⏵
                    ◉ File System   XDB
                                                              SYSMAN   ⏴
                    Location [/u02/fast_recovery_area]🔍   HR
                                                              OE   ⏴⏴
Fast Recovery Area Size(MB) [6000   ]   OUTLN

      Enable Archiving ☑   Password [   ]   Confirm Password [   ]

      To allow SSA users to schedule backups and perform restore operations, configure a Fast Recovery Area   **Master Account Privileges**
☑ TIP and select the Enable Archiving check box.

Listener Port   * Name [saimaster_role]

* Port Number [1521]🔍   Description [New database role to be assigned to master account.]

                                                              * Privileges [CREATE SESSION, ALTER SESSION, CREATE INDEXTYPE, CREATE ANY OPERATOR, CREATE ANY
                                                                PROCEDURE, CREATE ANY SEQUENCE, CREATE ANY INDEX, CREATE JOB, CREATE ANY
                                                                MATERIALIZED VIEW, CREATE ANY TABLE, CREATE ANY TRIGGER, CREATE ANY TYPE, CREATE
                                                                ANY VIEW, CREATE ANY SYNONYM, CREATE ANY DIRECTORY, SELECT ANY DICTIONARY, SELECT
                                                                ANY TABLE]

FIGURE 2-24. *Database details for service template*

In the Master Account Privileges section, name the master account role saimaster_
role. This role will be granted to the master account that is specified by the SSA user
when creating the self-service database. There is a list of privileges that will be granted
to the role. You can modify this list depending on your company requirements—for
example, if you feel that the SSA master account should not have privileges such as
CREATE ANY DIRECTORY, you can remove that privilege.

On the other hand, if you want to add more privileges, you can do so. In our
case, we have added the SELECT ANY TABLE privilege to the role in addition to the
existing privileges. This can be done if the requirement is that the master account
role should be able to select any data from any table in the database. So our final list
of privileges is as follows:

CREATE SESSION, ALTER SESSION, CREATE INDEXTYPE, CREATE ANY
OPERATOR, CREATE ANY PROCEDURE, CREATE ANY SEQUENCE, CREATE ANY
INDEX, CREATE JOB, CREATE ANY MATERIALIZED VIEW, CREATE ANY TABLE,

CREATE ANY TRIGGER, CREATE ANY TYPE, CREATE ANY VIEW, CREATE ANY
SYNONYM, CREATE ANY DIRECTORY, SELECT ANY DICTIONARY, SELECT
ANY TABLE

Click Next to access the Initialization Parameters screen (Figure 2-25).

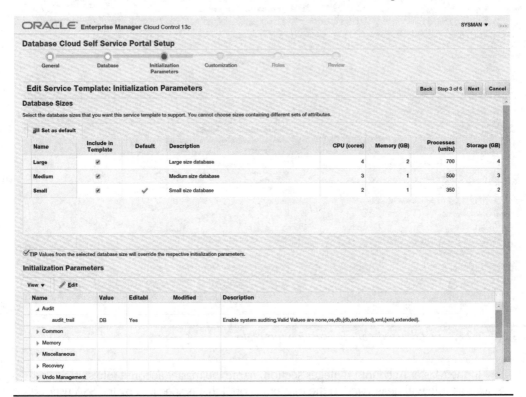

FIGURE 2-25. *Selecting initialization parameters for the service template*

Select the Database Sizes that the service template will support. These are the
pre-created sizes you created earlier in this chapter. The limits for each size are also
displayed. You can choose to include all of the sizes or only some of them in each
template.

This gives the SSA user SAI_DAS an option as to which database size to select.
Click Set As Default to make one of the database sizes the default, so that it is the
first choice for the SSA user when this service template is selected at the time of
self-service–database creation.

The initialization parameters for the database can also be edited. However, note
that the database size that is selected by the SSA user at request time will override
the corresponding initialization parameters such as sga_target, pga_aggregate_target,

processes, and cpu_count parameters. The Storage GB, as explained earlier, is not a hard limit on the database but is used only for thresholds and alerts.

Click Next to access the Customization screen (Figure 2-26).

Here you can specify the custom scripts to be executed before and after creating the service instance. A Post SQL Script can also be specified. In addition, custom

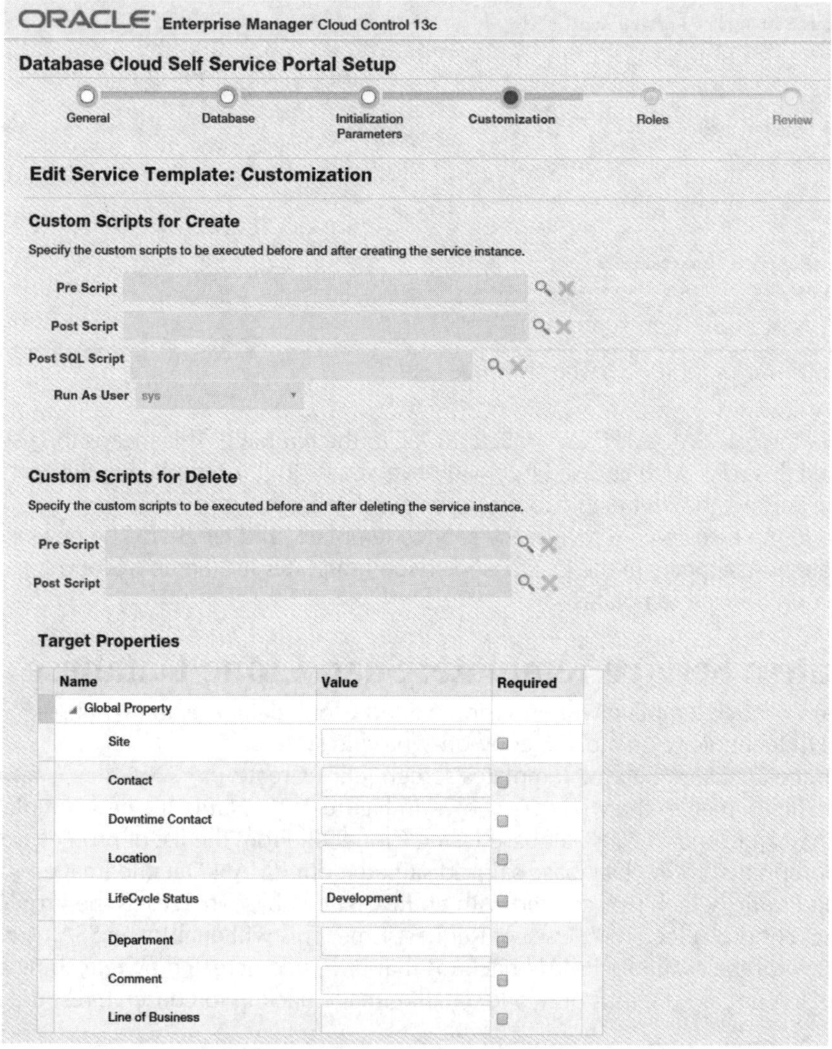

FIGURE 2-26. *Customization options for the service template*

scripts to be executed before and after deleting the service instance can be specified. All these are optional, of course.

Target Properties for the new self-service database can also be specified on this screen, such as the administrative contact, the downtime contact, the lifecycle status, the line of business, and so on.

Click Next to access the Roles screen (Figure 2-27).

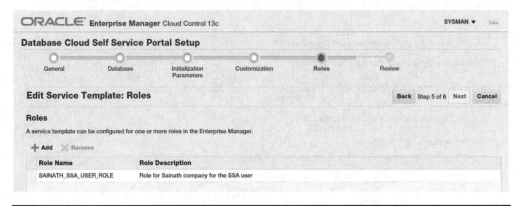

FIGURE 2-27. *Roles for the service template*

Add the role SAINATH_SSA_USER_ROLE to the template. This means the users assigned this role, such as SAI_DAS, will have access to this template in the Self Service Portal and will be able to create a new database.

Go to the next screen, review the service template, and create it. The new template now appears in the Database Service Templates list (Setup | Cloud | Database | Service Templates).

Create a Service Template: Snap Clone Database

This new service template will provision a Snap Clone database and will use CloneDB technology on a dNFS copy-on-write file system.

On the Database Service Templates screen, click Create.

The first screen of the wizard is shown in Figure 2-28. Name the new template Sainath Snap Clone 11204 Database Using CloneDB. From the list of profiles, select the appropriate profile, Database saiprod.sainath.com RMAN Datafile Image Backup Profile, which was created with an RMAN database image. As the Profile Version, choose Selected By User At Request Time. This will enable the SSA user to select any of the available RMAN backups that have been created by refreshing the profile. In our case, there is only one datafile image backup to conserve resources.

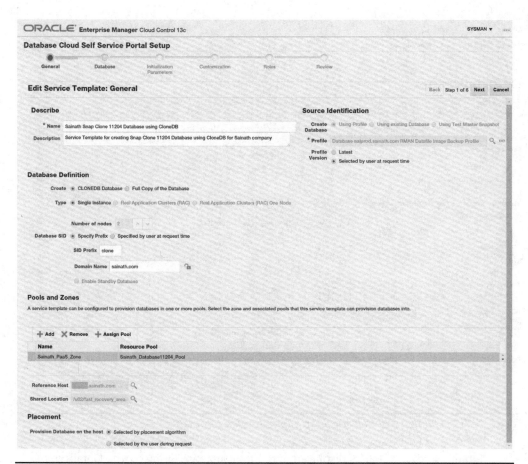

FIGURE 2-28. *Creating a service template for a Snap Clone database*

Because a datafile image backup has been created as the profile, an option appears dynamically in the Database Definition section to create a CLONEDB Database. Select CLONEDB Database and not Full Copy Of The Database. Use the SID Prefix of clone (you can use any SID prefix according to company standards) and set the Domain Name as sainath.com. Add the Sainath_PaaS_Zone and assign it to the Sainath_Database11204_Pool.

The other options on this screen are similar to what you have seen in the other template creation procedures. Click Next. The Database details screen appears (Figure 2-29).

FIGURE 2-29. *Database details for Snap Clone service template*

On this screen, a note is displayed under the Database Storage Area Details: "Database files location needs to be a NFS location." So we select an NFS location /u02/copy-on-write as the database storage area; this location has been set up previously as an NFS share at the Unix level on this database server. The instructions for how to do this are in the My Oracle Support (MOS) Document "Configure Direct NFS Client (DNFS) on Linux (11*g*)" (Doc ID 762374.1).

Check the Enable Fast Recovery Area option. You need to select a file system location such as /u02/fast_recovery_area for the FRA; ASM cannot be selected in this case because of Snap Clone requirements for CloneDB. Select a Fast Recovery Area Size (MB) of 6000. Also check the Enable Archiving check box for the new database.

Allow the SSA user to take up to 7 (maximum 10) backups for the new database. As the Backup Location, specify /u02/fast_recovery_area/clonebackups. Note that the backup does not use copy-on-write technology, so it is not a space-saver if multiple backups are performed by the SSA user. So in this case you do not need to use an NFS location for the backup location in the service template.

For the Listener Port, enter the port number that should be associated with the new database or the scan listener port number if you are using version 11.2 RAC or later.

Name the Master Account role saimaster_role and add the SELECT ANY TABLE privilege to the role in addition to the existing Privileges shown. This can be added if the master account role should be able to select any data from any table in the database.

On the next screen, the Initialization parameters screen, select the database sizes that the template will support. This gives the SSA user SAI_DAS an option as to which database size to select. Set the Small Database size as the default. Any such database size selected by the SSA user will override the corresponding initialization parameters such as sga_target, pga_aggregate_target, processes, and cpu_count parameters. The Storage GB is not a hard limit on the database but only used for thresholds and alerts.

Move to the next screen, which shows no custom scripts to add. Click Next. On the Roles screen, add the role SAINATH_SSA_USER_ROLE to the template. After this, review the service template and click Create on the review screen to save the template. The new template appears in the list of service templates, as you can see in Figure 2-30.

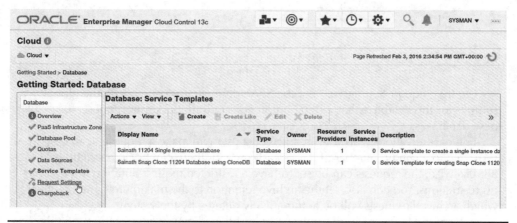

FIGURE 2-30. *List of service templates*

Enable Request Settings

Click Request Settings in the left panel of the Database setup screen, as shown in Figure 2-31.

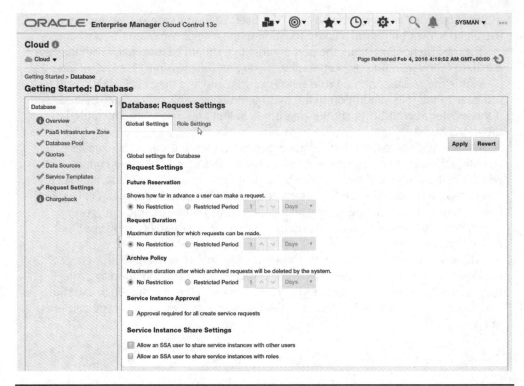

FIGURE 2-31. *Global Request Settings for the database*

On the Request Settings screen, the SSA administrator can choose the global settings for the database that will be enforced for all the SSA user requests for new databases.

Future reservations—how far in advance a user can make a request—can be restricted to a certain number of days in advance, or there can be no restrictions at all. Likewise, the requests can be set to have a restricted request duration in days, or no restrictions. You can also set the archive retention to the maximum duration after which archived requests will be automatically deleted by the system.

Enterprise Manager Cloud Control 13*c* introduced new request settings on this page. For the first time, Enterprise Manager includes a Service Instance Approval setting. With this setting, approval is required from the SSA administrator for *all* create service requests by the SSA user on the database side.

You can also set the Service Instance Share Settings, whereby you either allow an SSA user to share service instances with other users, or alternatively share the service instances with roles. This way, if one SSA user creates a database instance via self-service, then either other specified SSA users or all SSA users assigned a specified role will be able to see the new database instance in their own self-service consoles. They will be able to share monitoring and management. A development team might use this kind of setup.

Move to the Role Settings tab (Figure 2-32).

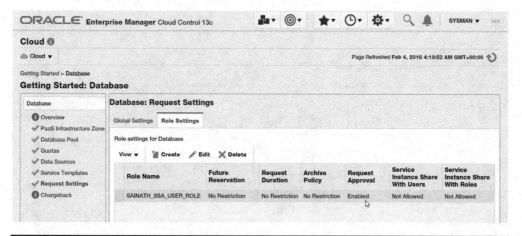

FIGURE 2-32. *Specify role settings.*

In this tab, you can specify different database request–related role settings for different roles. Click Create, select the appropriate role, and change the settings for that role. You can see that the SAINATH_SSA_USER_ROLE has been added, and Request Approval has been Enabled for this role. This means that whenever the SSA user SAI_DAS requests a database, the SSA administrator will need to approve the request. Once approved, the request will be automatically actioned.

Perhaps you could create a special role for certain requestors who want large production databases, so that special approval is required before the request is actioned. It would have been better, of course, if the request approval requirement could have been set at the individual service request level. In this way, you could specify that certain service requests require approval, such as those for large production databases or every production database. But at this point in time, it is not possible to set approval requirements at the service request level.

Configure Chargeback

Configuring chargeback of your database cloud is entirely optional. Chargeback can be used to allocate the costs of IT resources to the project managers, developers, or testers who consume them. Alternatively, the costs calculated can be used as "showback" without actually charging them. The Chargeback setup screen is shown in Figure 2-33. You create the charge plans, assign to targets, and optionally set up cost centers to aggregate costs among groups of SSA users.

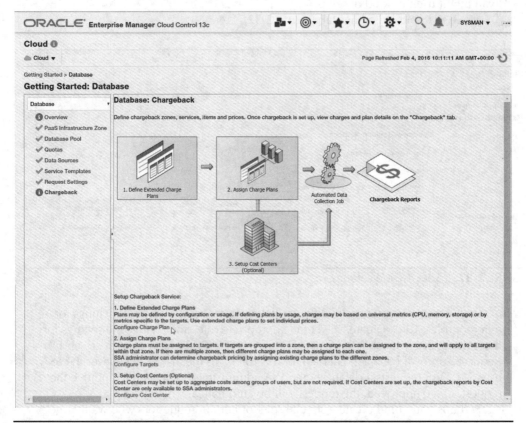

FIGURE 2-33. *Database Chargeback screen*

To use chargeback, you must have the Oracle Consolidation Planning and Chargeback Plug-in installed on the Oracle Management Server (OMS). Plug-in installation was explained in the "Deploy the Plug-ins" section earlier in this chapter. After the plug-in is installed, a super administrator (such as SYSMAN) in Enterprise Manager or a user who has been assigned the EM_CLOUD_ADMINISTRATOR role can proceed to configure the chargeback. The out-of-the-box EM_CBA_ADMIN (chargeback administrator) role also includes all the privileges for chargeback operations, so a user assigned this role could set up the chargeback, too.

Resource usage can be metered effectively by Enterprise Manager Cloud Control 13*c*, and this metering information can be used to calculate the charges applicable to the SSA users who request databases and consume resources. The SSA users can be internal project representatives or external users. In either case, they are able to provision the databases they require by simply raising a self-service request on their Self Service Portal.

Different types of charge plans can be used to calculate the chargeback. The Universal Charge Plan is available out of the box and is based on the metrics of CPU utilization, memory, and storage allocation. The Universal Charge Plan contains only these three metrics and no further metrics can be added. Since these are universal rates, they can be applied to most entity types, except some to which they are not applicable—such as Java 2 Platform, Enterprise Edition (J2EE) applications, for example. It is possible for a universal plan to use different rates based on different CPU architecture, as shown in Figure 2-34.

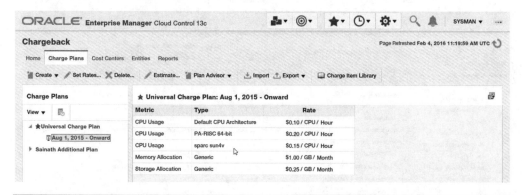

FIGURE 2-34. *Universal Charge Plan with different architectures*

In the screen shown in Figure 2-34, we have set up different rates for CPU usage based on the architecture. Company policy has determined that self-service requests for any entity (such as a database) based on PA-RISC 64-bit servers will be charged at a higher rate, 20 cents per CPU per hour, as compared to other servers that will be charged at a lower rate. This could have been levied to compensate for the cost of purchase or maintenance of these servers and is determined by company policy. Memory and storage allocation will be charged at a generic rate.

This universal plan has been in effect since August 2015. You cannot edit it: if you click Set Rates, you will see the message, "The selected charge plan revision Aug 1, 2015 - Onward is in effective from a previous report cycle. It cannot be edited. Create a new revision." To create a new revision, choose Create | Revision.

The new revision you create will take effect from the first day of the month in which you have created it. You can then change rates or add new rates. Note that any rates that you set will take effect from the beginning of the current month and will not affect the calculation of the previous months.

In addition, extended charge plans (also called Additional Plans) can be created that calculate charges based on specific entities. You can define rates based on configuration—for example, you can vary the rate depending on the database versions, or you can charge more for use of a particular database option. You can define actual usage-based rates. You can also define a flat charge independent of configuration or usage. The universal plan rates can also be adjusted or overridden by an extended charge plan.

Figure 2-35 shows an example of an extended (additional) plan that has been created.

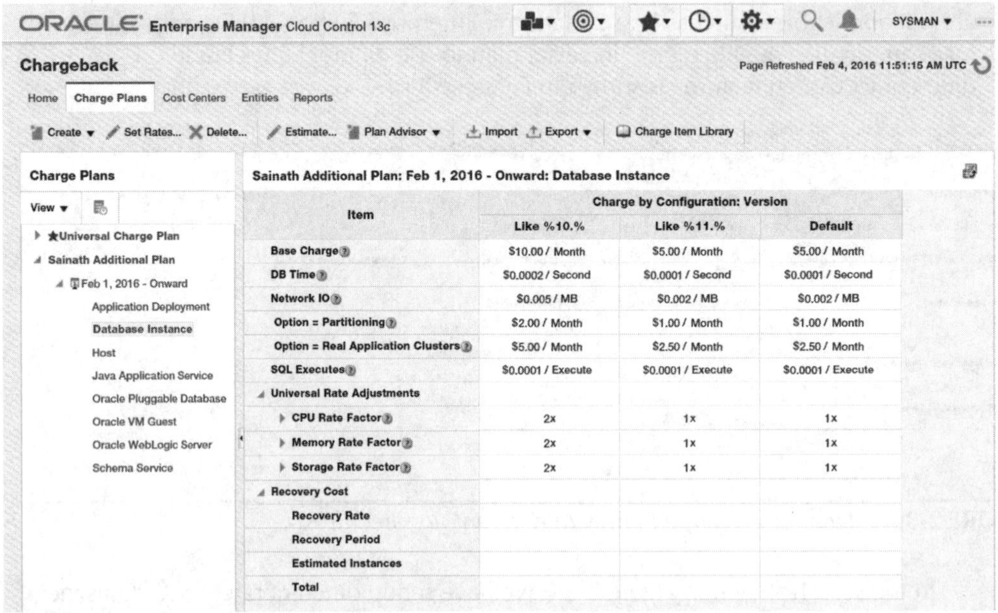

FIGURE 2-35. *Sainath additional plan*

The plan's charge rates for database instance are displayed. The same plan may contain different rates for database instance, schema service, pluggable database, host, WebLogic server, and other factors. This particular plan is a new revision from February 1 onward. It can be edited in the same month.

For the Database Instance, as you can see, two configurations based on version have been set up: one for 11*g* instances and another for 10*g* instances. To discourage older versions, the rates for 10*g* are higher (this is for example purposes only, to show what is possible).

First, we included a Base Charge, which is more if a 10*g* instance is requested by the SSA user, and less if an 11*g* instance is requested; this subtly influences SSA users to request the 11*g* version of the Database. All the other charges for an 11*g* Database request are lower as well. Usage charges—such as Network IO, SQL Executes, and

DB Time—have also been included. The latter figures have been kept the lowest since SQL executes and DB Time can climb very rapidly.

Additional database options such as Partitioning and Real Application Clusters will be charged extra as well in this plan. On top of that, the Universal Rates Adjustments are 1x for an 11*g* Database request and 2x for a 10*g* Database request.

If you click Set Rates, provided you are in the same month as the start date of the revision, you can then edit the rates; you can add new charge items if you click Add Item on that page. Select the Item Name to use for the Charge Item from a drop-down list. This list is derived from the Target Type. In the case of the Database Instance Target Type, this can be either a Base Charge, CPU Count, CPU Time, DB Time, Database Role, Disk Read (Physical) Operations, Disk Write (Physical) Operations, Edition, Uptime, Network IO, Option, RAC Node Count, Release, SQL Executes, or User Transactions. All these can be used as charge items.

Change Global Settings for Chargeback

You can also change the global settings for chargeback by moving to the Home page on the Chargeback screen and scrolling down to the Settings tab (Figure 2-36).

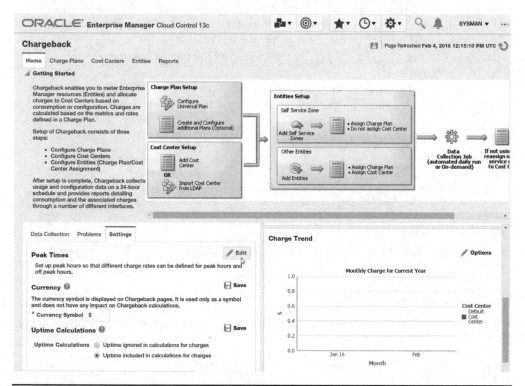

FIGURE 2-36.   *Settings for chargeback*

Here, you can change the Peak Times, Currency symbol, and Uptime Calculations. Set up peak hours so that different charge rates can be defined for peak hours and off-peak hours.

You can also change the default currency symbol ($) as displayed on chargeback screens. All charge plans including the Universal and Extended Plans will use this currency symbol, as well as every report. Changing the symbol does not convert the charge rates, however. The rate conversion, if required, must be done in a separate billing program that will draw the chargeback information from Enterprise Manager. (Note that Enterprise Manager is not responsible for generating chargeback bills; a separate billing program must be used.)

In the Settings tab, you can also decide whether uptime is to be included or ignored in the calculations for charges. By default, it will be included.

Add Cost Centers

Optionally, you can add cost centers using the Cost Centers tab on the Chargeback screen. You can set up a cost center to contain a number of entities, and the charges for all those entities can be aggregated by the cost center. Note that the chargeback per cost center can only be seen by the SSA administrator and not by the SSA user.

You can also arrange cost centers in a hierarchy, and this will result in charges being calculated in a rollup manner, with the topmost cost center incurring the charges of all the component cost centers. You can change this hierarchy in the future, if required.

An example hierarchy is shown in Figure 2-37. We have created a Sainath Development cost center under the Sainath Corporate cost center.

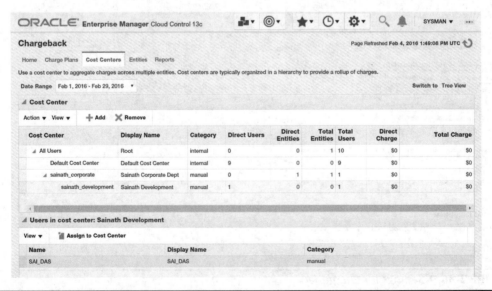

FIGURE 2-37. *Cost centers for chargeback*

You can select any of the cost centers and assign SSA users to another cost center by clicking the Assign To Cost Center button on this page. Any users who are not assigned to a cost center will be automatically placed in the Default Cost Center where their charges will be aggregated.

You can move cost centers by choosing Action | Move. Cost centers can also be deactivated by clicking the Remove button. The cost center remains active for historical purposes even after deactivation, but it is no longer possible to assign any user to or place any entity in a deactivated cost center.

You can also synchronize the cost centers on this page to an LDAP hierarchy used in your organization, by choosing Action | LDAP Settings, and Action | On-demand LDAP Sync.

Now move to the Entities tab (Figure 2-38).

FIGURE 2-38.   *Cost center and charge plan assignment for entities*

In this tab, you can add entities and assign charge plans and cost centers to those entities. Adding entities will start collecting metrics for those targets, on the basis of which chargeback will be calculated. Click the Add button to see the screen shown in Figure 2-39.

Here, you can select the targets that will be configured for chargeback and their usage modes. The following basic target types can be added: Host, VM Guest, Database Instance, and WebLogic Server. Be sure to select any zones that you have configured for use in the Self Service Portal.

We have added the PaaS Infrastructure Zone, the host, and the two database instances that will be used for SCHaaS and PDBaaS. The Usage Mode has been selected appropriately as Metered By Members for the zone that will be used for Database as a Service, Metered by Instance for the Host, Metered by Service for the SAIPROD 11*g* database that will be used for SCHaaS, and Metered by PDB for the AHUPROD 12*c* container database (CDB) to be used for PDBaaS.

Suppose, for example, that two application schemas, Sales and Inventory, are running as separate database services on one database. These application schemas

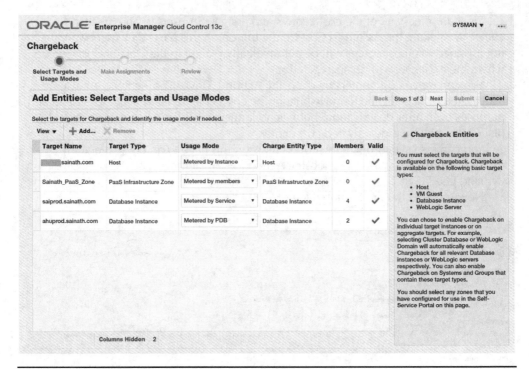

FIGURE 2-39. *Selecting targets and usage modes*

may belong to different cost centers, and therefore the metering and chargeback should pertain to each database service separately. So this particular database should be metered by service. If PDBs are being used in the same manner in a container database, then the metering should be by individual PDB.

Click Next to move to the Make Assignments screen (Figure 2-40).

The entities that you have added need to have a charge plan and cost center assigned to them. Select each row and use the buttons to assign a charge plan and a cost center. If a charge plan is not assigned directly to a target, it is inherited from the closest parent with a plan assignment. For example, setting a plan on a Host will result in all database instances on the host using the plan. For self-service zones, you can set the charge plan on the zone.

The cost center assignment, on the other hand, will determine to which cost center the charges will be allocated. The recommendation is that you should *not* set the cost center on any self-service entity. Only the entities that have *not* been created through self-service should have the cost center assigned in this step.

Since entities would be added and removed quickly in self-service, the SSA administrator would find it difficult to assign a charge plan manually to every new entity, or to assign an entity to a cost center. This assignment therefore happens

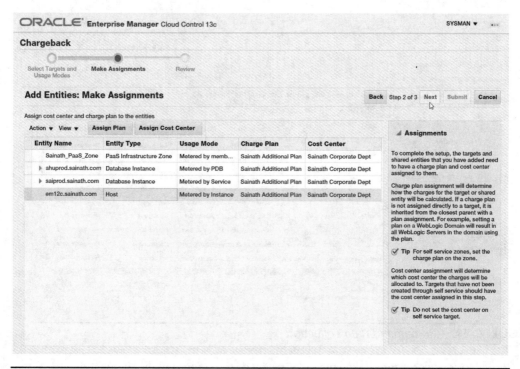

FIGURE 2-40.   *Add Entities: Make Assignments*

automatically in the case of entities that are created by self-service. For example, if a new database is created in a zone, it will inherit the charge plan of the zone.

Now move to the next step, review the information, and submit. Note that the metrics for those entities that have been added to chargeback are collected from the Enterprise Manager repository on a daily schedule. As a result, it may take up to 24 hours before charge data appears for any entities that have been added.

Move back to the Entities tab under Chargeback. You can see the newly added entities in the list (Figure 2-41).

The Latest Collection Status column says Not Started. When the chargeback setup is complete, it results in an ETL (Extract-Transform-Load) job running in Enterprise Manager by default once a day. You can also have the job run on demand by choosing Action | On-demand Data Collection to force the collection immediately.

The ETL job performs the following actions, in order: it extracts the monitoring and configuration data from the Enterprise Manager 13c repository tables, it performs transformations and aggregations to enable the data to be used for chargeback, it loads the data into different chargeback tables within the Enterprise Manager repository, and it then calculates the separate charges for the cost centers based on the assigned charge plans.

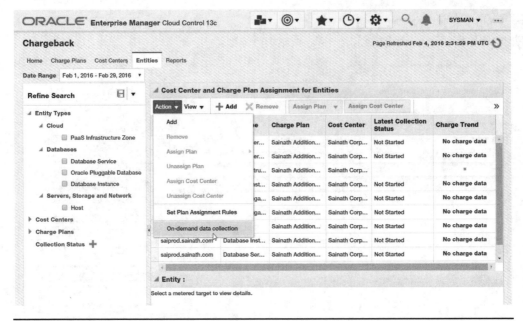

FIGURE 2-41. *On-demand data collection*

Hourly aggregation takes place for usage data, whereas daily aggregation is used for configuration data. As an example, User Transactions Per Service will be aggregated to every hour, whereas Database Edition will be aggregated to each day.

After the collection job has run and the aggregation is complete, the charge plans will be used to calculate the chargeback on the basis of the Daily Configuration data and the Hourly Usage data. A monthly reporting cycle is used. The usage and charge data for configured targets will be available from the Reports tab.

We will look at the calculated chargeback information after completing the creation of databases, schemas, and PDBs in later chapters.

Self-Service: Request and Create a Database Service

Finally, we come to the stage where the SSA user can log in to the Self Service Portal and make a request for a database to be provisioned. Because the database cloud is already set up by the cloud administrators, no more interaction is required with the administrator team (unless an approval requirement is set up, as explained earlier in this chapter). The SSA user can make a request for a new database, and the request will be automatically fulfilled by the Enterprise Manager Cloud mechanism—based on the quotas that have been allocated to the SSA user.

For example, if the SSA user has a quota of three databases, then only the first three of the database requests will be completed successfully. If the SSA user has a quota of 10GB of memory, only that amount of memory can be used for all the databases. The SSA user can monitor the consumption of resources and manage the provisioned databases via a GUI interface.

Begin by logging in to Enterprise Manager Cloud Control 13c as the SAI_DAS user. This is the SSA user that we created previously. The first page that appears for this user is the All Cloud Services page shown in Figure 2-42.

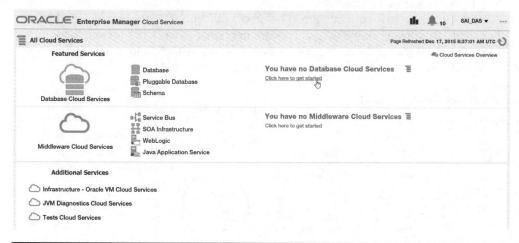

FIGURE 2-42. *All Cloud Services page for SSA user*

In the Database Cloud Services section, under Featured Services, select Click Here To Get Started. This brings up the Database Cloud Service Portal (Figure 2-43).

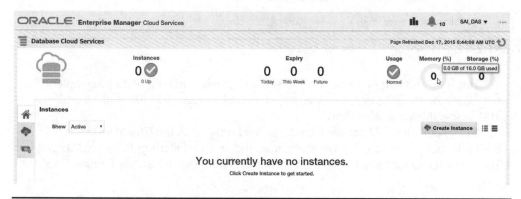

FIGURE 2-43. *Database Cloud Service Portal for SSA user*

For Database as a Service, the Database Cloud Service Portal is the home base for the SSA user. From here, the user can request new databases, monitor existing or past requests, and check the allocated quota allowance. Chargeback information is also available here.

By hovering your cursor over the Memory (%) and Storage (%) indicator dials at the top of the screen, you can see that 0GB has been used out of 16GB of the memory quota, and 0GB out of the 100GB of the storage quota. These are the quotas for the database cloud that have been granted (via a role) to the SSA user SAI_DAS by the SSA administrator.

The Usage circle is currently green colored, with Normal displayed along with a tick mark. This means all the usage items are in normal range. Click the circle for more details. This displays all the quotas available to SAI_DAS, and what has been used from the quotas, in a dial format, as shown in Figure 2-44.

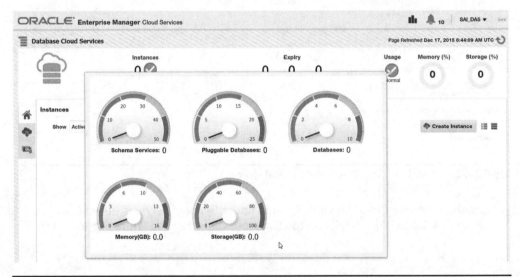

FIGURE 2-44. *Usage and quotas for SSA user*

This indicates that up to 50 schema services can be created, or 25 pluggable databases, or 10 databases. The Memory (GB) and Storage (GB) limits of 16 and 100, respectively, are also shown.

Now, back on the Database Cloud Service Portal, click the Create Instance button to view a pop-up window that shows the Service Offerings to be selected. These Service Offerings were created earlier by the SSA administrator (Figure 2-45).

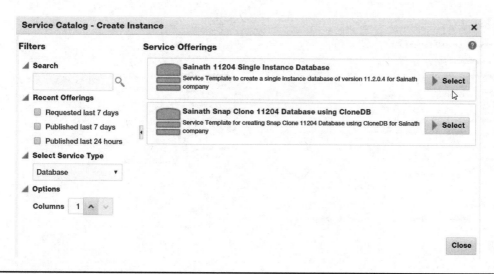

FIGURE 2-45. *Service Offerings*

For Select Service Type, choose Database. Two database service offerings have been set up and are available to the SAI_DAS user. Click the Select button next to the service offering named Sainath 11204 Single Instance Database to open the Create Database screen for the SSA user (Figure 2-46).

Enter a unique Database Service Name and a unique Master Account User Name and Password on this page. The username should not be a default account username such as SYS or SYSTEM. In this case, use SAITEST1 as the Database Service Name and SAIMASTER (you can use uppercase) as the Master Account User Name. This name will be used by the self-service user to log on to the database.

Select the Size for the new database, which is actually the database size. The Size settings here will override the settings in the database profile being used in the service template. The available database sizes have been set up previously for this chapter. We select the Small database size for this example. The limits for this size are displayed to the SSA user—CPU of two cores, Memory of 1GB, Process Count of up to 350, and Storage of 2GB.

The SSA user can also select the particular RMAN backup to be used for the self-service database request. This is available on a timeline depending on what backups have been created by the SSA administrator or cloud administrator (these backups were created by the administrator by refreshing the database profile, as explained earlier in this chapter).

Click the appropriate RMAN backup balloon in the timeline on this page. Explore the timeline and select the earliest backup that is available in the timeline. Later on, we will refresh this database to the second backup, so make sure the first backup is selected at this stage.

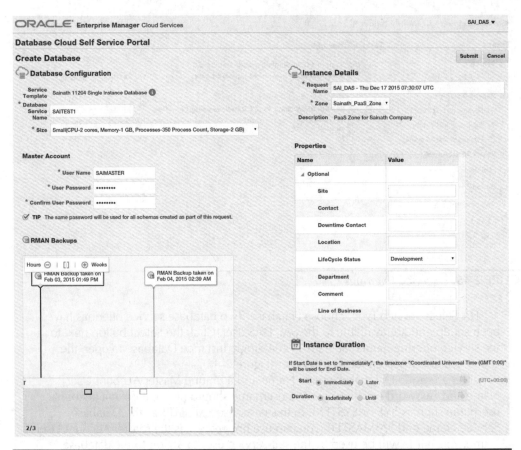

FIGURE 2-46. *Creating a database for the SSA user*

If the SSA user had access to multiple zones, the actual zone for deployment of the database could also be selected by the user. In our case, we only have one zone. The properties can also be set by the SSA user for this new database, along with the instance start and duration. You can set the duration of the database to a certain date or as indefinite. The created database will be available until this date, after which the database will be retired automatically.

Click Submit. This starts the Create Database request. Click the Requests tab, which is the second tab on the left pane of the screen (Figure 2-47), to see the status of the request.

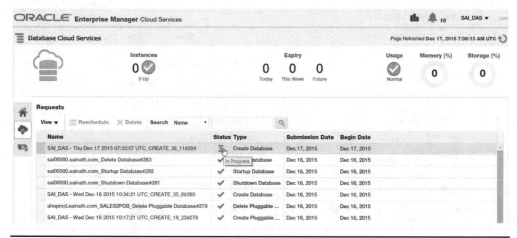

FIGURE 2-47. *Request in progress*

The Requests screen appears. The Create Database request is shown to be in progress. If an approval requirement was in place for all database requests or for the role of the SSA user, then the request status would show Pending Approval. This would then need to be approved by the SSA administrator, via Enterprise | Cloud | Cloud Home. The administrator would select the Pending Approval link from the Request Status graph on the Cloud Home page. The pending request would appear in a list, and the administrator would select it and click the Approve or Reject button.

You can examine the progress of the execution by drilling down on the hourglass icon, which displays the screen shown in Figure 2-48.

Detailed steps do not appear, since the self-service user SAI_DAS cannot examine the detailed execution of the steps. To examine the detailed steps, log in to Enterprise Manager as SYSMAN or the cloud administrator, and select Enterprise | Provisioning and Patching | Procedure Activity from the Cloud Control menu.

In the Deployment Procedure Manager, you can see that the latest process cloud request procedure owned by SAI_DAS, and of type cloud framework request has already succeeded. Drill down on the procedure to examine the detailed steps (Figure 2-49).

The process cloud request procedure completes in a few minutes. The output of each step can be examined by selecting the step. The Create Database Service step on this page shows that a new database sai00000.sainath.com was created, and a new service SAITEST1 was created and started.

The service name was input by the SSA user SAI_DAS, and the instance name sai00000 results from the prefix of sai having been specified in the service template when the template was created by the SSA administrator. The prefix of the instance

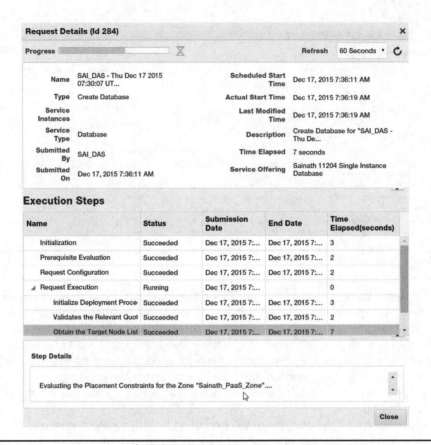

FIGURE 2-48. *Request Details screen*

name cannot be changed by the SSA user SAI_DAS using the self-service screens because the service catalog does not allow it.

Expand the Restore Database step, and you can see in the substeps that the database has been restored from an RMAN backup. This is shown in Figure 2-50.

Log onto the database pool host as the oracle UNIX user (the cloud administrator or DBA can do this, but not the SSA user). Type the command **lsnrctl status** to show the new service. Note the new service—lines are in boldface in the following output:

```
$ lsnrctl status

LSNRCTL for Linux: Version 12.1.0.2.0 - Production on 17-DEC-2015 07:48:31
Copyright (c) 1991, 2014, Oracle.  All rights reserved.
Connecting to (DESCRIPTION=(ADDRESS=(PROTOCOL=TCP)(HOST=xxxxx.sainath.com)
(PORT=1521)))
```

```
STATUS of the LISTENER
------------------------
Alias                    LISTENER
Version                  TNSLSNR for Linux: Version 12.1.0.2.0 - Production
Start Date               17-DEC-2015 05:34:32
Uptime                   0 days 2 hr. 13 min. 59 sec
Trace Level              off
Security                 ON: Local OS Authentication
SNMP                     OFF
Listener Parameter File
/u01/app/oracle/product/12.1.0/dbhome_1/network/admin/listener.ora
Listener Log File
/u01/app/oracle/diag/tnslsnr/xxxxx/listener/alert/log.xml
Listening Endpoints Summary...
  (DESCRIPTION=(ADDRESS=(PROTOCOL=tcp)(HOST=xxxxx.sainath.com)(PORT=1521)))
  (DESCRIPTION=(ADDRESS=(PROTOCOL=ipc)(KEY=EXTPROC1521)))
Services Summary...
Service "SAITEST1.sainath.com" has 1 instance(s).
  Instance "sai00000", status READY, has 1 handler(s) for this service...
Service "ahuprod.sainath.com" has 1 instance(s).
  Instance "ahuprod", status READY, has 1 handler(s) for this service...
Service "ahuprodXDB.sainath.com" has 1 instance(s).
  Instance "ahuprod", status READY, has 1 handler(s) for this service...
Service "emrep.sainath.com" has 1 instance(s).
  Instance "emrep", status READY, has 1 handler(s) for this service...
Service "emrepXDB.sainath.com" has 1 instance(s).
  Instance "emrep", status READY, has 1 handler(s) for this service...
Service "sai00000.sainath.com" has 1 instance(s).
  Instance "sai00000", status READY, has 1 handler(s) for this service...
Service "saiprod.sainath.com" has 1 instance(s).
  Instance "saiprod", status READY, has 1 handler(s) for this service...
Service "saiprodXDB.sainath.com" has 1 instance(s).
  Instance "saiprod", status READY, has 1 handler(s) for this service...
Service "sales.sainath.com" has 1 instance(s).
  Instance "ahuprod", status READY, has 1 handler(s) for this service...
The command completed successfully
```

The existence of the new instance sai00000 can also be verified at the UNIX level, by running the ps command with a grep for the pmon process. This is the process monitor, an important background process of an Oracle database. The pmon processes of all the Oracle instances are listed.

```
$ ps -aef | grep pmon
oracle     3327     1  0 05:34 ?        00:00:01 ora_pmon_saiprod
oracle     3458     1  0 05:34 ?        00:00:00 ora_pmon_ahuprod
oracle     3722     1  0 05:34 ?        00:00:00 ora_pmon_emrep
oracle     6042  5264  0 07:49 pts/0    00:00:00 grep pmon
oracle    32060     1  0 07:39 ?        00:00:00 ora_pmon_sai00000
```

FIGURE 2-49. *Successful completion of process cloud request*

FIGURE 2-50. *Restore Database step*

Log back into Enterprise Manager as the SSA user SAI_DAS. On the All Cloud Services Portal, you can see that one Database Instance has been created (Figure 2-51).

FIGURE 2-51. *Self-service database instance available*

Click the Instance link to move to the Database Cloud Service Portal (Figure 2-52). The name of the new self-service database is visible on the screen.

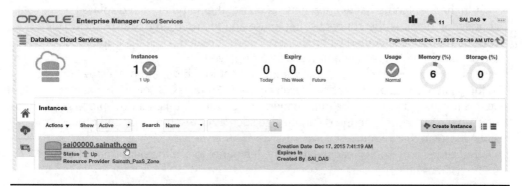

FIGURE 2-52. *Instance seen on Database Cloud Service Portal*

This is what the self-service user SAI_DAS will see. The user has used some of the quotas allocated by creating the first database. The new database, sai00000 .sainath.com, is shown with the Up Status. The user can now drill down to the SSA Home page (Figure 2-53) of the database.

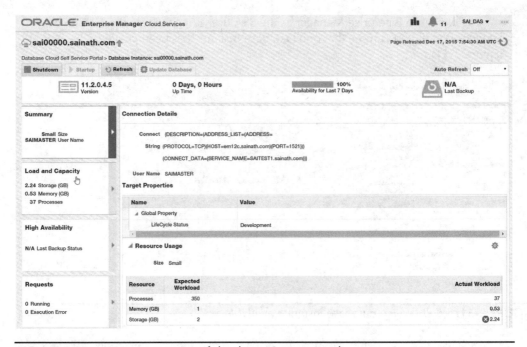

FIGURE 2-53. *SSA Home page of database: Summary tab*

On the SSA Home page of the new database, the Summary tab displays the connection details—the connect string to use and the username SAIMASTER. This was the username specified when the service was created. The target properties of the database and the resource usage is also displayed.

You can see that the SSA user is within the memory limit and processes limit set in the database size but has already exceeded the Storage GB set in the database size. Since the latter is a soft limit, an alert will be raised. It is not possible to go beyond the other limits in the database size such as cores, memory, and processes, since those are hard limits.

Click the Load And Capacity tab in the left panel to see the performance details of the database (Figure 2-54).

The self-service user can examine certain performance details of the new database such as the database activity, host CPU, active sessions, and memory usage breakdown. There is also a SQL Monitoring section for long-running SQL statements.

If required, the self-service user can start up and shut down the database using the buttons at the top of the Home page.

Now let's move to the High Availability tab, shown in Figure 2-55.

FIGURE 2-54.   *SSA Home page of database: Load And Capacity tab*

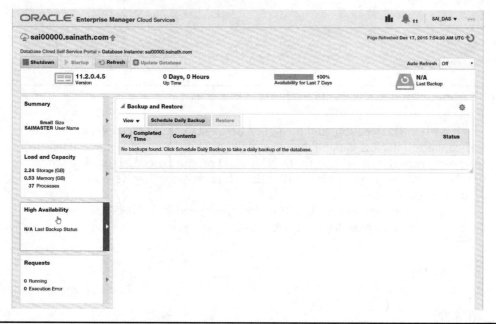

FIGURE 2-55.   *SSA Home page of database: High Availability tab*

The self-service user can schedule daily backups from this tab and restore from a previous backup via the Restore tab.

The self-service user can also use the connect string that is displayed in the Summary tab (shown in Figure 2-53) to connect to the database using other tools such as Oracle SQL Developer, via the database login of SAIMASTER.

In Figure 2-56, we have created a new database connection in Oracle SQL Developer, and we are using the connect identifier specified on the database service home page. The user name is SAIMASTER.

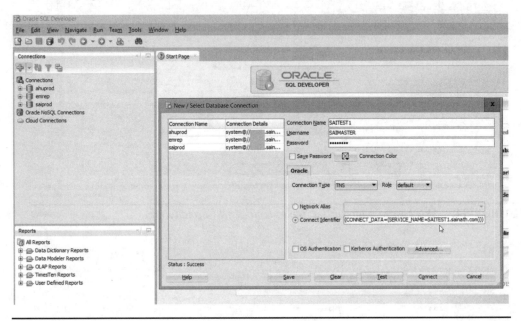

FIGURE 2-56. *New connection in Oracle SQL Developer*

First test the connection, and then click Connect to create the new connection and connect to it. Now expand the view of Other Users. Since this new database has been created from a copy of the SAIPROD production database, it also has the sample schemas such as HR, OE, SH, and so on, that were in the production database.

Select the HR user and expand its tables. The logged in SAIMASTER user can see the data in the Employees table (Figure 2-57).

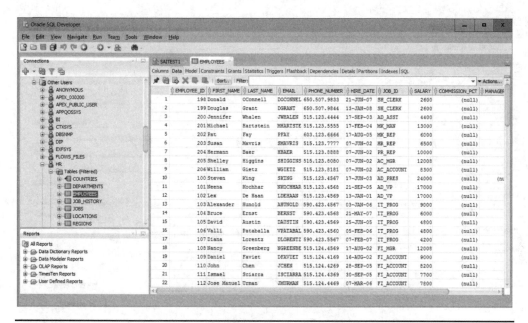

FIGURE 2-57. *Data in the Employees table*

If you scroll down, you can see that the employee count in this table in the newly created database is 107. Now go back to the SSA home page as the SSA user. If the data in the production or test master database has changed, the SSA administrator or cloud administrator can perform a refresh of the database profile used in the service template.

Once the refresh is completed by the admin team, the Refresh button is also available to the SSA user, as shown in Figure 2-58.

Click the Refresh button. This allows the SSA user to select the newer RMAN backups that are available from a timeline, to refresh the data in the SSA database sai00000. Select one of the available backups in the timeline and click Refresh.

Move back to the Requests screen (as shown previously in Figure 2-47) on the Database Cloud Self Service Portal. A refresh job has started and completes successfully after a few minutes. After this refresh is completed, the Refresh button on the SSA Home page is not available because there are no more newer backups available.

If the SSA user reconnects to the database using SQL Developer and reselects data from the HR.employees table, the SSA user can scroll down and see that there are 108 records instead of the original 107 records, thus showing that the data has been refreshed from the recent backup. A new employee has probably joined. This is just an example to show that a newer backup has been restored.

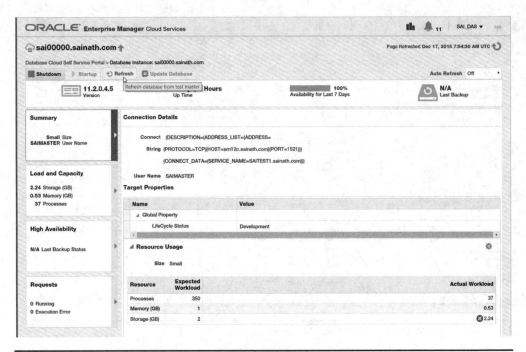

FIGURE 2-58. *Refresh the SSA database*

On the main Database Cloud Service Portal screen, the self-service user can delete the created database when it is no longer required (Figure 2-59).

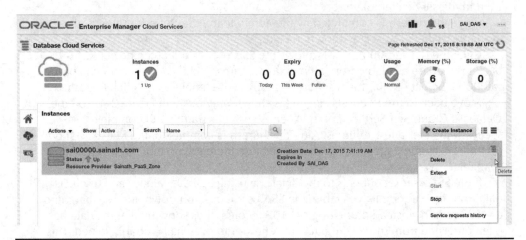

FIGURE 2-59. *Deleting the SSA database*

Simply clicking the Delete option in the menu starts a delete procedure that removes all traces of the database from the server. The quota used by this database is also released.

At the UNIX command-line level, the cloud administrator or DBA can verify that the database has been deleted. The pmon process for the database is no longer present, and the service has disappeared from the list of services in the listener output:

```
$ ps -aef | grep pmon
oracle    3327     1  0 05:34 ?        00:00:01 ora_pmon_saiprod
oracle    3458     1  0 05:34 ?        00:00:00 ora_pmon_ahuprod
oracle    3722     1  0 05:34 ?        00:00:00 ora_pmon_emrep
oracle   30437  5264  0 08:39 pts/0    00:00:00 grep pmon

$ lsnrctl status
LSNRCTL for Linux: Version 12.1.0.2.0 - Production on 17-DEC-2015 08:39:20
Copyright (c) 1991, 2014, Oracle.  All rights reserved.

Connecting to (DESCRIPTION=(ADDRESS=(PROTOCOL=TCP)(HOST=xxxxx.sainath.com)
(PORT=1521)))
STATUS of the LISTENER
------------------------
Alias                     LISTENER
Version                   TNSLSNR for Linux: Version 12.1.0.2.0 - Production
Start Date                17-DEC-2015 05:34:32
Uptime                    0 days 3 hr. 4 min. 48 sec
Trace Level               off
Security                  ON: Local OS Authentication
SNMP                      OFF
Listener Parameter File
/u01/app/oracle/product/12.1.0/dbhome_1/network/admin/listener.ora
Listener Log File
/u01/app/oracle/diag/tnslsnr/xxxxx/listener/alert/log.xml
Listening Endpoints Summary...
  (DESCRIPTION=(ADDRESS=(PROTOCOL=tcp)(HOST=xxxxx.sainath.com)(PORT=1521)))
  (DESCRIPTION=(ADDRESS=(PROTOCOL=ipc)(KEY=EXTPROC1521)))
Services Summary...
Service "ahuprod.sainath.com" has 1 instance(s).
  Instance "ahuprod", status READY, has 1 handler(s) for this service...
Service "ahuprodXDB.sainath.com" has 1 instance(s).
  Instance "ahuprod", status READY, has 1 handler(s) for this service...
Service "emrep.sainath.com" has 1 instance(s).
  Instance "emrep", status READY, has 1 handler(s) for this service...
Service "emrepXDB.sainath.com" has 1 instance(s).
  Instance "emrep", status READY, has 1 handler(s) for this service...
Service "saiprod.sainath.com" has 1 instance(s).
  Instance "saiprod", status READY, has 1 handler(s) for this service...
Service "saiprodXDB.sainath.com" has 1 instance(s).
  Instance "saiprod", status READY, has 1 handler(s) for this service...
Service "sales.sainath.com" has 1 instance(s).
  Instance "ahuprod", status READY, has 1 handler(s) for this service...
The command completed successfully
```

Self-Service: Request and Create a Snap Clone (CloneDB) Database Service

When you are logged in as SAI_DAS, on the Database Cloud Service Portal, click Create Instance to open a pop-up window with Service Offerings. These offerings have been pre-created by the cloud administrator (Figure 2-60).

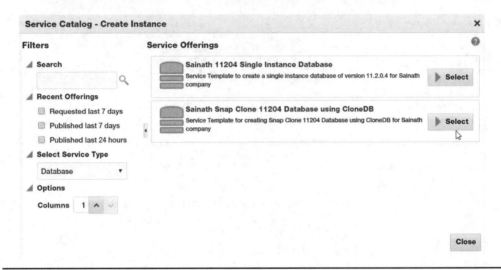

FIGURE 2-60. *Service Offerings*

Select the Snap Clone service offering to open the Create Database screen (Figure 2-61).

Enter the Service Name **SAICLONE1** and the User Name **SAIMASTER** with an appropriate password. As before, select the appropriate Size for the new database. The Size setting here will override the settings in the database profile that is being used in the service template.

The SSA user can also select the particular RMAN backup to be used for the self-service database request. This is available on a timeline, depending on what backups have been created by the SSA administrator or cloud administrator. Note that because you have selected the Snap Clone service offering, one or more RMAN image backups appear in the timeline, and not the normal RMAN backups that appeared when you created the non-clone database in the first service selection.

Be sure to click the appropriate RMAN backup balloon in the timeline on this screen. You can also change the properties or the instance start and duration if you wish. Click Submit.

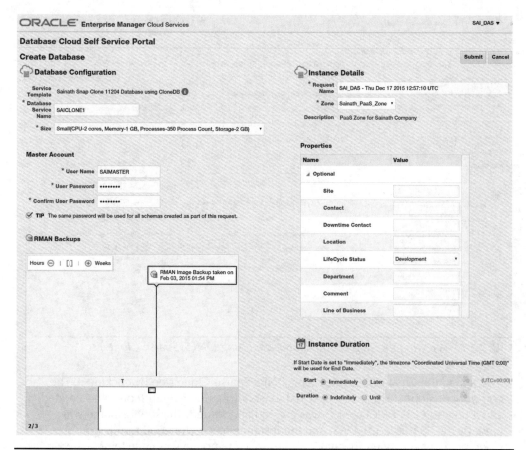

FIGURE 2-61. *Create Database: Snap Clone*

To examine the execution of the steps in detail, login as SYSMAN or the cloud administrator and select Enterprise | Provisioning and Patching | Procedure Activity. Locate the running Cloud Framework request and drill down to it.

The procedure completes in a few minutes. The output of each step can be seen by selecting it. You'll see the Create Database Using DNFS/Sparse Clone step that has been executed (Figure 2-62). This indicates a thin clone and not a full database has been created. You can also verify this at the UNIX level.

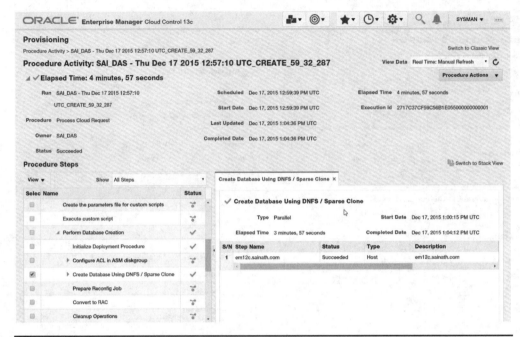

FIGURE 2-62.   *Viewing the step Create Database Using DNFS/Sparse Clone*

Expand the Create Database Using DNFS/Sparse Clone step by clicking it. The component steps show that a new database, clone000.sainath.com, was created, and a new service, SAICLONE1, was created and started. The service name was input by the SSA user SAI_DAS, and the instance name clone000 results from the clone prefix having been specified in the service template when the template was created by the SSA administrator.

At the UNIX level, the DBA or cloud administrator can execute commands to check the database and service creation. The pmon process and the service for the new database are shown in boldface in this output:

```
$ ps -aef | grep pmon
oracle    3327    1  0 05:34 ?        00:00:03 ora_pmon_saiprod
oracle    3458    1  0 05:34 ?        00:00:02 ora_pmon_ahuprod
oracle    3722    1  0 05:34 ?        00:00:02 ora_pmon_emrep
oracle   18843    1  0 13:04 ?        00:00:00 ora_pmon_clone000
oracle   23670 5264  0 13:13 pts/0    00:00:00 grep pmon

$ lsnrctl status
LSNRCTL for Linux: Version 12.1.0.2.0 - Production on 17-DEC-2015 13:13:33
Copyright (c) 1991, 2014, Oracle.  All rights reserved.

Connecting to (DESCRIPTION=(ADDRESS=(PROTOCOL=TCP)(HOST=xxxxx.sainath.com)
(PORT=1521)))
```

```
STATUS of the LISTENER
-----------------------
Alias                      LISTENER
Version                    TNSLSNR for Linux: Version 12.1.0.2.0 - Production
Start Date                 17-DEC-2015 05:34:32
Uptime                     0 days 7 hr. 39 min. 1 sec
Trace Level                off
Security                   ON: Local OS Authentication
SNMP                       OFF
Listener Parameter File
/u01/app/oracle/product/12.1.0/dbhome_1/network/admin/listener.ora
Listener Log File
/u01/app/oracle/diag/tnslsnr/xxxxx/listener/alert/log.xml
Listening Endpoints Summary...
  (DESCRIPTION=(ADDRESS=(PROTOCOL=tcp)(HOST=xxxxx.sainath.com)(PORT=1521)))
  (DESCRIPTION=(ADDRESS=(PROTOCOL=ipc)(KEY=EXTPROC1521)))
Services Summary...
Service "SAICLONE1.sainath.com" has 1 instance(s).
  Instance "clone000", status READY, has 1 handler(s) for this service...
Service "ahuprod.sainath.com" has 1 instance(s).
  Instance "ahuprod", status READY, has 1 handler(s) for this service...
Service "ahuprodXDB.sainath.com" has 1 instance(s).
  Instance "ahuprod", status READY, has 1 handler(s) for this service...
Service "clone000.sainath.com" has 1 instance(s).
  Instance "clone000", status READY, has 1 handler(s) for this service...
Service "emrep.sainath.com" has 1 instance(s).
  Instance "emrep", status READY, has 1 handler(s) for this service...
Service "emrepXDB.sainath.com" has 1 instance(s).
  Instance "emrep", status READY, has 1 handler(s) for this service...
Service "saiprod.sainath.com" has 1 instance(s).
  Instance "saiprod", status READY, has 1 handler(s) for this service...
Service "saiprodXDB.sainath.com" has 1 instance(s).
  Instance "saiprod", status READY, has 1 handler(s) for this service...
Service "sales.sainath.com" has 1 instance(s).
  Instance "ahuprod", status READY, has 1 handler(s) for this service...
The command completed successfully
```

Check the newly created database name and service. Use the Oracle-supplied oraenv script to change the Oracle UNIX variables before connecting to the database.

```
$ . oraenv
ORACLE_SID = [emrep] ? clone000
The Oracle base for ORACLE_HOME=/u01/app/oracle/product/11.2.0/dbhome_2 is /u01/app/
oracle

$ sqlplus / as sysdba
SQL*Plus: Release 11.2.0.4.0 Production on Thu Dec 17 13:15:11 2015
Copyright (c) 1982, 2013, Oracle.  All rights reserved.

Connected to:
Oracle Database 11g Enterprise Edition Release 11.2.0.4.0 - 64bit Production
With the Partitioning, OLAP, Data Mining and Real Application Testing options
```

```
SQL> select name from v$database;
NAME
---------
CLONE000

SQL> show parameter service
NAME                        TYPE        VALUE
--------------------------- ----------- ---------------------------
service_names               string      clone000.sainath.com,SAICLONE1


Check the datafiles for the new database, and their sizes in MB:

SQL> column name format A50
SQL> select name, bytes/1024/1024 MB from v$datafile;

NAME                                                 MB
-------------------------------------------------- --------
/u02/copy-on-write/clone000/ora_data_0.dbf         780
/u02/copy-on-write/clone000/ora_data_4.dbf         570
/u02/copy-on-write/clone000/ora_data_1.dbf         595
/u02/copy-on-write/clone000/ora_data_3.dbf           5
/u02/copy-on-write/clone000/ora_data_2.dbf         345.625
```

The datafiles are created on the Direct NFS (dNFS) file system /u02/copy-on-write. When we execute the du –h command on this file system, here are the results:

```
$ cd /u02/copy-on-write/clone000

$ du -h *.dbf
1.1M   newtmp_clone000_6158.dbf
15M    ora_data_0.dbf
4.9M   ora_data_1.dbf
16K    ora_data_2.dbf
16K    ora_data_3.dbf
6.8M   ora_data_4.dbf
```

This shows that the clone000 data files are sparse files that occupy lesser space than what is indicated in the v$datafile view. This is the proof that clone000 is a thin clone.

Logging back in as SAI_DAS, drill down to the newly created instance.

Click the instance name to open the Clone Database Home page (Figure 2-63).

The Storage Savings tab on the left pane shows DNFS Clone as the Clone Type of this database. Note the Space Efficiency indicator at the top of the screen, which shows the physical storage used as compared to the virtual storage.

Next, click the Storage Savings tab to see the breakdown of the virtual and physical storage used for each of the data files (Figure 2-64).

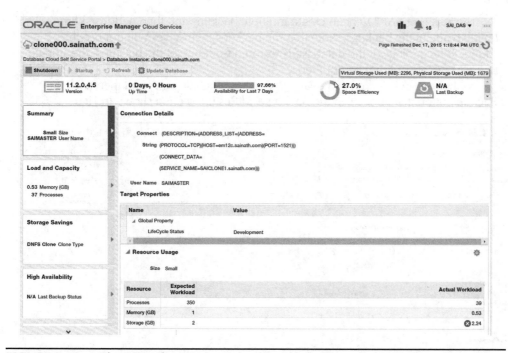

FIGURE 2-63.   *Clone Database Home page: Summary tab*

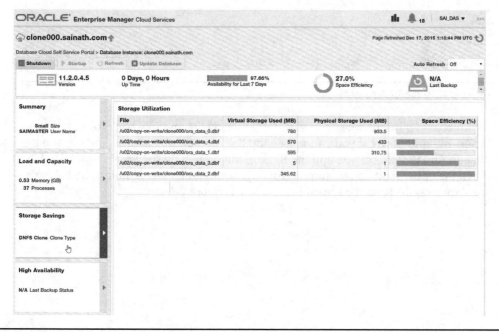

FIGURE 2-64.   *Clone database storage utilization*

The SSA user SAI_DAS can create multiple backups and then perform a time travel to any of the backups. Note that the backups themselves will not use the CloneDB technology. If the database is restored from one of the backups, the storage savings of CloneDB will be nullified.

For backups, click the High Availability tab on the left pane, and then click the Backup button that appears in the Backup And Restore section shown in Figure 2-65.

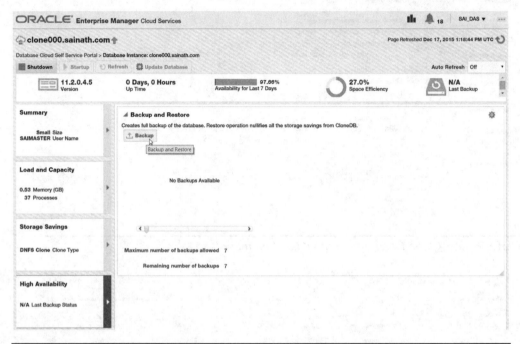

FIGURE 2-65. *Backup and Restore*

The backup is scheduled successfully. You can take multiple backups in this way. When you drill down, if you cannot see the Backup button, collapse and expand the Backup And Restore section and the Backup button will be shown.

In the upper-right corner, turn on Auto Refresh. After a few minutes, the backups are shown on the instance screen in a carousel (Figure 2-66).

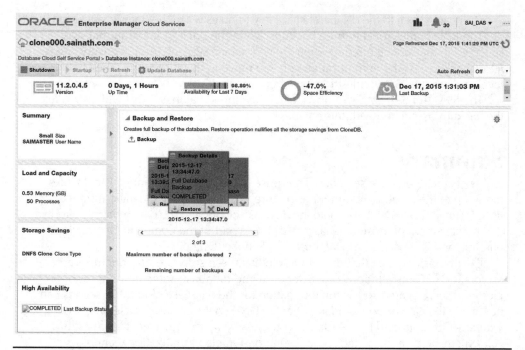

FIGURE 2-66.   *Backup And Restore carousel*

Note that the database goes into blackout mode when the backups are being taken, and the connection to the database may be lost. On the Database Cloud Service Portal, choose Show All to see the blacked-out database (Figure 2-67).

FIGURE 2-67.   *Choose Show All to see a blacked-out database*

Drill back down to the database after a few minutes when the status changes to Up.

The RMAN files for the three backups are in the backup location that was specified in the service offering when created, which was /u02/fast_recovery_area /clonebackups. As the administrator, you can move to this directory at the UNIX level and see the backup files that have been created.

The SSA user SAI_DAS can now delete the cloned database. This will also delete the backups associated with this database.

Summary

In this chapter, you have seen how Enterprise Manager Cloud Control 13c enables the setup of the database cloud infrastructure, the deployment of single-instance /RAC or Snap Clone databases onto the database cloud, and the day-to-day monitoring and management of those databases. This forms part of the complete Oracle cloud offering, and is described as Database as a Service (DBaaS).

Existing or new installations of Oracle Database software on nonclustered servers, or RAC installations of clusterware and database software on a set of clustered servers, are used as the foundation for the database cloud. The servers can be Oracle Exadata or non-Exadata, Oracle SUN Servers or non-Oracle hardware with any OS supported by the Oracle Enterprise Manager 13c Agent, such as IBM AIX, Microsoft Windows, and so on. Even non-Oracle virtualization technology, such as VMware, can be used provided the VMware images are treated as preexisting hosts with the OS installed.

The Oracle Database software can be installed on any of these platforms using the out-of-the-box Enterprise Manager provisioning deployment procedures, or by traditional Oracle software installation methods such as the Oracle Installer. Once the Oracle Database software is installed, the set of servers can be used as the DBaaS cloud infrastructure by setting up database zones, service catalogs, quotas, and chargeback plans as described in this chapter.

The aim of DBaaS is essentially to allow a self-service user to log in to a portal in Enterprise Manager Cloud Control 13c, request a new non-clone or Snap Clone database according to allocated quotas, and wait for the requests to be fulfilled automatically without human intervention, or with management approval (optionally).

When database creation is completed, the self-service user can monitor the new database, set up full and incremental database backups, shut down or start up the database, or retire (delete) it when it's no longer needed. Chargeback information is also available to the user at any point, as per the universal and extended charge plans that have been set up by the SSA administrator. (We will examine the chargeback reports after setting up Schema as a Service and PDB as a Service in the next few chapters.)

This ability to perform self-service provisioning of databases on demand reduces the overhead of going through the IT department, and increases efficiency and quality of service. For the first time, user teams such as internal projects or end users no longer need to be dependent on DBA teams to perform the actual provisioning of the databases required by their multiple projects.

The IT department concentrates on the back-end and ensures that the database cloud infrastructure is running smoothly, and tech support can also be called in if errors occur during the process of self-service requests being actioned by Enterprise Manager Cloud Control 13*c*. The other benefit to IT is that the end users of their database services are held accountable, as per published charge plans, for their allocations as well as day-to-day usage. Everyone stays a winner.

DBaaS, combined with the SCHaaS and Pluggable Database as a Service capabilities to be described in the coming chapters, demonstrate that there are a number of choices for self-service cloud provisioning in the Oracle cloud.

In the next chapter, we will take a look at the Schema as a Service capabilities of Enterprise Manager Cloud Control 13*c*.

CHAPTER
3

Schema as a Service

Y
ou have seen how easy it is for self-service users to request and deploy entire Oracle databases on demand on their private (onsite) database clouds using Oracle Enterprise Manager 13*c*. This is an excellent service for companies that normally allocate separate databases for each new project. But it may not be suitable for companies that prefer to allocate new schemas in existing databases. Consolidating multiple schemas in existing databases delivers a higher level of consolidation in these cases.

For example, a company may allocate a multi-node Real Application Cluster (RAC) database to use as the shared database for any new project or application. In this case, the DBA creates new schemas, tablespaces, and RAC database services on project demand, instead of creating a new separate database for each new project or application. This would save on memory and processing requirements for each new database, because every new database requires its own system global area (SGA) and program global area (PGA) memory areas, along with background processes that consume CPU bandwidth. Multiple schemas on the same database would instead share the database memory as well as background processes.

Avoiding multiple databases on the same server would also avoid interdatabase resource management issues, since services inside one large database could be controlled by the Oracle Database Resource Manager, a part and parcel of every Oracle Database. (In the large telecommunications company where I worked during the early 2000s, we had exactly this kind of schema consolidation inside a large database for different application projects.)

When the private database cloud and Database as a Service (DBaaS) arrived, it was eventually deemed necessary to address the specific requirements of the companies that preferred shared databases and schema-level consolidation and wanted their private cloud self-service users to request for and deploy schema services instead of new databases. In February 2013, Oracle released a number of new Enterprise Manager plug-ins that offered Schema as a Service (SCHaaS) solutions. This enabled an administrator to set up a database pool with existing databases, and enabled schemas to be self-serviced on those databases by Self Service Application (SSA) users.

Chapter 2 discussed the Enterprise Manager Cloud Control 13*c* capabilities for Database as a Service (DBaaS). We created the Platform as a Service (PaaS) Infrastructure Zone, set up the database pool, and created service templates for the self-service, single-instance database, as well as for a CloneDB thin clone database. We also tested provisioning those databases as the SSA user.

We will now look into the SCHaaS capabilities. The foundation of this service is a schema pool of pre-created Oracle Database instances on preinstalled database servers, which allows self-service users to request the creation of new schemas in these databases quickly and easily. Oracle Databases version 11*g* (or 10*g*) would normally be used for this purpose.

If you wanted to use Oracle 12*c* container databases (CDBs), you would instead use the capability of Pluggable Database as a Service (PDBaaS). However, technically, it is still possible to use Oracle 12*c* non-CDB databases for requesting schema services, but this is not recommended, because it would mean that you'd use an older architecture on a new way of doing things—the PDBs in a CDB.

The PaaS Infrastructure Zone is required as the basis of our schema pools. We created a PaaS Infrastructure Zone in Chapter 2, and we will use the same zone for SCHaaS here. So our first step will be to create the schema pool.

Create a Schema Pool

Log in as SYSMAN or a super administrator, or as an administrator assigned the EM_ SSA_ADMINISTRATOR role. Select Setup | Cloud | Database. The Database Cloud setup screen appears. By default, Database is selected in the drop-down list above the left pane. Select Schema from the drop-down list to open the Schema: Overview page (Figure 3-1), which shows the steps you'll follow for setting up SCHaaS.

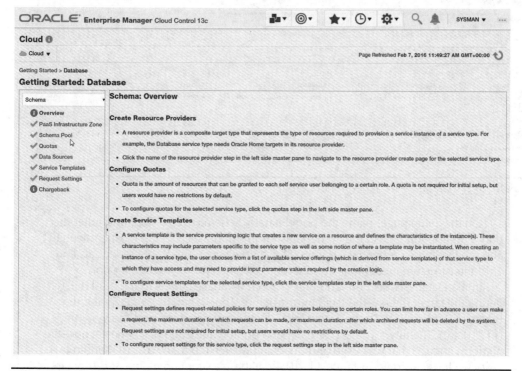

FIGURE 3-1.   *The Overview page shows the steps you'll take.*

The PaaS Infrastructure Zone was used in Chapter 2 for DBaaS and is also used here. Click Schema Pool in the left pane, and then click the Create button. The Create New Pool wizard starts, and the Setup page (Figure 3-2) is displayed.

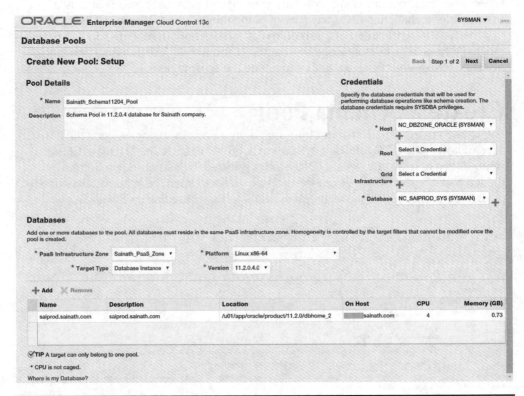

FIGURE 3-2. *Create New Schema Pool: Setup*

On the Setup page, name the pool Sainath_Schema11204_Pool and enter the pool's description. Select the credentials for this pool, such as the Host credentials and the Database credentials (with SYSDBA privileges). The Root credentials and Grid Infrastructure credentials are not required since this is a schema pool.

In the Databases section, add one or more database targets to the pool. First define the target filters—the PaaS Infrastructure Zone (Sainath_PaaS_Zone), the Platform (Linux x86-64), the Target Type (Database Instance), and the Version (11.2.0.4.0). The filters you set here depend on how the zone has been set up—the platform and OS that was used and the database version that was installed. In this case, we'll use a single-instance 11.2.0.4 database to contain all our self-service–created schemas.

Next, after specifying the target filters, you can add the database target by clicking the Add button. Select the saiprod.sainath.com database for the pool. This is an 11.2.0.4 database. The Oracle home location of the selected database is displayed, the host name, the CPUs that can be used by the database, and the memory allocated to the database. Note that all databases you select for the schema pool must reside in the same PaaS Infrastructure Zone.

It is important that you understand that a database can belong only to one schema pool. After this database is added to this pool, it cannot be used in any other schema pool. By the same token, if this database had already been used in another schema pool, it would not appear in the selection list when you clicked Add.

The databases you add to the schema pool need to be homogenous (using the same platform, version, configuration, and patch level), and this is controlled by the target filters that cannot be modified once the pool is created.

Click Next to open the Policies screen (Figure 3-3).

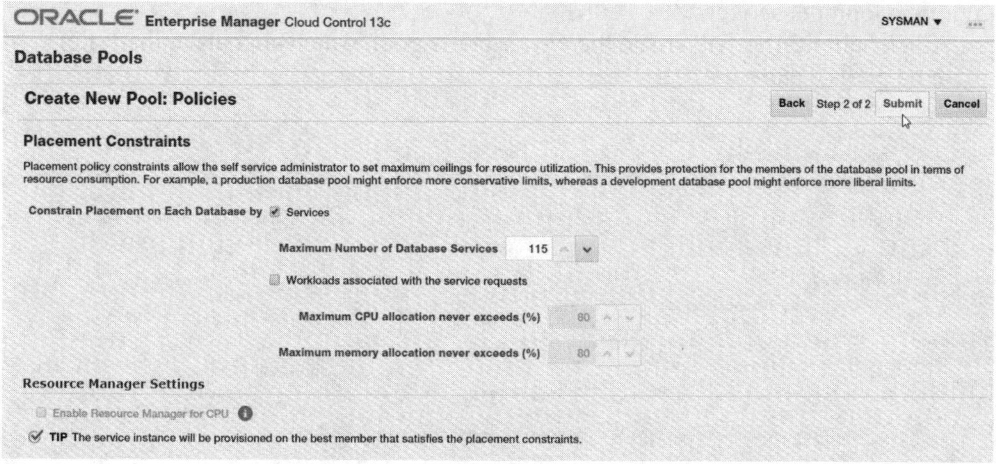

FIGURE 3-3. *Specify the placement constraints on the Policies screen.*

Here you can specify the placement constraints, which enable you to set maximum ceilings for resource utilization.

You can either create a placement constraint based on the maximum number of database services in each database (we have specified a maximum number of 115 database services whereas the default is 100), or based on the workloads associated with the service requests. In the latter case, the maximum CPU and memory allocation can also be set.

A range of small, medium, and large workloads with different CPU/memory /storage limits can be specified at the time of the service template creation, which will be discussed later in this chapter.

The CPU limits for the workloads can be enforced via the Oracle Database Resource Manager if you select Enable Resource Manager For CPU under Resource Manager Settings on this screen. If this option is selected, the Database Resource Manager will be used to create consumer groups that will be used to ensure that the service gets the requested CPU cycles on a system with full load.

Regarding the other limits that are not enforced via the Database Resource Manager, internal bookkeeping will be used. The service instance will be provisioned on the most suitable member that satisfies the placement constraints.

Note that a production database pool might enforce more conservative limits, whereas a development database pool might enforce more relaxed limits. For example, in a production database, you may decide to allow only 60 database services, not the default of 100 or the generous number of 115 we have used for our development services.

Click Submit. This will create the new schema pool, which appears in the list of schema pools (Figure 3-4).

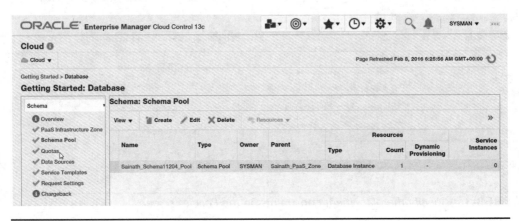

FIGURE 3-4. *The new schema pool appears in the list.*

Dealing with Quotas

Quotas control the amount of resources that a self-service user can request. They are a very important part of controlling the usage of the cloud. Because of its self-service nature, the cloud can easily be misused if no quotas are in force.

For example, without quotas, a developer could request 1000 schema services in an hour and bring an under-resourced database to its knees; if the developer were restricted to 25 new requests in the quota setting, however, requests would affect the database to a much lesser extent. Quotas need to be understood and set up carefully to make sure the right balance is achieved—not too much, not too little, and all depending on the underlying infrastructure and its capabilities.

Select Quotas from the left pane. Quotas have already been set up for our self-service users at the time of setting up DBaaS, as shown in Figure 3-5.

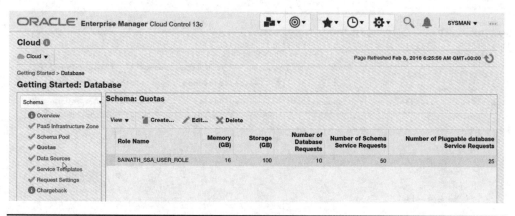

FIGURE 3-5. *Quotas were set up for the schema pool*

According to this quota setup, a user with the role of SAINATH_SSA_USER_ROLE can request a total number of 50 schemas, 10 databases, and 25 PDBs; a maximum of 100GB of storage and 16GB of memory can be used for all the services the user will create. Note that the quota is calculated separately for each SSA user, and these limits apply only to services created through the Self Service Portal.

If the SSA user were granted additional privileges by mistake, the user could then be able to create databases or schemas or PDBs outside the Self Service Portal, and these would not apply toward the limits. The SSA administrator must ensure that this does not happen by controlling the privileges that are granted.

Creating a Data Profile

Data profiles and service templates are at the center of self-service provisioning. The data profiles are the gold copies of one or more schemas that will be used in the provisioning, and the service templates are the actual locked-down deployment procedures (a series of executable steps defined in Enterprise Manager) that will be presented to the self-service user for selection from a catalog of services.

We now need to set up a data profile for the schema self-service provisioning. Click Data Sources in the left pane, and then select the Data Profiles step. Click Create to open the Reference Target screen (Figure 3-6).

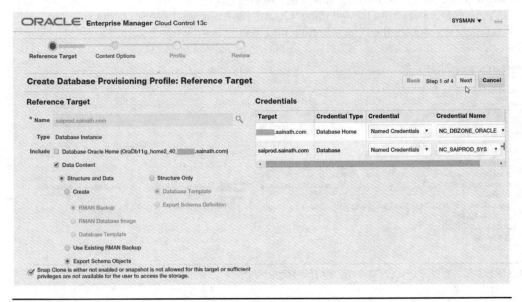

FIGURE 3-6. *Create Data Profile: Reference Target screen*

Select the reference target database saiprod.sainath.com. Choose the Data Content and Structure And Data options. Since we are creating a schema profile, select Export Schema Objects under Structure And Data. The actual schemas that are to be included will be specified in the next step.

Also, select the Named Credentials for the database home (the Oracle user at the UNIX level), as well as for the database (with SYSDBA privileges). Click Next to open the Content Options screen (Figure 3-7).

From the list of schemas in the reference database, select the HR schema to be used in the export. System schemas and schemas without any objects are not listed.

In the Directory Locations section, select a database directory that can be used. You can also customize the dump file name if you want, or set a maximum file size in MB. Under Log, set the Directory and File Name.

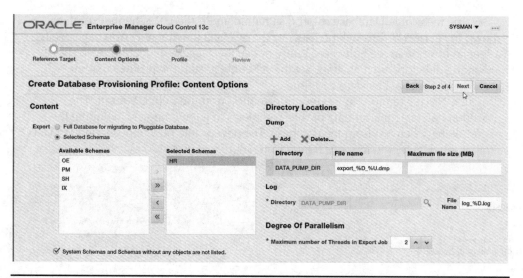

FIGURE 3-7. *Create Data Profile: Content Options screen*

Under Degree Of Parallelism, select the number of threads to perform the export operation (default is 1). We have increased the threads to 2. Increasing the number of threads helps reduce the time to create the profile, but more system resources will be used.

Click Next to open the Profile Information screen (Figure 3-8).

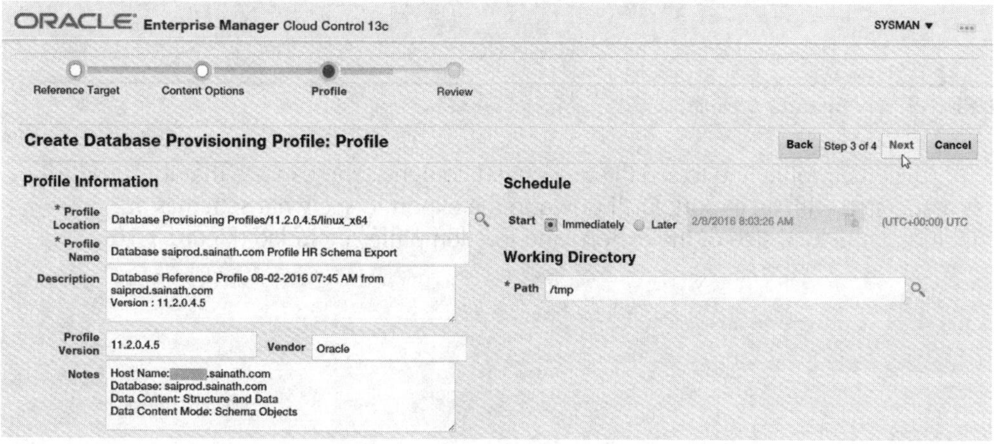

FIGURE 3-8. *Create Data Profile: Profile Information screen*

Name the profile Database saiprod.sainath.com Profile HR Schema Export, as shown in Figure 3-8. This will be used for the SCHaaS functionality. You can specify a special location in the Software Library or use the suggested location. Also specify a working directory, such as /tmp. Set the schedule to start the profile creation immediately or at a later date and time.

Click Next. Examine the review information and then click Submit. The procedure to create the schema profile completes in a few minutes, including the export of the schema(s) from the database. The new profile now appears on the Data Profiles tab (Figure 3-9) in the Schema: Data Sources screen.

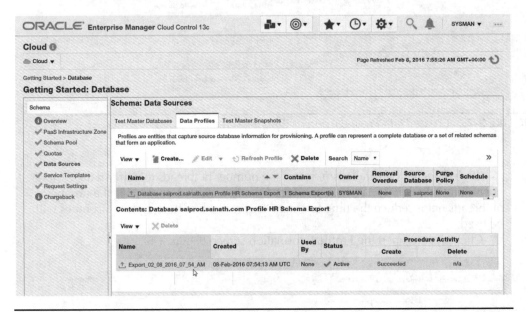

FIGURE 3-9. *New data profile*

Click the profile line to see the associated contents. You can see that this profile is associated with an export. Drill down to the export to see what schemas are included, the total size of the export, and the dump files included (Figure 3-10).

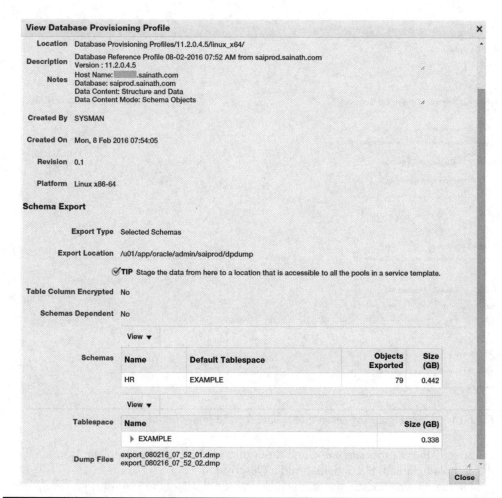

View Database Provisioning Profile   ✕

Location	Database Provisioning Profiles/11.2.0.4.5/linux_x64/
Description	Database Reference Profile 08-02-2016 07:52 AM from saiprod.sainath.com Version : 11.2.0.4.5
Notes	Host Name: ▮▮▮▮▮.sainath.com Database: saiprod.sainath.com Data Content: Structure and Data Data Content Mode: Schema Objects
Created By	SYSMAN
Created On	Mon, 8 Feb 2016 07:54:05
Revision	0.1
Platform	Linux x86-64

Schema Export

Export Type	Selected Schemas
Export Location	/u01/app/oracle/admin/saiprod/dpdump

☑**TIP** Stage the data from here to a location that is accessible to all the pools in a service template.

Table Column Encrypted	No
Schemas Dependent	No

View ▼

	Name	Default Tablespace	Objects Exported	Size (GB)
Schemas	HR	EXAMPLE	79	0.442

View ▼

	Name	Size (GB)
Tablespace	▶ EXAMPLE	0.338

Dump Files	export_080216_07_52_01.dmp export_080216_07_52_02.dmp

Close

FIGURE 3-10. *Detailed profile information*

Creating a Service Template for the HR Schema

The next step is to create a service template, the actual service definition that is offered to self-service users in a service catalog, a list of such services. We want this template to use the HR schema profile we created from the saiprod database.

From the left pane of the Database screen, select Service Templates, and then click Create. You'll see the Create New Service Template screen (Figure 3-11).

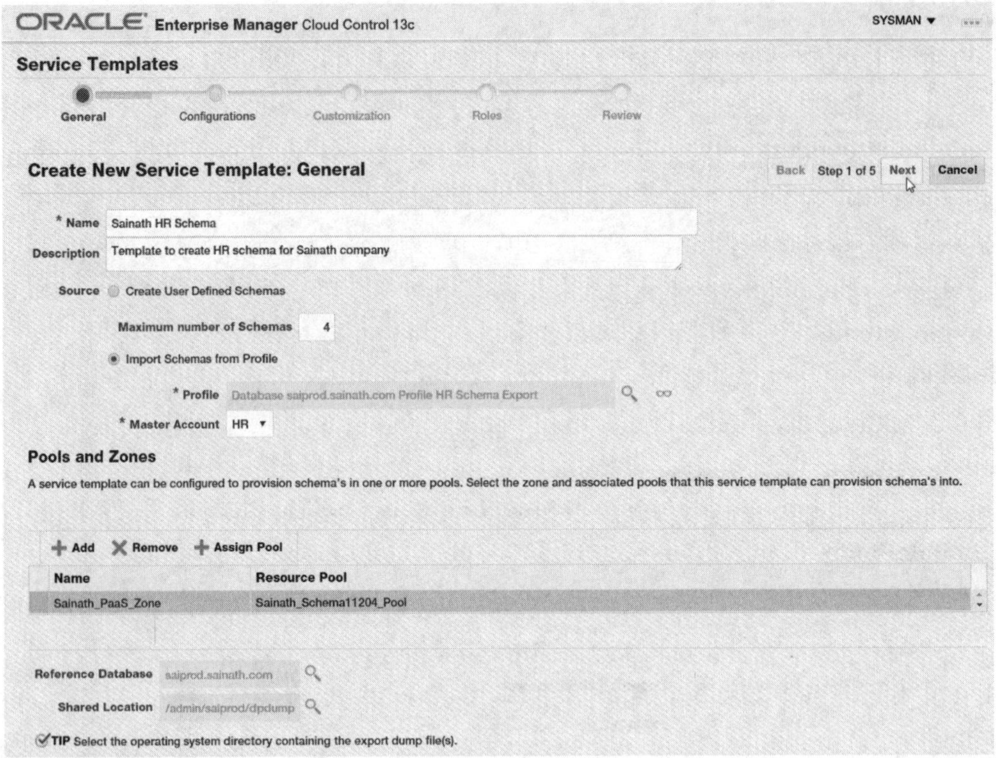

FIGURE 3-11. *Creating a new service template for the HR schema*

Specify the appropriate name and description for the service template. Name this template Sainath HR Schema. Add a Description.

For the schema Source, the SSA administrator can allow the SSA users to name and create their own user-defined schemas (with a maximum specified). Choose Create User Defined Schemas and set a Maximum value. Alternatively, the schema(s) to be created by the SSA users can be imported from an existing data profile.

If using a Data Profile, choose Import Schemas From Profile. The SSA administrator knows what schemas are present in the profile; select one of the schemas to be a master account that will have access to all the other schemas in the profile. This master account selection will be done at the service template creation stage itself, in this case by the SSA administrator.

This doesn't apply to user-defined (empty) schemas, since the SSA administrator does not know what schemas will be named and created by the SSA users at request time. With user-defined schemas, the SSA users themselves will decide and select the master account schema from the list of their user-defined schemas if they have selected the service offering for user-defined schemas.

In this service template, we have chosen Import Schemas From Profile and selected the Database saiprod.sainath.com Profile HR Schema Export as the Profile; this was created in the previous step. The master account is selected as the HR schema since there is no other schema in the profile—only the HR schema has been exported. If there were multiple schemas in the profile, you could have selected any one of the schemas as the master.

In the Pools And Zones section, first add the PaaS Infrastructure Zone Sainath_PaaS_Zone, then select the zone from the list, and then click Assign Pool.

Assign the schema pool Sainath_Schema11204_Pool that we created in the previous section. Since the schema pool we have selected refers to the saiprod database, the Reference Database is automatically populated as saiprod.sainath .com. However, you need to enter the shared location manually, as the export dump directory **/u01/app/oracle/admin/saiprod/dpdump**—the location of the DATA_PUMP_DIR directory when the profile was created.

A service template can be configured to provision schemas in one or more schema pools, so you can assign multiple schema pools if they are present, which means you are specifying multiple databases in which the self-service schemas can be created.

Note that in our case, we are using the same database, saiprod.sainath.com, for the source data as well as the destination for the self-service schemas to be created. In real life, this would not be the case. You would create the schemas in a different development or test database.

Click Next. The Configurations screen is displayed (Figure 3-12).

Under the Workloads section, create an expected workload size by clicking the Create button. The workload signifies the expected CPU, memory, and storage requirements for each service that will be created. Multiple workloads can be created here, which can be then selected by the SSA user when creating the schema. At least one workload must be created.

Specify a workload for the new service, and name it SAI_SMALL_WORKLOAD. Specify 0.25 CPU cores, 0.5GB memory, and 0.5GB storage for the small workload. Create another workload, SAI_MEDIUM_WORKLOAD, with more CPU cores, memory, and storage allocated. Use 0.75 CPU cores, 1GB memory, and 1GB storage for the medium workload.

Note that these are not hard limits; they are only for budgeting purposes, and alerts will be raised to the SSA administrator if the SSA created schema exceeds these limits. The only exception is the limit of CPU cores—if, when creating the schema pool, the SSA administrator had ticked Enable Resource Manager For CPU, the Oracle Database Resource Manager will be used to ensure that the new service gets the requested CPU cycles on a system with full load, thus guaranteeing quality of service for the new schema service so far as CPU usage is concerned.

On the same page, under Schema Privileges, you can assign privileges either from existing database roles or create a new database role. We select the latter, and specify a new database role, SAINATH_HR_SCHEMA_ROLE (uppercase is important), to be created.

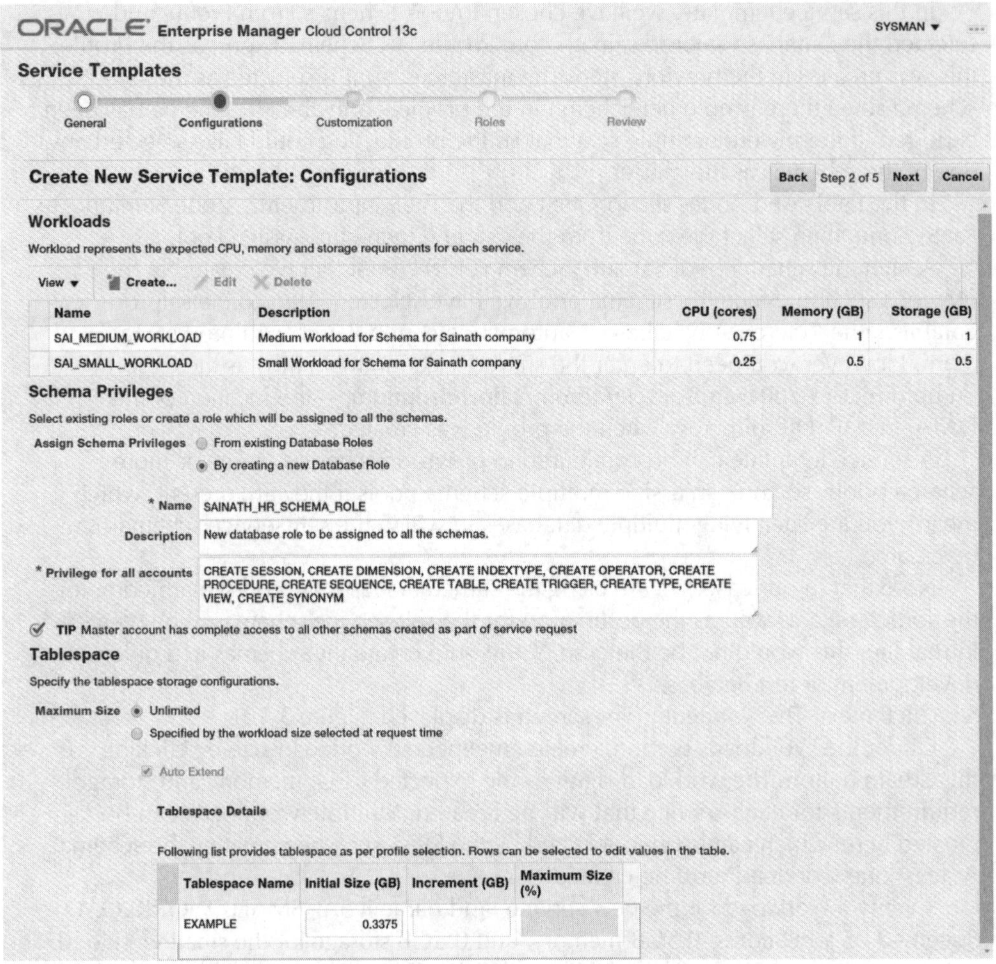

FIGURE 3-12. *Service Template for HR Schema: Configurations*

The privileges for this role are displayed on this page, and you can add to them if required or remove some of the privileges as per company policy. The default privileges are

CREATE SESSION, CREATE DIMENSION, CREATE INDEXTYPE, CREATE OPERATOR, CREATE PROCEDURE, CREATE SEQUENCE, CREATE TABLE, CREATE TRIGGER, CREATE TYPE, CREATE VIEW, CREATE SYNONYM

Also note that the master account is supposed to have total access to all the other schemas created as part of the service request.

Finally, specify the Tablespace storage configuration—the initial size, whether to auto extend, the increment size, and the maximum size (this can be the same as the maximum workload size specified). We have selected Unlimited.

Click Next to continue. In the Customization screen, you can specify the custom scripts to be executed before and after creating or deleting the service instance. You cannot specify a SQL script. No scripts are specified in our case. The target properties can also be set on this screen. Click Next.

The Roles screen appears, where you can select the SAINATH_SSA_USER_ROLE; this means any user granted this role will be able to see and use this service template. After this, review the information, and then save the service template.

Creating a Service Template for User-Defined Schemas

Let's create a second service template for a schema, this time to allow the SSA user to create user-defined schemas—that is, empty schemas that can be named by the SSA user. Select Service Templates from the left pane, and click Create. In the next screen (Figure 3-13), name the new template Sainath User Defined Schema.

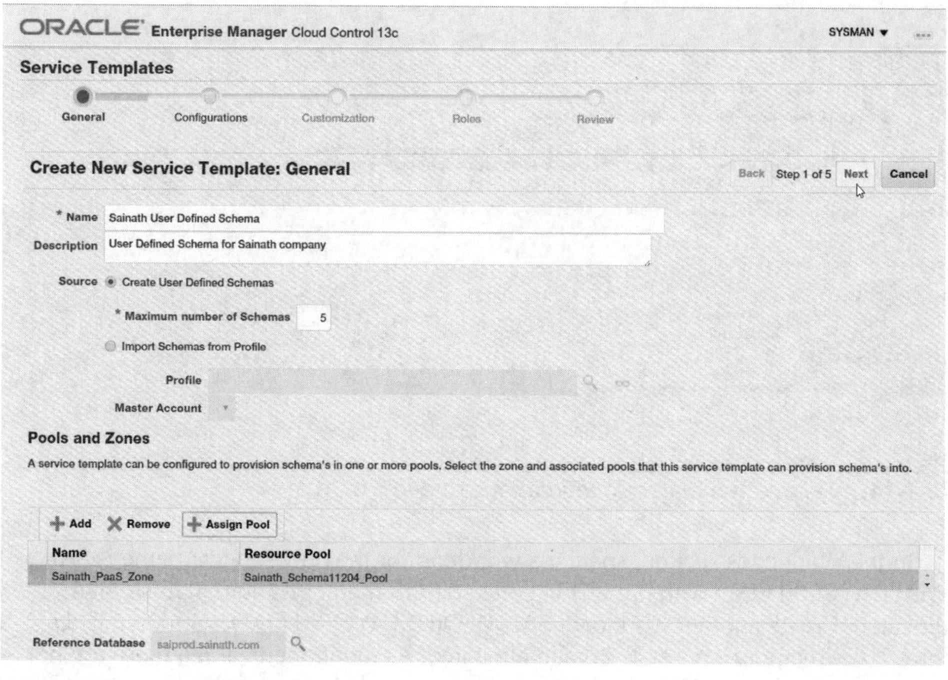

FIGURE 3-13.   *Creating a service template for user-defined schema*

Under Source, select Create User Defined Schemas. Enter **5** as the maximum number of schemas to be created (the default is 4, and the maximum is 9).

As before, add the Sainath_PaaS_Zone and assign the Resource Pool Sainath_Schema11204_Pool to the zone. The Reference Database field is automatically populated as saiprod.sainath.com. Click Next to move to the next screen, shown in Figure 3-14.

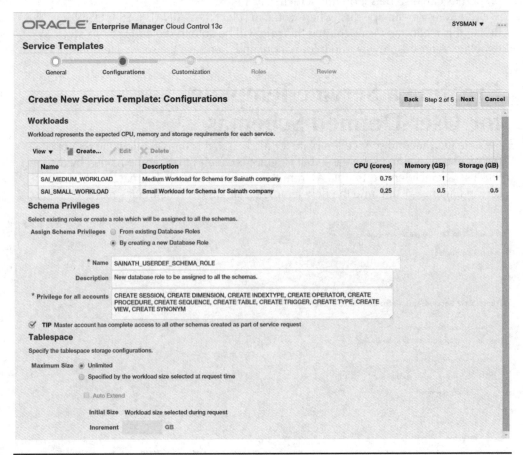

FIGURE 3-14. *Service Template: Configurations screen*

In the Workloads section, specify a workload for the new service: name is SAI_SMALL_WORKLOAD with 0.25 CPU cores, 0.5GB memory, and 0.5GB storage allocated. Create another workload, SAI_MEDIUM_WORKLOAD, with 0.75 CPU cores, 1GB memory, and 1GB storage allocated. As mentioned earlier, these are not hard limits; they are only for budgeting purposes, and alerts will be raised to the SSA administrator if the SSA created schema exceeds these limits. The only exception is the limit of CPU cores, since the Database Resource Manager setting, if enabled in the schema pool, can be used to ensure quality of service for the new schema service(s) so far as CPU usage is concerned.

Multiple workloads can be created here, which can be selected by the SSA user when creating the user-defined schemas. At least one workload must be created.

On the same screen, choose an appropriate name, and specify a new database role, SAINATH_USERDEF_SCHEMA_ROLE (uppercase important), to be created. Keep the existing privileges. The default privileges are the same as earlier:

> CREATE SESSION, CREATE DIMENSION, CREATE INDEXTYPE, CREATE OPERATOR, CREATE PROCEDURE, CREATE SEQUENCE, CREATE TABLE, CREATE TRIGGER, CREATE TYPE, CREATE VIEW, CREATE SYNONYM

For the Tablespace, specify the Maximum Size as Unlimited. The step that follows enables you to specify the custom scripts and the target properties. Next, add the previously created role, SAINATH_SSA_USER_ROLE, to the template. Examine the review information and then create the new service template.

The two new service templates for schema now appear in the Service Templates list, as shown in Figure 3-15.

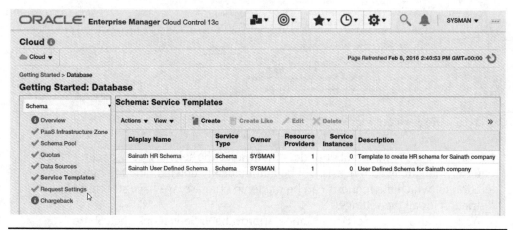

FIGURE 3-15. *Service Templates list with new schemas*

Request Settings

The request settings control the manner in which self-service users can make requests for a schema service—how far in advance a request can be made, the request archive retention, and the maximum duration for which requests can be made. These serve as further controls of the self-service nature of the cloud.

Click Request Settings in the left pane to open the Request Settings screen shown in Figure 3-16.

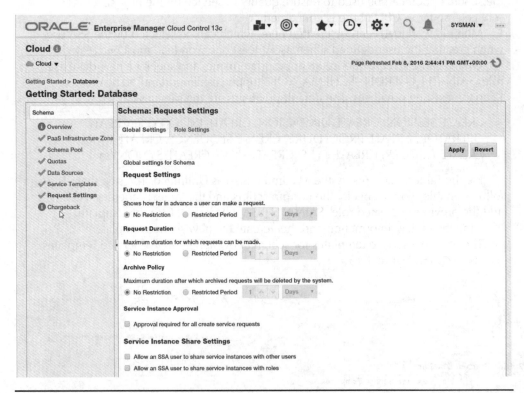

FIGURE 3-16. *Request Settings screen*

You can specify the number of days in advance the self-service user can make a request, when archived requests will be automatically deleted, and the maximum duration for which the requests can be made. In our case, we have selected No Restriction for all the settings.

You can also set up Service Instance Approval and Service Instance Share Settings. In addition, you can move to the Role Settings tab and assign different settings to different roles.

Configuring Chargeback

The final setup step is to configure chargeback for SCHaaS. Using the chargeback capability, the resource usage of the schemas and associated database services that are created by the SSA user can be calculated based on various criteria. A dollar figure can then be presented to the self-service user or project.

As explained in Chapter 2, we entered charge rates into a Universal Charge Plan and also created an Extended Plan called Sainath Additional Plan. In this plan, we added charge rates for schema service; these are shown in Figure 3-17.

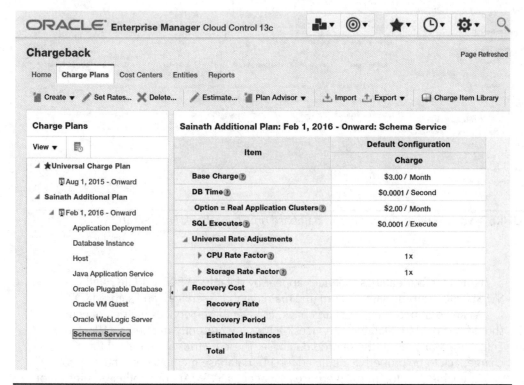

FIGURE 3-17. *Charge rates for schema service*

We have set up a Base Charge for each schema service, an extra configuration charge if the database used for the schema is a RAC database, usage charges on top of these for DB time per service, and SQL Executes per service. Other available options that you can charge for are Disk Read (Physical) Operations Per Service, Disk Write (Physical) Operations Per Service, User Transactions Per Service, and others. Note that all these can easily build up costs.

The creation and assignment of cost centers and assignment of the additional charge plan to various entities including the zone and the saiprod database was completed and explained in Chapter 2. As a result of this, services belonging to the database saiprod are shown in the Entities tab (Figure 3-18) of the Chargeback screen.

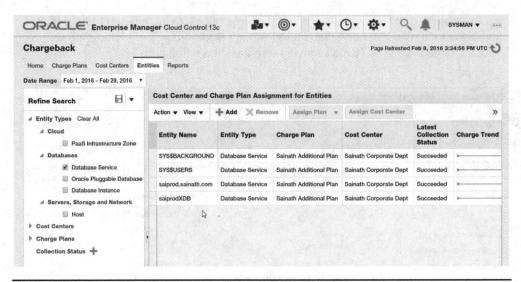

FIGURE 3-18. *Services from saiprod database on Chargeback Entities tab*

Note that four database services appear by default: SYS$BACKGROUND, SYS$USERS, saiprod.sainath.com (the main database service), and saiprodXDB.

As an additional step for chargeback, EM Database Services metric collection should be enabled. Database Services Metrics are currently not being collected by Enterprise Manager for the saiprod database. These metrics are required for chargeback to be properly calculated for 11*g* database members of schema pools.

To enable this, log in to Enterprise Manager as SYSMAN or another administrator with the appropriate rights. Move to the saiprod database home page, and select Oracle Database | Monitoring | Metric And Collection Settings.

Use the drop-down box to change the view to All Metrics. Scroll down to the EM Database Services Metric, and click the Disabled link. On the screen that appears, click the Enable button and edit the collection settings (Figure 3-19).

After clicking the Enable button, you can specify the Collection Frequency and whether the metric data collected will be used for historical trending or alerting. You can also change the upload interval.

Click Continue. A message is displayed: "The settings have been modified but not saved to the repository. You can make further changes to the settings and click the OK button to save the data." Click the OK button to save.

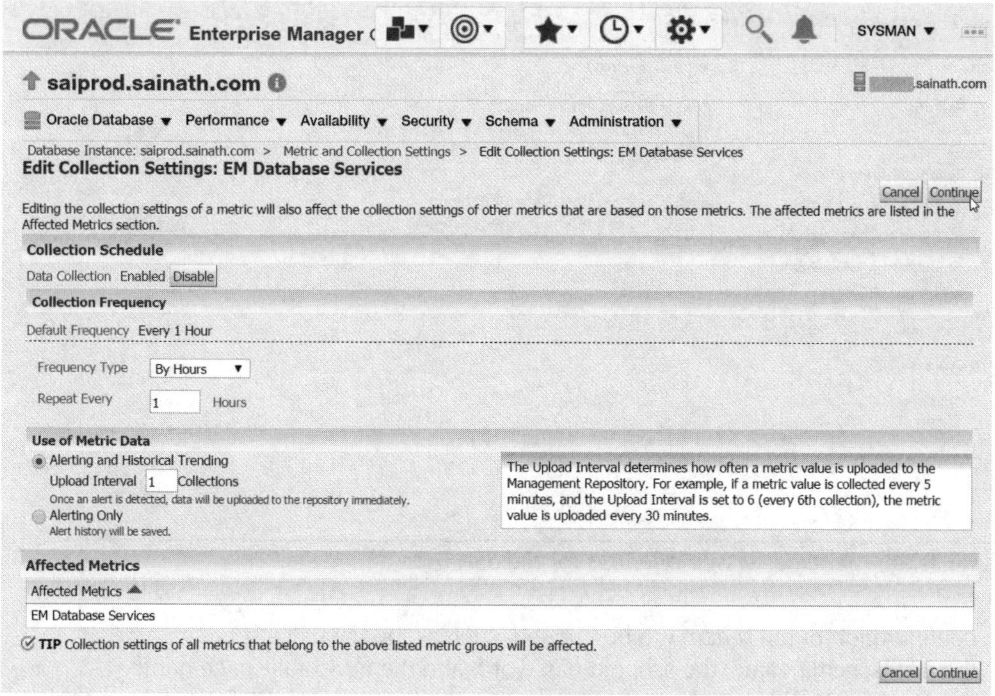

FIGURE 3-19. *Edit Collection Settings: EM Database Services*

Self Service: Request and Create a Schema Service

You've now configured a Self Service Portal for SCHaaS. It's time to try out your new creation. The following steps walk you through the process of logging in as the self-service user and seeing for yourself what you can do in this portal.

Log in to Enterprise Manager Cloud Control 13*c* as the SAI_DAS user, the SSA user we created previously. On the All Cloud Services console, under Featured Services in the Database Cloud Services section, select Click Here To Get Started. This brings up the Database Cloud Service Portal. Click Create Instance.

You'll see a pop-up window with the service offerings to select. The service offerings have been pre-created by the cloud/SSA administrator. We have selected Schema under Select Service Type so that only schema service offerings are displayed in the list (Figure 3-20). This list of services is the Service Catalog.

Select the Sainath HR Schema service offering, which opens the Create Schema screen shown in Figure 3-21, where the SSA user SAI_DAS can specify the

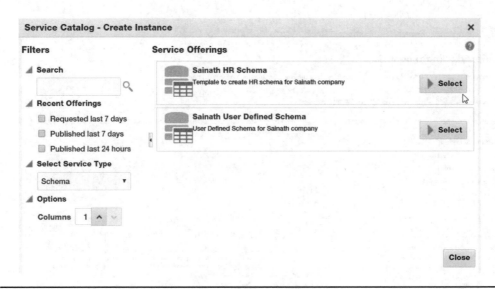

FIGURE 3-20. *Schema service offerings for the SSA user*

configuration of the schema to be created, such as the database service name, the new schema name, the schema password, and the new tablespace name.

As user SAI_DAS, we have input a database service name HRNEW1 (this can be any name you want). Also select the appropriate workload, either SAI_MEDIUM_WORKLOAD or SAI_SMALL_WORKLOAD from the drop-down box. This workload was set up at the time of the service offering creation by the SSA administrator/cloud administrator and has different settings for CPU cores, memory, and storage. Again, these are soft limits for budgeting and alert purposes, unless the Oracle Database Resource Manager has been enabled for ensuring the CPU cycles to the new service.

The schema prefix is automatically generated from the name of the SSA user— SAI_DAS. This can be removed so that the schema prefix is blank. After this, rename the schema by clicking the Rename Schemas icon. (Note: When renaming the schemas, select the schema line first.)

Type a Schema Name of **HRNEW1**. The tablespace name can be entered as **HRNEW1DATA**. The service properties can be changed if required, and the creation of the service can be set to start immediately or to start later at a specified date and time. The duration of the service can also be set at this stage. Click Submit.

Note that if at this point of submission, an error, "Please enter a different Database Service Name," appears, simply enter a service name that is different from the schema name.

The request is shown as running (the hourglass icon) in the Status column of the Requests tab on the Database Cloud Services screen (Figure 3-22).

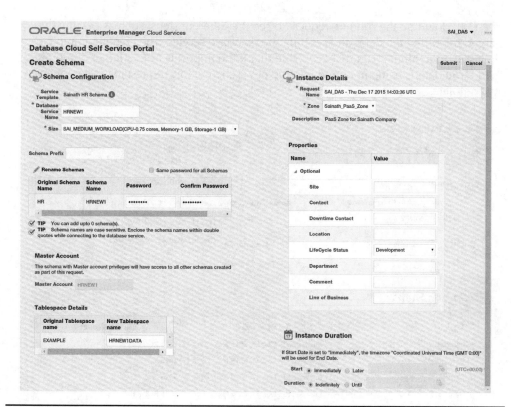

FIGURE 3-21.   *Configuring the schema in the Create Schema screen*

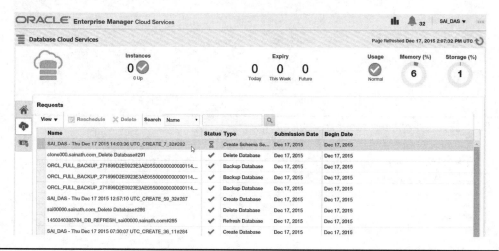

FIGURE 3-22.   *Running schema creation request*

Drill down on the running request to see the different steps, such as placing the target, importing the data, and creating the database service. The creation completes in less than a minute (Figure 3-23). Note that if the import is from a larger dump file and more data is being imported into the new schema, this request may take longer to complete.

FIGURE 3-23. *Completed schema service request*

The new schema service, HRNEW1, is shown as up and running in the Database Cloud Services screen (Figure 3-24).

FIGURE 3-24. *Newly created schema service*

The SSA user can drill down to the Schema Service home page from the Database Cloud Services screen. The home page is shown in Figure 3-25.

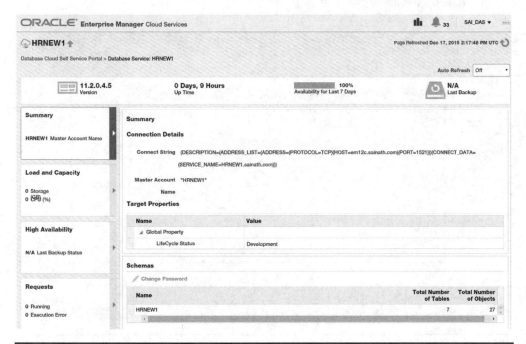

FIGURE 3-25. *Home page of the schema service*

In the Summary tab, you'll see the target properties and the schemas included in the new service, along with the number of tables and objects belonging to each schema. You can see that the HRNEW1 schema has 7 tables and 27 objects in total.

The home page has other tabs as well, such as the Load And Capacity tab that displays resource usage and performance information such as active sessions. The High Availability tab enables the SSA user to create new export dump backups and restore from such backups directly without involving the cloud administrator or DBA. This places more power, and the corresponding responsibility, in the hands of the SSA user.

The Transparent Network Substrate (TNS) Connect String of the new database service is displayed on the Summary tab:

```
(DESCRIPTION=(ADDRESS_LIST=(ADDRESS=(PROTOCOL=TCP)(HOST=xxxxx.sainath
.com)(PORT=1521)))(CONNECT_DATA=(SERVICE_NAME=HRNEW1.sainath.com)))
```

This connect string, along with the master account login of HRNEW1, can be used in any client software, such as Oracle SQL Developer, to connect to this database service. In Figure 3-26, for example, we have created a new database connection in Oracle SQL Developer and are using the connect identifier specified on the schema service home page.

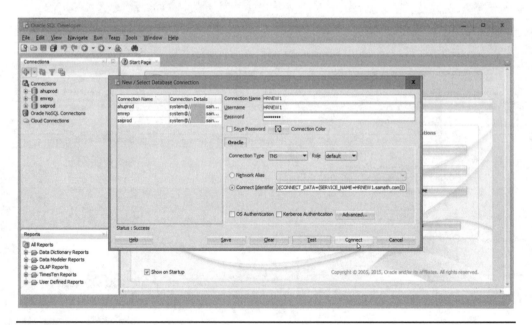

FIGURE 3-26. *SQL Developer connecting to new service*

Using SQL Developer, we connect to the HRNEW1 database service and see the list of tables (Figure 3-27) in this schema, which is a copy of the original HR schema from the saiprod database.

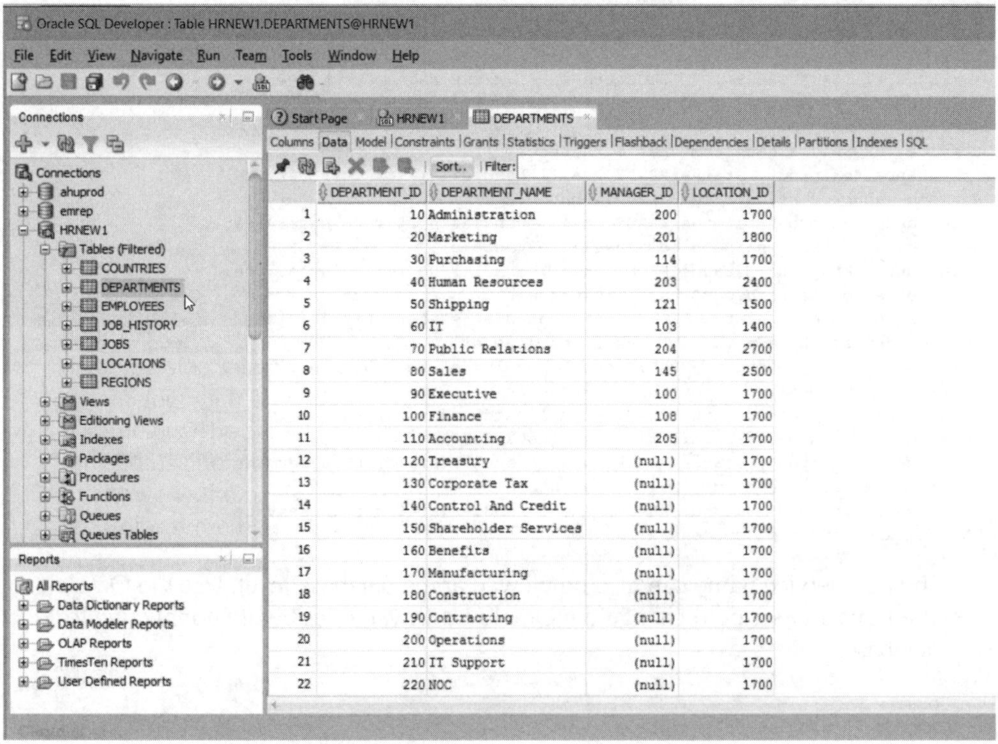

FIGURE 3-27.   *List of tables in new schema*

At the UNIX level, the database administrator (not the SSA user) can see the changes in the listener services. The new service, HRNEW1.sainath.com, has been added as shown in this `lsnrctl status` output (highlighted in boldface):

```
$ lsnrctl status
LSNRCTL for Linux: Version 11.2.0.4.0 - Production on 17-DEC-2015 14:22:04
Copyright (c) 1991, 2013, Oracle.  All rights reserved.

Connecting to (ADDRESS=(PROTOCOL=tcp)(HOST=)(PORT=1521))
STATUS of the LISTENER
------------------------
Alias                     LISTENER
Version                   TNSLSNR for Linux: Version 12.1.0.2.0 - Production
Start Date                17-DEC-2015 05:34:32
Uptime                    0 days 8 hr. 47 min. 32 sec
Trace Level               off
Security                  ON: Local OS Authentication
SNMP                      OFF
Listener Parameter File
/u01/app/oracle/product/12.1.0/dbhome_1/network/admin/listener.ora
```

```
Listener Log File
/u01/app/oracle/diag/tnslsnr/xxxxx/listener/alert/log.xml
Listening Endpoints Summary...
  (DESCRIPTION=(ADDRESS=(PROTOCOL=tcp)(HOST=xxxxx.sainath.com)(PORT=1521)))
  (DESCRIPTION=(ADDRESS=(PROTOCOL=ipc)(KEY=EXTPROC1521)))
Services Summary...
Service "HRNEW1.sainath.com" has 1 instance(s).
  Instance "saiprod", status READY, has 1 handler(s) for this service...
Service "ahuprod.sainath.com" has 1 instance(s).
  Instance "ahuprod", status READY, has 1 handler(s) for this service...
Service "ahuprodXDB.sainath.com" has 1 instance(s).
  Instance "ahuprod", status READY, has 1 handler(s) for this service...
Service "emrep.sainath.com" has 1 instance(s).
  Instance "emrep", status READY, has 1 handler(s) for this service...
Service "emrepXDB.sainath.com" has 1 instance(s).
  Instance "emrep", status READY, has 1 handler(s) for this service...
Service "saiprod.sainath.com" has 1 instance(s).
  Instance "saiprod", status READY, has 1 handler(s) for this service...
Service "saiprodXDB.sainath.com" has 1 instance(s).
  Instance "saiprod", status READY, has 1 handler(s) for this service...
Service "sales.sainath.com" has 1 instance(s).
  Instance "ahuprod", status READY, has 1 handler(s) for this service...
The command completed successfully
```

The new service name can also be viewed at the database level. Use the Oracle-supplied `oraenv` script to change the Oracle UNIX variables before connecting to the database.

```
$ . oraenv
ORACLE_SID = [clone000] ? saiprod
The Oracle base for ORACLE_HOME=/u01/app/oracle/product/11.2.0/dbhome_2 is /u01/app/
oracle

$ sqlplus / as sysdba
SQL*Plus: Release 11.2.0.4.0 Production on Thu Dec 17 14:23:51 2015
Copyright (c) 1982, 2013, Oracle.  All rights reserved.

Connected to:
Oracle Database 11g Enterprise Edition Release 11.2.0.4.0 - 64bit Production
With the Partitioning, OLAP, Data Mining and Real Application Testing options

SQL> show parameter service
NAME                          TYPE        VALUE
----------------------------- ----------- ----------
service_names                 string      HRNEW1
```

Back on the database Self Service Portal, the new service can be deleted by the SSA user by selecting Delete from the menu bar icon at the right, as shown in Figure 3-28.

FIGURE 3-28.   *Deleting the schema service*

This starts the deletion procedure. The schema and service are deleted in the space of a minute.

Self Service: Request and Create User-Defined Schemas

So far, the SSA administrator exported a schema(s) from production into a data profile, and this schema was renamed and re-created when the SSA user selected the corresponding service offering from the Service Catalog. But what if the SSA user instead wants to create multiple blank schemas, without any data? The second service offering for user-defined schemas will be able to achieve this.

When you are logged in as SAI_DAS, on the Database Cloud Services Portal, click Create Instance. This brings up a pop-up window with service offerings pre-created by the cloud administrator (Figure 3-29).

Select the Sainath User Defined Schema service offering. Then, on the Create Schema screen (Figure 3-30), type in the details.

Enter the database service name **CAMPAIGN1** and select a medium workload size.

Next, specify the multiple schemas you want to access with this service, by clicking Create to add new schema lines as required. You can add up to five schemas, which is the limit specified in the service template by the SSA administrator.

In this example, we have specified three new schemas: COMPANY1, COMPANY2, and MARKETMASTER (use uppercase for the schema names). For each schema, enter the tablespace name as well as the password to be used. As the master account with access to all the other schemas, we have selected the third schema, MARKETMASTER.

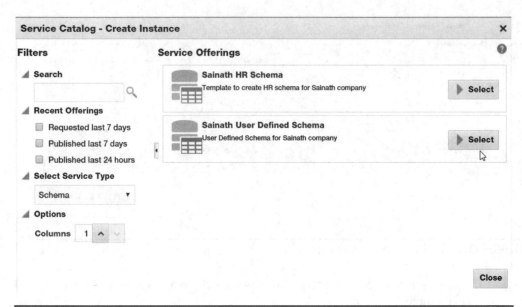

FIGURE 3-29.   *Selecting the user-defined schema service offering*

You can change the service properties, schedule the request to start immediately or at a later date and time, and also specify the duration of the request, after which it will be deleted automatically. Click Submit. The request starts executing and completes successfully in just over a minute.

The newly created service, CAMPAIGN1, appears in the list of service instances (Figure 3-31) for the SAI_DAS user.

Drill down on the CAMPAIGN1 service instance to see the new service home page (Figure 3-32).

The connect string and the master account MARKETMASTER is displayed. This can be used to connect to the service using tools such as SQL Developer. The list of schemas in the service, and the total number of tables and objects in each schema, are also displayed in the Schemas section.

The other tabs display resource usage and performance information such as active sessions. The High Availability tab enables SSA user to create new export dump backups and restore from such backups directly.

At the same time, the cloud administrator or DBA (not the SAI_DAS user) can examine the new users and tablespaces that have been created at the database level, along with their preallocated file sizes, as shown in the next code example.

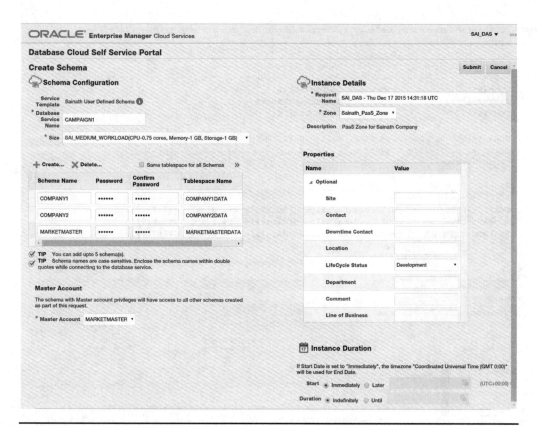

FIGURE 3-30. *Create Schema screen for the user-defined schema*

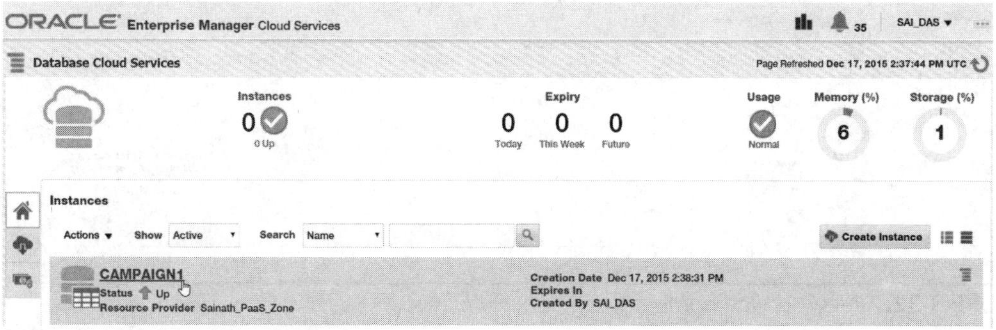

FIGURE 3-31. *New schema service instance in list*

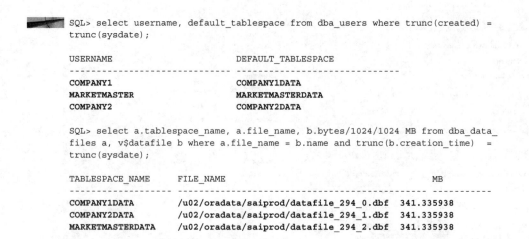

```
SQL> select username, default_tablespace from dba_users where trunc(created) =
trunc(sysdate);

USERNAME                        DEFAULT_TABLESPACE
------------------------------  ------------------------------
COMPANY1                        COMPANY1DATA
MARKETMASTER                    MARKETMASTERDATA
COMPANY2                        COMPANY2DATA

SQL> select a.tablespace_name, a.file_name, b.bytes/1024/1024 MB from dba_data_
files a, v$datafile b where a.file_name = b.name and trunc(b.creation_time) =
trunc(sysdate);

TABLESPACE_NAME      FILE_NAME                                          MB
-------------------  ------------------------------------------------  -----------
COMPANY1DATA         /u02/oradata/saiprod/datafile_294_0.dbf   341.335938
COMPANY2DATA         /u02/oradata/saiprod/datafile_294_1.dbf   341.335938
MARKETMASTERDATA     /u02/oradata/saiprod/datafile_294_2.dbf   341.335938
```

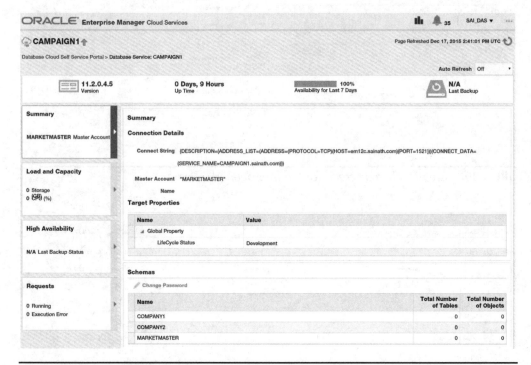

FIGURE 3-32. *New service home page*

The new service can also be seen at the UNIX level:

```
$ lsnrctl status
LSNRCTL for Linux: Version 11.2.0.4.0 - Production on 17-DEC-2015 14:44:57
Copyright (c) 1991, 2013, Oracle.  All rights reserved.

Connecting to (ADDRESS=(PROTOCOL=tcp)(HOST=)(PORT=1521))
STATUS of the LISTENER
------------------------
Alias                     LISTENER
Version                   TNSLSNR for Linux: Version 12.1.0.2.0 - Production
Start Date                17-DEC-2015 05:34:32
Uptime                    0 days 9 hr. 10 min. 25 sec
Trace Level               off
Security                  ON: Local OS Authentication
SNMP                      OFF
Listener Parameter File
/u01/app/oracle/product/12.1.0/dbhome_1/network/admin/listener.ora
Listener Log File
/u01/app/oracle/diag/tnslsnr/xxxxx/listener/alert/log.xml
Listening Endpoints Summary...
  (DESCRIPTION=(ADDRESS=(PROTOCOL=tcp)(HOST=xxxxx.sainath.com)(PORT=1521)))
  (DESCRIPTION=(ADDRESS=(PROTOCOL=ipc)(KEY=EXTPROC1521)))
Services Summary...
Service "CAMPAIGN1.sainath.com" has 1 instance(s).
  Instance "saiprod", status READY, has 1 handler(s) for this service...
Service "ahuprod.sainath.com" has 1 instance(s).
  Instance "ahuprod", status READY, has 1 handler(s) for this service...
Service "ahuprodXDB.sainath.com" has 1 instance(s).
  Instance "ahuprod", status READY, has 1 handler(s) for this service...
Service "emrep.sainath.com" has 1 instance(s).
  Instance "emrep", status READY, has 1 handler(s) for this service...
Service "emrepXDB.sainath.com" has 1 instance(s).
  Instance "emrep", status READY, has 1 handler(s) for this service...
Service "saiprod.sainath.com" has 1 instance(s).
  Instance "saiprod", status READY, has 1 handler(s) for this service...
Service "saiprodXDB.sainath.com" has 1 instance(s).
  Instance "saiprod", status READY, has 1 handler(s) for this service...
Service "sales.sainath.com" has 1 instance(s).
  Instance "ahuprod", status READY, has 1 handler(s) for this service...
The command completed successfully
```

Back on the Self Service Portal, the new service can be deleted by the SSA user SAI_DAS by selecting Delete. The deletion completes in about a minute, removing the service and associated schemas from the database.

Summary

Oracle's private database cloud management capabilities grew to encompass Schema as a Service (SCHaaS), in addition to the previously released Database as a Service (DBaaS), and Infrastructure as a Service (IaaS). The SCHaaS capability is powered by automated deployment procedures supplied by Oracle out-of-the-box, to satisfy cloud users who want to consolidate at the schema level instead of creating entirely new databases every time.

The cloud administrator or SSA administrator goes through the procedure of setting up the schema Self Service Portal by creating PaaS Infrastructure Zones, schema pools, quotas, data profiles, service templates, request settings, and, optionally, chargeback plans. Once these are completed and the rights are assigned to the appropriate SSA role, the SSA user can log into the Self Service Portal and issue a service request for a new schema service—one based on an exported schema(s) or on empty schema(s).

After successful completion of the service request, the same SSA user can drill down to the home page of the provisioned service for self-management, examine the resource usage and performance details of the service, and also perform export backups or restores of the schema data associated with the service. For additional security, the cloud administrator can deploy Oracle Database Vault at the database server level, thus ensuring security isolation. Budgeting of resources for schema services, and alerting the SSA administrator if those limits are exceeded, can also be achieved via the use of workloads in each service template. The Oracle Database Resource Manager can be enabled at the schema pool level, and this can ensure quality of service for the new schema service(s) in so far as the CPU cycles are concerned.

With the introduction of the Schema as a Service (SCHaaS) capability in Enterprise Manager, it became possible for Oracle private cloud users to self-service the provisioning of schemas in existing databases. Cloud consolidation was driven further by a considerable degree, and this also served to reduce the proliferation of databases or virtual machines being deployed for every single application.

In the next chapter, we will take a look at the PDB as a Service capabilities of Enterprise Manager Cloud Control 13*c*. It is true that PDBaaS enables the Oracle Database Cloud Service to achieve the highest level of consolidation—more so than schemas or databases can achieve.

CHAPTER
4

Pluggable Database
as a Service

I n the previous chapters, we looked at setting up and using Database as a Service (DBaaS) in Enterprise Manager for self-service requests of single-instance and Snap Clone databases, and Schema as a Service (SCHaaS) for self-service requests of schemas in existing databases. But what about the new concept of pluggable databases?

Although schemas have been around for a long time, pluggable, or multitenant, database architecture was introduced in Oracle Database 12*c*. From this version onward, a container database (CDB) could contain many self-contained pluggable databases (PDBs) with their own local users and tablespaces. These were like separate databases, except that they shared the CDB's memory and background processes.

This architecture was specifically designed for the cloud, since it allowed the highest level of consolidation and afforded more isolation than schema consolidation. If you have multiple schemas in a database, you can grant cross-schema privileges so that one schema user can select, update, or delete data in another schema's tables. In the case of PDBs, the only way for one PDB to access the data in another PDB would be via database links—just like separate databases.

Each PDB has its own separate set of schemas and tablespaces. You can unplug PDBs from one CDB and plug them into another, and you can use Recovery Manager (RMAN) to backup and restore individual PDBs, but you cannot use RMAN in the same way for schemas. (Note that the Oracle Enterprise Edition Multitenant Option license is required if you create more than one PDB in a CDB database.)

In this chapter, we'll look at the Pluggable Database as a Service (PDBaaS) capabilities, introduced in Enterprise Manager in late 2013. The previously named Oracle Cloud Management 12.1.0.7 plug-in released in October 2013 added the PDBaaS capability. Using this capability, cloud self-service users could request the creation of pluggable databases themselves. This was the next stage of the private database cloud.

The PDBaaS capability requires a PDB pool of one or more Oracle 12*c* CDBs that have been pre-created by the cloud administrator. Once the PDBaaS cloud has been set up, the self-service user can request new PDBs in those CDBs using the Self Service Portal, with a preset quota allocation.

The PaaS Infrastructure Zone is the basic foundation of the PDB pool, just as it was for the schema pool and the database pool. The zone has already been created, and we will use the same zone for PDBaaS. So the next step will be to create the PDB pool itself.

Creating a Pluggable Database Pool

To create a PDB pool, log in as a super administrator (such as SYSMAN) or as an administrator assigned the EM_SSA_ADMINISTRATOR role. Choose Setup | Cloud | Database. In the Cloud Database setup screen, select Pluggable Database from the drop-down list at the top of the left pane. The Pluggable Database: Overview screen (Figure 4-1) shows the steps you'll need to follow to set up PDBaaS.

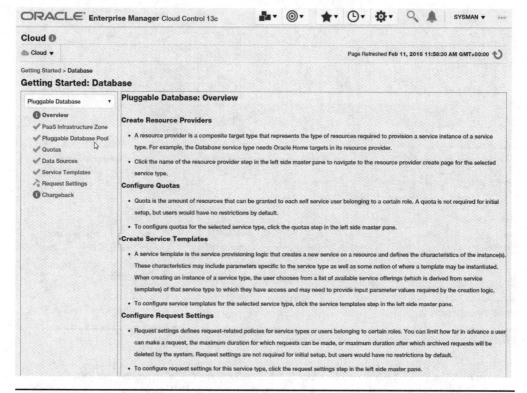

FIGURE 4-1.   *PDB cloud setup: overview of steps*

The PaaS Infrastructure Zone has already been set up. Click Pluggable Database Pool in the left pane, and then click the Create button. The Create New Pool wizard starts with the Setup screen (Figure 4-2).

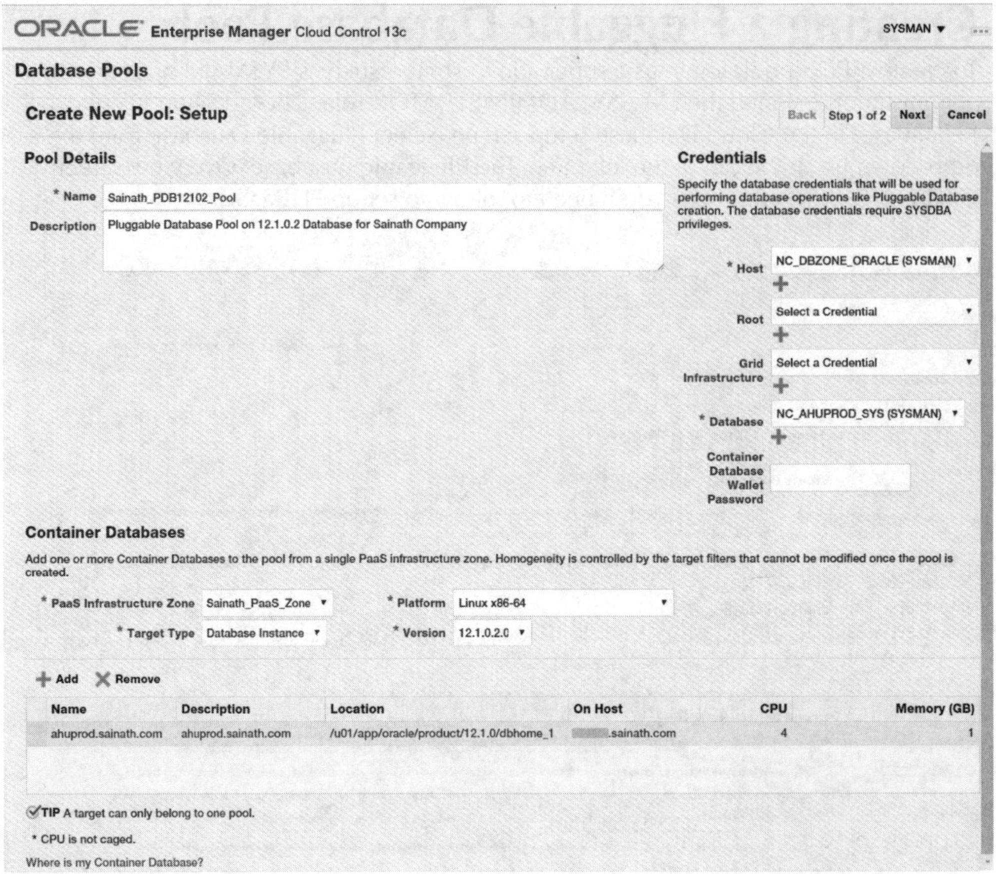

FIGURE 4-2. *Create New Pool: Setup screen*

Name the pool Sainath_PDB12102_Pool and enter the pool's Description:
Pluggable Database Pool on 12.1.0.2 Database for Sainath Company.

Select the Credentials for this pool, such as the Host credentials and the
Database credentials (with SYSDBA privileges) for the 12c CDB that will be used.
The Root credentials and Grid Infrastructure credentials are not required, since this
is a PDB pool. One additional credential can be specified on this page—the
Container Database Wallet Password. Specify this if you want to support encryption
for the PDBs that will be created. The password you enter here must be used to open
the wallet from the keystore.

In the Container Databases section, you can add one or more CDB targets to
the pool. First, you need to define the target filters—the PaaS Infrastructure Zone
(Sainath_PaaS_Zone), the Platform (Linux x86-64), the Target Type (Database

Instance), and the Version (12.1.0.2.0). The filters you set here depend on how the zone has been set up—the platform that has been used, and the CDB version that has been installed. We will use a single-instance 12.1.0.2 CDB to house all our Self Service Application (SSA)–created PDBs.

Specify the target filters, and then add the CDB by clicking the Add button. Select the ahuprod.sainath.com database for the pool. This is a 12.1.0.2 container database. Next, the Oracle home location of the selected database is displayed, as well as the host name, the CPUs that can be used by the database, and the memory in GB allocated to the database. Note that all container databases you select for the PDB pool must reside in the same PaaS Infrastructure Zone.

A CDB can belong to one PDB pool only, so after this database is added to this pool, it cannot be used in any other PDB pool. Likewise, if this database had already been used in another PDB pool, it will not appear in the selection list when you click Add.

Note that the databases you add to the pool need to be homogenous (using the same platform, version, configuration and patch level), and this is controlled by the target filters that cannot be modified once the pool is created.

Click Next to open the Policies screen (Figure 4-3), where you can specify the Placement Constraints to set maximum ceilings for resource utilization.

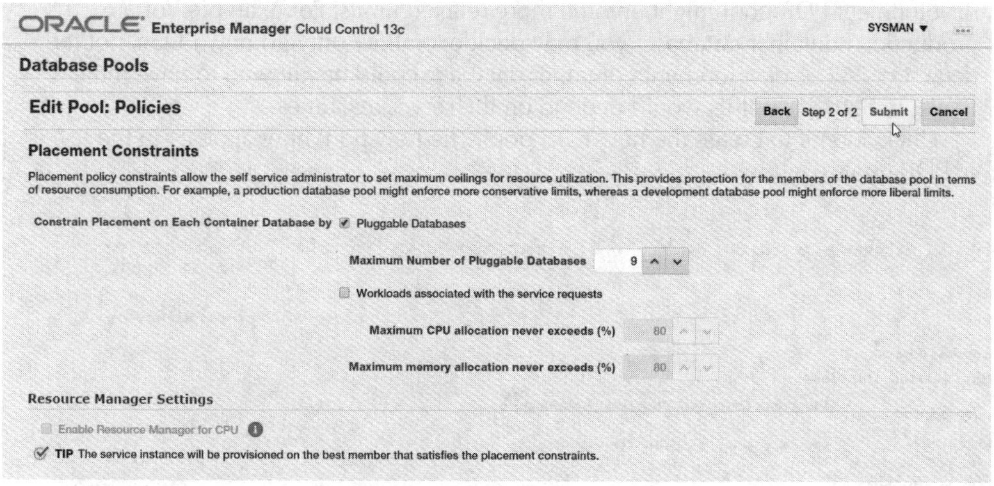

FIGURE 4-3. *Specify Placement Constraints in the Policies screen.*

You can create a Placement Constraint based on the Maximum Number Of Pluggable Databases in each CDB (we have specified a maximum number of 9 PDBs only; the default is 252), or based on the Workloads Associated With The

Service Requests. In the latter case, you can also set the maximum CPU and memory allocations.

The maximum CPU defines the maximum limit of the CPU allowed for each CDB, beyond which a PDB service request cannot be placed on that database. The number of CPU cores available for the CDB is derived from the initialization parameter cpu_count if explicitly set for instance caging, or the CPU count of the host itself if there is no instance caging. On the other hand, the maximum memory allocation represents the total system global area (SGA) allocated for each CDB.

A range of small, medium, and large workloads with different CPU, memory, session, and storage limits can be specified at the time of the service template creation (later on in this chapter). The CPU limits for these workloads can be enforced via the Oracle Database Resource Manager if you select Enable Resource Manager For CPU under Resource Manager Settings on this screen. If this is selected, the Resource Manager will be used to create consumer groups, and these consumer groups will ensure that the PDB service gets the requested CPU cycles on a system with full load.

Regarding the other limits that are not enforced via the Database Resource Manager, internal bookkeeping will be used. The service instance will be provisioned on the most suitable member that satisfies the placement constraints.

Note that a production PDB pool might enforce conservative limits, whereas a development PDB pool might enforce more relaxed limits. For example, for a production container database, you may decide to allow only 20 new PDBs, not the default of 252. A development container database could be allowed to have more PDBs. In both cases, this would depend on the server resources.

Click Submit to create the new PDB pool. The new pool now appears in the list of PDB pools (Figure 4-4).

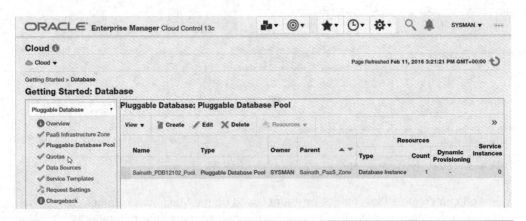

FIGURE 4-4. *New PDB pool appears in the list*

Setting Up Quotas

Quotas control the amount of resources that a self-service user can request. They form a very important part of controlling the usage of the cloud. Because of its self-service nature, the cloud could easily be misused if no quotas were in force. A developer could potentially request hundreds of PDBs in a short space of time, and this could bring an under-resourced CDB to its knees, but if the same developer were restricted to a quota of just 10 new PDB requests, that would not affect the destination CDB as much.

Quotas need to be understood and set up carefully, with balance between allowing too much and allowing too little. The kind of balance you set up depends on the capacity of the underlying infrastructure.

Select Quotas from the left pane. Quotas have already been set up for our self-service users at the time of setting up Database as a Service, as shown in Figure 4-5.

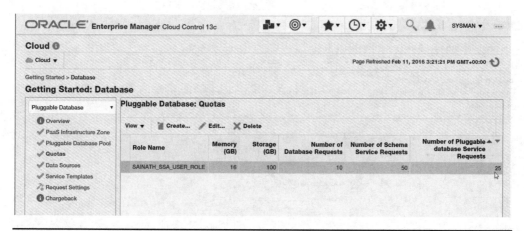

FIGURE 4-5. *Quotas were created previously.*

According to the previous quota setup, any user belonging to the role SAINATH_SSA_USER_ROLE can request a total number of 50 schemas, 10 databases, and 25 PDBs, and can use a maximum of 100GB of storage and 16GB of memory for all the services the user will create. Note that the quota is calculated separately for each SSA user, and these limits apply only to services created through the Self Service Portal. The SSA user (if granted additional privileges by mistake) could create databases or schemas or PDBs outside the Self Service Portal, and these would not apply toward the limits. The SSA administrator must therefore ensure that this does not happen by controlling the privileges that are granted.

Creating a Data Profile for PDB

You can set up a data profile as a gold copy of the source PDB that will be used in the provisioning. The service templates that will use such data profiles are the actual locked-down deployment procedures (a series of executable steps predefined in Enterprise Manager) that are presented to the self-service user as possible selections from a service catalog.

We'll now create a data profile from an existing PDB. The ahuprod.sainath.com CDB that we are using in the PDB pool for creation of self-service PDBs also contains a copy of a production PDB named SALES that we will use as the source for the profile.

Log in to Enterprise Manager as an administrator with sufficient DBA rights on the ahuprod.sainath.com CDB. Drill down to the CDB Home screen, and from the Database menu, select Oracle Database | Provisioning | Provision Pluggable Databases. The Provision Pluggable Databases screen opens (Figure 4-6).

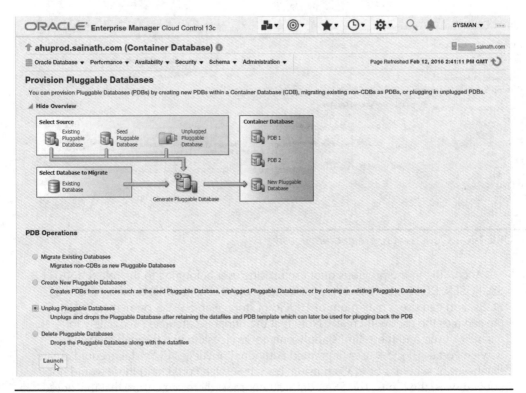

FIGURE 4-6. *Provision Pluggable Database screen*

Under PDB Operations, select Unplug Pluggable Databases and then click Launch. The first page of the wizard opens (Figure 4-7).

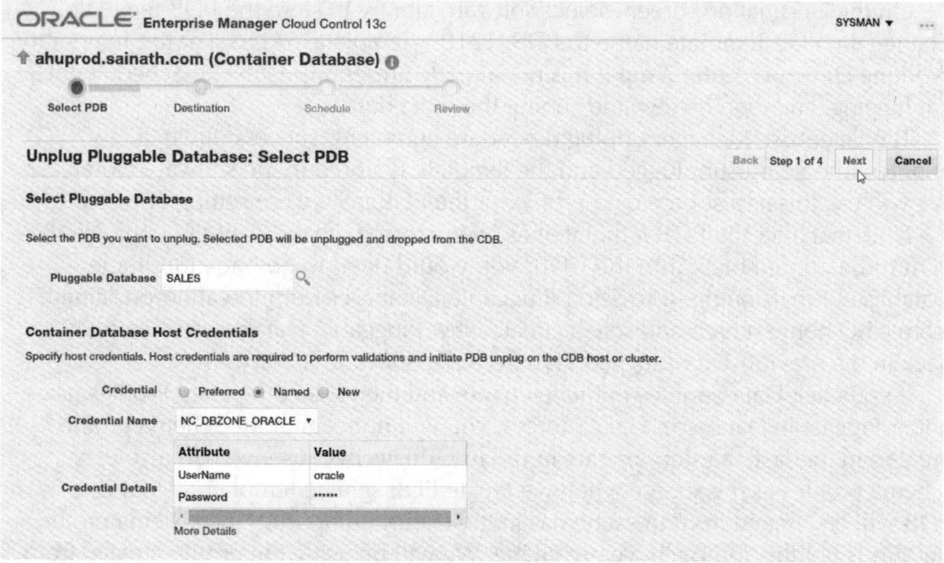

FIGURE 4-7. *Unplug Pluggable Database wizard Select PDB screen*

Select SALES as the Pluggable Database that is to be unplugged. Also choose the Container Database Host credentials. Click Next to open the Destination screen (Figure 4-8).

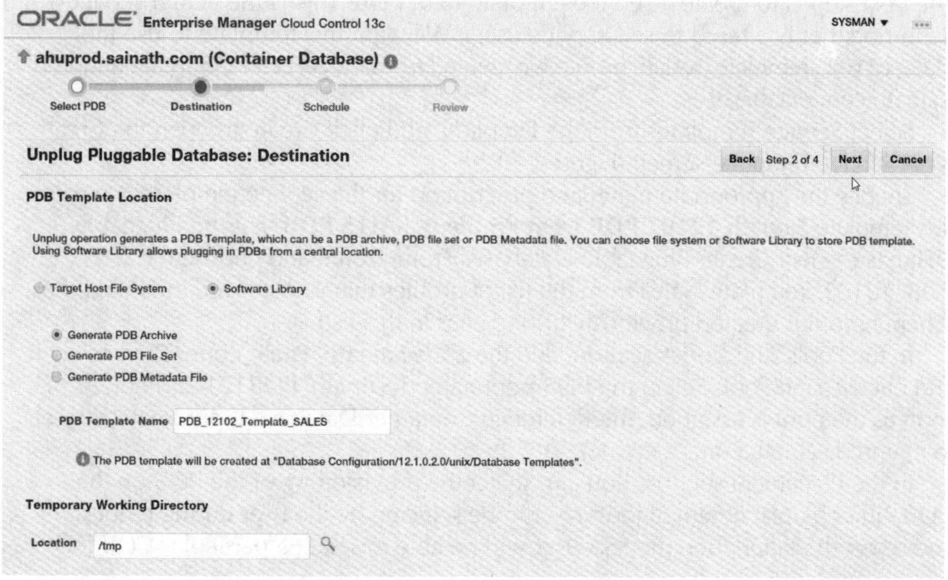

FIGURE 4-8. *Select the Software Library destination.*

On the Destination screen, select Software Library to store the PDB template. Change the PDB Template name to PDB_12102_Template_SALES. For the Temporary Working Directory, enter **/tmp** if it is not already present. Click Next. Schedule the unplugging, and then review and submit the procedure.

The Enterprise Manager unplug procedure completes successfully in a few minutes. The PDB is unplugged and the template is stored in the software Library. We will use this as a source data profile for the PDBaaS we are setting up.

Note that after the PDB template has been created, if you want the unplugged PDB to be copied back into the CDB, you would need to go back to Oracle Database | Provisioning | Provision Pluggable Databases from the ahuprod.sainath .com CBD home screen and select Create New Pluggable Databases. Then plug back in the previously unplugged PDB from the Software Library.

If you click Data Sources in the left pane, and then select the Data Profiles tab, under Pluggable Database: Data Sources, you will notice that the schema profile created in the last chapter appears in the list. This is because we can also use schema profiles as the source when we create PDB service templates—that is, a PDB will be created from the schemas in the export dump from the schema profile. But this is not the approach we are taking. We will be using the profile created from the unplugged PDB instead.

Creating a Service Template from a PDB Profile

The next step is to create a service template for a PDB. This is the actual service definition that is offered to self-service users. We want this template to use the PDB_12102_Template_SALES profile we created from the SALES PDB in the ahuprod .sainath.com database.

Select Service Templates from the left pane, and click Create to open the Create New Service Template screen (Figure 4-9).

Specify the appropriate name and description for the service template. Name this template **Sainath 12102 PDB from Profile of SALES PDB**. For the Pluggable Database, select Create Pluggable Databases From Profile and choose the PDB_12102_Template_Sales from the list of profiles that is displayed (note that the schema profiles created previously also appear in this list).

In the Pools And Zones section, add the zone **Sainath_PaaS_Zone**. Then select it and click Assign Pool. Select the PDB pool named Sainath_PDB12102_Pool. As soon as the pool is assigned, the Reference Container Database is automatically set to ahuprod.sainath.com.

In the Placement section, you can select the provisioning of the PDB on the CDB either by placement algorithm or to be selected by the user during request. If you select the latter, then the SSA user will be able to select a particular CDB for

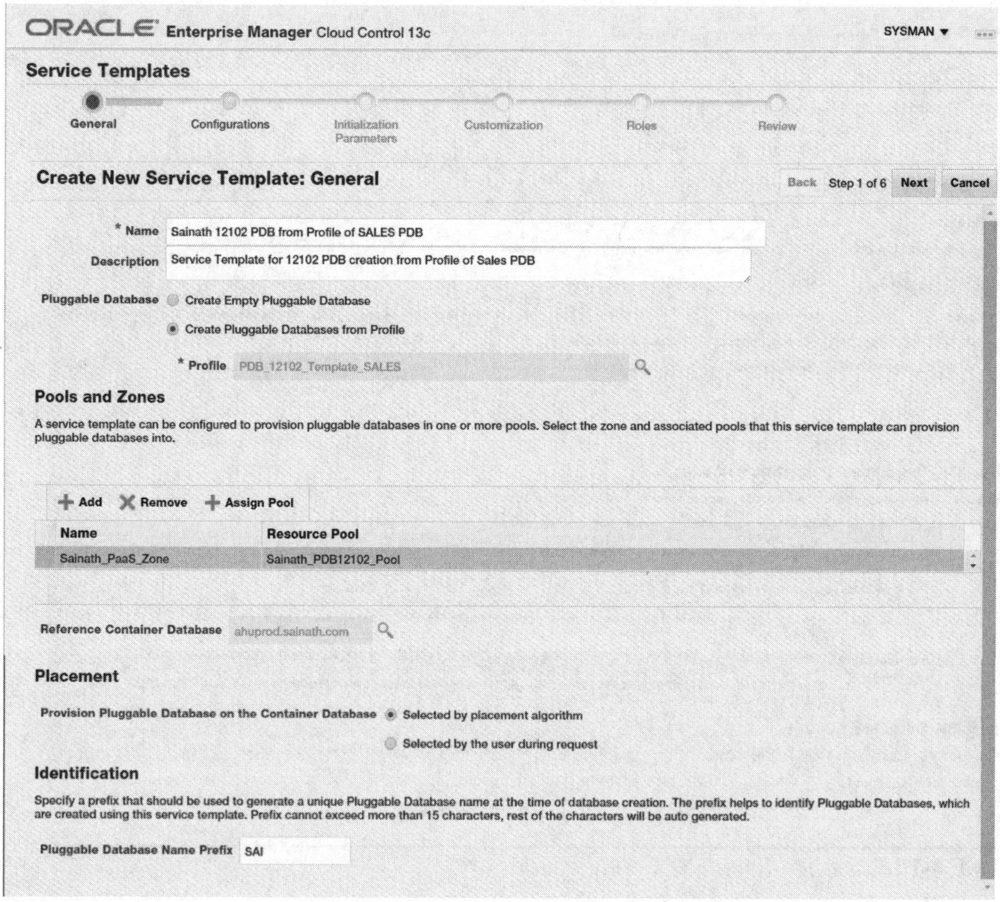

FIGURE 4-9. *Create New Service Template from SALES PDB profile*

placement when requesting for the new PDB. In our case, because there is only one CDB in the PDB pool we have created, the selection by the user does not apply, so we leave it at the default setting—Selected By Placement Algorithm.

Enter **SAI** as the Pluggable Database Name Prefix. The prefix will help to identify the PDBs that are created using this service template. Note that the PDB name prefix cannot exceed more than 15 characters.

Click Next to open the Configurations screen (Figure 4-10).

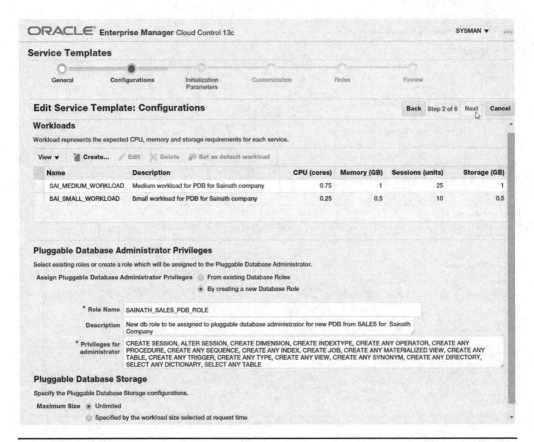

FIGURE 4-10. *Service Template: Configurations*

Under the Workloads section, create an expected workload size by clicking the Create button. At least one workload must be created. The workload signifies the expected CPU, Memory, Sessions, and Storage requirements for each PDB service that will be created. Multiple workloads can be created here, which then can be selected by the SSA user when creating the PDB. One of the workloads can be set as the default workload.

Specify a workload for the new PDB service; name it SAI_SMALL_WORKLOAD. In this workload, specify the CPU Cores as 0.25, Memory as 0.5GB, Sessions as 10 units, and Storage as 0.5GB. Create another SAI_MEDIUM_WORKLOAD with more CPU cores, memory, sessions, and storage allocated. Use 0.75 CPU Cores, 1GB Memory, Sessions as 25 units, and 1GB Storage for the medium workload.

Note that these figures are just examples and will vary depending on the server resources you have available and the type of PDBs that are being offered in the service catalog. Production PDBs will normally have larger workload offerings.

Regarding the limits set in these workloads for CPU cores, if when creating the PDB pool, you had selected Enable Resource Manager For CPU in the Policies screen (refer back to Figure 4-3), then the Oracle Database Resource Manager will be used to ensure that the new PDB service gets the requested CPU cycles on a system with full load. This guarantees quality of service (QoS) for the new PDB service so far as CPU usage is concerned.

The memory is a soft limit used for budgeting purposes only. Alerts will be raised with the SSA administrator if the PDB service usage exceeds the specified memory limit. This will also apply to the CPU cores limit in the workload, if the Resource Manager is not enabled in the PDB pool. The sessions limit from the workload is used in the sessions initialization parameter for the PDB when it is created, so it is a hard limit. Regarding the storage limit in the workload, it is a soft limit unless the maximum size of the PDB is set to Specified By The Workload Size Selected At Request Time, which is a setting under the Pluggable Database Storage section on this same screen. This will make it a hard limit.

Under the Pluggable Database Administrator Privileges section, specify a new database role SAINATH_SALES_PDB_ROLE (uppercase important) to be created for the PDB administrator. Take a note of the privileges granted to this role. If company policy permits, allow privileges such as SELECT ANY TABLE to remain in the list of privileges so that the new role will be able to select from any table in the PDB. The default list of privileges is as follows:

CREATE SESSION, ALTER SESSION, CREATE DIMENSION, CREATE INDEXTYPE, CREATE ANY OPERATOR, CREATE ANY PROCEDURE, CREATE ANY SEQUENCE, CREATE ANY INDEX, CREATE JOB, CREATE ANY MATERIALIZED VIEW, CREATE ANY TABLE, CREATE ANY TRIGGER, CREATE ANY TYPE, CREATE ANY VIEW, CREATE ANY SYNONYM, CREATE ANY DIRECTORY, SELECT ANY DICTIONARY, SELECT ANY TABLE

At the bottom of the Configurations screen, under the Pluggable Database Storage section, specify the PDB storage configuration. The Maximum Size can be set to be Unlimited or Specified By The Workload Size Selected At Request Time. If you specify the latter, it means that the workload storage size limit will be enforced, and the PDB will not be able to grow beyond this limit. The workload storage size limit will become a hard limit.

Note that if you had selected a schema profile as the source for this service template, the tablespaces in the profile will also be displayed at the bottom of the screen, and it is possible to edit the initial size of the tablespace that will be created. If the schema profile contained encrypted tablespaces, you would be asked to enter the wallet password here.

Click next to open the Initialization Parameters screen, where you can change only a few PDB-level initialization parameters, such as cursor_sharing and open_cursors. Click Next to see the Customization screen, where you can specify the custom scripts to be executed before and/or after creation and/or deletion of the PDB service. However, no SQL scripts can be specified here.

You can also enter the target property values that will be applied to the new PDB service. If you select the Required check box for one or more of these target properties, the SSA user will be forced to fill in these properties when requesting the service. You can also select and lock the Lifecycle Status property, so that it cannot be changed by the SSA user at request time.

After this, in the Roles screen, add the role SAINATH_SSA_USER_ROLE to the service template. Then review the information and proceed to create the PDB service template.

Creating a Service Template for an Empty PDB

The next step is to create a service template to create an empty PDB. This is the second PDB service definition that will be offered to self-service users.

Select Service Templates from the left pane, and click Create to open the Create New Service Template screen (Figure 4-11).

In the General screen, specify the appropriate name and description for the Service template. Name this template Sainath 12102 Empty PDB. Select Create Empty Pluggable Database. As a result, there is no need to select any profile.

In the Pools And Zones section, add the zone **Sainath_PaaS_Zone**, select it, and click Assign Pool. Select the PDB pool named Sainath_PDB12102_Pool. As soon as the pool is assigned, the Reference Container Database is automatically set to ahuprod.sainath.com.

In the Placement section, you can select the provisioning of the PDB on the CDB either by placement algorithm or to be selected by the user during request. If you select the latter, then the SSA user will be able to select a particular CDB for placement when requesting the new PDB. In our case, since there is only one CDB in the PDB pool we have created, the selection by the user does not apply, so we leave it at the default setting—Selected By Placement Algorithm.

Enter **SAI** as the Pluggable Database Name Prefix. The prefix will help to identify the PDBs that are created using this service template. Note that the PDB name prefix cannot exceed more than 15 characters.

Click Next to open the Configurations screen (Figure 4-12).

Under the Workloads section, create an expected workload size by clicking the Create button. The workload signifies the expected CPU, memory, sessions, and storage requirements for each PDB service that will be created. Multiple workloads can be created here, which can be then selected by the SSA user when creating the PDB.

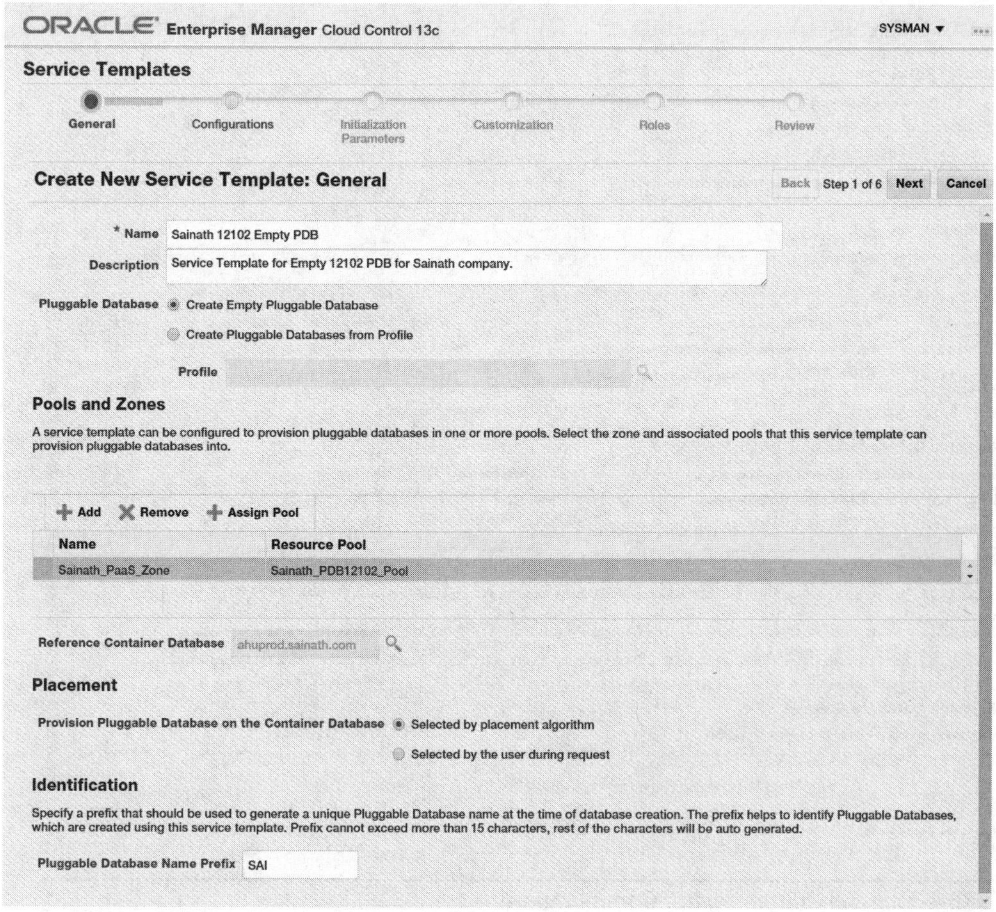

ORACLE' Enterprise Manager Cloud Control 13c | SYSMAN ▼

Service Templates

General — Configurations — Initialization Parameters — Customization — Roles — Review

Create New Service Template: General | Back | Step 1 of 6 | Next | Cancel

* Name | Sainath 12102 Empty PDB

Description | Service Template for Empty 12102 PDB for Sainath company.

Pluggable Database | ● Create Empty Pluggable Database

○ Create Pluggable Databases from Profile

Profile

Pools and Zones

A service template can be configured to provision pluggable databases in one or more pools. Select the zone and associated pools that this service template can provision pluggable databases into.

➕ Add ✖ Remove ➕ Assign Pool

Name	Resource Pool
Sainath_PaaS_Zone	Sainath_PDB12102_Pool

Reference Container Database | ahuprod.sainath.com

Placement

Provision Pluggable Database on the Container Database ● Selected by placement algorithm

○ Selected by the user during request

Identification

Specify a prefix that should be used to generate a unique Pluggable Database name at the time of database creation. The prefix helps to identify Pluggable Databases, which are created using this service template. Prefix cannot exceed more than 15 characters, rest of the characters will be auto generated.

Pluggable Database Name Prefix | SAI

FIGURE 4-11. *Create New Service Template for an empty PDB*

Specify a workload for the new PDB service, and name it SAI_SMALL_ WORKLOAD. In this workload, specify the CPU cores as 0.25, Memory as 0.5GB, Sessions as 10 units, and Storage as 0.5GB. Create another SAI_MEDIUM_ WORKLOAD with 0.75 CPU cores, 1GB memory, Sessions as 25 units, and 1GB Storage. These figures are just examples and will vary depending on the server resources you have available. One of the workloads can be set as the default workload. At least one workload is required to be created.

Regarding the limits set in these workloads, the same principles of hard or soft limits apply as discussed earlier in the chapter in the section "Creating a Service Template from a PDB Profile."

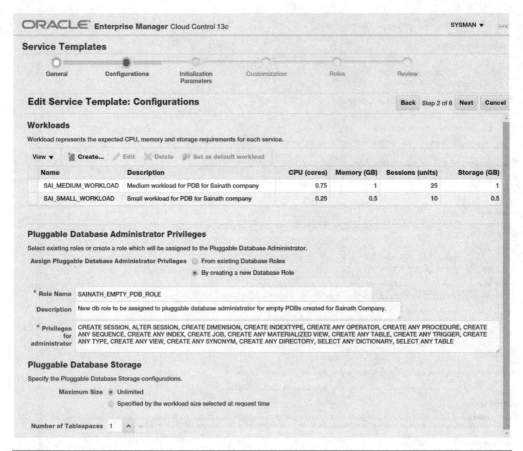

FIGURE 4-12. *Service Template: Configurations*

Under the Pluggable Database Administrator Privileges section, specify a new database role, SAINATH_EMPTY_PDB_ROLE (uppercase important) to be created for the PDB administrator. Take a note of the privileges granted to this role. If company policy permits, allow privileges such as SELECT ANY TABLE to remain in the list of privileges so that the new role will be able to select from any table in the PDB. The default list of privileges is as follows:

CREATE SESSION, ALTER SESSION, CREATE DIMENSION, CREATE INDEXTYPE, CREATE ANY OPERATOR, CREATE ANY PROCEDURE, CREATE ANY SEQUENCE, CREATE ANY INDEX, CREATE JOB, CREATE ANY MATERIALIZED VIEW, CREATE ANY TABLE, CREATE ANY TRIGGER, CREATE ANY TYPE,

CREATE ANY VIEW, CREATE ANY SYNONYM, CREATE ANY DIRECTORY, SELECT ANY DICTIONARY, SELECT ANY TABLE

At the bottom of the Configurations screen, under the Pluggable Database Storage section, specify the PDB storage configuration. The Maximum Size can be set to be Unlimited or Specified By The Workload Size Selected At Request Time. If you specify the latter, it means that the workload storage size limit will be enforced, and the empty PDB will not be able to grow beyond this limit.

You can also specify the Number Of Tablespaces to be created in the new PDB. The default is 1, and you can enter up to 30 new tablespaces to be created in each new empty PDB.

Click Next to open the Initialization Parameters screen, where you can change only a few PDB-level initialization parameters, such as cursor_sharing and open_cursors. Click Next to see the Customization screen, where you can specify the custom scripts to be executed before and/or after creation and/or deletion of the PDB service. However, no SQL scripts can be specified on this screen.

You can also enter the target property values that will be applied to the new PDB service. If you select the Required check box for one of more of these target properties, then the SSA user will be forced to fill in these properties when requesting the service. You can also select and lock the Lifecycle Status property so that it cannot be changed by the SSA user at request time.

In the Roles screen, add the role SAINATH_SSA_USER_ROLE to the service template. Then review the information and click Create to save the service template for creating an empty PDB.

The two new service templates for PDB now appear in the service template list, as shown in Figure 4-13.

FIGURE 4-13. *Service Template List*

Setting Up Request Settings

As the next step, you can optionally set up the request settings, which control the manner in which the self-service users can make requests for a PDB service. These help you further control the self-service nature of the cloud.

Click Request Settings in the left pane to see the screen shown in Figure 4-14.

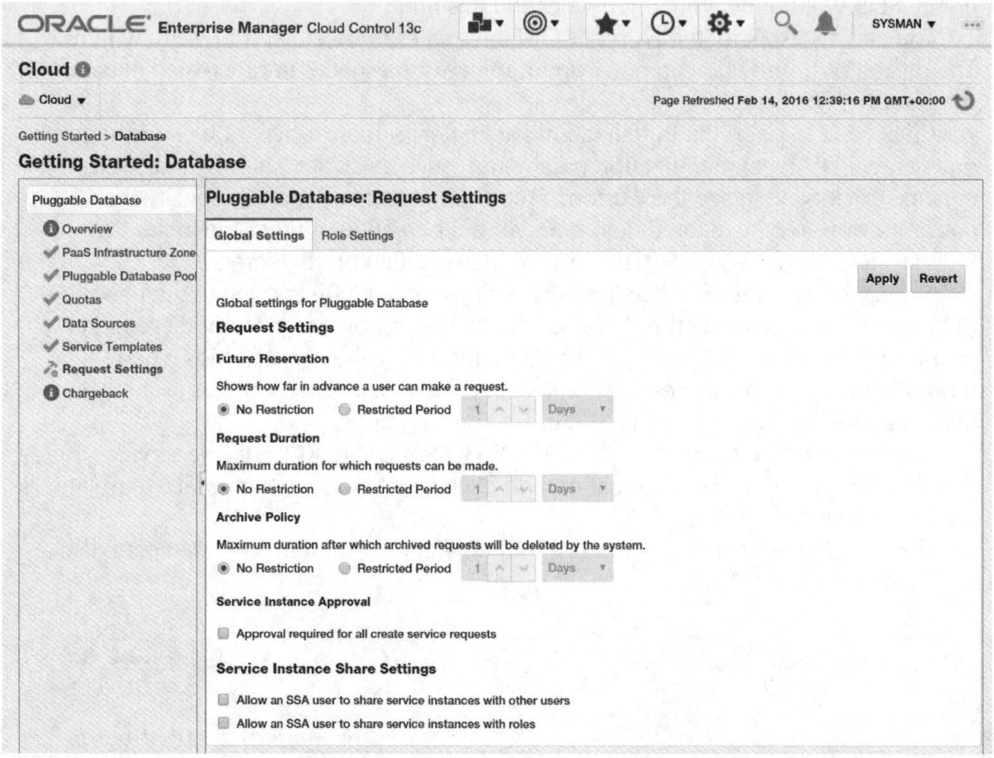

FIGURE 4-14. *Pluggable Database: Request Settings*

You can specify the number of days in advance the self-service user can make a request, when archived requests will be automatically deleted, and the maximum duration for which the requests can be made. We have selected No Restriction for all the settings.

Service Instance Approval and Service Instance Sharing can also be enabled. You can also move to the Role Settings tab and assign different settings to different roles.

Configuring Chargeback

The final setup step is to configure the chargeback for PDBaaS. Using the chargeback capability, the resource usage of the PDBs that are created by the SSA user can be calculated based on various criteria. A dollar figure can then be presented to the self-service user or project.

As explained in Chapter 2, we entered charge rates into a Universal Charge Plan and created an Extended Plan called Sainath Additional Plan. In this plan, we added charge rates for Oracle Pluggable Database. These rates are shown in Figure 4-15.

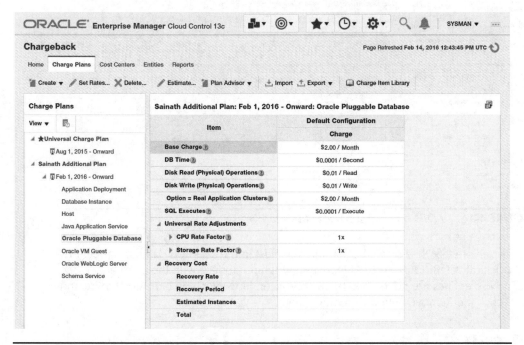

FIGURE 4-15.   *Sainath Additional Plan: Charge Rates for Oracle Pluggable Database*

We have set up a base charge for each PDB service, plus an extra configuration charge if the container database used for the PDB is a RAC container database, and usage charges on top of these for DB Time and SQL Executes per PDB service.

Other available options that you can charge for are CPU Count, CPU Time, Disk Read (Physical) Operations, Disk Write (Physical) Operations, User Transactions, and so on—each of these per PDB service. Note that these usage charges can easily build up the total chargeback figure, so you need to set them with some restraint.

The creation and assignment of cost centers and assignment of the additional charge plan to various entities including the zone and the ahuprod CDB has already been completed and explained in Chapter 2. As a result of this, you can see the PDBs belonging to the CDB ahuprod.sainath.com in the Entities tab (Figure 4-16) of the Chargeback screen.

FIGURE 4-16. *PDBs on Chargeback Entities tab*

Note that the two PDBs that already exist in the ahuprod database appear by default: CDBROOT and SALES. These will not interfere with the chargeback because these entities are not owned by the SSA user. However, you can select them and click the Remove button to remove them.

Self Service: Request and Create a PDB Service for SALES PDB

You've now configured a self-service portal for PDBaaS. It's time to try out your new creation. The following steps walk you through the process of logging in as the self-service user to see for yourself what you can do in this portal.

Log in to Enterprise Manager Cloud Control 13*c* as the SAI_DAS user. This is the SSA user we created previously. On the All Cloud Services page that appears, under Featured Services, in the Database Cloud Services section, select Click Here To Get Started. This brings up the Database Cloud Service Portal. Click Create Instance.

A pop-up window shows the service offering to be selected. The service offerings have been pre-created by the cloud/SSA administrator. We have kept the default All under Select Service Type so that all the service offerings available to the SSA user SAI_DAS are displayed in the service catalog (Figure 4-17). These include the Database, Schema, and PDB service offerings in the list.

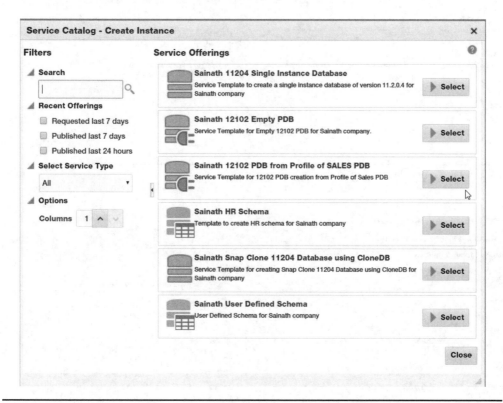

FIGURE 4-17. *All available service offerings for the SSA user SAI_DAS*

The service offerings in the service catalog cannot be displayed in a particular order; however if you change Columns to 2 or 3 instead of the default 1, the service catalog appears in a condensed form. In this case, we have changed Columns to 2 (Figure 4-18).

Select the Sainath 12102 PDB From Profile of SALES PDB service offering. The Create Pluggable Database screen appears (Figure 4-19).

Enter the details for the new PDB you are requesting. As the PDB Name, enter **SALES2PDB**, and as the Database Service name, enter **SALES2**. Note that the PDB Name and the Database Service name *must* be different to avoid the error, "Please enter a different service name."

Select the Medium workload. Enter the PDB Administrator Name **SALES2PDBADMIN** (use uppercase) along with a password you choose. Change the

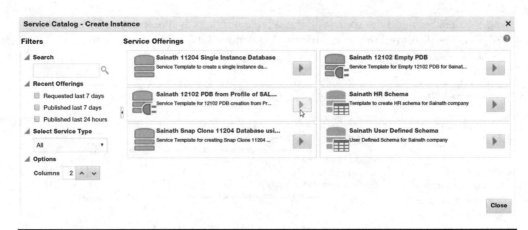

FIGURE 4-18. *Service catalog in two-column mode*

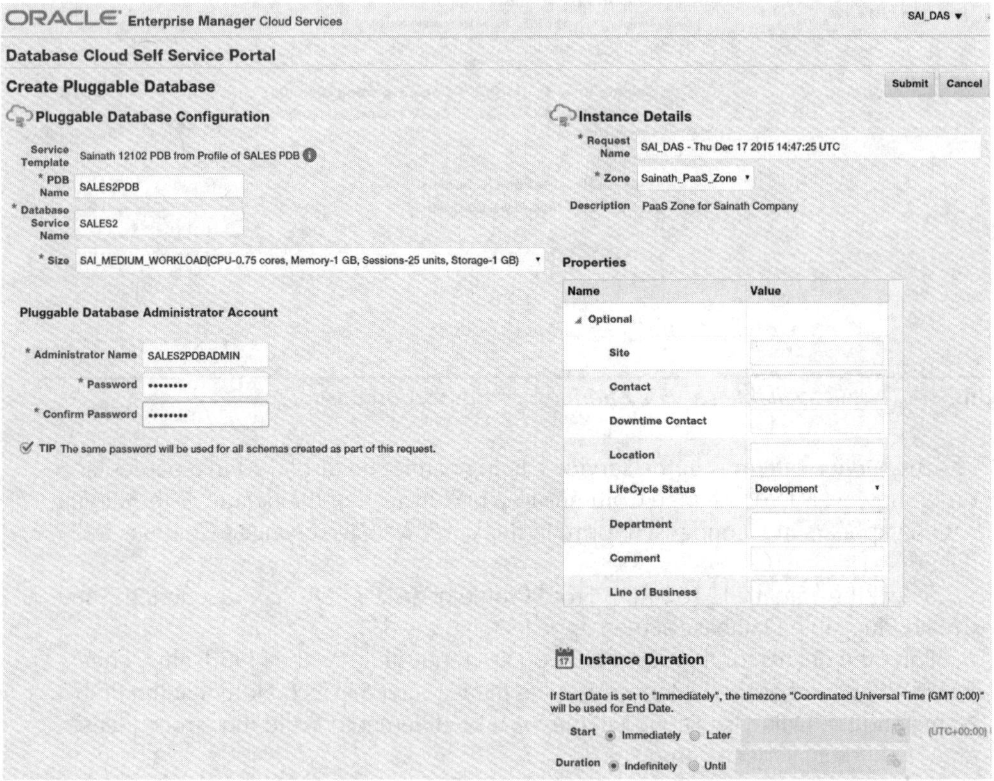

FIGURE 4-19. *Creating a new PDB via self-service*

properties if you want, and in the Instance section, set the Start and Duration. Then submit the request.

Move to the Requests tab in the left pane. The PDB creation is shown as running in the list of requests that appears (Figure 4-20).

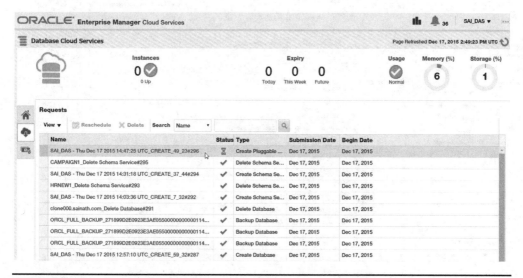

FIGURE 4-20. *Status of request to create PDB*

If you drill down on the request, the steps appear in brief, since the self-service user SAI_DAS cannot examine the detailed execution of the steps. To see the steps in full, log in to Enterprise Manager as SYSMAN or the cloud administrator, and select Enterprise | Provisioning and Patching | Procedure Activity. The PDB Create procedure is shown in the lists of procedures. Drill down to the steps (Figure 4-21).

The steps show that a PDB was created, and because the profile was from an unplugged PDB, the procedure has also executed datapatch successfully, as shown in the step Apply Datapatch. Datapatch is the Oracle command-line utility used to patch Oracle Database 12c CDBs and PDBs.

The procedure to create the new PDB completed in under 5 minutes. The new PDB SALES2PDB is now visible in the list of pluggable database targets (Figure 4-22) in Enterprise Manager, as viewed by SYSMAN or the cloud administrator by choosing Targets | Databases.

FIGURE 4-21. *Detailed steps of PDB creation*

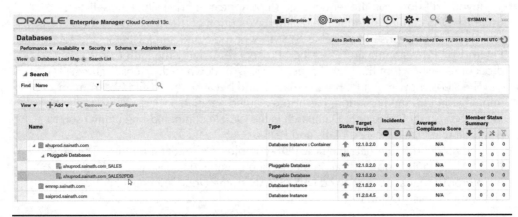

FIGURE 4-22. *Pluggable database targets*

The new service is also visible at the UNIX level. The command `lsnrctl status` displays the list of services as follows:

```
$ lsnrctl status
LSNRCTL for Linux: Version 11.2.0.4.0 - Production on 17-DEC-2015 14:58:08
Copyright (c) 1991, 2013, Oracle.  All rights reserved.
Connecting to (ADDRESS=(PROTOCOL=tcp)(HOST=)(PORT=1521))
STATUS of the LISTENER
------------------------
Alias                     LISTENER
Version                   TNSLSNR for Linux: Version 12.1.0.2.0 - Production
Start Date                17-DEC-2015 05:34:32
Uptime                    0 days 9 hr. 23 min. 36 sec
Trace Level               off
Security                  ON: Local OS Authentication
SNMP                      OFF
Listener Parameter File
/u01/app/oracle/product/12.1.0/dbhome_1/network/admin/listener.ora
Listener Log File
/u01/app/oracle/diag/tnslsnr/xxxxx/listener/alert/log.xml
Listening Endpoints Summary...
   (DESCRIPTION=(ADDRESS=(PROTOCOL=tcp)(HOST=xxxxx.sainath.com)(PORT=1521)))
   (DESCRIPTION=(ADDRESS=(PROTOCOL=ipc)(KEY=EXTPROC1521)))
Services Summary...
Service "ahuprod.sainath.com" has 1 instance(s).
  Instance "ahuprod", status READY, has 1 handler(s) for this service...
Service "ahuprodXDB.sainath.com" has 1 instance(s).
  Instance "ahuprod", status READY, has 1 handler(s) for this service...
Service "emrep.sainath.com" has 1 instance(s).
  Instance "emrep", status READY, has 1 handler(s) for this service...
Service "emrepXDB.sainath.com" has 1 instance(s).
  Instance "emrep", status READY, has 1 handler(s) for this service...
Service "saiprod.sainath.com" has 1 instance(s).
  Instance "saiprod", status READY, has 1 handler(s) for this service...
Service "saiprodXDB.sainath.com" has 1 instance(s).
  Instance "saiprod", status READY, has 1 handler(s) for this service...
Service "sales.sainath.com" has 1 instance(s).
  Instance "ahuprod", status READY, has 1 handler(s) for this service...
Service "sales2.sainath.com" has 1 instance(s).
  Instance "ahuprod", status READY, has 1 handler(s) for this service...
Service "sales2pdb.sainath.com" has 1 instance(s).
  Instance "ahuprod", status READY, has 1 handler(s) for this service...
The command completed successfully
```

Two new services are visible—sales2pdb.sainath.com and sales2.sainath.com—the first for the new PDB and the second for the corresponding new service. Both names were selected by the SSA user at the time of submitting the request.

Log in to Enterprise Manager as the SSA user SAI_DAS. The new pluggable database is shown in the Self Service Portal of SAI_DAS (Figure 4-23).

FIGURE 4-23. *New SALES2PDB in Self Service Portal*

Drill down on the new PDB to display the PDB Home screen (Figure 4-24) as viewed by the self-service user.

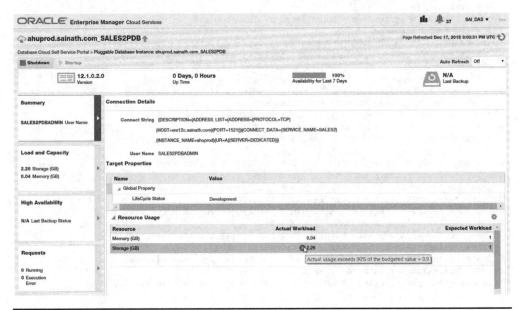

FIGURE 4-24. *Home screen of the new PDB*

The self-service user SAI_DAS can perform a startup and shutdown of the PDB by clicking the corresponding buttons at the top of the screen. SAI_DAS can also see the performance details of this new PDB, including SQL monitoring of long-running SQL statements under the Load And Capacity tab.

And in the High Availability tab, SAI_DAS can schedule daily backups of the PDB—or restore from a previous backup. The first backup will take a full database copy, followed by an incremental backup to disk each day. These disk backups are retained so that a full database recovery or a point-in-time recovery can be performed to any time within the past 30 days.

As SAI_DAS, we had selected the medium workload size, and the Storage Limit was specified as 1GB in that workload. However, the new PDB SALES2PDB was created from a service offering built on a profile of an existing PDB SALES with multiple sample schemas, and the total size was larger than 1GB.

As a result, immediately after creation, the storage limit has been breached. So you see that an alert is displayed in the Summary page under the Resource Usage section, indicating that the actual usage exceeds 90 percent of the budgeted value. The expected workload for storage was 1GB, but the actual workload is 2.26GB.

The self-service user SAI_DAS can also use the Connect String displayed on the Summary page to connect to the PDB using other tools such as Oracle SQL Developer, via the PDB administrator login of SALES2PDBADMIN. The SQL Developer create connection screen is shown in Figure 4-25.

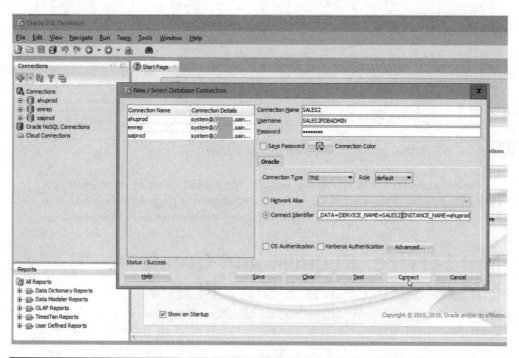

FIGURE 4-25. *SQL Developer connecting to SALES2 service*

Connect to the new service, and drill down to the schema list in the PDB using the SQL Developer screen. Select the SH schema and examine the tables it owns. Look at the data of one of the tables, as shown in Figure 4-26. These schemas and tables are from the source PDB SALES, which had the sample schemas installed. When the new self-service PDB was created by SAI_DAS, it was a copy of the SALES PDB and all its data.

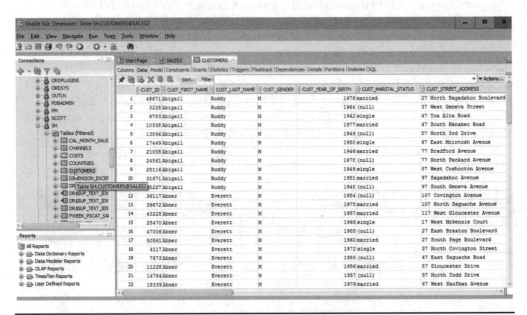

FIGURE 4-26. *Tables and data in SH schema in new PDB*

On the main Database Portal, it is possible for the self-service user to delete the PDB when it is no longer required. Select the PDB on that page and choose Delete from the Actions menu. The deletion completes successfully in a few minutes.

Self Service: Request and Create a PDB Service for Empty PDB

When you are logged in as SAI_DAS, on the Database Cloud Services Portal, click Create Instance. The service offerings available to SAI_DAS are presented as a service catalog in a pop-up window (Figure 4-27).

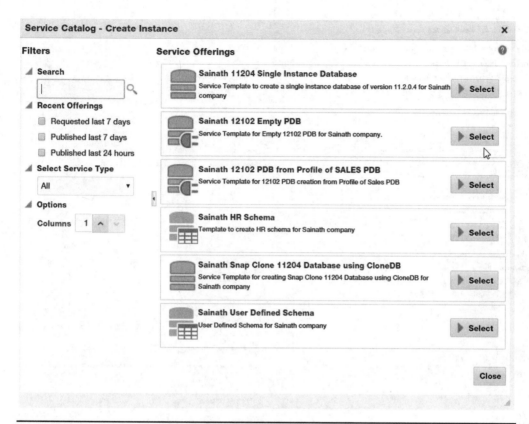

FIGURE 4-27. *Service catalog offerings for SAI_DAS*

Select Sainath 12102 Empty PDB to open the Create Pluggable Database screen (Figure 4-28).

For the PDB Name, type **TEST2PDB**, and for the Database Service Name, type **TEST2**. Note that the PDB Name and the Database Service Name *must* be different to avoid the error, "Please enter a different service name."

Select one of the workloads according to your requirements. Then enter the PDB Administrator name **TEST2PDBADMIN** (use uppercase) along with a password you choose. Type **TEST2DATA** as the Tablespace Name. You can also change the Properties of the service and the instance Start and Duration. Then submit the request.

The request completes successfully in a little over 3 minutes. The new empty PDB TEST2PDB appears in the list of service instances, as shown in Figure 4-29.

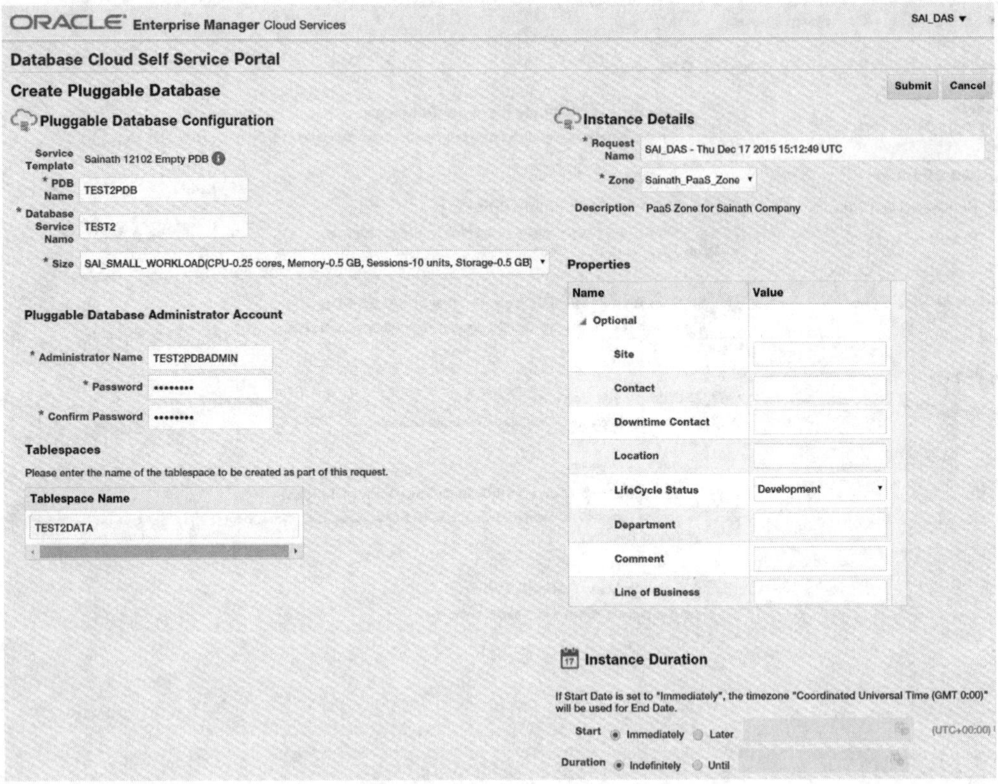

FIGURE 4-28. *Create Pluggable Database screen*

FIGURE 4-29. *Empty PDB TEST2PDB in the service instance list*

Drill down to the PDB Home screen (Figure 4-30) to see the performance details, startup and shutdown capability, and backup capability. The Connect String displayed can be inserted into SQL Developer to connect to the new PDB.

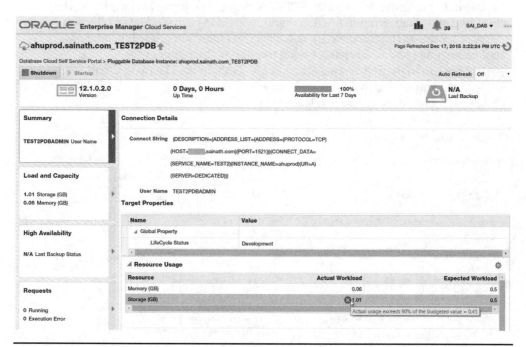

FIGURE 4-30.   *Home screen of new PDB*

Note that an alert has been raised about the storage in this case, too, because we have used the small workload, which has a lower storage limit. Because this is an empty PDB, it is obvious that our storage limit for small workloads may be too small. So perhaps it is time for the SSA administrator to revisit the workloads in the service templates and set them to more realistic figures for future use by SAI_DAS.

On the main Database Portal screen, it is possible for the self-service user to delete the created PDB when it is no longer required by selecting the PDB on that page and choosing Actions | Delete. The PDB is deleted in a few minutes.

Viewing Chargeback Results

Chargeback plans have been set up by the SSA administrator for the database instance, schema, and pluggable database.

For a quick look at chargeback results, as the SAI_DAS user, create a database, schema, and pluggable database via the Self Service Portal. The three services will appear in the list of services. Wait 15 minutes or more after creation, so that the metrics are collected for the targets. While you are waiting, you can run some test SQL queries on the database.

Log in to Enterprise Manager as SYSMAN. Select Enterprise | Chargeback. Then click the Entities tab. From the Action menu, select On-demand Data Collection.

Wait for the job to complete successfully. The collection job will handle all applicable usage and fixed charges since the start of the report cycle.

Log back in to the Self Service Portal as SAI_DAS. In the Database Cloud Services section, you can see the three service instances that have been created. Click the Chargeback icon in the left pane (Figure 4-31).

FIGURE 4-31. *Created service instances*

You'll see the Charge Trend for the SSA user SAI_DAS (Figure 4-32).

You can see that the total chargeback from January 15, 2016, to February 15, 2016, has been calculated as $4.16. The main charge of $3.75 (in the lower-right corner) is from SQL Executes, according to the Charge Trend bar chart. Someone seems to have run extensive queries on one of the service instances. No prizes for guessing who that was.

Note that there is only one bar in the graph for the date of February 15; this is because the three services were created on that date only, and no other services were created by SAI_DAS in the entire month.

Open the Details tab on the same page (Figure 4-33).

FIGURE 4-32.   *Charge trend for SAI_DAS*

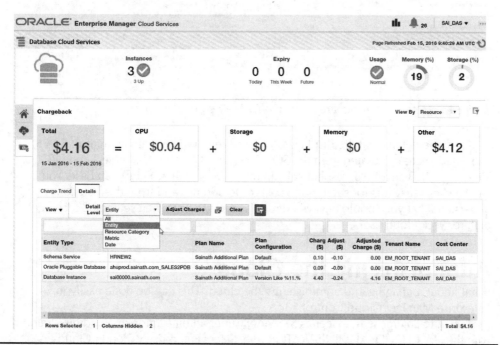

FIGURE 4-33.   *Details tab for chargeback*

The Details tab displays the charge plans that were used and shows that most of the chargeback is coming from the database instance. You can drill down further to the charges by changing the selection in Detail Level drop-down box, as shown in the screenshot. The current Detail Level is Entity. Change the Detail Level to Metric (Figure 4-34).

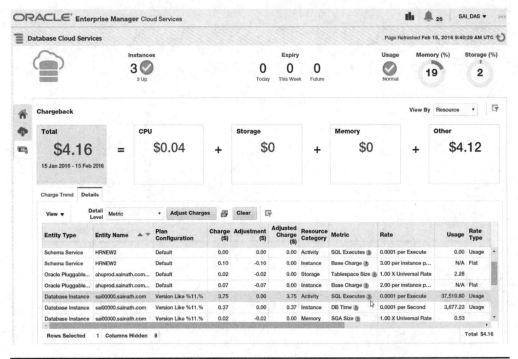

FIGURE 4-34. *Details tab for chargeback with a Metric detail level*

From the details that are displayed, you can see that the main charges of $3.75 and $0.37 were calculated from the SQL Executes (37,510.80 executes) and DB Time (3,677.23 seconds), respectively, in the sai0000.sainath.com database. You can see how easy it is for such usage charges to add up, and from this you can understand that you should always exercise some restraint when setting up a charge plan for your cloud users.

Administering the Cloud

What about managing and administering the cloud? This can be done easily in Enterprise Manager Cloud Control 13*c*.

Log in to Enterprise Manager as SYSMAN, super administrator, or an administrator with the EM_CLOUD_ADMINISTRATOR role. Select Enterprise | Cloud | Cloud

Home to bring up the Cloud Home screen shown in Figure 4-35. In this screen, the cloud administrator can monitor the entire cloud infrastructure that has been set up in Enterprise Manager.

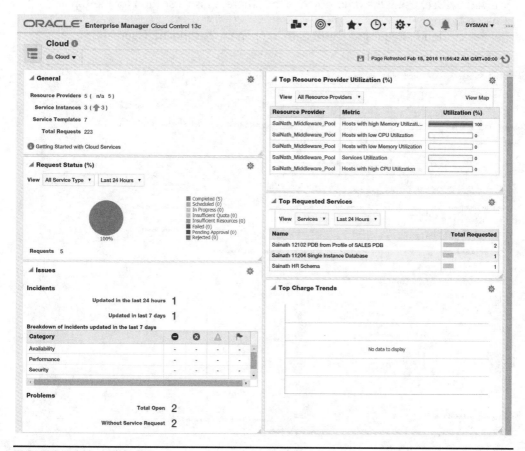

FIGURE 4-35. *Cloud Home screen*

In the General section, you can see the status of the Resource Providers (the Zones and Pools), along with the Service Instances that have been created, the Service Templates that are available, and the total number of requests so far. You can drill down on any of these.

In the Request Status section, you can further examine the status of the service requests to see which requests have failed, which had insufficient quota or resources, which are pending approval, and so on. You can also drill down and see other details—for example, if you wanted to approve or reject any pending requests or check those with insufficient quotas or resources.

Incidents and Problems with any of the cloud components are displayed in the Issues section. Other sections display the Top Resource Provider Utilization (%), and the Top Requested Services Viewed By Service, that you can also change to viewed by User using the drop-down menu. There is also a section for the Top Charge Trends.

Select Cloud | Requests | Dashboard to open the dashboard (Figure 4-36).

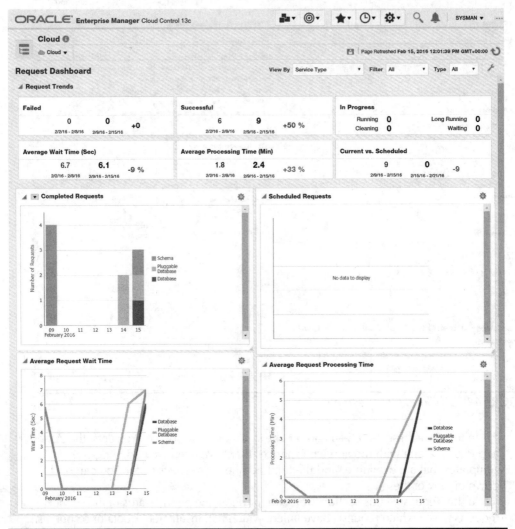

FIGURE 4-36. *Cloud Requests Dashboard*

Here, the cloud administrator can monitor the Request Trends—the failures, successes, average wait times (seconds), average processing times (minutes), and the current versus scheduled trends. The In Progress pane displays Running, Long Running, Waiting, and Cleaning requests.

In the other sections, the Completed Requests, Scheduled Requests, the Average Request Wait Time, and the Average Request Processing Time can be viewed, with breakdowns on Database, Schema, or Pluggable Database for each graph.

The cloud administrator can perform other management activities from the Cloud Home screen. Select Cloud | Members | Topology to see a graphical view of the cloud infrastructure. Select Cloud | Resource Providers to see a list of the zones and pools that have been set up. This enables the cloud administrator to edit existing providers or create new ones.

Select Cloud | Service Templates to see all the service templates that have been created; you can also edit or create, grant, revoke, reassign, publish, or unpublish any of the service templates. Select Cloud | Service Instances to see the different instances that have been created by self-service users; the cloud administrator can start or stop, delete, or extend any of these instances.

Select Cloud | Requests | Show to display a full list of all cloud requests, which the cloud administrator can approve, reject, reschedule, clean up failed requests, or delete requests.

In this way, Enterprise Manager Cloud Control 13*c* enables monitoring and management of the cloud infrastructure and the day-to-day working of the cloud, using exactly the same portal that was used to set it up.

Summary

We have now had a look at Oracle's Private Database Cloud Management Capabilities using the Enterprise Manager Cloud Control 13*c* Portal. Database as a Service, Schema as a Service, and Pluggable Database as a Service are all possible to be set up by the cloud administrator. Consequentially, the self-service user can log on to the Self Service Portal of Enterprise Manager and request any of these services.

Note that in the case of all these three database cloud services, the Standard Edition of Oracle Database cannot be used, since licensing of the Enterprise Manager Cloud Management for Database Pack and the Database Lifecycle Management (DBLM) Pack is not allowed on the Standard Edition.

In the next chapter, we will take a look at setting up the hybrid database cloud with Enterprise Manager, and show how Enterprise Manager agents are installed on the Oracle public cloud, so that an on-premise Enterprise Manager installation can effectively monitor and manage cloud databases as well as on-premise databases, and that pluggable databases can be moved from one installation to another. After that, we will look at using the Cloud REST API to perform database/schema/PDB services requests on the private database cloud, instead of using the Enterprise Manager self-service console.

CHAPTER
5

Hybrid Database Cloud

Oracle Enterprise Manager 12.1.0.5 has been available since June 2015. Beginning with this release, you can use an on-premise Enterprise Manager OMS (Oracle Management Service) to install hybrid cloud agents on Oracle public cloud (OPC) database servers and WebLogic servers via an Enterprise Manager Hybrid Cloud Gateway mechanism.

This was the first time this was possible in Enterprise Manager, and it opened up an entirely new world of Hybrid Cloud Management. You could now use an on-premise Enterprise Manager to monitor and manage both on-premise and cloud databases. You could compare database, WebLogic Server and host server configurations, and apply compliance standards equally. You could also clone Oracle 12*c* pluggable databases (PDBs) and Java applications from on-premise to a cloud container database (CDB) or WebLogic Server and back again—all via the on-premise Enterprise Manager console.

The most powerful feature of Enterprise Manager from this release onward is that it is able to manage the hybrid cloud from a single management interface. So you can have databases and WebLogic servers on company premises and OPC-based databases and WebLogic servers all managed via one central on-premise Enterprise Manager installation.

Normal Enterprise Manager agents are installed on your on-premise servers, and special hybrid cloud agents are installed (via the push mechanism of Enterprise Manager) on your cloud servers. The hybrid cloud agents work through a Hybrid Cloud Gateway, one of your on-premise Enterprise Manager agents that has been designated as such. The Hybrid Cloud Gateway works as a specialized Secure Shell (SSH) tunnel of sorts.

Once the hybrid cloud agents start talking to the OMS, you, as the database administrator, can see all your databases and WebLogic servers either on-premise or on the cloud, and you can clone PDBs and Java applications easily to and from the cloud via Enterprise Manager.

In addition, you can also use the other features of the Enterprise Manager packs, such as diagnostics, tuning, DBLM, and so on in the hybrid cloud. For example, as part of DBLM, you can perform configuration comparisons between on-premise and cloud databases or WebLogic servers or host servers, and also compliance checks. In this way, you can make sure your entire enterprise cloud—on-premise as well as public cloud—is compliant and adheres to configuration guidelines with controlled configuration deviations.

In this chapter, we will look at the steps for setting up the hybrid cloud via Enterprise Manager Cloud Control 13*c*. We will follow the presteps and then install a hybrid cloud agent via the Hybrid Cloud Gateway. Next, we will go through the steps of configuration management and comparisons for the hybrid cloud, and then we will test the cloning of PDBs to the cloud.

Presetup steps for the hybrid cloud include setting up one of your OMS agents as the hybrid gateway agent, creating SSH keys for the OMS server, and creating a named credential with SSH key credentials for the hybrid cloud.

Presetup for Hybrid Cloud

For the hybrid cloud capability, the following pre-steps are required on your Enterprise Manager installation. We will execute these one by one.

Step 1: Register the Agent

Register any agent in your Enterprise Manager local (on-premise) installation as the hybrid gateway agent. Preferably choose an agent that is not your main OMS server agent—that is, the agent can be on one of your target servers that is not too heavily loaded with monitoring and managing its own targets.

The Enterprise Manager command line interface (EMCLI) is used to register the hybrid gateway agent. Log in as the Oracle UNIX user, and move to where EMCLI is installed on your target server. Log in first to EMCLI as SYSMAN, and then issue the `register` command, as shown next. (The host name is hidden for privacy reasons.)

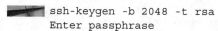

```
./emcli login -username=sysman
./emcli register_hybridgateway_agent -hybridgateway_agent_list='xxxxx.sainath.com:3872'
```

This registers the agent as a hybrid gateway agent. There are ways to register an additional agent as a slave or secondary agent that can take over the monitoring if the master or primary agent goes down, but for now we will set up only one agent since this is an example run.

Note that if you have a lot of cloud database servers, you should not use only one gateway agent to communicate to all of these. Instead, set up multiple gateway agents to talk to different cloud servers. For example, one gateway agent can be used to talk to 5–10 cloud servers, another can be used to talk to other cloud servers, and so on. The architecture in this case is very important and needs to be set up in a well-planned manner.

This relationship between which gateway agent talks to which hybrid cloud agent is set up when the hybrid agent is installed on each cloud server, as we will see later on. When installing the agent on one or multiple servers, you select the gateway agent to use.

Step 2: Generate SSH Keys

The next step is to generate SSH keys for the OMS server. Log in to the OMS host as the Oracle UNIX user and type the following:

```
ssh-keygen -b 2048 -t rsa
Enter passphrase
```

Importantly, you should not use a passphrase; just press ENTER. The SSH keys you generate will be used in an Enterprise Manager named credential that we will create in the next step, and a passphrase is not supported for use with SSH keys in named credentials.

The ssh-regkey utility generates two files in the .ssh subdirectory under the Oracle Unix user's home, as seen here:

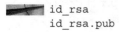

```
id_rsa
id_rsa.pub
```

Step 3: Create a Named Credential

The next step is to create a named credential for use with the hybrid cloud.

Log in to the Enterprise Manager console as SYSMAN or a super administrator. Choose Setup | Security | Named Credentials.

Create a named credential NC_OPC_DBCS. This should be selected with Authenticating Target Type as Host, Credential Type as SSH Key Credentials, and Scope as Global.

Note that if SSH Key Credentials does not appear in the drop-down list of Credential Type, then you need to run the workaround listed in My Oracle Support (MOS) Note 1640062.1. The workaround you can use is a PL/SQL block mentioned in the note, which is to be executed as SYSMAN in the OMS repository.

On the Create Credential screen (Figure 5-1), in the SSH Private Key and SSH Public Key fields, cut and paste the appropriate SSH keys from the Oracle home's .ssh directory on the OMS server. You generated these SSH keys in Step 1.

For User Name, enter **oracle**. You can also expand the Access Control section and grant access to this credential to other Enterprise Manager administrators.

Don't test the named credential; just save it (because, at this point of time, the cloud database server is not a managed target in Enterprise Manager, and as such it cannot be used for testing the named credential).

Step 4: Changing SELINUX to Permissive

When you are running the Enterprise Manager clone-to-cloud deployment procedure later on in this chapter (in the section "Cloning to Oracle Cloud"), the Secure Copy Files step may fail with the error message, "rsync: Failed to exec ssh: Permission denied (13)," in certain cases where the local OMS server has been set up with enforcing SELINUX security.

A quick workaround to this is to change SELINUX to permissive in the file /etc/selinux/config, as the root UNIX user on the OMS server:

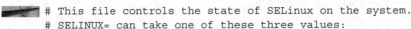

```
# This file controls the state of SELinux on the system.
# SELINUX= can take one of these three values:
#       enforcing - SELinux security policy is enforced.
```

```
#       permissive - SELinux prints warnings instead of enforcing.
#       disabled - No SELinux policy is loaded.
SELINUX=permissive
# SELINUXTYPE= can take one of these two values:
#       targeted - Targeted processes are protected,
#       mls - Multi Level Security protection.
SELINUXTYPE=targeted
```

Reboot your system after you make this change. After the reboot is completed, confirm as the root UNIX user that the `getenforce` command returns `Permissive`:

```
# getenforce
Permissive
```

Note that if your company mandates that `SELINUX` should be set to `enforcing` for security reasons, you will need to configure `SELINUX` to allow `RSYNC` to be executed from the agent (via script).

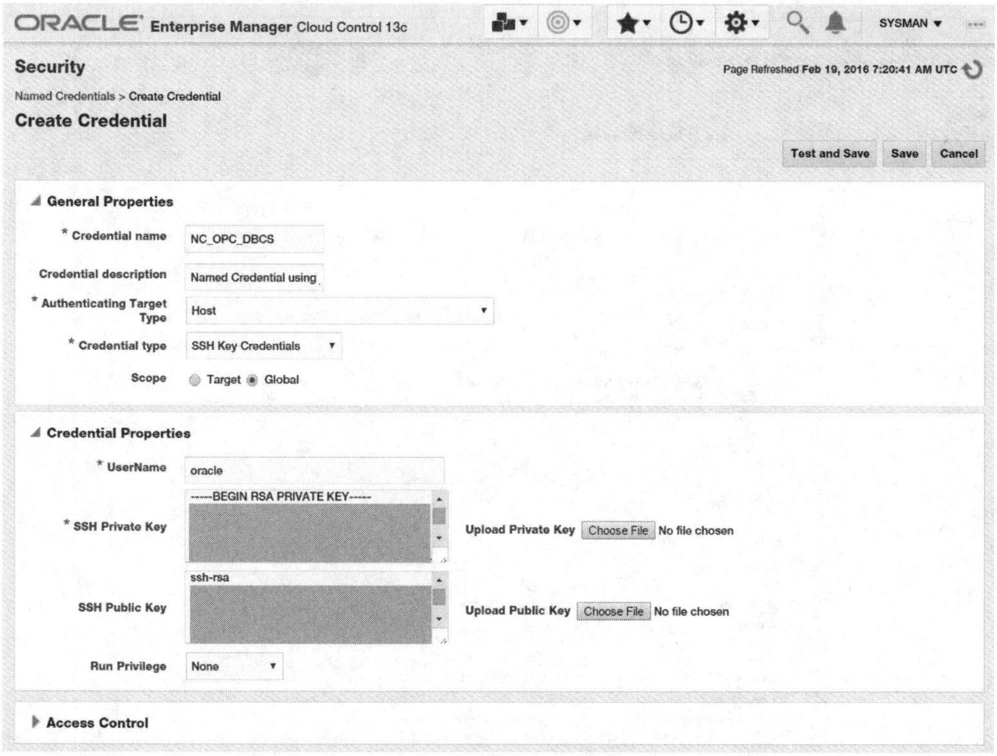

FIGURE 5-1.   *Creating a named credential using SSH key credentials*

This is more complicated than the quick workaround described earlier. You will need to work with your security administrator for the correct steps to set up SELINUX to allow individual commands such as RSYNC.

Other Requirements

The other requirements for the hybrid cloud are obvious. You will need an account (either trial or production) for the OPC at cloud.oracle.com, for the Database Cloud Service.

You will have created an Oracle Database Service (a server with an Oracle Database) on the Oracle public cloud in advance, and it would be up and running.

You will need the IP address of this cloud database server, which will be used in this hybrid cloud setup. You would have also set up PuTTY access from your laptop to the cloud database server.

Figure 5-2 shows an example setup of a Oracle public cloud database server, AHUTESTSERVER, that has been created. (The IP address and other fields are blanked out in this screenshot for privacy reasons.)

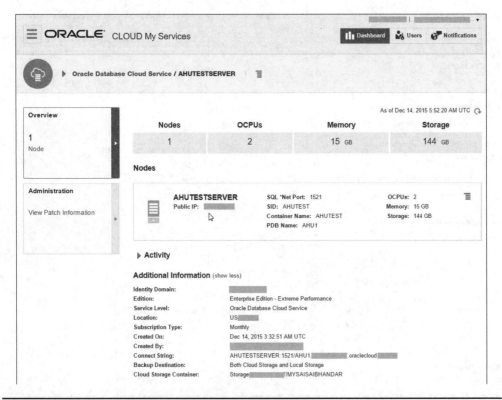

FIGURE 5-2. *Oracle public cloud database server setup*

Note that we have created the "Extreme Performance" type of Enterprise Edition database on the OPC, so that the Enterprise Manager Management Packs, such as Diagnostics, Tuning, Database Lifecycle Management (DBLM), etc., can be used on the cloud database. In Figure 5-2, "Extreme Performance" is displayed in the Edition field.

Next, we'll prepare to test the cloud and install the cloud agent.

Testing the Hybrid Cloud

Log in as the Oracle UNIX user to the Enterprise Manager 13c OMS, and change to the .ssh directory under the Oracle home:

```
cd .ssh
```

Using vi, open the file id_rsa.pub in this directory and copy the text to the clipboard. This is the OMS server public key. This was generated during one of the presetup steps earlier in this chapter.

From your on-premise workstation, open an SSH session using PuTTY to the Oracle public cloud database server, and as the Oracle UNIX user, type the following:

```
cd ~/.ssh
vi authorized_keys
```

In this file, paste the OMS server public key (make sure there are no line breaks), and save the file. Then, from a UNIX session on the OMS server, ssh to the Oracle public cloud database server using the IP address. Accept the connection when asked.

You are now ready to test out the hybrid cloud capability.

Installing the Cloud Agent

Log in to the Enterprise Manager console as SYSMAN or a super administrator. Choose Setup | Add Target | Add Targets Manually to open the screen shown in Figure 5-3.

In the section Add Host Targets, click Install Agent On Hosts. You'll see the Add Host Targets: Host And Platform screen (Figure 5-4).

Type in the IP address of the OPC database server host. For the Platform, select Linux x86-64 (the only one that can be chosen for the hybrid cloud at the time of writing). Click Next.

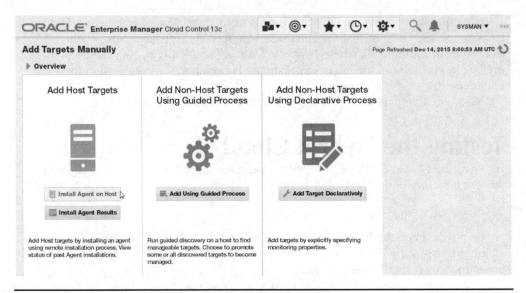

FIGURE 5-3. *Add Targets Manually Overview screen*

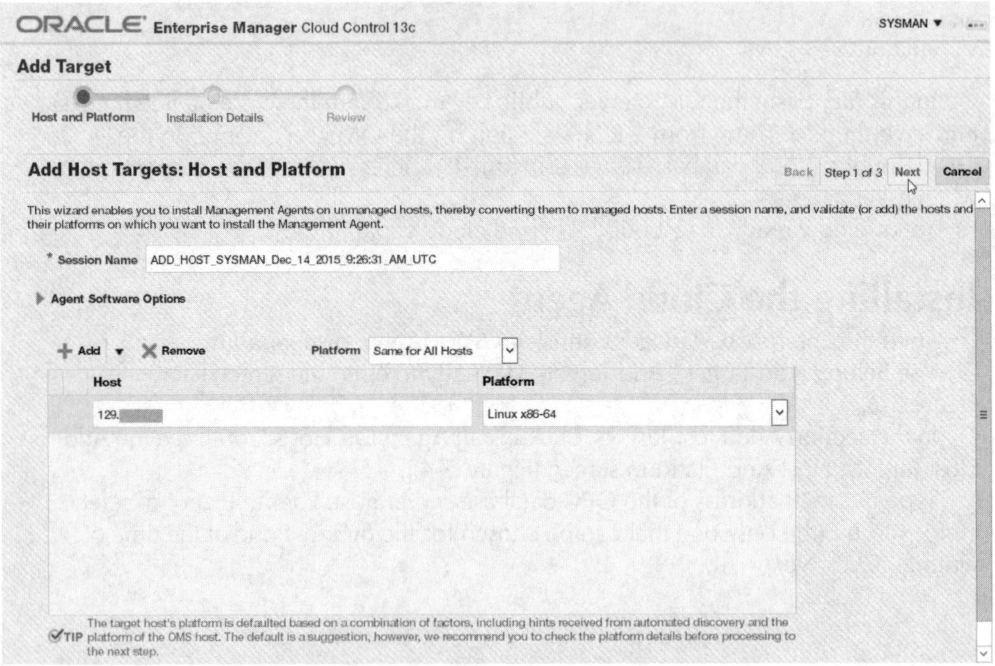

FIGURE 5-4. *Adding host targets*

A warning informs you that you have used an IP address or short name, and the host name is not fully qualified. The full text of the warning is as follows:

The host names specified include IP addresses or short names. It is advised to provide Fully Qualified Host Names, such as foo.mydomain.com, that are persistent over the life of the targets. It is recommended for ease of maintenance and overall security. However, you can choose to ignore this warning and proceed by clicking Next.

Note that if you want to use a full host name for this IP address, you will need to add the host name and address to /etc/hosts on the OMS server as well on the OPC database server before the agent install; otherwise the emctl `secure agent` command, which is run by Enterprise Manager at the end of the agent install procedure, will not work.

Ignore the warning and click Next to see the Installation Details screen (Figure 5-5). The Agent Software Version that will be installed is 13.1.0.0.0.

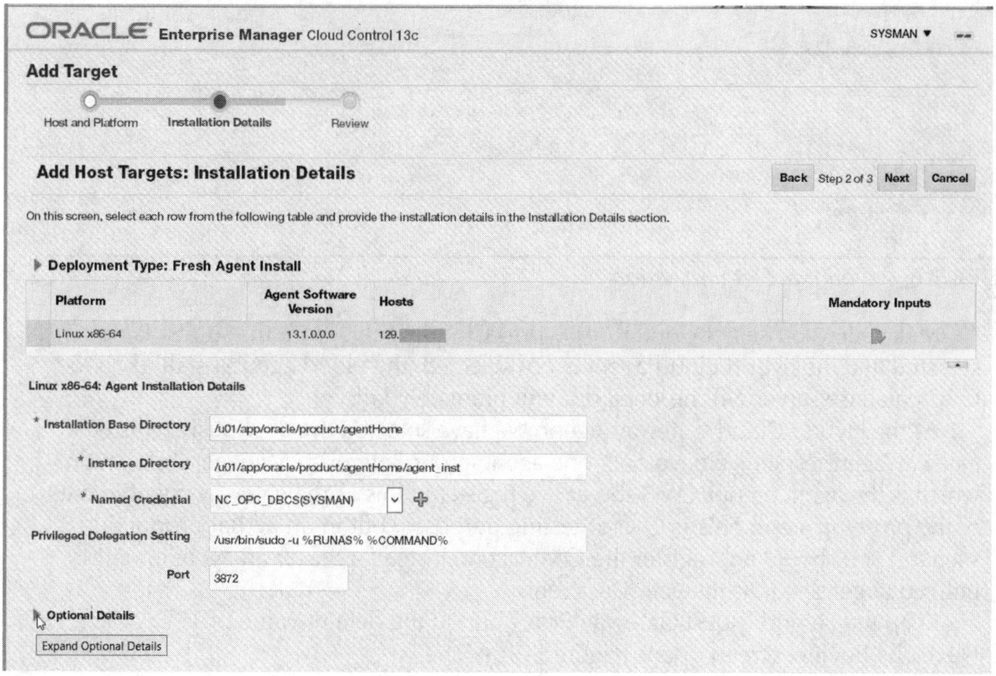

FIGURE 5-5. *Add Host Targets: Installation Details*

On this screen, enter the Installation Base Directory for the agent. Adhering to cloud database standards, which are derived from the earlier well-known Oracle Flexible Architecture (OFA) standards, this directory is installed at /u01/app/oracle/ product, where other Oracle database software has been installed when the OPC database server was created.

You can use any name for the base directory. We have used agentHome, so the full directory path is /u01/app/oracle/product/agentHome.

On entering the base directory, the Instance Directory in the next line is automatically generated as agent_inst under /u01/app/oracle/product/agentHome.

As the Named Credential, select NC_OPC_DBCS. This named credential uses SSH key credentials and was pre-created with the SSH private and public keys of the OMS server.

A very important thing to do at this stage is to expand the Optional Details section by clicking it. The expanded details are shown in Figure 5-6.

FIGURE 5-6. *Optional Details section*

Make sure you select Configure Hybrid Cloud Agent. Note that if this is not selected and the hybrid cloud agent is not selected, the cloud agent installed on the OPC database server will proceed but will ultimately fail.

As the Hybrid Cloud Gateway Agent, we have selected the previously registered gateway agent. Since we have only one agent in our Enterprise Manager installation, which is the agent on our OMS server, we registered this as the gateway agent in one of the presetup steps. This is OK for testing purposes, but in an actual production scenario you should not register the OMS agent. Instead, register an agent on a less utilized target server as the gateway agent.

Keep the Hybrid Cloud Gateway Proxy port at the default value of 1748. Click Next. The Review screen opens (Figure 5-7).

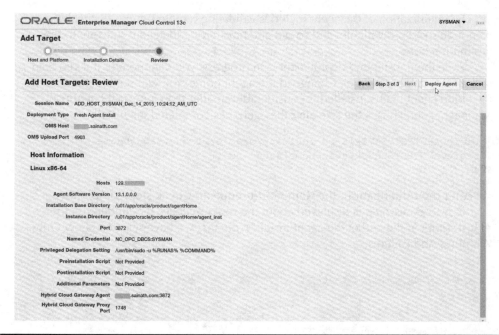

FIGURE 5-7. *Add Host Targets: Review*

Review the information and click Deploy Agent. The procedure starts. The first step is the agent's initialization, as shown in Figure 5-8, followed by remote prerequisite checks and then the actual deployment.

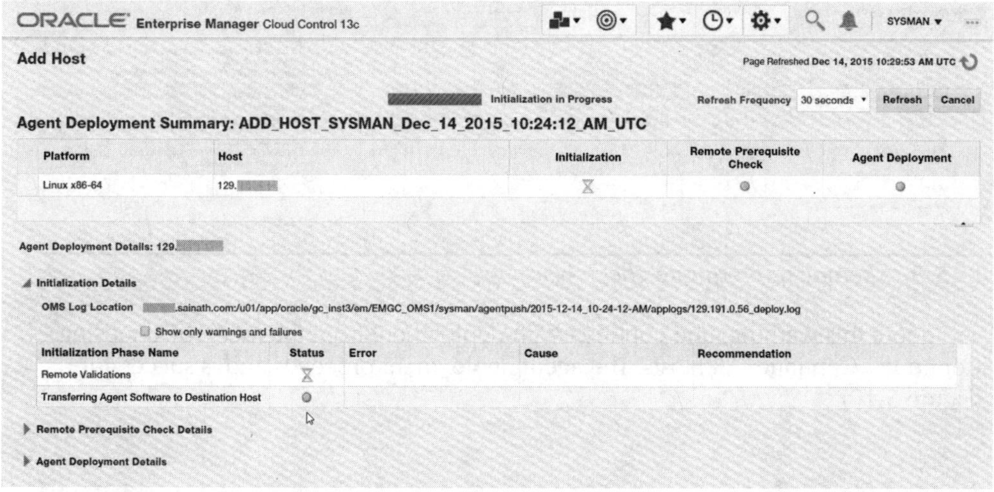

FIGURE 5-8. *Agent deployment: initialization in progress*

The initialization of the agent includes validating remote settings (a check to see if enough space is available, and so on) and transferring the agent software to the destination host.

While the transfer and deployment is in progress, you can monitor it if you SSH to the OPC database server. Change to the agent home. You will see that the size of the cloud agent that is installed is considerably smaller than a normal Enterprise Manager agent. (This is the size after the agent has completed the install.)

```
[oracle@AHUTESTSERVER]$ cd /u01/app/oracle/product/agentHome
[oracle@AHUTESTSERVER agentHome]$ du -hs .
944M.
```

After the initialization, the Remote Prerequisite Check step completes (Figure 5-9). A warning is displayed about the root privileges required to run the root.sh script at the end of the agent install. Note that we have selected Show Only Warnings And Failures.

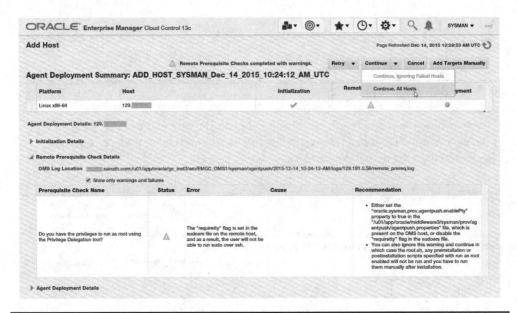

FIGURE 5-9. *Remote prerequisite check warning*

Ignore this warning, and continue with deployment from the menu by choosing Continue | Continue, All Hosts. The agent deployment proceeds and is successful (Figure 5-10).

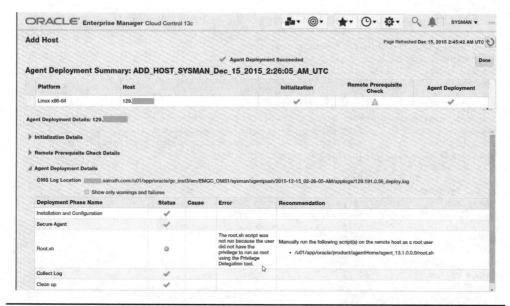

FIGURE 5-10. *Successful agent deployment*

As the displayed message indicates, you now need to run the root.sh script key manually. You can use PuTTY to do this. Log in as the OPC UNIX user to the cloud database server, and then `sudo -s` to root. Change to the agent home directory that was mentioned in Figure 5-10, and run the root.sh script. Note that this is important for proper agent functioning.

You can also SSH to the OPC server from the OMS server, and check the status of the agent as follows:

```
$ ssh <IP Address of OPC Server>
Authorized uses only. All activity may be monitored and reported.
```

On the cloud server, check where the agent has been installed by examining the contents of the /etc/oragchomelist file. This file has the directory locations of the agent home.

```
[oracle@AHUTESTSERVER ~]$ cat /etc/oragchomelist
/u01/app/oracle/product/agentHome/agent_13.1.0.0.0:/u01/app/oracle/product/agentHome/
agent_inst
```

The first directory in the list is the agent home. Move to the bin subdirectory under this home:

```
[oracle@AHUTESTSERVER ~]$ cd /u01/app/oracle/product/agentHome/agent_13.1.0.0.0/bin
```

From this subdirectory, check the status of the agent via the following command:

```
[oracle@AHUTESTSERVER bin]$ ./emctl status agent
Oracle Enterprise Manager Cloud Control 13c Release 1
Copyright (c) 1996, 2015 Oracle Corporation.  All rights reserved.
---------------------------------------------------------------
Agent Version          : 13.1.0.0.0
OMS Version            : 13.1.0.0.0
Protocol Version       : 12.1.0.1.0
Agent Home             : /u01/app/oracle/product/agentHome/agent_inst
Agent Log Directory    : /u01/app/oracle/product/agentHome/agent_inst/sysman/log
Agent Binaries         : /u01/app/oracle/product/agentHome/agent_13.1.0.0.0
Core JAR Location      : /u01/app/oracle/product/agentHome/agent_13.1.0.0.0/jlib
Agent Process ID       : 17969
Parent Process ID      : 17923
Agent URL              : https://129.xxx.x.xx:3872/emd/main/
Local Agent URL in NAT : https://129.xxx.x.xx:3872/emd/main/
Repository URL         : https://129.xxx.x.xx:1748/empbs/upload
Started at             : 2015-12-15 02:43:48
Started by user        : oracle
Operating System       : Linux version 2.6.39-400.109.1.el6uek.x86_64 (amd64)
Number of Targets      : 2
Last Reload            : (none)
Last successful upload                       : 2015-12-15 02:55:20
Last attempted upload                        : 2015-12-15 02:55:20
Total Megabytes of XML files uploaded so far : 0.22
Number of XML files pending upload           : 0
Size of XML files pending upload(MB)         : 0
Available disk space on upload filesystem    : 28.24%
Collection Status                            : Collections enabled
Heartbeat Status                             : Ok
Last attempted heartbeat to OMS              : 2015-12-15 02:56:57
Last successful heartbeat to OMS             : 2015-12-15 02:56:57
Next scheduled heartbeat to OMS              : 2015-12-15 02:57:57

---------------------------------------------------------------
Agent is Running and Ready
```

The hybrid agent is up and running—and its XML files are also being uploaded via the hybrid gateway back to the on-premise Enterprise Manager repository. So everything is fine.

Discovering the Database and Listener on the Cloud Server

In the Enterprise Manager console, log in as SYSMAN or a super administrator and choose Targets | Hosts. Because an agent has been installed on the cloud server, you can see the cloud server IP in the list of hosts monitored by Enterprise Manager (Figure 5-11). This is the line beginning with 129. and has been masked for privacy reasons.

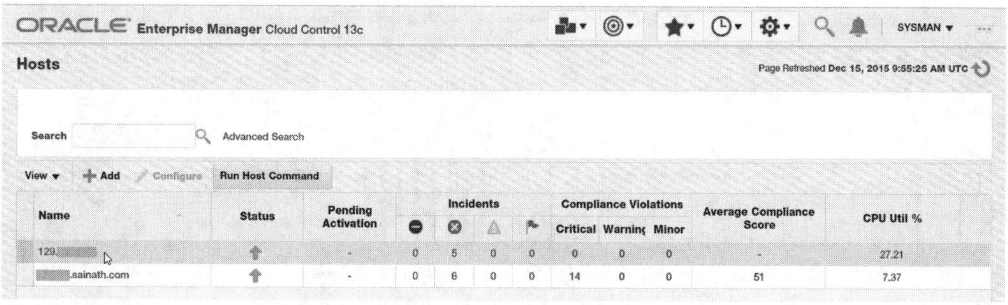

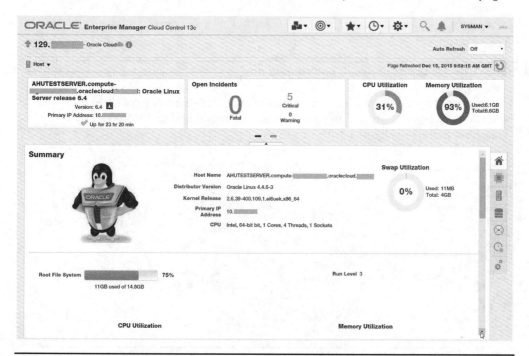

FIGURE 5-11. *Host list*

Drilling down to the cloud host displays the Host home page (Figure 5-12). The host configuration details along with the CPU, memory, and swap utilization, plus open incidents are shown. Note that the host appears like a normal Enterprise Manager host, except for the "Oracle Cloud" words and icon at the top-left corner of the home page.

FIGURE 5-12. *Cloud Host home page*

Scroll down to see the other details of the cloud host, such as the performance details (Figure 5-13). Separate graphs show the CPU Utilization, Memory Utilization, CPU Threads Utilization, Filesystem Distributions, and Network Usage.

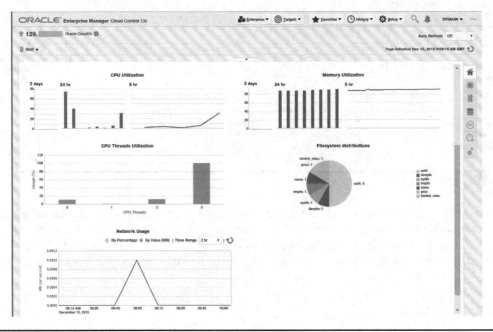

FIGURE 5-13. *Performance details of the cloud host*

Choose Targets | Databases. Currently, the cloud database has not been discovered so is not visible in the list of databases monitored and managed by Enterprise Manager (Figure 5-14).

FIGURE 5-14. *The cloud database is not yet visible.*

Choose Add | Oracle Database. The first step of the discovery process is displayed (Figure 5-15).

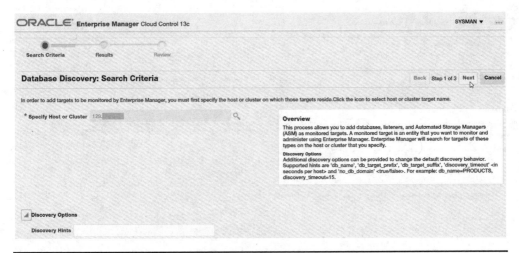

FIGURE 5-15. *Database Discovery: Search Criteria*

On this page, specify the IP address of the OPC database server. You can also specify discovery hints, as explained. Click Next.

At this point, before proceeding, unlock the dbsnmp user in the OPC database and change the user password. This will be needed for monitoring the cloud database. You can do this by sshing to the OPC server, using the oraenv database utility to change the environment to the AHUTEST database, and then logging in to SQL*Plus as sysdba and making the change. This is shown here:

```
$ ssh <IP Address of OPC Server>
Authorized uses only. All activity may be monitored and reported.

[oracle@AHUTESTSERVER ~]$ . oraenv
ORACLE_SID = [AHUTEST] ?
The Oracle base has been set to /u01/app/oracle

[oracle@AHUTESTSERVER ~]$ sqlplus / as sysdba
SQL*Plus: Release 12.1.0.2.0 Production on Tue Dec 15 10:08:07 2015
Copyright (c) 1982, 2014, Oracle.  All rights reserved.
Connected to:
Oracle Database 12c EE Extreme Perf Release 12.1.0.2.0 - 64bit Production
With the Partitioning, Oracle Label Security, OLAP, Advanced Analytics
and Real Application Testing options

SQL> alter user dbsnmp account unlock identified by <password you want>
  2  /

User altered.
```

When you click Next, the OPC database and listener will both be discovered, as shown in Figure 5-16. Select both the database and the listener.

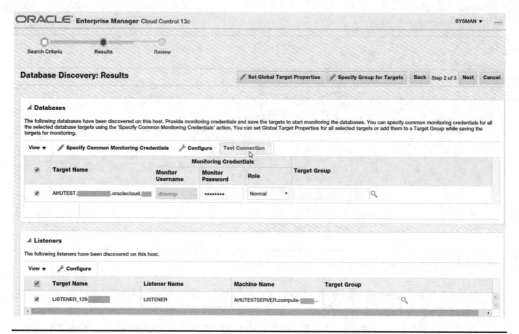

FIGURE 5-16. *Database Discovery: Results*

Enter the Monitor Username **dbsnmp** and the Monitor Password you have used in the `alter` statement. Click Test Connection, and make sure the connection test is successful.

Click Next. The Review screen (Figure 5-17) appears with the discovered CDB, PDBs, and listener on the cloud server.

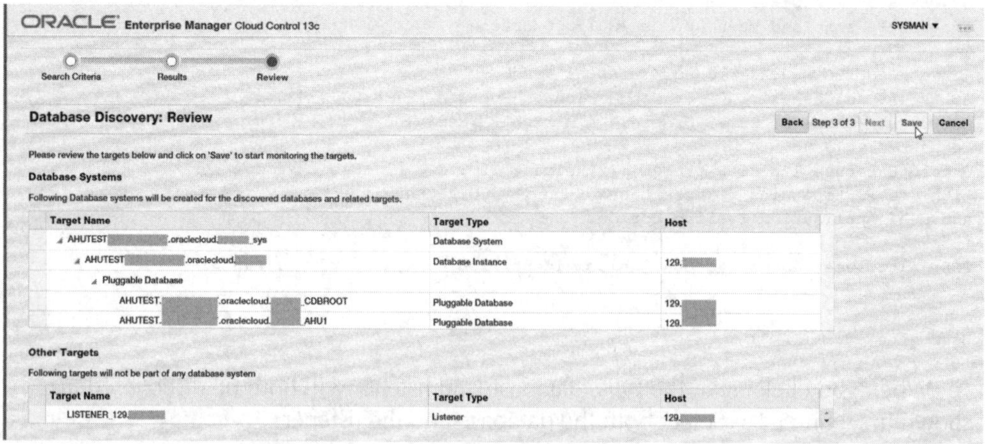

FIGURE 5-17. *Reviewing the discovered targets*

Click Save. The cloud database now appears in the list of Enterprise Manager database targets (Figure 5-18).

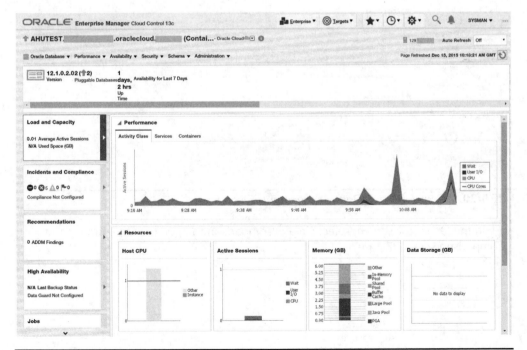

FIGURE 5-18. *Database target list*

The status is shown as Pending, but you can drill down to the details on the database home page (Figure 5-19).

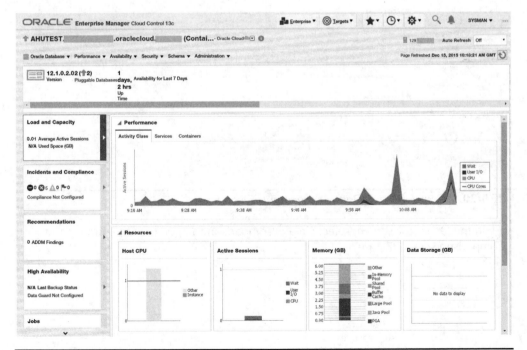

FIGURE 5-19. *Home page of cloud database*

The cloud database home page appears just like a normal database target in Enterprise Manager, except that the "Oracle Cloud" words and icon are visible at the top-left of the screen. You can monitor and manage it just like a normal on-premise database.

Comparing On-Premise and Cloud Database Configurations

You can now compare configurations. Choose Enterprise | Configuration | Comparison And Drift Management from the Enterprise Manager console. The Overview screen that opens is shown in Figure 5-20.

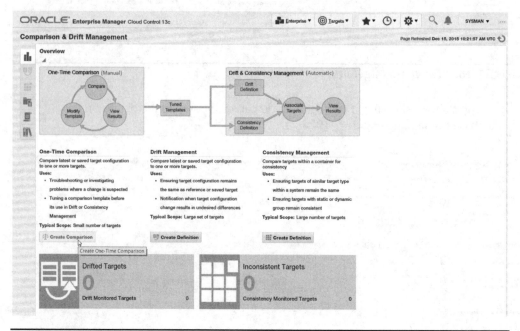

FIGURE 5-20. *Comparison & Drift Management: Overview*

In the Overview screen, select Create Comparison to open the One-Time Comparison screen (Figure 5-21).

FIGURE 5-21. *One-Time Comparison screen*

For the Reference Target (Current), select the on-premise 12c database ahuprod .sainath.com. In the Compared Targets list, select and add the Cloud database AHUTEST. For the Comparison Template, select the Database Instance Template. A comparison template helps avoid the system alerting you on obvious differences.

Note that clicking the Advanced button enables you to select a saved or current reference target, as shown in Figure 5-22.

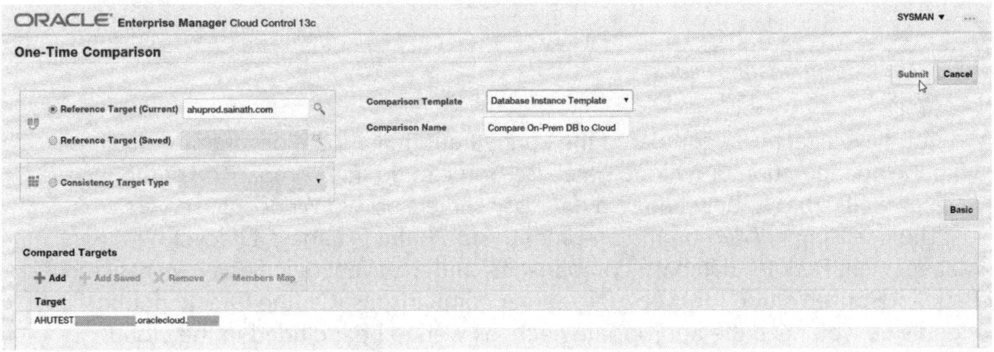

FIGURE 5-22. *Advanced mode: selecting a current or saved reference target*

Click Submit. The results of the configuration comparison are displayed, as shown in Figure 5-23.

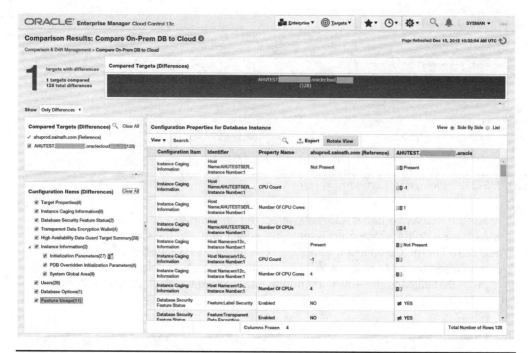

FIGURE 5-23.   *Comparison results*

You have effectively compared the configuration of a local on-premise database with the configuration of a cloud database. You can do this comparison at the server level as well—that is, between two database servers or two WebLogic servers.

The licensing needed on the on-premise side is the Database Lifecycle Management Pack for database comparisons, and the WebLogic Server Management Pack Enterprise Edition for WebLogic Server comparisons. On the Oracle public cloud side, you need the appropriate packs as well to be included in the cloud database version you select, such as Enterprise Edition Extreme Performance. This also applies to other capabilities such as compliance checks.

You can save a configuration at a certain date and time as a gold configuration (for example, immediately after setting up a database server) and then run a configuration comparison of your current configuration to the gold configuration at regular intervals, to alert you of any differences.

You can also set up compliance standard enforcement for the hybrid cloud, so that you can apply your corporate compliance standards to all your enterprise databases, no matter where they are. When this is set up, Enterprise Manager is able to enforce the same compliance standards on the Oracle public cloud as well as on-premises databases.

Cloning PDBs from On-Premise to Cloud

One of the main features of the hybrid cloud is that it is possible to move on-premise PDBs easily to an Oracle cloud CDB. For example, you may be moving a PDB to the cloud so that some development work can be completed.

Before you start this test, note a few things. There is a current restriction in the process that says that the patch set level of the PDB being cloned needs to be the same as the cloud CDB. Suppose, for example, that the 12*c* CDB ahuprod has been patched to the October 2015 Database PSU (Patch Set Update). This means all the PDBs in this CDB are also on this PSU.

The cloud database, on the other hand, may have a different patch set level, depending on when you created it. Up to the first week of a particular month, all cloud databases when created may have an older PSU automatically applied. In the next few weeks of the month, all new cloud databases created may have the latest PSU automatically applied.

You can check this by going to your cloud service console, drilling down to your cloud database, and drilling down on View Patch Information in the Administration box on the server screen, as shown in Figure 5-24.

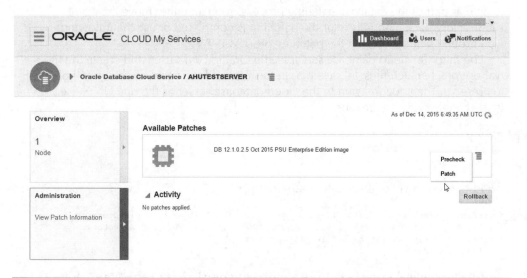

FIGURE 5-24. *Patching your cloud database to the latest PSU*

As of December 2015, if this screen tells you "No patches available," it means the cloud database is on the latest October PSU, which should be fine. If it shows the October PSU on this screen, then it means the cloud database is on the earlier PSU, so you should apply the October PSU first on the database.

You can also check the current PSU by moving to the OPatch directory under the Oracle home on the cloud server, and issuing the command `opatch lsinventory`. This will display the patches that have been applied on the Oracle home.

Be sure to read the next section, "Preserving the Agent Home When Patching the Cloud Database" before you start the patching process.

Note that if there are any patch conflicts and the patch application on the cloud database fails, you may need to force apply the patch for the patching to complete successfully.

After you have completed the PSU patch application, you can proceed with the actual cloning, since the source and destination CDBs are now at the latest PSU.

Preserving the Agent Home When Patching the Cloud Database

If you have installed the Enterprise Manager Agent under /u01/app/oracle (the Oracle base directory), and if you then use the cloud database patching menu to apply a later PSU to the database, the agent home will be moved to /u01/app.ORG /oracle as part of the database patching process. You can either move the agent subdirectory back manually after the patching is completed or use the following workaround before you start the patching process.

Log in to the cloud database server as the Oracle UNIX user, and create the file /var/opt/oracle/patch/files_to_save.ora. In this file, add the agent directory (full path) to preserve. Then, log in again to the cloud database server as the opc UNIX user. Issue the following commands:

```
sudo -s
cd /var/opt/oracle/patch
vi dbpatchm.cfg
```

In this root-owned file, locate these lines:

```
# create /var/opt/oracle/patch/files_to_save.ora with full path of directory or
# files to preserve any special files you may have in your /u01/app directory.
# set this to yes, if you have files_to_save.ora
special_files="no"
```

Change the line `special_files="no"` to **`special_files="yes"`**. Save the file.

After you follow these steps, the next time you perform any patching from the cloud database patching menu, the agent directory will be preserved in the original location and you will not need to move it back manually after the patching has completed.

Because of the dynamic nature of the Oracle database cloud and its continuous evolution, the workaround explained previously may no longer be needed if the agent directory is automatically preserved by the cloud database patching process.

Cloning to Oracle Cloud

Log in as SYSMAN or a super administrator to the Enterprise Manager console. You can currently see both on-premise databases (ahuprod) and cloud databases (AHUTEST) in a single screen by choosing Targets | Databases.

As shown in Figure 5-25, right-click the on-premise PDB SALES, which is in the ahuprod CDB, and choose Oracle Database | Cloning | Clone To Oracle Cloud.

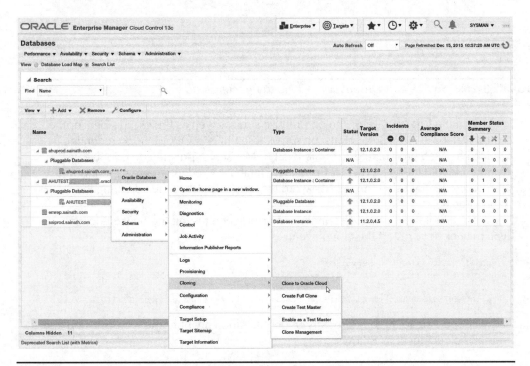

FIGURE 5-25. *Cloning to the Oracle cloud*

The Source And Destination screen opens (Figure 5-26).

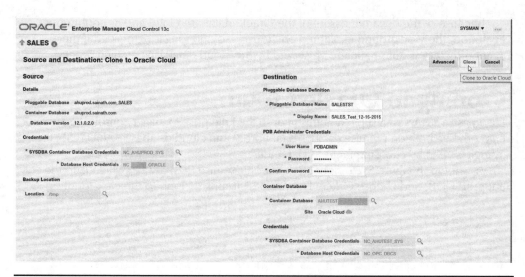

FIGURE 5-26. *Source and Destination: Clone to Oracle Cloud*

Fill in the Credentials for the on-premise side, as well as the cloud side. For the cloud Database Host Credentials, be sure to use the NC_OPC_DBCS credential, which has been pre-created with the local (OMS) server private and public keys. For the cloud database SYSDBA Container Database Credential, create a new named credential using the sys password that you specified when creating the cloud database.

Note that if there is an I/O connection error when testing the new credential, you may need to restart the cloud agent:

```
$ ssh <IP Address of OPC Server>
Authorized uses only. All activity may be monitored and reported.

[oracle@AHUTESTSERVER ~]$ cd /u01/app/oracle/product/agentHome/agent_13.1.0.0.0/bin
```

After moving to the bin directory under the cloud agent home, you can stop and start the cloud agent as follows:

```
[oracle@AHUTESTSERVER bin]$ ./emctl stop agent
Oracle Enterprise Manager Cloud Control 13c Release 1
Copyright (c) 1996, 2015 Oracle Corporation.  All rights reserved.
Stopping agent ... stopped.

[oracle@AHUTESTSERVER bin]$ ./emctl start agent
Oracle Enterprise Manager Cloud Control 13c Release 1
Copyright (c) 1996, 2015 Oracle Corporation.  All rights reserved.
Starting agent ................ started.
```

Enter the name of the Destination PDB on the cloud side as SALESTST, since this will be a test pluggable database. Enter a more descriptive display name if you wish. Also select a User Name and Password for the administrator of the new PDB.

At this point, you can click Clone to start the procedure. Or click the Advanced button at the top of the page. This switches to Advanced mode, and a multiple page workflow appears (Figure 5-27).

FIGURE 5-27. *Advanced mode*

Click Next. The Clone To Oracle Cloud: Configuration screen opens (Figure 5-28).

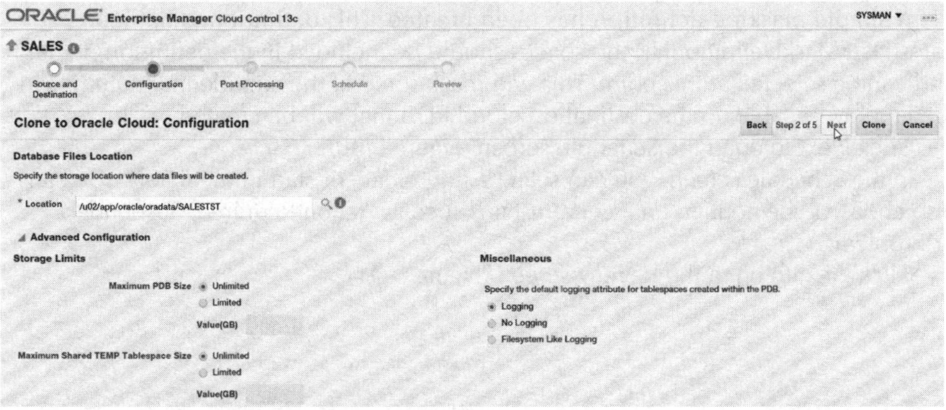

FIGURE 5-28. *Clone to Oracle Cloud: Configuration*

According to cloud database standards based on Oracle Flexible Architecture (OFA) standards, the PDB data files will reside at /u02, in the /u02/app/oracle/oradata/<*PDB name*> directory. You can also enter storage limits if you wish, such as the maximum PDB size or the maximum shared TEMP tablespace size. The default logging attribute for tablespaces created with the PDB can also be specified—Logging, No Logging, or Filesystem Like Logging.

Click Next to open the Post Processing screen (Figure 5-29).

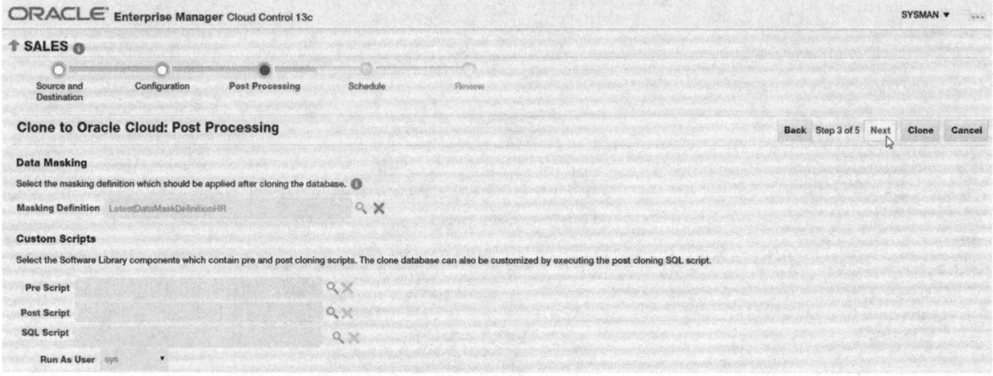

FIGURE 5-29. *Clone to Oracle Cloud: Post Processing*

This screen shows the importance of the advanced mode, because it is possible to select a data masking definition if it has been created for the source database.

Masking is seamlessly integrated with Enterprise Manager, which makes sure that confidential data is masked when being cloned from an on-premise production database to a cloud development database.

A simple masking definition has been created. This definition is named LatestDataMaskDefinitionHR (no spaces should be included in the definition name) and can be selected at this point. This will mask some of the confidential columns in the Employees table, in the destination cloud PDB that will be created.

Click Next to open the Schedule screen (Figure 5-30).

In the Schedule screen, you can select a future date or start immediately. You can also choose to be notified on a certain status such as Action Required, Suspended, or Problems.

Click Next to open the Review screen (Figure 5-31).

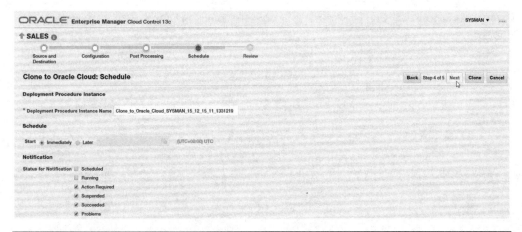

FIGURE 5-30. *Clone to Oracle Cloud: Schedule*

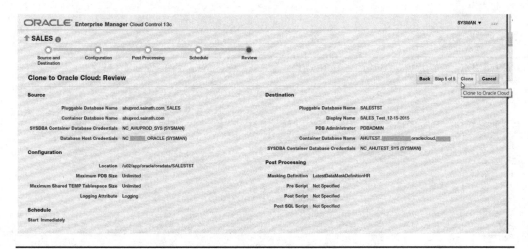

FIGURE 5-31. *Clone to Oracle Cloud: Review*

Review the information and click Clone. The procedure starts to execute (Figure 5-32).

In the Procedure Steps list, you can see a Secure Copy Files step. Note that the rsync UNIX command is being used by the procedure to fast-copy files to the cloud.

The clone-to-cloud completes successfully in under 16 minutes (depending on the PDB size and the Internet connectivity), as shown in Figure 5-33. You can examine each step and its output here.

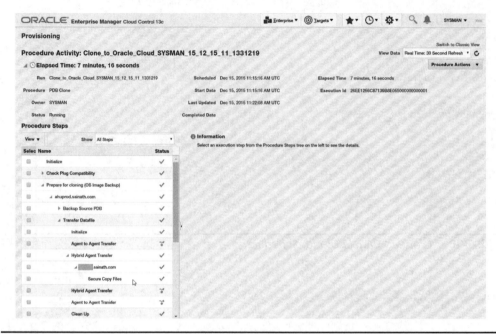

FIGURE 5-32. *Cloning to cloud execution*

FIGURE 5-33. *Completed clone-to-cloud*

When you choose Targets | Databases, you can now see the new SALES Test PDB under the cloud CDB AHUTEST (Figure 5-34).

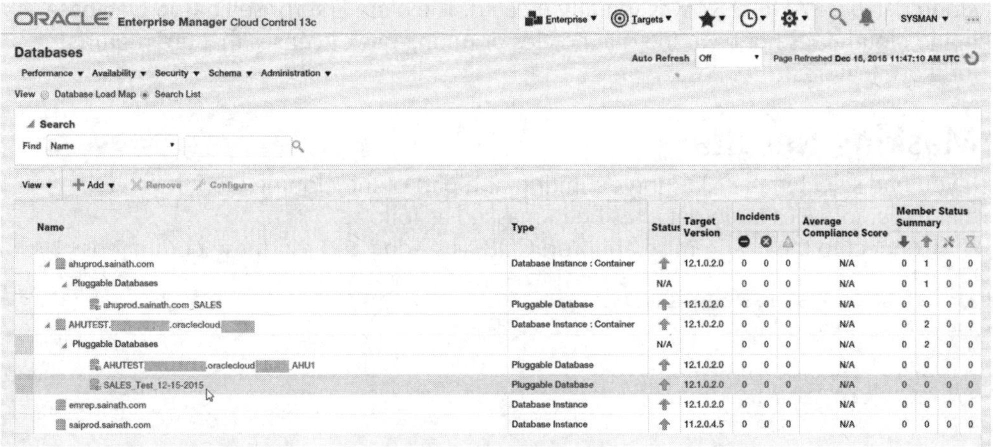

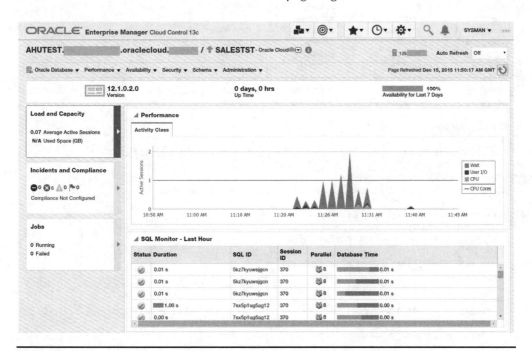

FIGURE 5-34. *Cloned PDB appears under cloud CDB*

Drill down to the Sales Test PDB home page (Figure 5-35).

FIGURE 5-35. *PDB home page*

The "Oracle Cloud" words and icon are visible on the top of the page. Note that database performance details may not be displayed if the plain Enterprise Edition Database had been selected instead of Extreme or High Performance when the cloud database AHUTEST was initially created. The plain Enterprise Edition Database in the cloud does not have the diagnostics or tuning pack licenses that are required for these features.

Masking Results

If you had selected the Masking definition as a part of the cloning workflow, verify that the employees table data has been masked as follows.

Connect to the on-premise ahuprod CDB as sysdba and run these commands:

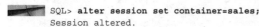

```
SQL> alter session set container=sales;
Session altered.

SQL> colu first_name format A15
SQL> colu last_name format A15
SQL> colu email format A15

SQL> select first_name, last_name, email, salary from hr.employees where rownum < 10
  2  /

FIRST_NAME      LAST_NAME       EMAIL            SALARY
--------------- --------------- --------------- -------
Steven          King            SKING            24000
Neena           Kochhar         NKOCHHAR         17000
Lex             De Haan         LDEHAAN          17000
Alexander       Hunold          AHUNOLD           9000
Bruce           Ernst           BERNST            6000
David           Austin          DAUSTIN           4800
Valli           Pataballa       VPATABAL          4800
Diana           Lorentz         DLORENTZ          4200
Nancy           Greenberg       NGREENBE         12008

9 rows selected.
```

This is the source data. Now check the same rows in the cloud PDB:

```
$ ssh <IP Address of OPC Server>
Authorized uses only. All activity may be monitored and reported.

[oracle@AHUTESTSERVER ~]$ . oraenv
ORACLE_SID = [AHUTEST] ?
The Oracle base has been set to /u01/app/oracle

[oracle@AHUTESTSERVER ~]$ sqlplus / as sysdba
SQL*Plus: Release 12.1.0.2.0 Production on Tue Dec 15 12:06:29 2015
Copyright (c) 1982, 2014, Oracle.  All rights reserved.
Connected to:
Oracle Database 12c EE Extreme Perf Release 12.1.0.2.0 - 64bit Production
With the Partitioning, Oracle Label Security, OLAP, Advanced Analytics
and Real Application Testing options
```

```
SQL> alter session set container=salestst;
Session altered.

SQL> colu first_name format A15
SQL>  colu last_name format A15
SQL>  colu email format A25
SQL> select first_name, last_name, email, salary from hr.employees where rownum <10
  2  /

FIRST_NAME     LAST_NAME     EMAIL                        SALARY
-----------    -----------   -------------------------    -------
attcaf         awdaaf        attcaf.awdaaf@company.com     432507
akuqdd         akqacd        akuqdd.akqacd@company.com     496210
aaagcc         aaqacc        aaagcc.aaqacc@company.com     492911
aavcfe         azaafe        aavcfe.azaafe@company.com     226338
akuqdd         aamamd        akuqdd.aamamd@company.com     226338
abdlcd         akqacd        abdlcd.akqacd@company.com     432507
aaatxd         aqxaxd        aaatxd.aqxaxd@company.com     433877
aaalnc         aeranc        aaalnc.aeranc@company.com     407701
aumvav         azuaav        aumvav.azuaav@company.com     741111

9 rows selected.
```

You can see that the employee data has been masked successfully, according to the masking definition that was selected during the clone-to-cloud procedure.

Verifying the APEX Version of CDBs

Note that if the Oracle Application Express (APEX) versions on the two databases (on-premise and cloud) do not tally, the plug-in of the PDB to the cloud database during the cloning process may not complete successfully. The PDB on the cloud database may be left open in restricted mode. This will be apparent when you try to drill down to the new cloned PDB in Enterprise Manager, and it tries this for a few minutes and then reports that the PDB is in restricted mode.

The reason for this can be found in the view PDB_PLUG_IN_VIOLATIONS on the cloud database:

```
SQL> select name, cause, type, message from PDB_PLUG_IN_VIOLATIONS where status !=
'RESOLVED';
NAME        CAUSE   TYPE    MESSAGE
----------  ------  ------  --------------------------------------------------------
SALESTST1   APEX    ERROR   APEX mismatch: PDB installed version 4.2.5.00.08 CDB
installed version 5.0.0.00.31
```

You can verify that the APEX versions are different. On the cloud database (which was created without choosing Configure PDB Demos when creating the cloud database server), run the following:

```
SQL> select version_no from apex_release;
VERSION_NO
----------
5.0.0.00.31
```

```
SQL> select comp_name, status, schema from dba_registry where upper(comp_name) like
'%EXPRESS%';
COMP_NAME                      STATUS       SCHEMA
---------------------------    ----------   ------------
Oracle Application Express     VALID        APEX_050000
```

On the on-premise database, the results of the same commands are shown here:

```
SQL> select version_no from apex_release;
VERSION_NO
----------
4.2.5.00.08

SQL> select comp_name, status, schema from dba_registry where upper(comp_name) like
'%EXPRESS%';
COMP_NAME                      STATUS       SCHEMA
---------------------------    ----------   ------------
Oracle Application Express     VALID        APEX_040200
```

The solution for this issue was to download the APEX 5.0 version (not the 5.0.1 version) from www.oracle.com/technetwork/developer-tools/apex/downloads/index.html, and then to apply this APEX version on the on-premise database, before you start the cloning.

The runtime APEX can be installed by a single command:

```
@apxrtins.sql SYSAUX SYSAUX TEMP /i/
```

After this is complete, the on-premise PDB will have the correct APEX version. This is verified here:

```
SQL> select version_no from apex_release;
VERSION_NO
----------
5.0.0.00.31

SQL> select comp_name, status, schema from dba_registry where upper(comp_name) like
'%EXPRESS%';

COMP_NAME                      STATUS       SCHEMA
---------------------------    ----------   ------------
Oracle Application Express     UPGRADING    APEX_050000
```

The cloning from the on-premise PDB to the cloud CDB can then proceed without any issues. However, if the cloud database reports a new version of APEX later than 5.0, you will need to follow the procedure outlined earlier in this section while using the later version of APEX and installing it on the ahuprod database.

Cloning from Oracle Cloud

You can also clone PDBs from the cloud back to on-premise. For example, suppose you complete your development on the cloud PDB, and then bring back the PDB to an on-premise CDB for testing purposes.

Right-click the cloud PDB and choose Oracle Database | Cloning | Clone From Oracle Cloud (Figure 5-36). This procedure will bring the PDB back to the on-premise CDB.

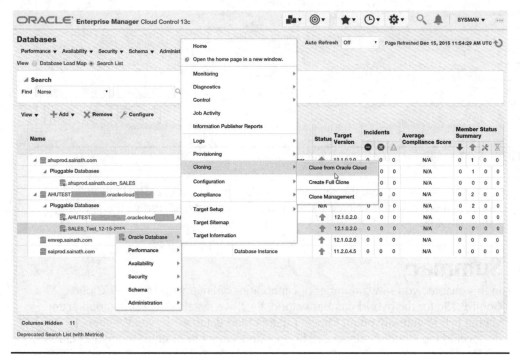

FIGURE 5-36.   *Cloning from Oracle cloud*

This opens the Clone Details screen (Figure 5-37), where you can select the source PDB and the destination CDB that is on-premise.

Specify the credentials on either side, and click Clone. The procedure will clone the PDB from the cloud back to an on-premise CDB.

This should complete successfully in most cases, but at times, when a special cloud patch has been applied at the cloud database level by the Oracle cloud team, that patch is not available to be rolled back by the datapatch utility at the on-premise PDB level. This will result in the clone procedure failing at the Apply Datapatch stage.

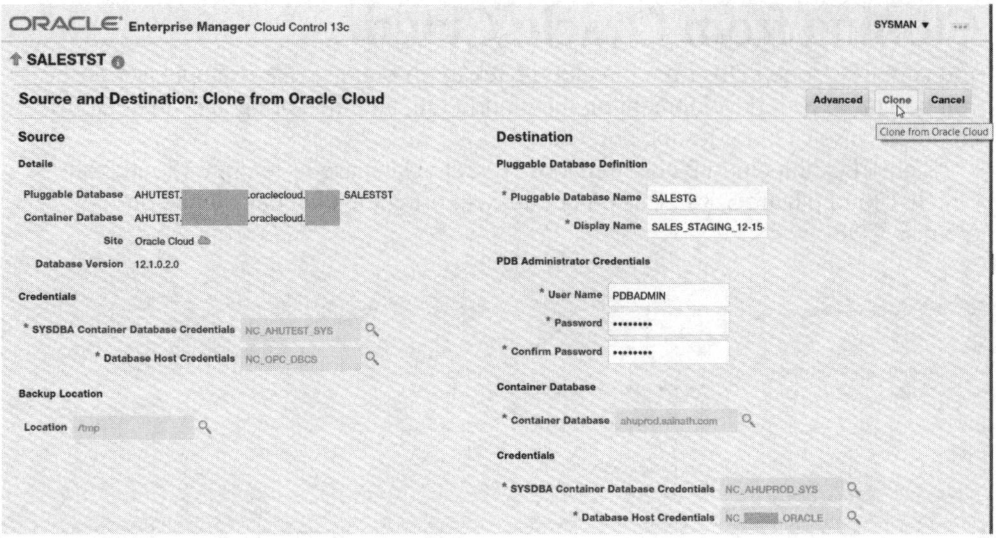

FIGURE 5-37. *Selecting the source and destination*

In such a case, ignore the step and continue the procedure. The PDB will be cloned but opened in restricted mode. You will then have to resolve the patching issue manually.

Summary

In this chapter, you saw a number of capabilities of Enterprise Manager Cloud Control 13*c* for the hybrid database cloud. First, we installed a hybrid cloud agent via the hybrid gateway on an Oracle public cloud database server. We then discovered the cloud database and listener and started to monitor the hybrid cloud.

We looked at configuration comparisons and configuration management for the hybrid cloud and discussed compliance standards enforcement. After this, we completed the cloning of a PDB from on-premise to the cloud, and we looked at moving a PDB back in the opposite direction. In conclusion, you can see that Enterprise Manager is able to work effectively with the Oracle Database hybrid cloud.

In the next chapter, we will look at using the Cloud REST API to perform Database as a Service, Schema as a Service, and PDB as a Service without using the Enterprise Manager self-service console.

CHAPTER
6

Using the Cloud REST API

I n previous chapters, you learned how to set up the private database cloud and how the self-service user can use the Enterprise Manager Self Service Portal to create databases, schemas, or pluggable databases (PDBs) on demand.

But what if your company chooses not to use the Enterprise Manager Self Service Portal? Perhaps the company has created and customized its own orchestration engine outside Enterprise Manager—in a sense, its own private cloud portal—which is able to provision multiple technologies in its private cloud, not just Oracle databases or middleware. Such a portal/orchestration engine can, of course, be built using Oracle technology. For example, you could use the Oracle WebCenter Suite, the Oracle SOA Suite, and Oracle Business Profit Management (BPM) software to build a powerful cloud portal/orchestrator with approvals and business rules included.

If the self-service user requested a production database, which would require approval from management, Oracle BPM would route it to the appropriate manager via e-mail and, once approved, the database would be provisioned. Or approvals could be required based on the cost of the database service above a certain limit. Non-Oracle technology, such as databases or middleware from other vendors, could be provisioned as well with this orchestrator. Manual services such as performance tuning or data migration could also be offered at an extra cost (thus increasing the value of the IT department) and a business catalog created, all outside Enterprise Manager.

Beginning with the previously named Oracle Cloud Management Plug-in 12.1.0.2, RESTful web services-based API support for Database as a Service (DBaaS) has been provided in Enterprise Manager. (Representational State Transfer, or REST, is an architecture style for designing networked applications.) Support has been steadily enhanced in later versions of the plug-in, including support for Cloud REST APIs for Schema as a Service, Snap Clone, and RMAN-based cloning in Oracle Cloud Management Plug-in 12.1.0.6; support for pluggable Database as a Service in the 12.1.0.7 version of the plug-in; support for CloneDB in DBaaS in 12.1.0.8; and so on. The Cloud REST API of Enterprise Manager continues to be enhanced by Oracle.

This Cloud REST API support is of great importance when you are using orchestration engines. The orchestrator can call the Cloud REST API of Enterprise Manager to do the actual provisioning for you.

In this chapter, we will use the Cloud REST API to query the available cloud services and then request the self-service provisioning of a database, schema, and PDB service—just as we did in the previous chapters using the Enterprise Manager Self Service Portal.

We can also monitor the progress of the creation of each of these services using the Cloud REST API. Then, after creation is completed, we will use the Cloud REST API to destroy each of the created services. Let's get started.

Installing the REST Client

First, you must install a REST client application in your browser. If you're using Google's Chrome browser, search for the "Postman REST Client" extension and add it. If you're using the Mozilla Firefox browser, install the "RESTClient" extension.

For this example, we will use the Postman REST client in Chrome, which is shown in Figure 6-1 after it has been installed and started up.

FIGURE 6-1.   *Postman REST client in Chrome*

For the full Database as a Service REST API syntax, you can refer to the extensive official Oracle documentation: Chapter 44, "Database as a Service SSA User REST APIs" in the *Enterprise Manager Cloud Administration Guide* (Release 13.1). We will use some of the examples listed in the Oracle documentation to demonstrate the working of the Cloud REST API with Enterprise Manager. (It is always a good idea to refer to the documentation as you work with Oracle products.)

Presteps

Before attempting any requests via the Cloud REST API, you'll need to complete some presteps. Enterprise Manager needs to be up and running in the background, because it will be doing the actual provisioning. If you're using a VirtualBox with Enterprise Manager 13c installed and on which DBaaS, SCHaaS, and PDBaaS has already been set up, first make sure that the VirtualBox is up and running and that you have started the Enterprise Manager OMS and agents, as you have done for the previous chapters.

Next, make sure your browser can connect to https://<hostname>.sainath .com:7802/em (assuming that this is the name of the installation; note that this is an imaginary hostname), and accept the security certificate so that it proceeds to the Enterprise Manager login screen, as explained next.

Enter **https://\<hostname\>.sainath.com:7802/em** in your browser. A message may appear: "Your connection is not private," as shown in Figure 6-2. Click Advanced and then click Proceed To *\<link\>*.

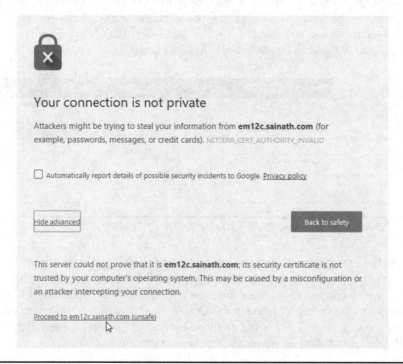

FIGURE 6-2. *Making the connection*

In the Enterprise Manager login screen, do not log in at this point. Instead, proceed to Step 1.

This prestep (of allowing the connection and accepting the security certificate) that we have just completed is necessary; otherwise, Postman will return an error when you issue the request in Step 1. The error will look like this:

```
Could not get any response: This seems to be like an error connecting
to https://<hostname>.sainath.com:7802/em/cloud.
```

Now let's begin to use the Cloud REST API to view details of the cloud resources, to issue creation requests for new databases, to issue requests for schemas and PDBs, to monitor the progress of their creation, and then to issue deletion requests for the services you have created.

Step 1: Viewing Details

You can view the details of all the cloud resources accessible to a particular Self Service Application (SSA) user, such as SAI_DAS. Use the top-level /em/cloud. This is a GET Request, and the request configuration should include the following:

URI	/em/cloud (Note: Do not use this URL; instead, use https://<hostname>.sainath.com:7802/em/cloud, as explained in the next paragraph)
Request headers	Authorization: basic ZGVtb3VzZXI6ZGVtb3VzZXI= X-specification-Version: 10001
Body	None
Request method	GET

Start the REST client. Prefix the request URL with https://<hostname>.sainath .com:7802 to give a full request URL of https://<hostname>.sainath.com:7802/em/ cloud for this particular action of viewing the cloud resources.

In the Authorization tab, select Basic Auth, and type **SAI_DAS** as the Username and **welcome1** as the Password. This is a Self Service Application (SSA) user who has been created previously by the cloud administrator (in a previous chapter).

After you have entered the basic authentication details, click Update Request, as shown in Figure 6-3. This generates the authorization header.

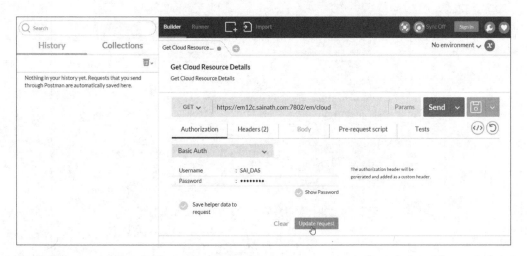

FIGURE 6-3.   *Requesting cloud resource details*

Now click the Headers tab (Figure 6-4).

FIGURE 6-4. *The Headers tab*

Enter the following for the second header: **X-specification-Version: 10001**. Make sure GET is chosen for the Request Method. Then click the Send button.

The response is displayed after a few seconds, providing the details of all the cloud resources available to the SSA user, as shown in Figure 6-5.

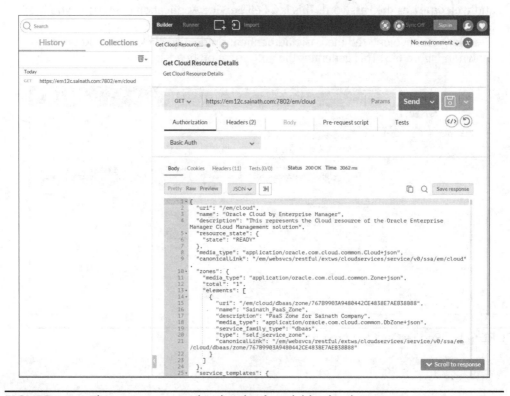

FIGURE 6-5. *The response provides details of available cloud resources.*

For your reference, the output of the cloud resources details is reproduced next. It contains important information such as the zone details and the service template details that are available to the SAI_DAS user. The output shows that several service templates for creating databases, schemas, and PDBs via self-service are all available to the SAI_DAS user. These were set up by the cloud administrator, as you saw in the previous chapters.

Information about the zone and available service templates will be used in the steps that follow. Have a quick look at the parts of the output highlighted in boldface and the parts marked with `Author's Note`. Then skip to the end of the output.

Cloud Resources Details Output

```
{
  "uri": "/em/cloud",
  "name": "Oracle Cloud by Enterprise Manager",
  "description": "This represents the Cloud resource of the Oracle Enterprise Manager
Cloud Management solution",
  "resource_state": {
    "state": "READY"
  },
  "media_type": "application/oracle.com.cloud.common.Cloud+json",
  "canonicalLink": "/em/websvcs/restful/extws/cloudservices/service/v0/ssa/em/cloud",
  "zones": {
    "media_type": "application/oracle.com.cloud.common.Zone+json",
    "total": "1",
    "elements": [
      { (Author's Note: This is the main PaaS zone set up in the image)
        "uri": "/em/cloud/dbaas/zone/767B9903A9480442CE4838E7AEB38B88",
        "name": "Sainath_PaaS_Zone",
        "description": "PaaS Zone for Sainath Company",
        "media_type": "application/oracle.com.cloud.common.DbZone+json",
        "service_family_type": "dbaas",
        "type": "self_service_zone",
        "canonicalLink": "/em/websvcs/restful/extws/cloudservices/service/v0/ssa/em/
cloud/dbaas/zone/767B9903A9480442CE4838E7AEB38B88"
      }
    ]
  },
  "service_templates": { (Author's Note: This is the List of Service Templates)
    "media_type": "application/oracle.com.cloud.common.ServiceTemplate+json",
    "total": "6",
    "elements": [
      { (Author's Note: This is the Service template for a single 11g database)
        "uri": "/em/cloud/dbaas/dbplatformtemplate/0C21CF0F90EA6AEAE055000000000001",
        "name": "Sainath 11204 Single Instance Database",
        "description": "Service Template to create a single instance database of
version 11.2.0.4 for Sainath company",
        "media_type": "application/oracle.com.cloud.common.DbPlatformTemplate+json",
        "service_family_type": "dbaas",
        "type": "dbaas",
        "canonicalLink": "/em/websvcs/restful/extws/cloudservices/service/v0/ssa/em/
cloud/dbaas/dbplatformtemplate/0C21CF0F90EA6AEAE055000000000001"
      },
```

```
      { (Author's Note: This is the Service Template for a CloneDB 11g database)
        "uri": "/em/cloud/dbaas/dbplatformtemplate/0C226670F4C70ECDE055000000000001",
        "name": "Sainath Snap Clone 11204 Database using CloneDB",
        "description": "Service Template for creating Snap Clone 11204 Database using
CloneDB for Sainath company",
        "media_type": "application/oracle.com.cloud.common.DbPlatformTemplate+json",
        "service_family_type": "dbaas",
        "type": "dbaas",
        "canonicalLink": "/em/websvcs/restful/extws/cloudservices/service/v0/ssa/em/
cloud/dbaas/dbplatformtemplate/0C226670F4C70ECDE055000000000001"
      },
      { (Author's Note: This is the Service Template for a 12c SALES PDB)
        "uri": "/em/cloud/dbaas/pluggabledbplatformtemplate/0C5B81D424A60E3
9E055000000000001",
        "name": "Sainath 12102 PDB from Profile of SALES PDB",
        "description": "Service Template for 12102 PDB creation from Profile of Sales
PDB",
        "media_type": "application/oracle.com.cloud.common.PluggableDbPlatformTemplat
e+json",
        "service_family_type": "dbaas",
        "type": "dbaas",
        "canonicalLink": "/em/websvcs/restful/extws/cloudservices/service/v0/ssa/em/
cloud/dbaas/pluggabledbplatformtemplate/0C5B81D424A60E39E055000000000001"
      },
      {(Author's Note: This is the Service Template for an empty 12c PDB)
        "uri": "/em/cloud/dbaas/pluggabledbplatformtemplate/0C5B81D424AE0E3
9E055000000000001",
        "name": "Sainath 12102 Empty PDB",
        "description": "Service Template for Empty 12102 PDB for Sainath company.",
        "media_type": "application/oracle.com.cloud.common.PluggableDbPlatformTemplat
e+json",
        "service_family_type": "dbaas",
        "type": "dbaas",
        "canonicalLink": "/em/websvcs/restful/extws/cloudservices/service/v0/ssa/em/
cloud/dbaas/pluggabledbplatformtemplate/0C5B81D424AE0E39E055000000000001"
      },
      {(Author's Note: This is the Service Template for HR Schema)
        "uri": "/em/cloud/dbaas/schemaplatformtemplate/0C308CF48B1616C
2E055000000000001",
        "name": "Sainath HR Schema",
        "description": "Template to create HR schema for Sainath company",
        "media_type": "application/oracle.com.cloud.common.
SchemaPlatformTemplate+json",
        "service_family_type": "dbaas",
        "type": "dbaas",
        "canonicalLink": "/em/websvcs/restful/extws/cloudservices/service/v0/ssa/em/
cloud/dbaas/schemaplatformtemplate/0C308CF48B1616C2E055000000000001"
      },
      { (Author's Note: This is the Service Template for User Defined Schemas)
        "uri": "/em/cloud/dbaas/schemaplatformtemplate/0C308CF48B1D16C
2E055000000000001",
        "name": "Sainath User Defined Schema",
        "description": "User Defined Schema for Sainath company",
        "media_type": "application/oracle.com.cloud.common
.SchemaPlatformTemplate+json",
        "service_family_type": "dbaas",
```

```
      "type": "dbaas",
      "canonicalLink": "/em/websvcs/restful/extws/cloudservices/service/v0/ssa/em/
cloud/dbaas/schemaplatformtemplate/0C308CF48B1D16C2E055000000000001"
    }
  ]
 },
 "service_family_types": {
   "media_type":
<truncated>
```

All the cloud resource information is shown in this output and is available to the SAI_DAS user. Now let's use this information as we issue the requests to create services. Let's start by creating a single instance database.

Step 2: Creating a Database

Let's create a self-service database by passing a request on the DB Zone. This is a POST request; according to the Oracle documentation, the request configuration should include the following:

URI	/em/cloud/dbaas/zone/82CF1C28FA20A183C99D138FF8065F19 (Note: Do not use this URL; instead, use the URL shown following this table)
Request headers	Authorization: basic ZGVtb3VzZXI6ZGVtb3VzZXI= Content-Type: application/oracle.com.cloud.common .DbPlatformInstance+json Accept: application/oracle.com.cloud.common .DbPlatformInstance+json

Click the + icon in Postman to open a new blank tab.

Use the Request URL from the "Cloud Resources Details Output" from Step 1: /em/cloud/dbaas/zone/767B9903A9480442CE4838E7AEB38B88

This is the main PaaS zone setup in the image. Prefix this with https://<hostname> .sainath.com:7802 to get the full request URL, like so:

https://<hostname>.sainath.com:7802/em/cloud/dbaas/zone/767B9903A9480 442CE4838E7AEB38B88

Add the three headers mentioned in the table. Change the method to POST instead of GET. Type in Username **SAI_DAS** and Password **welcome1** as the basic authentication, and click Update Request. The Authorization string will change.

In the Body tab in Postman, click the "raw" radio button. In the empty box, type the following (optionally, to avoid typing, you can use the zip file as discussed in the section "Importing Postman Collections from JSON Files (Optional)" later in this chapter):

```
{
        "based_on": "/em/cloud/dbaas/dbplatformtemplate/0C21CF0F90EA6AE
AE055000000000001",
        "name": "Database Request from Sai_Das using RESTful API",
        "description": "This is a Request to create a 11204 database by Sai_Das using
the RESTful API",
        "params":
        {
            "username": "saimaster",
            "password": "welcome1" ,
            "database_sid" : "sai" ,
            "service_name" : "saitest1",
            "db_size_name": "Small",
            "database_profile_version":"RMAN Backup_02_03_2015_13_49_PM"
                }
    }
}
```

Notice that we have used the following string:

```
"/em/cloud/dbaas/dbplatformtemplate/0C21CF0F90EA6AEAE055000000000001"
```

This is the string from the "Cloud Resources Details Output" from step 1, and it refers to the service template that was set up for a single-instance 11g database. Following are the other details we have specified:

```
        "username": "saimaster",
        "password": "welcome1" ,
        "database_sid" : "sai" ,
        "service_name" : "saitest1",
        "db_size_name": "Small",
        "database_profile_version":"RMAN Backup_02_03_2015_13_49_PM"
```

The username *saimaster* and password *welcome1* are the master account username and password that will be created. The database SID will be *sai* and the database service will be *saitest1*.

One of the parameters used in the body is `database_profile_version`. You can get the correct version of the profile used in this template by logging in to the Enterprise Manager console as SYSMAN or a cloud administrator.

In the Enterprise Manager console, choose Setup | Cloud | Database. Then click Data Sources and then open the Data Profiles tab. Select the RMAN Full Backup profile in the top section of this tab.

The profile versions that are available for this profile are displayed in the Contents section, as shown in Figure 6-6. These are the actual RMAN backups that have been completed by the cloud administrator or the SSA administrator.

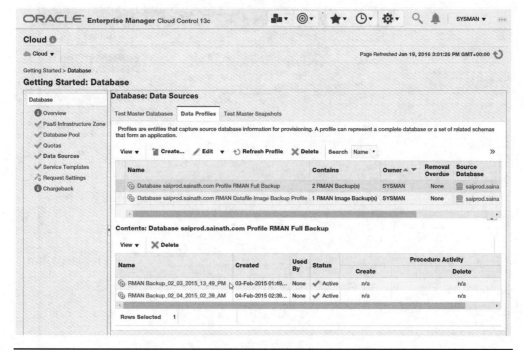

FIGURE 6-6.   *Getting the name of the profile version*

Note the name of the first profile version listed on this screen. Enter this name in the body of the request as the database_profile_version. This is the first backup that is available for the profile. Later on, we will refresh the SSA database to the second backup that is available for the same profile. The available backups are shown in Figure 6-6.

In the body of the Postman request, we also specified `"db_size_name"`: `"Small"` as one of the parameters. `db_size_name` is explained in Chapter 5 of the *Enterprise Manager Command Line Interface* (EMCLI) documentation. Search for `create_database_size`, which is an SSA verb that has been provided. `db_size_name` is used to specify a database size that will override values in the service template. We used EMCLI commands to create three database sizes, as explained in Chapter 2. In the Postman request, we requested a "small" database size.

The Postman request is now ready. Click Send. The response is shown in Figure 6-7. Notice that the words "INITIATED" and "SCHEDULED" are shown in the response and displayed in the box at the bottom of the screen.

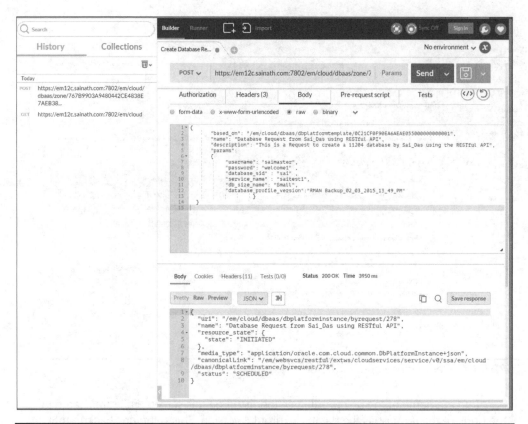

FIGURE 6-7. *Initiating the database creation request*

Note that the URI displayed in the response will be different each time the database is created. Make a note of the URI that is displayed in the response. You'll use this URI in the steps that follow—in checking the progress of the creation and in the deletion of the newly created database. The URI in the response in Figure 6-7 is /em/cloud/dbaas/dbplatforminstance/byrequest/278.

Checking the Progress of Database Creation via the Enterprise Manager API

Now let's check the progress of the database creation request. We do this first via the Enterprise Manager Self Service Portal or as the cloud administrator.

Log in to the Enterprise Manager Self Service Portal at https://<hostname>.sainath .com:7802/em as the SSA user SAI_DAS with password welcome1.

Click the Database Cloud Services link under All Cloud Services. Select the
Requests tab on the left panel. In the Status area, you can see that the creation of the
new database is in progress (Figure 6-8).

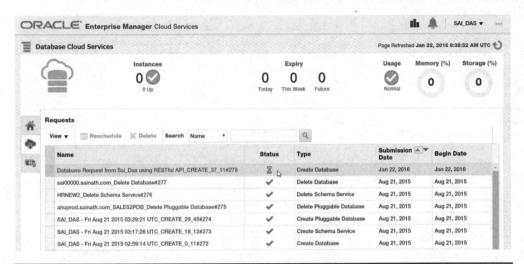

FIGURE 6-8.   *Request in progress in the Self Service Portal*

Drilling down, you can see the creation steps as shown to the SSA user.
Alternatively, you can log in to Enterprise Manager as the super administrator
SYSMAN or as a cloud administrator and see the database creation by choosing
Enterprise | Provisioning And Patching | Procedure Activity.

The Deployment Procedure Activity screen shows that a Cloud Framework
Request has been executed. The name of the request indicates that it has been
initiated via the Cloud REST API.

Drilling down, you can see that the procedure and all its steps completed in just
over 5 minutes (Figure 6-9).

Checking the Progress of Database Creation via the Cloud REST API

An alternative way to view the database creation progress is via the Cloud REST API
itself. To do this, you perform a GET operation on the resource identified by the
return URI.

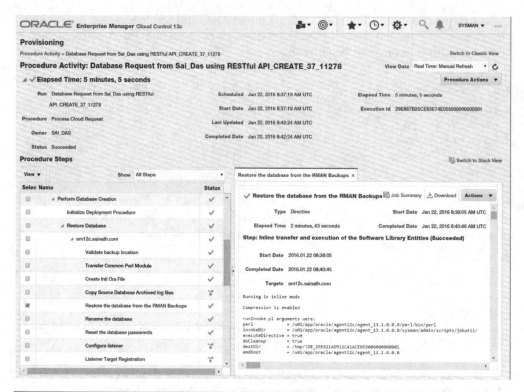

FIGURE 6-9. *DBaaS create procedure completed steps*

The request configuration should be as follows:

URI	/em/cloud/dbaas/dbplatforminstance/byrequest/<*your request number*>
Request headers	Authorization: basic ZGVtb3VzZXI6ZGVtb3VzZXI= Accept: application/oracle.com.cloud.common .DbPlatformInstance+json
Body	None
Request method	GET

Click the + icon in Postman to open a new blank tab. As the Request URL, enter **/em/cloud/dbaas/dbplatforminstance/byrequest/278**, which was included earlier in the response from the database creation step (see Figure 6-7). We have prefixed this with https://<hostname>.sainath.com:7802 to get the full request URL: https://<hostname> .sainath.com:7802/em/cloud/dbaas/dbplatforminstance/byrequest/*278*.

In every case, the request number returned by the initial database creation request will be different. Use the correct request number that was returned in your case, instead of *278*.

Put in the two headers, as shown in the preceding table. Keep the GET method. Type in Username **SAI_DAS** and Password **welcome1** in the Basic Authentication area, and click Update Request. The authorization string will change. Click the Send button.

The response will show "CREATING" for the State and "IN-PROGRESS" for the Status if the database is still being created.

Once the database is created, the responses will show "READY" and "RUNNING" for the State and Status, respectively. In this way, you can check the status of the request by reissuing the request repeatedly.

The full text of the READY and RUNNING responses also include the connect string that can be used to connect to the newly created database using tools such as Oracle SQL Developer. The text shows the database version, the master username of saimaster, and other attributes of the database.

Once the request completes, the newly created database will appear in the Self Service Portal of Enterprise Manager, and the SSA user can drill down to the database's home page, take a backup, shut it down or startup, and also connect to it using Oracle SQL Developer by using the connect string shown on the database home page.

Step 3: Refreshing the Database That Was Requested and Created

After the SSA database has been created, it is possible for the SSA user SAI_DAS to refresh the database to a more recent backup of the source database, provided such a backup was performed by the cloud administrator or SSA administrator (as explained in an earlier chapter).

A POST operation is performed on the URI of the resource to refresh the DB service instance. Use the following request configuration values:

URI	/em/cloud/dbaas/dbplatforminstance/byrequest/<*your request number*>
Request headers	Authorization: basic ZGVtb3VzZXI6ZGVtb3VzZXI= Content-Type: application/oracle.com.cloud.common.DbPlatformInstance+json Accept: application/oracle.com.cloud.common.DbPlatformInstance+json

Body	`{`
	`"operation" : "REFRESH_DATABASE",`
	`"database_profile_version": "<Use correct profile version>"`
	`}`

Request method	POST

Click the + icon in Postman to open a new blank tab. As the Request URL, enter **/em/cloud/dbaas/dbplatforminstance/byrequest/278**, which was included in the response from the database creation step. Prefix this with **https://<hostname> .sainath.com:7802** to get the full Request URL: https://<hostname>.sainath .com:7802/em/cloud/dbaas/dbplatforminstance/byrequest/*278*.

In every case, the request number returned by the initial database creation request will be different. Use the correct request number that was returned in your case instead of *278*.

Add the three headers shown in the table. Change the method to POST instead of GET. Type in Username **SAI_DAS** and Password **welcome1** in the Basic Authentication area, and click Update Request. The Authorization string will change.

Type in the following for the body of the request:

```
{
"operation" : "REFRESH_DATABASE",
"database_profile_version": "RMAN Backup_02_04_2015_02_39_AM"
}
```

One of the parameters used in the body is `database_profile_version`. You can get the correct version of the profile used in this template by logging in to the Enterprise Manager console as SYSMAN or a cloud administrator and choosing Setup | Cloud | Database.

Click Data Sources and then open the Data Profiles tab. Select the RMAN Full Backup profile in the top section on this tab. The profile versions that are available for this profile, appear in the Contents section below on the same page (Figure 6-6, shown earlier). These are the actual RMAN backups that have been completed by the cloud administrator or the SSA administrator.

Note the second profile version that is listed in the Contents section in Figure 6-6, and add this to the body of the request. This is the second backup that is available for the profile. Specifying this backup in the body of this request will refresh the SSA database with the data in the second backup.

Click the Send button.

The response shows "INITIATED" and the successfully submitted REFRESH_DATABASE operation on the service instance. The refresh operation has its own request ID, which you can use to monitor the progress of the refresh as described.

After the refresh is complete, you can log in to the database using SQL Developer and verify that the data is from the later backup.

On the Database Cloud Service Portal screen, user SAI_DAS can also click the Delete button to delete this database; we will use the Cloud REST API to do so, however, which is described next.

Step 4: Deleting the Database That Was Requested and Created

A DELETE operation is performed on the URI of the resource to delete a database service instance. Use the following request configuration values:

URI	/em/cloud/dbaas/dbplatforminstance/byrequest/**<your request number>**
Request headers	Authorization: basic ZGVtb3Nzc1ExI6ZGVtb3Nzc1QI= Accept: application/oracle.com.cloud.common .DbPlatformInstance+json
Body	None
Request method	DELETE

Click the + icon in Postman to open a new blank tab. As the Request URL, enter **/em/cloud/dbaas/dbplatforminstance/byrequest/278**, which was included in the response from the database creation step. Prefix this with **https://<hostname>.sainath.com:7802** to get the full Request URL as follows: https://<hostname>.sainath.com:7802/em/cloud/dbaas/dbplatforminstance/byrequest/*278*.

In every case, the request number returned by the initial database creation request will be different. Use the correct request number that was returned in your case, instead of *278*.

Add in the two headers mentioned in the table. Change the method to DELETE instead of GET. Type in Username **SAI_DAS** and Password **welcome1** in the Basic Authentication area, and click Update Request. The authorization string will change. Click the Send button (Figure 6-10).

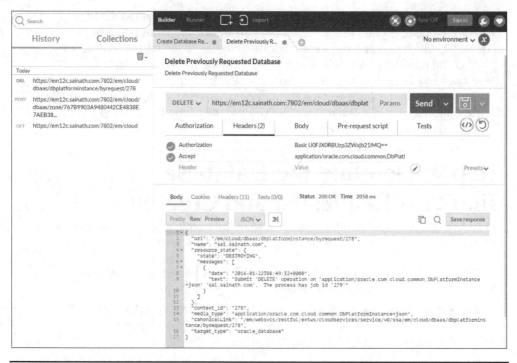

FIGURE 6-10. *Deleting the database request*

"DESTROYING" is shown in the response.

Log in to Enterprise Manager as SAI_DAS. The database deletion is shown as progressing and completes successfully in about 2 minutes.

Step 5: Creating a Schema

Now let's create a schema by passing a request on the schema platform template. A POST is performed. The request configuration to use is as follows:

URI	/em/cloud/dbaas/schemaplatformtemplate/ CC3BBB665A6BC6FFE040F00AEF252456
	(Note: Do not use this URI; instead, use the URL shown following this table)
Request headers	Authorization: basic ZGVtb3VzZXI6ZGVtb3VzZXI=
	Content-Type: application/oracle.com.cloud.common .SchemaPlatformInstance+json
	Accept: application/oracle.com.cloud.common .SchemaPlatformInstance+json

Click the + icon in Postman to open a new blank tab. Use the request URL from the "Cloud Resources Details Output" from Step 1:

```
uri": "/em/cloud/dbaas/schemaplatformtemplate/0C308CF48B1616C2E055000000000001",
```

This refers to the service template that was set up in this Enterprise Manager installation for creating the HR schema (the new schema will be created in the existing 11*g* database saiprod).

Prefix this with **https://<hostname>.sainath.com:7802** to get the full request URL: https://<hostname>.sainath.com:7802/em/cloud/dbaas/schemaplatformtemplate/ 0C308CF48B1616C2E055000000000001

Put in the three headers mentioned in the table. Change the method to POST instead of GET. Type in Username **SAI_DAS** and Password **welcome1** in the Basic Authentication area, and click Update Request. The authorization string will change.

In the Body tab in Postman, click the "raw" radio button. In the empty box, type the following:

```
{
    "based_on": "/em/cloud/dbaas/schemaplatformtemplate/0C308CF48B1616C
2E055000000000001",
    "name": "Schema Request from sai_das using RESTful API",
    "params": {
        "schema": [
            {
                "username": "HRNEW3",
                "original_name": "HR",
                "password": "welcome1"
            }
        ],
        "workload_name": "SAI_MEDIUM_WORKLOAD",
        "service_name": "HRNEW3",
        "masterAccount": "HRNEW3",
        "tablespaces": [
            {
                "old_tablespace_name": "EXAMPLE",
                "new_tablespace_name": "HRNEWDATA"
            }
        ]
    },
"zone" : "/em/cloud/dbaas/zone/767B9903A9480442CE4838E7AEB38B88"
}
```

The JSON (JavaScript Object Notation) text can also be tested on the site http:// jsonlint.com/ to double-check its validity.

Back in Postman, add the correct body text and click Send (Figure 6-11).

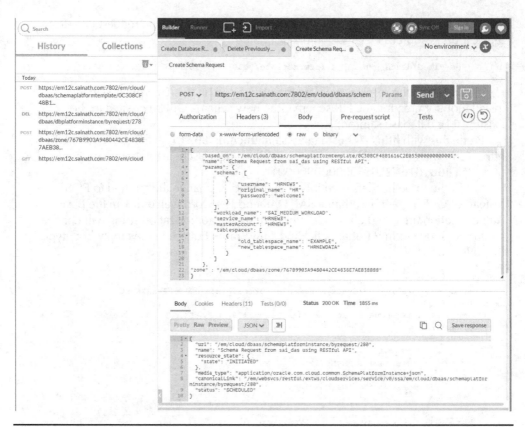

FIGURE 6-11. *Posting the schema creation request*

"INITIATED" and "SCHEDULED" are the responses displayed in the box at the bottom of the screen.

Note that the URI displayed in the response will be different each time the schema is created. Make a note of the URI, because it will be used in the next steps of this chapter—checking the progress of the creation and deleting the newly created schema. The URI in the response shown in Figure 6-11 is /em/cloud/dbaas/schemaplatforminstance/byrequest/280.

Checking the Progress of the Schema Creation Request via EM13*c* Screens

Log in to the Enterprise Manager Self Service Portal at https://<hostname>.sainath .com:7802/em as the SSA user SAI_DAS.

In the drop-down box, choose Databases. You can see the creation of the new schema has succeeded. Drilling down, you can see the creation steps as shown to the SSA user.

Alternatively, you can log in to Enterprise Manager as the super administrator SYSMAN or as a cloud administrator and see the schema creation by choosing Enterprise | Provisioning And Patching | Procedure Activity.

The Deployment Procedure Manager shows that a Cloud Framework Request type of Request has already succeeded. The Run name shows that it has been initiated via the RESTful API and that it is a Schema request.

Drilling down, you can see that the procedure and all its steps completed in under 2 minutes (Figure 6-12). Note the "Import data from dump files" step, indicating that the schema was created from an export dump file.

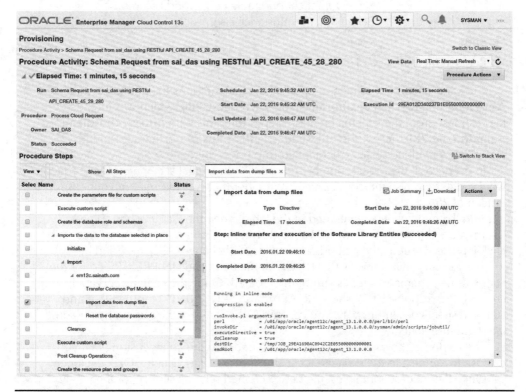

FIGURE 6-12. *Schema create procedure completed steps*

Checking the Progress of the Schema Creation Request via the Cloud REST API

An alternative way to view the progress of the schema service creation is via the Cloud REST API itself. Use a GET operation on the resource identified by the return URI to see the progress of the creation request.

Use the following request configuration. Note that the correct request number should be used as returned by the initial creation request.

URI	/em/cloud/dbaas/schemaplatforminstance/byrequest/*<your request number>*
Request headers	Authorization: basic ZGVtb3VzZXI6ZGVtb3VzZXI= Accept: application/oracle.com.cloud.common .SchemaPlatformInstance+json
Body	None
Request method	GET

Click the + icon in Postman to open a new blank tab. As the Request URL, enter **/em/cloud/dbaas/schemaplatforminstance/byrequest/280**, which was included in the response from the schema creation step. Prefix this with **https://<hostname>.sainath.com:7802** to get the full Request URL: https://<hostname>.sainath.com:7802/em/cloud/dbaas/schemaplatforminstance/byrequest/*280*.

In every case, the request number returned by the initial schema creation request will be different. Use the correct request number that was returned in your case, instead of *280*.

Add the two headers mentioned in the table. Keep the GET method. Type in Username **SAI_DAS** and Password **welcome1** in the Basic Authentication area, and click Update Request. The authorization string will change. Click the Send button.

The response will show "CREATING" for the State and "IN-PROGRESS" for the Status if the schema service is still being created. Once the schema service is created, the responses will show "READY" and "RUNNING" for the State and Status, respectively. In this way, you can check the status of the request by reissuing the request repeatedly.

The response shows the database version and also the connect string that you can use to connect to the new service, using tools such as Oracle SQL Developer.

Once the request completes, the newly created schema service for the newly imported schema will appear in the Enterprise Manager Self Service Portal and the SSA user can drill down to the service home page—where the user can perform an export or restore of the data in this service. The connection string can be copied and pasted into tools such as Oracle SQL Developer to access the schema service HRNEW3 directly using the HRNEW3/welcome1 login.

On the Database Cloud Self Service Portal screen, user SAI_DAS can also click the Delete button to delete this schema service; however, we will now use the Cloud REST API to do so.

Step 6: Deleting the Schema Service That Was Requested and Created

A DELETE operation is performed on the URI of the resource to delete the schema service. Use the following request configuration values:

URI	/em/cloud/dbaas/schemaplatforminstance/byrequest/<*your request number*>
Request headers	Authorization: basic ZGVtb3VzZXI6ZGVtb3VzZXI= Accept: application/oracle.com.cloud.common .SchemaPlatformInstance+json
Body	None
Request method	DELETE

Click the + icon in Postman to open a new blank tab. As the Request URL, type **/em/cloud/dbaas/schemaplatforminstance/byrequest/280**, which was included in the response from the schema creation step. Prefix this with **https://<hostname>.sainath.com:7802** to get the full Request URL: https://<hostname>.sainath.com:7802/em/cloud/dbaas/schemaplatforminstance/byrequest/*280*.

In every case, the request number returned by the initial schema creation request will be different. Use the correct request number that was returned in your case, instead of *280*.

Add the two headers mentioned in the table. Change the method to DELETE instead of GET. Type in Username **SAI_DAS** and Password **welcome1** in the Basic Authentication area, and click Update Request. The authorization string will change. Next, click the Send button (Figure 6-13).

"DESTROYING" is shown in the response.

Log in to Enterprise Manager as SAI_DAS. The schema deletion is shown as progressing. It completes successfully in a little over 1 minute.

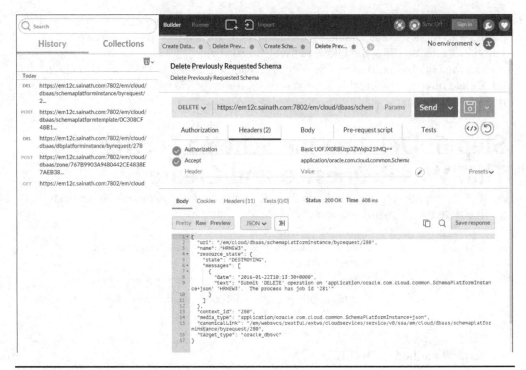

FIGURE 6-13. *Deleting the schema service request*

Step 7: Creating a Pluggable Database

We can now create a PDB by passing a request on the Pluggable DB Platform Template. A POST is performed. Use the following request configuration as per Oracle documentation:

URI	/em/cloud/dbaas/pluggabledbplatformtemplate/ CC3BBB665A6BC6FFE040F00AEF252456 (Note: Do not use this URI; instead, use the URL shown following this table)
Request headers	Authorization: basic ZGVtb3VzZXI6ZGVtb3VzZXI= Content-Type: application/oracle.com.cloud.common .PluggableDbPlatformInstance+json Accept: application/oracle.com.cloud.common.Pluggable DbPlatformInstance+json

Click the + icon in Postman to open a new blank tab. Use the Request URL from the "Cloud Resources Details Output" from Step 1:

```
"uri": "/em/cloud/dbaas/pluggabledbplatformtemplate/0C5B81D424A60E3
9E055000000000001"
```

This refers to the service template that was set up in this Enterprise Manager installation for creating the Sales PDB (the new PDB is to be created in the existing 12*c* container database ahuprod).

Prefix this with **https://<hostname>.sainath.com:7802** to get the full request URL: https://<hostname>.sainath.com:7802/em/cloud/dbaas/pluggabledbplatform template/0C5B81D424A60E39E055000000000001

Add in the three headers mentioned in the table. Change the method to POST instead of GET. Type in Username **SAI_DAS** and Password **welcome1** in the Basic Authentication area, and click Update Request. The Authorization string will change.

In the Body tab in Postman, click the "raw" radio button. In the empty box, type the following:

```
{
    "zone": "/em/cloud/dbaas/zone/767B9903A9480442CE4838E7AEB38B88",
    "name": "PDB Request from sai_das using RESTful API",
    "params": {
        "username": "SALES3PDBADMIN",
        "password": "welcome1",
        "workload_name": "SAI_MEDIUM_WORKLOAD",
        "pdb_name": "SALES3PDB",
        "service_name": "SALES3",
        "tablespaces": [
            "EXAMPLE",
            "USERS"
        ],
        "target_name ": "ahuprod"
    }
}
```

In the body, we have used the correct DBaaS zone according to the Cloud Resources Details output in Step 1. The username SALES3PDBADMIN is the administrative user for the new PDB. The PDB name is SALES3PDB, and the service name as SALES3. The workload selected is SAI_MEDIUM_WORKLOAD.

The new PDB will have the same tablespaces used in the PDB template in the service template. The main data is in the tablespaces EXAMPLE and USERS, so these are specified in the body of the request. When the PDB is created, unlimited quota on these tablespaces will be granted to the administrative user SALES3PDBADMIN.

The administrative user SALES3PDBADMIN is assigned the PDB_DBA role when created, and also the SAINATH_SALES_PDB_ROLE (with more system privileges), which was specified at the time the service template was created by the cloud administrator. (Refer to Chapter 4 for the complete list of privileges specified in the service template.)

The target_name is the CDB in which the new PDB will be created. In this case, the CDB that will be used is the 12.1.0.2 ahuprod database.

The valid JSON can also be tested on the site http://jsonlint.com/.

Back in Postman, type in the correct body text and click Send (Figure 6-14).

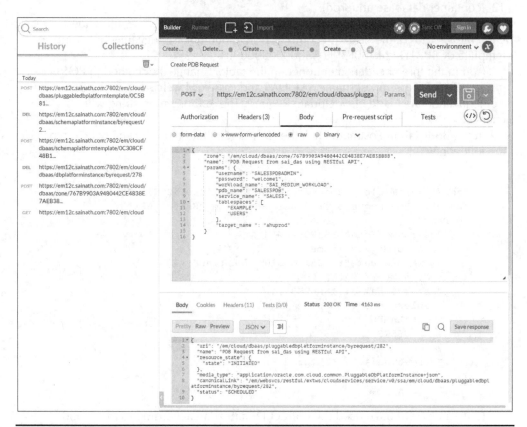

FIGURE 6-14. *Posting the PDB creation request*

"INITIATED" and "SCHEDULED" are shown in the response in the box at the bottom of the screen.

Note that the URI displayed in the response will be different each time the PDB is created. Make a note of the URI, because it will be used in the next steps of this chapter. The URI in the response shown in Figure 6-14 is /em/cloud/dbaas/ pluggabledbplatforminstance/byrequest/282.

Checking the Progress of the PDB Creation Request via EM13c Screens

Log in to the Enterprise Manager Self Service Portal at https://<hostname>.sainath .com:7802/em as the SSA user SAI_DAS with password welcome1.

From the drop-down box, choose Databases. You can see the creation of the new PDB has succeeded. Drilling down, you can see the creation steps as shown to the SSA user.

Alternatively, you can log in to Enterprise Manager as the super administrator SYSMAN or as a cloud administrator and see the PDB creation by choosing Enterprise | Provisioning And Patching | Procedure Activity.

The Deployment Procedure Manager shows that the Pluggable Database as a Service procedure has already succeeded. Drilling down, you can see that the procedure and all its steps completed in under 5 minutes (Figure 6-15). The steps show that a new PDB and its service have been created.

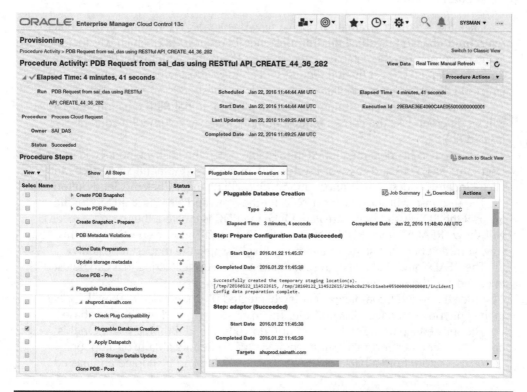

FIGURE 6-15.   *PDB completed procedure creation steps*

Checking the Progress of the PDB Creation Request via the Cloud REST API

You can also view the progress of the PDB creation via the Cloud REST API by performing a GET operation on the resource identified by the return URI.

The following request configuration should be used. Note that the correct request number should be used as returned by the initial PDB creation request.

URI	/em/cloud/dbaas/pluggabledbplatforminstance/byrequest/<*your request number*>
Request headers	Authorization: basic ZGVtb3VzZXI6ZGVtb3VzZXI= Accept: application/oracle.com.cloud.common.PluggableDbPlatformInstance+json
Body	None
Request method	GET

Click the + icon in Postman to open a new blank tab. As the Request URL, enter **/em/cloud/dbaas/pluggabledbplatforminstance/byrequest/282**, which was included in the response from the database creation step. Prefix this with **https://<hostname> .sainath.com:7802** to get the full request URL: https://<hostname>.sainath.com:7802/ em/cloud/dbaas/pluggabledbplatforminstance/byrequest/*282*.

In every case, the request number returned by the initial PDB creation request will be different. Use the correct request number that was returned in your case instead of *282*.

Add the two headers mentioned in the table. Keep the GET method. Type in the Username **SAI_DAS** and Password **welcome1** in the Basic Authentication area, and click Update Request. The Authorization string will change. Click the Send button.

The response will show "CREATING" for the State and "IN-PROGRESS" for the Status if the PDB is still being created. Once the PDB is created, the response receive will show "READY" and "RUNNING" for the State and Status, respectively. In this way, you can check the status of the request by reissuing the request repeatedly.

The READY and RUNNING response shows the connect string that can be used to connect to the new service, as well as the database version.

Once the request completes, the newly created pluggable database will appear in the Enterprise Manager SSA console. The instance type is Pluggable Database.

The self-service user SAI_DAS can drill down to the PDB home page. On this page, the user can perform a shutdown or startup, schedule a daily backup, or perform a restore from a backup. The connection string can be copied and pasted into tools such as Oracle SQL Developer to access the PDB service SALES3 directly, using the SALES3PDBADMIN/welcome1 login.

On the Database Cloud Self Service Portal page, SAI_DAS can also click the Delete button to delete this PDB via self-service, however, we will use the Cloud REST API way to do so in the next step.

Step 8: Deleting the Pluggable Database That Was Requested and Created

A DELETE operation is performed on the URI of the resource to delete the PDB. Use the following request configuration values:

URI	/em/cloud/dbaas/pluggabledbplatforminstance/ byrequest/<*your request number*>
Request headers	Authorization: basic ZGVtb3VzZXI6ZGVtb3VzZXI= Accept: application/oracle.com.cloud.common.Pluggable DbPlatformInstance+json
Body	None
Request method	DELETE

Click the + icon in Postman to open a new blank tab. As the Request URL, enter **/em/cloud/dbaas/pluggabledbplatforminstance/byrequest/282**, which was included in the response from the schema creation step. Prefix this with **https://<hostname> .sainath.com:7802** to get the full request URL: https://<hostname>.sainath.com:7802/ em/cloud/dbaas/pluggabledbplatforminstance/byrequest/*282*.

In every case, the request number returned by the initial PDB creation request will be different. Use the correct request number that was returned in your case, instead of *282*.

Add the two headers mentioned in the table. Change the method to DELETE instead of GET. Type the Username **SAI_DAS** and Password **welcome1** in the Basic Authentication area, and click Update Request. The Authorization string will change (Figure 6-16). Then click the Send button.

"DESTROYING" is shown as the response.

Log into Enterprise Manager as SAI_DAS. The PDB deletion is shown as running. It completes successfully in about 1 minute.

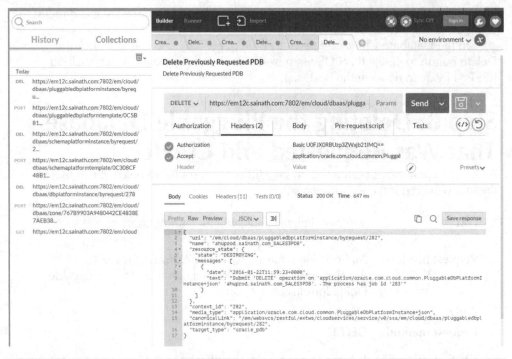

FIGURE 6-16. *Deleting a PDB request*

Importing Postman Collections from JSON Files (Optional)

This final step is optional. To save you time in testing the requests in this chapter, we have supplied a zip file. Download the file 353_06_ServicesCollectionsJSON.zip, which contains a number of JSON files that will be used to create multiple collections for the services in Postman in Chrome.

Unzip this file to a directory on your computer. The following five text files are in the zip:

- A_GetCloudResourceDetails.json.txt

- B_CreationofServices.json.txt

- C_MonitoringCreationRequests.json.txt

- D_RefreshofDatabase.json.txt

- E_DeletionofServices.json.txt

In Postman, move to the Collections tab. Click the Import icon at the top of the screen. Select the five files. Order by name when you select, so that the alphabetical order is maintained.

The Collections are immediately added, and they appear in Postman, under the Collections tab. Expand the collections to show the multiple requests that have been created inside each collection (Figure 6-17).

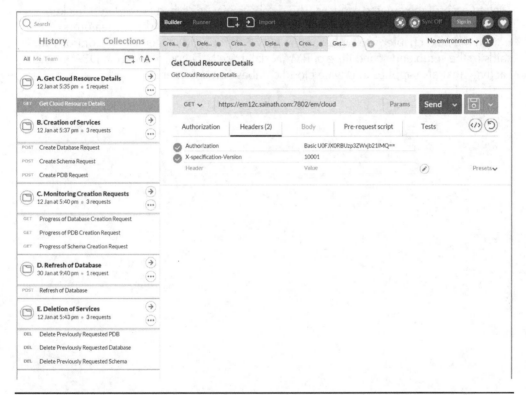

FIGURE 6-17.   *Postman JSON collections expanded*

You can easily test out the Cloud REST API by clicking each of the requests in the collection. This populates the request details on the Postman screen. Select Basic Auth as the Authorization, and enter the username and password of the SSA user. Click Update Request. Then click the Send button to perform the request.

Note that when using the monitoring creation requests, or the deletion requests, you must remember to replace the request number in the body of the request with the actual request number from the creation request that was just completed. This is because these monitoring and deletion requests require the actual request number, and you can get that only from the response when the corresponding creation request has actually been processed.

Summary

In this chapter, we used the Postman REST client and posted requests to the Cloud REST API of Enterprise Manager. First of all, we queried the available cloud services, and then requested the self-service provisioning of a database, schema, and PDB service. The progress of the creation of each of these services was monitored using the API, and after creation was complete, the Cloud REST API was again used to delete each of the created services. The database was refreshed to the latest backup before it was deleted. We also saw how to use the Postman collections feature.

In the next chapter, we will examine how Enterprise Manager Cloud Control 13*c* aids in the setup and scheduling of RMAN database backups, a common DBA activity that also applies to private cloud database environments.

CHAPTER
7

Managing Database
Backups

Oracle supplies a powerful utility to back up and recover Oracle Databases. Oracle Recovery Manager (RMAN) is included along with the Oracle Database software install. This chapter shows how the private cloud administrator or DBA can set up and schedule RMAN database backups using Enterprise Manager Cloud Control 13*c* instead of the older, more time-consuming, manual method of UNIX shell scripting and cron jobs.

RMAN scripts have traditionally been used by DBAs to run complete or incremental database backups. The scripts are placed in a shell script wrapper at the UNIX level, and backups are scheduled using the UNIX cron job facility. These hand-written RMAN and shell scripts need to be tested, verified, and maintained manually. Although this is manageable for one or two databases, the same task would need to be repeated with every new database or every new database server that is provisioned— and the time spent on setting up such backups, testing and verifying the scripts, and maintaining them would increase correspondingly.

Using Enterprise Manager streamlines and automates the procedure. RMAN scripts can be generated seamlessly in Enterprise Manager after you answer a few questions, and they can be automatically scheduled via the centralized Enterprise Manager job system, removing the need for creating wrapper shell scripts and cron jobs.

Using Enterprise Manager would also make it unnecessary to maintain any customized RMAN scripts continuously with every new database release. And when new versions of the Oracle Database are released, the Oracle Enterprise Manager Database plug-in would automatically accommodate any special features in that release. RMAN script maintenance would no longer be necessary. New RMAN features, such as compression, encryption, block change tracking, and so on, would be available when you set up the backup in Enterprise Manager.

Scheduling the RMAN backups using the Enterprise Manager job system would enable the use of the built-in alerting mechanism of Enterprise Manager, so that the administrator would be automatically alerted when a backup job fails, rather than being required to log in to each server and check the backup logs one-by-one (as we used to do in the last century). Using Enterprise Manager for database backups reduces the requirement to script for errors, or write and schedule health-check scripts to check for backup failures and errors. You get the picture.

In this way, the private cloud administrator can set up and schedule regular RMAN database backups for the pre-12*c* database pools used for schema self-service provisioning, or the 12*c* container database (CDB) pools used for pluggable database (PDB) self-service provisioning.

What about the single-instance or Real Application Cluster (RAC) databases and/ or PDBs that can be created on the fly by the Self Service Application (SSA) users? In this case, SSA users can schedule Oracle-suggested RMAN daily backups directly from the console—both for instances as well as PDBs. Note that in the case of schemas, only an export dump is possible for the SSA user.

Backups in the Past

When I worked for a large Australia-based company at the start of the 21st century, Oracle databases were backed up cold (offline) by making a OS-level copy of the database files and control files. This progressed to hot (online) backups. As the years went on, we started to use RMAN to back up databases, but we still used UNIX shell scripts and the UNIX cron utility.

In the next phase, however, as Enterprise Manager was being implemented in the company, the database teams began performing RMAN backups using Enterprise Manager. We realized immense benefits immediately, such as time savings and efficiency in setting up and managing RMAN backups. This gradual transition, from manual backups to scripting, then to RMAN scripting, and finally to Enterprise Manager, was also reflected in other companies around the world.

Let's look back at the past of database backups. The very early backups were offline (cold) backups: the database was shut down manually, and an OS file copy of all the database files and control files was taken. This OS copy served as the database backup and would be stored directly on tape—in those days, disk space was limited and expensive.

DBAs then started to write UNIX shell scripts to do the actual work. The database would be shut down and the database files and control files were copied to the tape using OS file copy commands, after which the scripts would start up the database.

Scheduling of such backup jobs was achieved via the UNIX cron job utility, which was used to schedule UNIX jobs. An appropriate schedule was set up in the Oracle user's crontab file. This resulted in the UNIX cron job utility executing the backup script at the appropriate time.

Some level of automation was definitely achieved by the scripts, but backup still required the manual effort of writing, setting up, and testing the scripts. The backup scripts also needed to be maintained to cater for any system changes in the future. For example, a different tape drive or a different backup location could be used, perhaps to disk. Or the database name could be changed, or new databases on the same server would need to be backed up, perhaps by the same script looping through the database name entries in oratab. For all these changes, someone would need to maintain and change the backup scripts, test them again, set them up again, and debug them again if there were any problems found during testing.

Version 7 of the Oracle Database (around 1988) introduced the technology of online (hot) backups for the first time. Now the database could stay open at the same time the backup was taking place, and transactions could continue normally. However, each tablespace had to be placed in a special backup mode by issuing a command such as `alter tablespace <my tablespace name> begin backup`. With this command, the checkpoint System Change Number (SCN) in all datafile headers for that tablespace was frozen; however, extra redo was also generated by the database to aid in recovering fractured blocks (blocks that were in the process of being changed when being backed up by the OS utility).

So, the script heroes in the company came to the rescue again. The scripts were revamped to connect to the database, get a list of all the tablespaces, and then put all the tablespaces in backup mode. The OS file copy to tape would then be executed. After checking that the OS copy was successful, the tablespaces were removed from backup mode.

RMAN Benefits

The RMAN utility was introduced in Oracle Database version 8 as a new backup method for Oracle Databases. With the arrival of RMAN, we no longer needed to put the tablespaces in backup mode. The utility, when backing up the blocks in a datafile, was itself aware of any fractured blocks and came back to reread these blocks later on when they were no longer fractured. A simple technical solution, RMAN resulted in the generation of less redo with correspondingly less strain on the database. As such, it became the backup solution of choice for any Oracle Database.

Nevertheless, there was a lot of initial resistance from DBAs to the use of RMAN. This was probably because a separate catalog database had to be created to hold the backup history. Many DBAs, including myself, thought it didn't make sense to create a new database just to back up an existing database. This was back in the days when there were few databases around, and server resources were limited. The catalog database also had to be backed up via a logical backup (export and import), creating more administrative overhead.

To rectify this dependence on the catalog database, later versions of RMAN (from Oracle 8*i* onward) enabled the control file of the database to itself function as the RMAN catalog. So you could now back up a database using RMAN and retain the history of the backups in the control file. A limited history in this manner was held in the control file, but if you wanted an older history, it was always possible to restore an older control file.

The RMAN control file method of database backups began to be accepted worldwide, and DBAs started to use RMAN to back up their production databases. But RMAN had, of course, inherited the history of the cron and UNIX shell scripts that had been used to perform offline or online database backups.

The script heroes simply modified the scripts to perform the backup using the RMAN commands. The tablespaces no longer needed to be placed in or out of backup mode, so those commands were removed. Everything else stayed the same, including the use of the UNIX cron job facility.

In some companies, the simple English-like RMAN commands supplied by Oracle were buried under layers of customized scripts. This made it more difficult for new DBAs to understand these scripts, also made it more tedious for debugging and future enhancements.

We can contrast this with the Enterprise Manager approach: you can set up and schedule database backups very easily, without writing any script (Enterprise Manager will create the RMAN script and schedule it) and without using the UNIX cron job utility, by using Oracle Enterprise Manager Cloud Control. This results in time and cost savings, increased productivity, and automation of the entire approach, as you will now find out for yourself.

Initial Backup Steps

Let's suppose that you want to back up a database that is already a target in the Enterprise Manager system—that is, the Enterprise Manager Agent has been installed on the database server and the database has been discovered and promoted as a managed target.

Move to the Database home page by choosing Target (the circular archery target icon) | Databases, and click the Database name. When the home page is displayed (make sure you are logged in to the database with SYSDBA credentials), you can set up the Fast Recovery Area (FRA) to help in automating the backups.

Choose Target | Availability | Backup & Recovery | Recovery Settings and scroll down the page to the Fast Recovery area shown in Figure 7-1.

Specify a location for the FRA and the size in GB. Before you click Apply, remember to specify an appropriate size depending on the size of the database and how exactly you will be backing up—for example, if you will be using image copies of your datafiles or only compressed backup sets (which will take up much less space). You can resize the FRA later on, but if it runs out of space, archive logs (if in ARCHIVELOG Mode) may stop being generated, and the database will not process any transaction after that until the space issue is resolved.

After you set up the FRA, you can enable ARCHIVELOG Mode for the database. This enables you to take online backups and point-in-time recovery. You can enable ARCHIVELOG Mode on the same page where you set up the FRA, as shown in Figure 7-1 in the Media Recovery section.

After you've set the ARCHIVELOG Mode, Enterprise Manager will prompt you to restart the database and take a whole database backup immediately after the database has been restarted.

The database is now opened in ARCHIVELOG Mode, and you can proceed with setting up the backup.

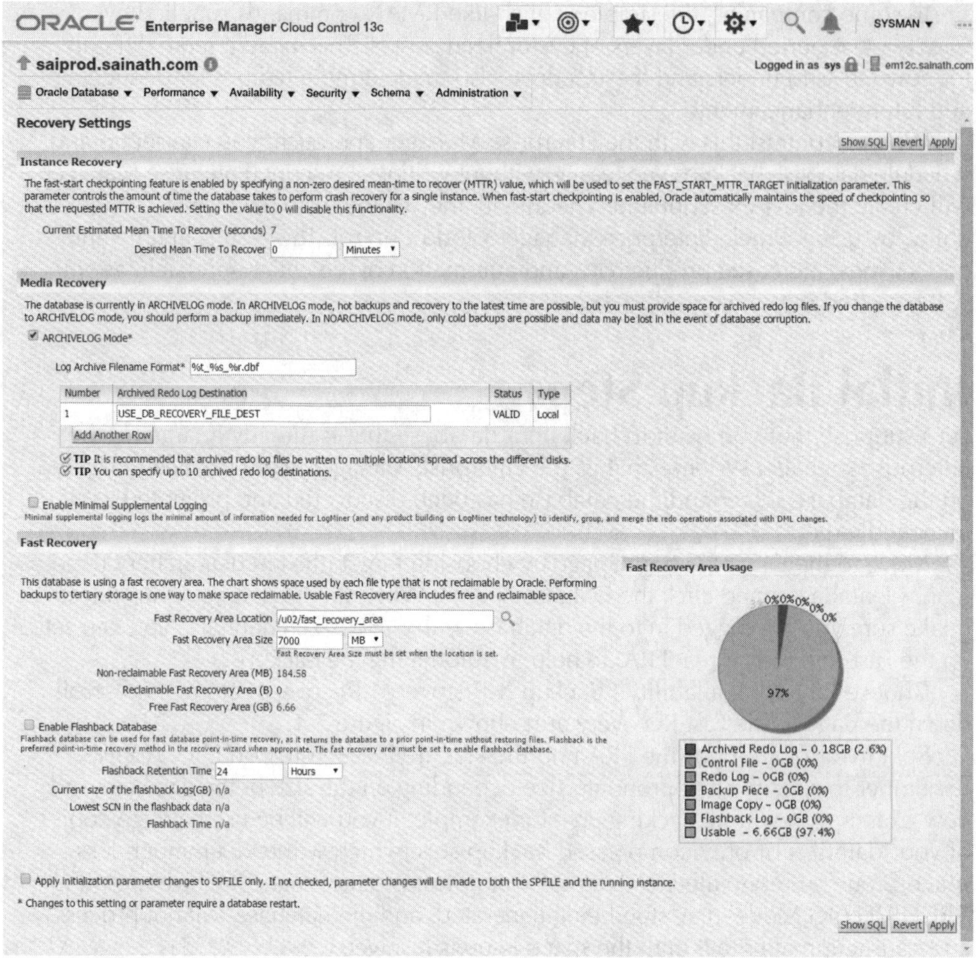

FIGURE 7-1. *Setting up the Fast Recovery section and ARCHIVELOG Mode*

Backup Settings

From the Database home page, choose Target | Availability | Backup & Recovery | Backup Settings (Figure 7-2).

In the Disk Settings section of the Device tab, select a Parallelism of 1 (the default) and a Disk Backup Type as Compressed Backup Set. Selecting a larger parallelism will increase the number of concurrent RMAN streams to the disk backup location. Use this feature with care, because the correct setting depends on how much the disk can handle. Using a high setting will increase the speed of the backup, with results depending on the disk subsystem structure.

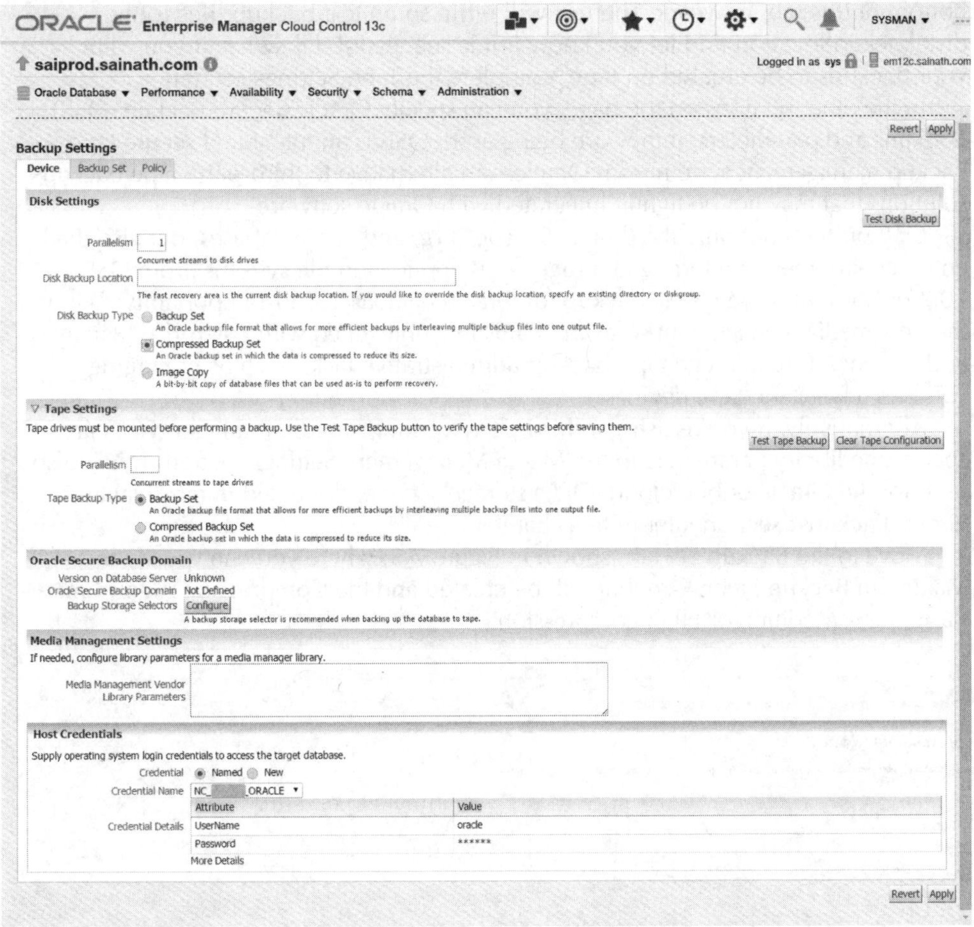

FIGURE 7-2. *Entering backup settings*

The Disk Backup Type offers several options: Backup Set, Compressed Backup Set, or Image Copy. Select the Compressed Backup Set option for the best use of the backup space. This sort of backup compression was introduced in Oracle 10*g* and was welcomed by DBAs.

Instead of a backup set, you can also select an Image Copy as the backup type. This will create an exact copy of each datafile. This is useful for fast recovery, as will be discussed later in this chapter.

Leave the Disk Backup Location field blank to enable use of the FRA, provided it has been set up.

Click the Test Disk Backup button to make sure the disk backup is set up properly. This requires that you first complete the Host Credentials section at the bottom of this tab, however. The test will write some test backup files to the disk backup location and let you know if it is successful. Likewise, if you want your backups to be created on tape, complete the Tape Settings section.

In the other sections on the page, you can specify Oracle Secure Backup (OSB) domains and parameters, if they are being used. OSB is an integrated secure tape backup management system from Oracle—an alternative to third-party tape backup solutions that may not be tightly integrated with Oracle software.

OSB protects not only the Oracle 9i, 10g, 11g, and 12c databases, but also the entire environment, including heterogeneous application file systems (from OSB 10.2 onward). It is the fastest backup for Oracle databases. Most importantly, OSB is the only media management software that is fully integrated with Enterprise Manager and can therefore manage tape backup administrative tasks such as managing volumes (tapes) and tape devices.

Alternatively, if you're using a third-party vendor's media manager, you can specify the library parameters in the Media Management Settings section. This is also used for the Oracle public cloud (OPC) storage service, discussed in the "Database Group Backups" section later in this chapter.

Move to the Backup Set tab, shown in Figure 7-3, where you can specify the Maximum Backup Piece Size that will be created and the Compression Algorithm: Basic, Low, Medium, or High compression.

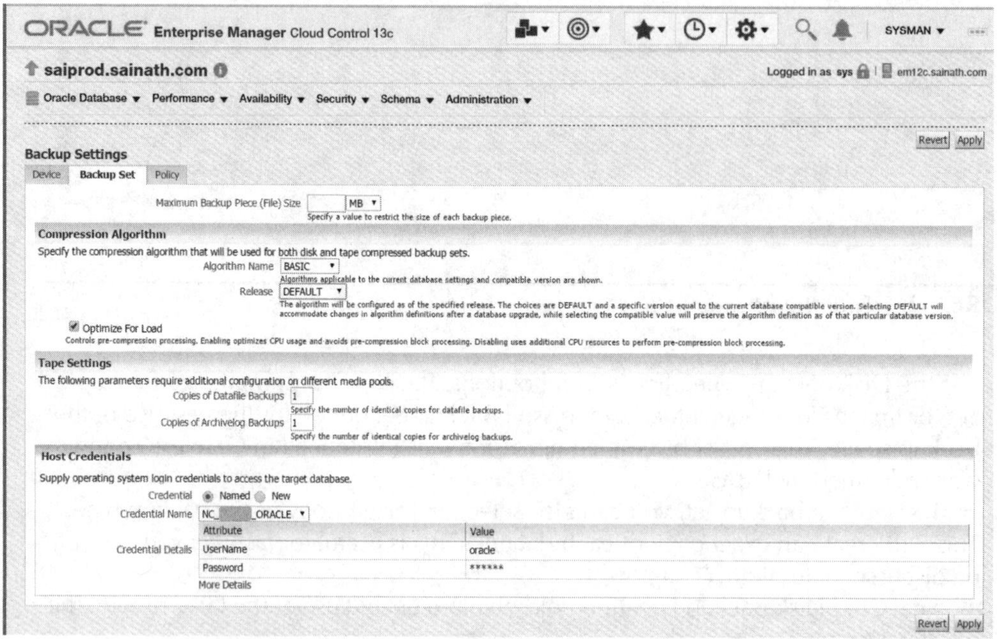

FIGURE 7-3. *Specify sizes and algorithms in the Backup Set tab.*

Under Compression Algorithm, you can choose either Default or a specific release version such as 11.2.0.0.0 for the Release. This setting allows preservation of the algorithm definition for that database version.

You can also optimize the CPU usage of the compression, in particular by avoiding precompression block processing.

Click the Policy tab, shown in Figure 7-4. Here, you can specify that the database control file and server parameter file (SPFILE) are backed up automatically with every database backup or database structural change.

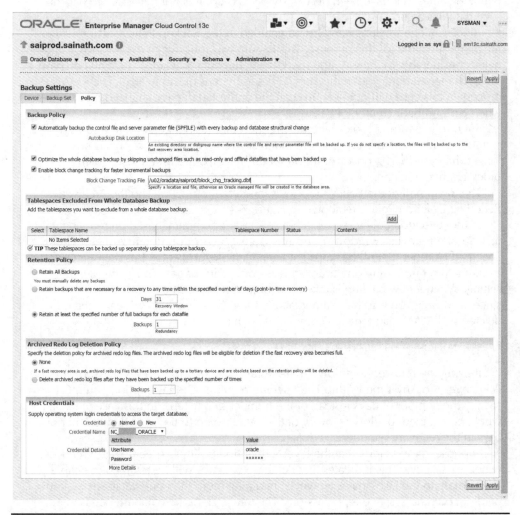

FIGURE 7-4. *Specify the backup files in the Backup Policy tab.*

Setting up the database control file and SPFILE backup as automatic is strongly recommended, because these are very important files for the database. Because you are using the NOCATALOG Mode of RMAN, it is of utmost importance that you ensure the safety of the control file and make certain it is backed up, since the history of all the backups is contained in the control file.

If the Autobackup Disk Location is not specified in the Backup Policy section, it will default to the Fast Recovery Area.

You can also optimize the database backup by skipping unchanged read-only or offline datafiles that have been previously backed up. It is not necessary to backup such datafiles again.

Block Change Tracking can also be enabled in the Backup Policy section with a file name specified for this purpose. This feature was introduced in Oracle 10*g* and helps considerably to increase the speed of incremental backups, since all database block changes are tracked in this special file (only tens of MB in size). The RMAN process in this case will not need to scan the entire datafile for changed blocks when performing incremental backups.

Such full scanning took place during incremental backups in 9*i*, and as a result, the incremental backups were much slower in that version. This is no longer the case in 10*g* onward. Incremental backups are much faster with block change tracking.

The lower half of the Policy tab shows the Retention Policy and the Archived Redo Log Deletion Policy, as shown in Figure 7-4.

In the Retention Policy section, choose a retention policy based on redundancy instead of a recovery window. To do this, select the option Retain At Least The Specified Number Of Full Backups For Each Datafile, and enter **1** as the number of backups to retain at any one time—this is your redundancy. This is the default setting. When a new backup is taken, the older backup will be marked as obsolete, since only 1 backup is to be retained at any time. Obsolete backups can then be deleted by RMAN maintenance commands such as:

```
DELETE NOPROMPT OBSOLETE DEVICE TYPE DISK;
```

If using the recovery window, in the Retain Backups That Are Necessary For A Recovery To Any Time Within The Specific Number Of Days option you must specify the number of days instead of the number of backups. In this case, backups would be retained to allow recovery of the database up to the specified number of days in the recovery window.

Suppose, for example, that the RMAN retention policy is specified as a recovery window of 7 days. This indicates that database backups will be retained to enable recovery up to the last 7 days. However, retaining more than one database backup on disk could have space repercussions. The total size of the database needs to be considered, as well as the types of backups taken each day (full or incremental), the amount of archive logs generated each day (since archive log backups are also included), and the amount of finite space allocated to the database's FRA.

The DBA needs to keep all these factors in mind and closely monitor the database backup space available over the next few weeks—adjusting the recovery window if required, or perhaps changing the Retention Policy to redundancy instead of a recovery window.

In the Archived Redo Log Deletion Policy section, you can specify the deletion policy for archived redo logs, and they can be made eligible for deletion when the FRA becomes full. There are two options. If you select None, this will disable the Archived Redo Log Deletion Policy. Assuming that the FRA is set, the archived redo logs that have been backed up and are obsolete according to the retention policy setting will be deleted by the RMAN maintenance commands.

If you select the option Delete Archived Redo Logs After They Have Been Backed Up The Specified Number Of Times, you must specify the number of backups to a tertiary device, after which the archived redo logs will be deleted.

If this database is a primary database in a Oracle Data Guard configuration, more options will be available on this page. The options are different for a primary database and a standby database.

With a primary database, in addition to these two options is one more option, Delete Archived Redo Log Files, with two suboptions:

- **After They Have Been Applied To All Standby Databases**   Archived redo logs will be deleted after being applied or consumed on all remote destinations. The destinations may or may not be mandatory.

- **After They Have Been Shipped To All Standby Databases**   Archived redo logs will be deleted after transfer to all remote destinations. The destinations may or may not be mandatory.

You can also select both Delete Archived Redo Log Files and Delete Archived Redo Logs After They Have Been Backed Up The Specified Number Of Times to delete the archived redo logs that have been applied or shipped to all remote destinations, and also after taking into consideration whether the specified number of archived log backups have been backed up to a tertiary device.

In the case of a standby database, there are three main options:

- None

- Delete Archived Redo Log Files After They Have Been Applied To The Standby Database

- Delete Archived Redo Logs After They Have Been Backed Up The Specified Number Of Times

Choose an option and then click OK to save the backup settings in the control file of the database, since you are not using an RMAN catalog database.

You can confirm the changed settings by logging into RMAN at the command prompt and executing the `show all` command, which displays the RMAN configuration. First, change the Oracle environment parameters using the `oraenv` command and specifying the appropriate system ID (SID):

```
[oracle@myhostname ~]$ . oraenv
ORACLE_SID = [] ? saiprod
The Oracle base for ORACLE_HOME=/u01/app/oracle/product/11.2.0/dbhome_2 is /u01/app/
oracle
```

Then log into RMAN and issue the `show all` command:

```
[oracle@myhostname ~]$ rman target=/ nocatalog

Recovery Manager: Release 11.2.0.4.0 - Production on Mon Jan 11 15:00:14 2016
Copyright (c) 1982, 2011, Oracle and/or its affiliates.  All rights reserved.
connected to target database: SAIPROD (DBID=2261730455)
using target database control file instead of recovery catalog

RMAN> show all;

RMAN configuration parameters for database with db_unique_name SAIPROD are:
CONFIGURE RETENTION POLICY TO REDUNDANCY 1; # default
CONFIGURE BACKUP OPTIMIZATION ON;
CONFIGURE DEFAULT DEVICE TYPE TO DISK; # default
CONFIGURE CONTROLFILE AUTOBACKUP ON;
CONFIGURE CONTROLFILE AUTOBACKUP FORMAT FOR DEVICE TYPE DISK TO '%F'; # default
CONFIGURE DEVICE TYPE DISK BACKUP TYPE TO COMPRESSED BACKUPSET PARALLELISM 1;
CONFIGURE DATAFILE BACKUP COPIES FOR DEVICE TYPE DISK TO 1; # default
CONFIGURE ARCHIVELOG BACKUP COPIES FOR DEVICE TYPE DISK TO 1; # default
CONFIGURE MAXSETSIZE TO UNLIMITED; # default
CONFIGURE ENCRYPTION FOR DATABASE OFF; # default
CONFIGURE ENCRYPTION ALGORITHM 'AES128'; # default
CONFIGURE COMPRESSION ALGORITHM 'BASIC' AS OF RELEASE 'DEFAULT' OPTIMIZE FOR LOAD
TRUE ; # default
CONFIGURE ARCHIVELOG DELETION POLICY TO NONE; # default
CONFIGURE SNAPSHOT CONTROLFILE NAME TO '/u01/app/oracle/product/11.2.0/dbhome_2/dbs/
snapcf_saiprod.f'; # default
```

You can see that your modifications in the Backup Settings tabs of Enterprise Manager Cloud Control 13*c* have been saved as the configuration settings in RMAN. These are stored in the control file of the SAIPROD database.

The `# default` comment shows the unchanged configuration settings; conversely, the settings without this comment have been modified. The settings for the backup optimization is ON, controlfile autobackup is ON, and there is a parallelism of 1 using a backup set that is compressed. These are all the settings that we had changed in the preceding pages.

Scheduling a Full Backup

Now let's schedule the database backup.

In the Enterprise Manager Cloud Control 13c console, from the home page of the SAIPROD database, choose Target | Availability | Backup & Recovery | Schedule Backup. The Schedule Backup screen is shown in Figure 7-5.

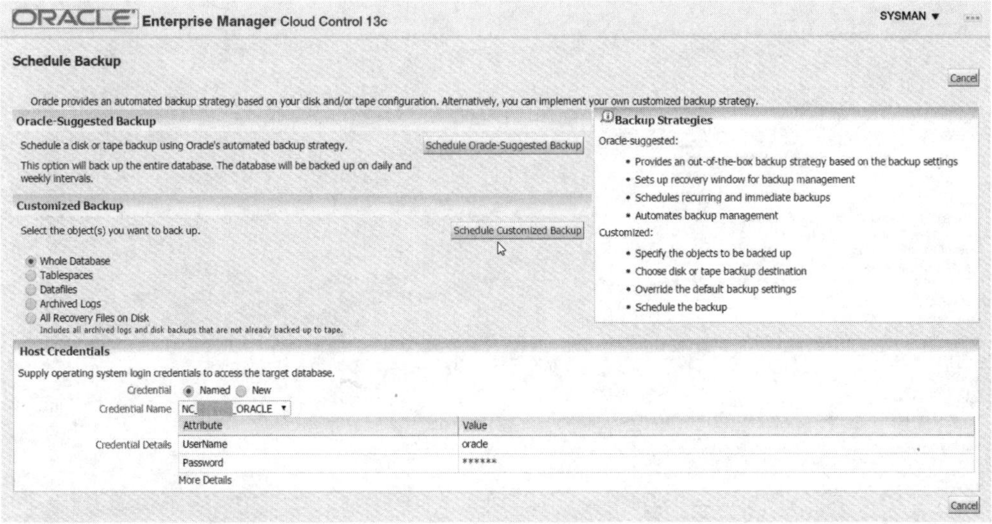

FIGURE 7-5. *Schedule Backup screen*

In the Customized Backup section, choose Whole Database. You can also back up individual tablespaces, datafiles, or only the archived logs in this section of the page. Pluggable database will appear in this list only if it is a 12c CDB. (The SAIPROD database is an 11g database and is used for schema self-service, as you have seen in the earlier chapters.)

The last option on this section is to back up All Recovery Files On Disk. Selecting this option enables you to back up the FRA of the database to tape. You can create the FRA only in an Oracle Database 10g or later (it is not possible in older versions). This is where all the RMAN backup pieces, image copies, and archive logs are stored. Hence, backing up the FRA is effectively a "backup of your backup."

The recommendation from Oracle is to back up the database to a less expensive disk (that is, not tier 1 or tier 2 disks) instead of tape, so that at least one database backup exists on disk. This backup location on disk is the FRA. This then enables the DBA to perform a fast recovery from the available disk-based backup in case of any production issues, rather than spend time waiting for the tape to be located and then the tape backup to be restored to the disk.

Oracle's practical concept of disk-based recovery is instrumental in reducing expensive outage to the business in the event of any such required database restores. The FRA can then be backed up to tape once a week, to enable offsite tape backups as well as onsite disk backups. This would be a suitable Oracle backup strategy.

After you have made your selection, click Schedule Customized Backup. The Schedule Customized Backup: Options screen is shown in Figure 7-6.

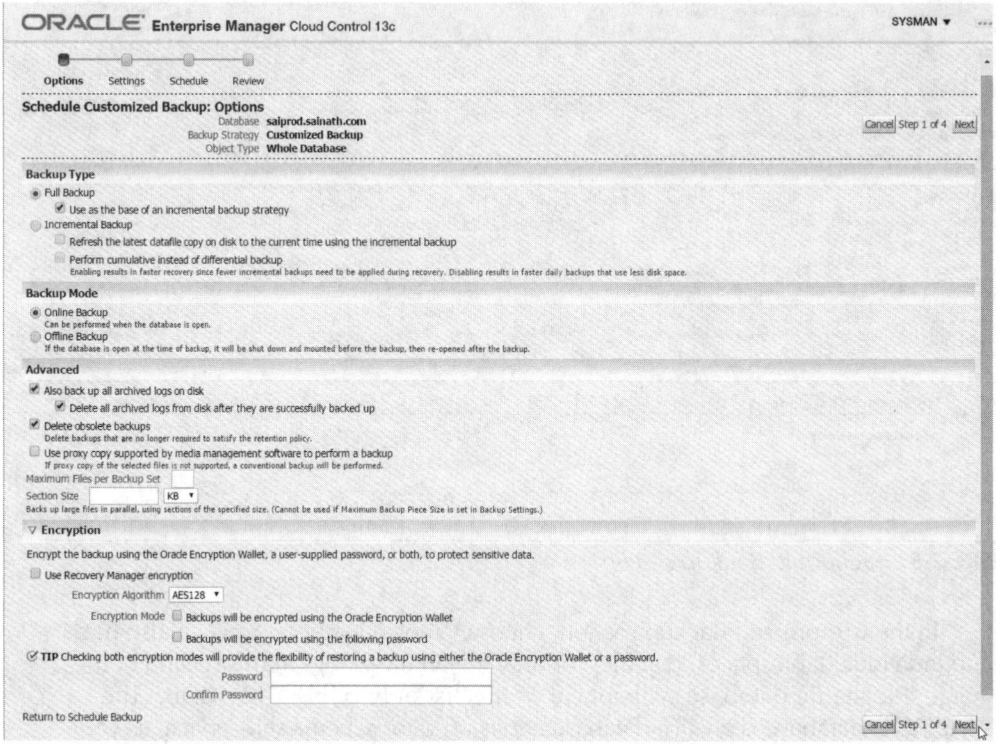

FIGURE 7-6. *Options for scheduling a customized backup*

For the Backup Type, select Full Backup. Also select the Use As The Base Of An Incremental Backup Strategy.

We'll set up a full backup of this type on Sundays and an incremental backup of the database to take place every day. For the Backup Mode, choose Online Backup. (Note that the database needs to be in ARCHIVELOG Mode for online backups to work; otherwise, only offline backups are possible.)

Scroll down to the Advanced section (Figure 7-6). Select the options Also Backup All Archived Logs On Disk and Delete All Archived Logs From Disk After They Are Successfully Backed Up. Selecting these options configures the backup to include all archive logs with the full database backup and deletes the archive logs from disk after they are backed up. Select the option Delete Obsolete Backups so that backups marked as obsolete will be deleted—these are no longer required according to the retention policy.

Expand the Encryption area on this page by clicking it. The Encryption settings applicable to your target database version are displayed. Backup Encryption was first introduced in Oracle 10*g* Release 2 and is available for all later versions such as Oracle 11*g* Releases 1 and 2.

Note that Oracle's Advanced Security Option is required if you want to create encrypted backups on disk with RMAN. You must make sure you are licensed to use this option; being licensed for the Oracle Database Enterprise Edition (EE) does not automatically mean you are licensed to use the Advanced Security Option. The alternative is to use Oracle Secure Backup (OSB) to create encrypted backups on tape. Again, you must make sure you are licensed to use this product. Oracle Secure Backup must be installed separately.

If you choose Use Recovery Manager Encryption, then as the Encryption mode you can select Encryption Using The Oracle Wallet as well as Encryption Using The Password. Specify the password in the appropriate field and confirm. This will encrypt the backup using both of these methods. This also offers greater flexibility, because you can use either the wallet or the password when the RMAN backup needs to be restored. By default, AES128 is selected as the Encryption Algorithm. We have decided not to use encryption in this case.

Click Next to move to the Settings screen shown in Figure 7-7.

FIGURE 7-7. *Setting destination media for backup*

The Disk Backup Location is displayed as the FRA. This is configured in our case as /u02/fast_recovery_area.

Click Next page to move to the Scheduling screen, where you set the day and time you want your backup to run. There are three options, as shown in Figure 7-8.

You can schedule the backup to run once either immediately or at a later time, or repeatedly at a schedule you define.

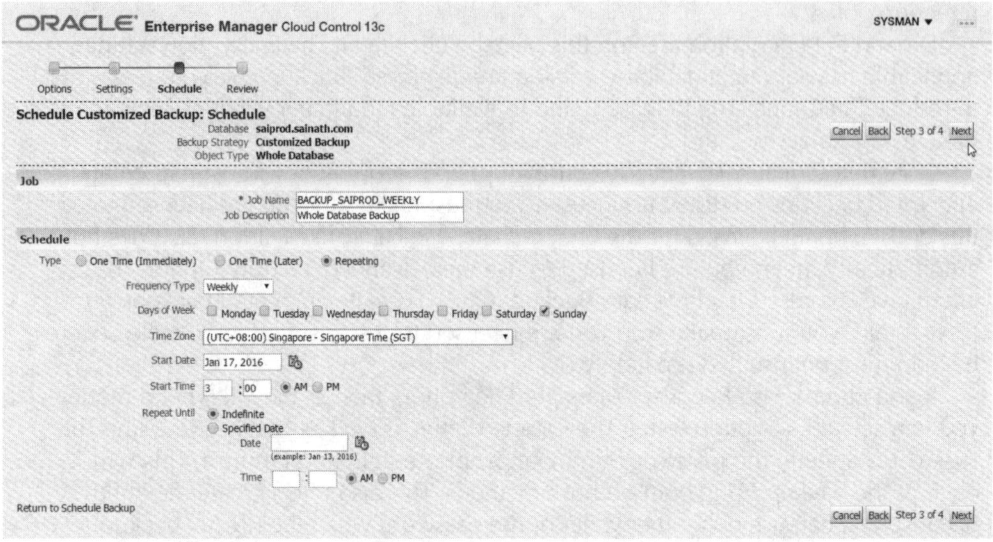

FIGURE 7-8. *Setting the schedule*

The One Time (Later) and Repeating options enable you to specify the start date and time you want the backup to run and the Time Zone associated with the time you specify. Choosing the Repeating option also lets you select the Frequency Type (for example, days or weeks) and the Frequency. For example, if you select Days as the Frequency Type and 1 as the Frequency, the backup will run once every day at the time you have specified.

In addition, whatever Frequency Type and Frequency you select, you can repeat it either indefinitely or until a specified date and time. The current time is shown as the suggested setting for the backup. We suggest 3:00 A.M. the following morning so that the backup will start at a time of low activity.

For Frequency Type, Weekly is selected since we want a full database backup to be performed each week. Under the Days Of The Week, select Sunday. Select the Repeat Until Indefinite radio button, so that the backup schedule will be continued indefinitely with no end date or time.

Click Next to open the Scheduled Customized Backup: Review screen shown in Figure 7-9.

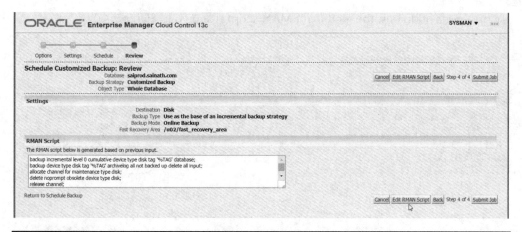

FIGURE 7-9. *Review of the scheduled backup*

As you can see, Enterprise Manager Cloud Control 13c has generated the RMAN script that will be used in the backup, based on the input criteria you identified in the previous screens. The script is as follows:

```
backup incremental level 0 cumulative device type disk tag '%TAG' database;
backup device type disk tag '%TAG' archivelog all not backed up delete all input;
allocate channel for maintenance type disk;
delete noprompt obsolete device type disk;
release channel;
```

The RMAN commands perform a full database and archive log backup. The archive logs are deleted after backup. After this, the maintenance commands that delete obsolete disk backups are executed. These actions are derived from what we had previously specified in the Cloud Control backup setup and backup schedule wizard pages.

Clicking Edit RMAN Script enables you to make modifications to the generated script before you submit it. Note that once modifications are made, it is not possible to return to the previous pages of the wizard. Nevertheless, you may want to change the RMAN script to include extra maintenance commands, such as the following, that will cross-check backups and archive logs and delete the backups and archive logs that have expired:

```
allocate channel for maintenance device type disk;
crosscheck backup;
delete noprompt expired backup;
delete noprompt obsolete device type disk;
crosscheck archivelog all;
delete noprompt expired archivelog all;
release channel;
```

After the additions, the modified RMAN script is shown in Figure 7-10.

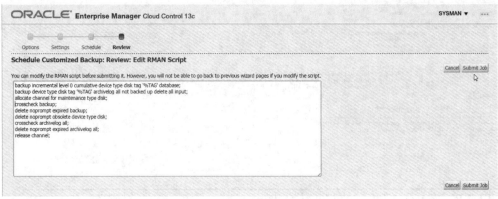

FIGURE 7-10. *Edit RMAN script*

Click the Submit Job button. After the job is submitted successfully, you can select View Job to display the status and the progress of the job. To view the output in detail, click the Backup step.

The RMAN output is displayed in the right pane; a partial view is shown in Figure 7-11. The full output log can be downloaded by clicking the Download button. You can download it at your end.

Understanding the Output

On studying the RMAN output log, you can gain a clear understanding of the entire sequence of events that occurred during the backup job.

First, a compressed full backup set for the database is created. This is an incremental level 0 cumulative backup that can be used as the basis of an incremental backup strategy. After this database backup is completed, a control file and SPFILE autobackup are created, because we identified earlier that we wanted these files to be automatically backed up with each backup.

A compressed archived log backup set is then created to back up the archive logs. After successful backup, because of the included delete input clause, RMAN deletes the archive logs from their disk location.

But what if you require any of these deleted archive logs during a database recovery? Oracle, during such a recovery—complete or incomplete—uses the archive logs to apply all the changes to restore the database to any point of time (the main purpose of archive logging). So some or all of the archive logs may be needed by the recovery.

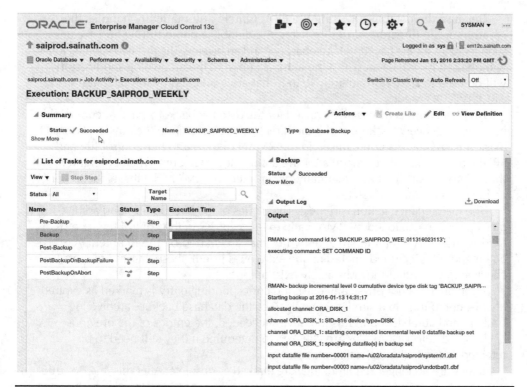

FIGURE 7-11. *RMAN output*

To achieve this in the past, DBAs performed a manual restore of the archive logs from their compressed UNIX tar archives and then place the restored archive logs in a directory accessible by the Oracle-controlled recovery. DBAs had to do manual searches for the necessary archive log files. This kind of manual searching and restoring of the archive logs is no longer needed in the case of RMAN, because this powerful utility from Oracle automatically locates the archive log backup sets needed and extracts the archive logs that are required for the recovery.

This is another tremendous benefit of using RMAN as your Oracle database backup mechanism. When the backup is completed, we see that the database backups, archive log backups, control file and SPFILE autobackups—all comprising RMAN backup pieces—are created in the appropriate subdirectories in the FRA as follows:

```
/u02/fast_recovery_area/SAIPROD/backupset/2016_01_13
/u02/fast_recovery_area/SAIPROD/autobackup/2016_01_13
/u02/fast_recovery_area/SAIPROD/archivelog/2016_01_13
```

Because the database is using the FRA, Oracle automatically handles the creation of the directory structure using the database name PROD and creates subdirectories for the backupset, autobackup, and archivelog. The first two subdirectories will be used for the backup and the autobackup, and the archivelog subdirectory will be used to store normal archive logs that are generated by the database in ARCHIVELOG Mode.

Another subdirectory is also created for the date the backups have occurred. This happens with every backup, and if the directory structure up to the day level doesn't exist, it is created. As you can see in the RMAN output, another control file and SPFILE autobackup takes place after the archive logs back up. Once configured, these autobackups will automatically occur after any RMAN database backup or archive logs backup completes.

The maintenance actions are next. The names of the backup files and archive log files have been cataloged by RMAN and exist as entries in the control file records. During the RMAN maintenance activities that are started by the maintenance commands you included (including the extra ones listed), these entries are cross-checked to verify that they physically exist on disk.

If the file does not physically exist, the corresponding entry is marked as expired (that is, not found). In a similar manner, since the database backup, archive log backup, and autobackup in this job have succeeded, the entries of the previous backup and autobackup files are checked to determine if they still need to be retained according to the retention policy.

If they are no longer required, they are marked as obsolete. After this, the `delete noprompt expired` and `delete noprompt obsolete` commands are used one after the other to delete all the expired or obsolete database backup, archive log backup, and controlfile backup entries, and also the archive log file entries from the controlfile records. In the case of obsolete records, the actual physical backup files are also deleted from the disk. The maintenance commands are obviously very important for space management.

Managing Backups

Enterprise Manager also lets you manage the current backups of the database. To do this, choose Availability | Backup & Recovery | Manage Current Backups from the Database menu to open the Manage Current Backups screen, shown in Figure 7-12. Here you can search for backups with a status of All, Available, Expired, Unavailable, or Other.

You can select to search contents of Datafile, Archived Redo Log, SPFILE, or Control File backups, with a Completion Time of Within A Month, A Week, Two Days, One Day, Within 8 Hours—or all of these.

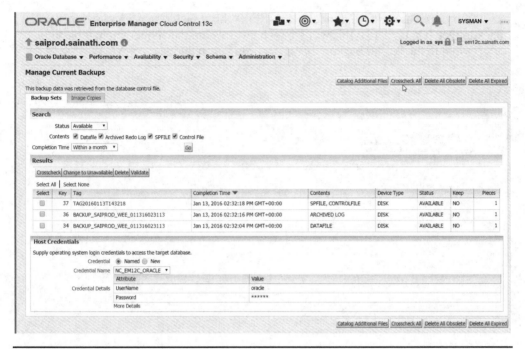

FIGURE 7-12. *Managing current backups*

You can use the options on this screen to perform the RMAN maintenance commands, such as Crosscheck All, Delete All Obsolete, and Delete All Expired. This is a fast and easy way to perform RMAN maintenance if you are running out of space.

You can also Catalog Additional Files, such as operating system copies of datafiles you may have taken, filer snapshot files, and so on. Cataloging enables RMAN to use these files.

Scheduling an Incremental Backup

We have prepared a full backup of the database to take place on every Sunday. The next step is to schedule a daily incremental backup.

Select Availability | Backup & Recovery | Schedule Backup from the Home page of the PROD database. In the Schedule Backup screen, select Whole Database in the Customized Backup section. Then click Schedule Customized Backup.

We proceed as we have done previously, but this time we select an Incremental Backup type (Figure 7-13). This will create a level 1 cumulative incremental backup as opposed to the level 0 backup that is occurring each Sunday.

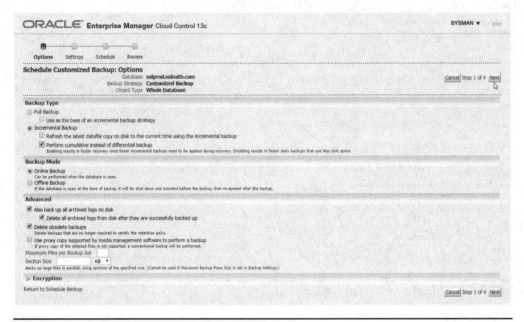

FIGURE 7-13. *Selecting an incremental backup*

Everything else stays the same as what we set up earlier, but the scheduling of this backup will be different, as shown after we click Next, in Figure 7-14.

As you can see in Figure 7-14, the incremental backup has been scheduled to take place on every day of the week except Sunday (when the full backup is taking place). The time selected is the same as before—3:00 A.M.—when database activity is assumed to be the lowest.

The RMAN script generated for the incremental backup is displayed in the Review screen, shown in Figure 7-15.

The RMAN script issues the `backup incremental level 1 cumulative…` `database` command.

After successful completion, examine the output. As you can see, the incremental backup of the database takes place followed by the autobackup of the control file and SPFILE. This is followed by the archive log backup and another autobackup.

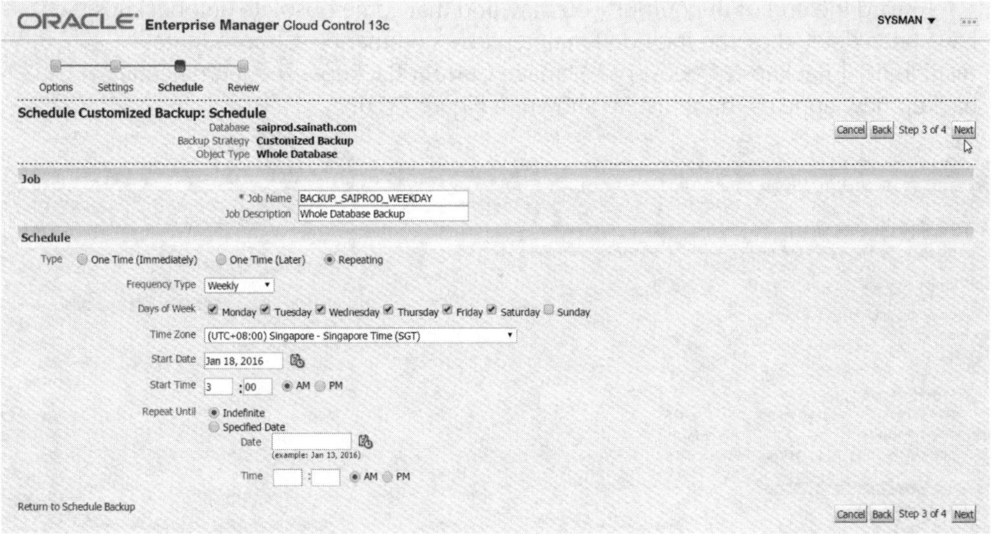

FIGURE 7-14. *Scheduling an incremental backup*

FIGURE 7-15. *Generated RMAN script for incremental backup*

Toward the end of the output, you may find that some obsolete autobackups have been deleted by the included maintenance commands. Choose Target | Availability | Backup & Recovery | Manage Current Backups. The incremental backup now appears in the list, as shown in Figure 7-16.

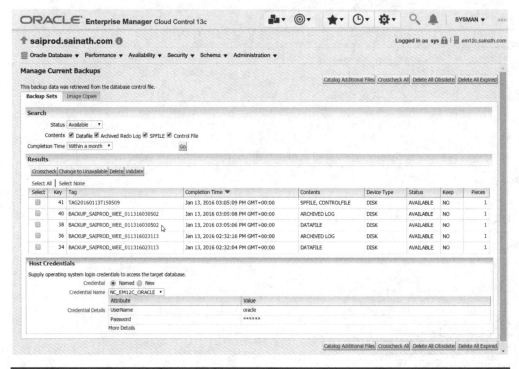

FIGURE 7-16. *List of backups*

Oracle Suggested Backups

On the Schedule Backup screen, you can also create an Oracle Suggested Backup, as shown in Figure 7-17.

If you choose to create this backup, an RMAN script is generated to perform backups according to this strategy. Using this automatically generated script, RMAN will perform a full database copy on the first backup. This will create datafile copies rather than RMAN backup pieces. Consequently, every day, an incremental cumulative backup will be performed that updates the datafile copies with all the changes.

The backups on disk are retained so that you can perform a full database recovery or a point-in-time recovery to any time within the past day. This means the datafile copy backup will always be up to date with production. The advantage is that you

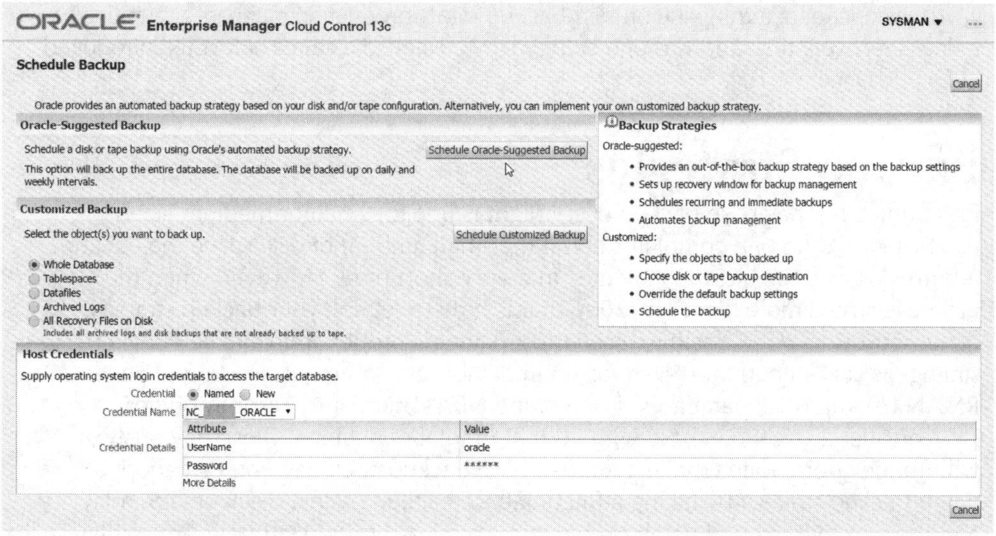

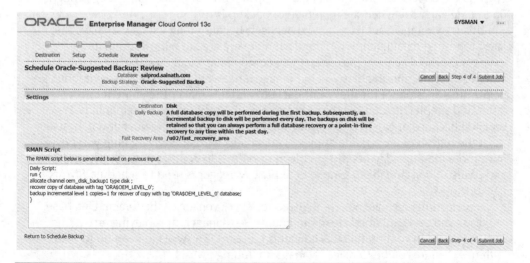

FIGURE 7-17. *Oracle suggested backups*

can easily switch over to this backup and use it as a production database in an emergency, without any restore of the backup or recovery of the database.

The generated RMAN script for the Oracle Suggested Backup is shown in Figure 7-18.

FIGURE 7-18. *RMAN script for Oracle suggested backup*

This concept of turning the on-disk backup into a production database dramatically reduces recovery time and was one of the many advanced features of RMAN introduced in Oracle Database 10*g*.

Backup Strategies

Executing a full database backup every night is fine for small or medium-sized databases, and no one complains about the small amount of disk space the backup requires or why the backup executes in a very short time. However, when the database size is more than, say, 200GB, it is time to rethink your backup strategy.

In most real-world database scenarios, having a proper and validated backup strategy is very important—even for small databases. And regular testing of your RMAN backup of all databases is one of the DBA's mandatory responsibilities.

Consider a larger database with 500GB in total of database files. Obviously, it will not be appropriate to take a full database backup each day. You can adopt a better backup strategy by taking a full database backup once a week on a Sunday and then an incremental database backup Monday through Saturday. This will enable you to recover the database to any point in time during the previous week by first restoring Sunday's full database backup and then applying the appropriate incremental backups.

The Oracle Database (10*g* and later) offers an extremely useful facility in RMAN that is not known to many DBAs. You can take an image copy of all the datafiles of a database once in a while, and then take an incremental backup each day that will actually refresh the image copy of the database with all the incremental changes. The datafile copies become the same as in production since they are being brought up to date each day when the incremental backup is run.

This is extremely useful for large databases, because they will always have the latest refreshed datafile copies in the flash recovery area to fall over to in an emergency. The datafile copies actually become the production database in this case. Technically, this enables you to manage a recovery of the database without performing a restore of the files from backup, and this makes the entire recovery faster and simpler. If you use a backup strategy that is based on incrementally updated backups, it can help minimize the media recovery time of your database.

If the refresh of the datafile copies occurs daily, then at recovery time you never have more than one day of redo (archived or online) to apply. This facility is visible and easily understandable if Oracle Enterprise Manager is used to schedule RMAN backups.

New features such as these, enhanced for every version of the Oracle Database, are displayed and explained clearly in Enterprise Manager, thus playing an important role in continuing DBA education. Every DBA wants to keep up to date with new features of the Oracle Database, including RMAN.

You can now set up the level 1 incremental backup for every weekday as before, but with this refreshing of the image copy as well, to keep the image copy up to date with your production database.

Database Group Backups

Beginning with Enterprise Manager Cloud Control 12*c*, DBAs can set up and schedule RMAN backups of an entire group of databases in one shot. This can be done for any databases from version 10.2 onward. All older versions of Oracle Database that are certified targets in Enterprise Manager, such as 9.2.0.8, cannot use the group backup feature, but their backups can still be set up individually from their Home page in Enterprise Manager.

Group backups can help ease the administrative burden because you would not need to set up and schedule backups of every database target in Enterprise Manager.

The first step is to set up a Database Group. From the Enterprise Manager main menu, choose Target | Groups. There are no groups displayed yet. Select Create | Group to create a group on the Add Target screen (Figure 7-19).

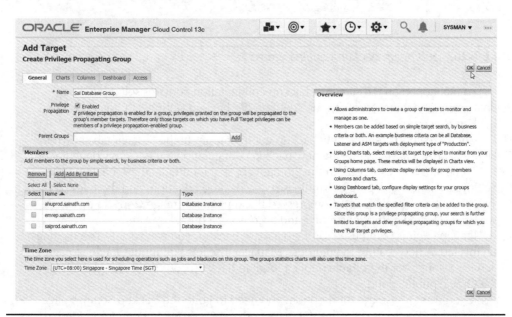

FIGURE 7-19. *Creating the Sai Database Group*

We are adding the Sai Database Group with three database targets as members of the group.

After you click OK and have created the group, open the Group home page by choosing Target | Groups and clicking the group name from the list. On the Group home page is a new menu option named Backup Configurations. This capability first appeared in Enterprise Manager Cloud Control 12*c*. Select this option to open the Backup Configurations screen (Figure 7-20).

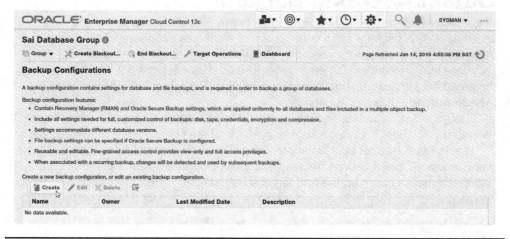

FIGURE 7-20. *Setting up backup configurations*

As mentioned on the screen, a backup configuration contains settings to back up a group of databases. It can also contain file backup settings if Oracle Secure Backup is used.

Click Create to create a new backup configuration. In the Storage tab shown in Figure 7-21, we have named the new backup configuration Sai Backup Configuration.

Three tabs are displayed. In the Storage tab, specify the database backup Disk Settings such as the degree of Parallelism, the Backup Location, and the Backup Type—a normal Backup Set, Compressed Backup Set, or Image Copy. In this case, we have selected a Parallelism of 3 and a Compressed Backup Set.

If a tape unit is being used for the database backup, you can specify Tape Settings on this tab. A new feature in Enterprise Manager 13*c* lets you input Oracle Storage Service Settings (for the Oracle public cloud) to back up your databases directly to the Oracle public cloud.

If you want to use the third option, you need to go to the Backup Settings page (refer back to Figure 7-2) for this database and enter a properly configured Media Management Vendor property to send backups to the Oracle cloud.

Note that before using the Oracle cloud as a backup destination for your database, you must first install the Oracle Database Cloud Backup Module and configure

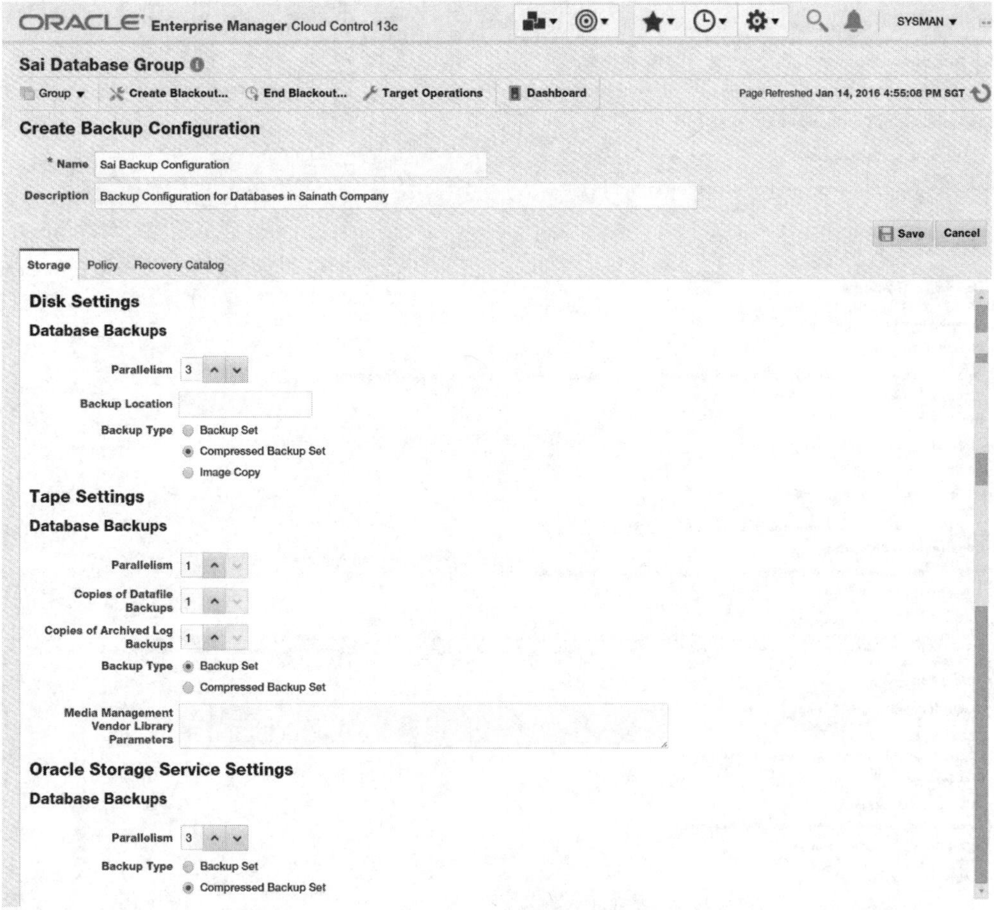

FIGURE 7-21. *Storage tab for Sai Backup Configuration*

RMAN of that database to use Oracle Database Backup Service as the backup destination. This is outside the scope of this chapter and is explained in the Oracle documentation manual "Using Oracle Database Backup Service" at https://docs.oracle.com/cloud/latest/dbbackup_gs/CSDBB/toc.htm.

As the next step, move to the Policy tab (Figure 7-22), where you can specify whether you want to override the RMAN retention policy set at the database level. In this case, we have chosen not to do so.

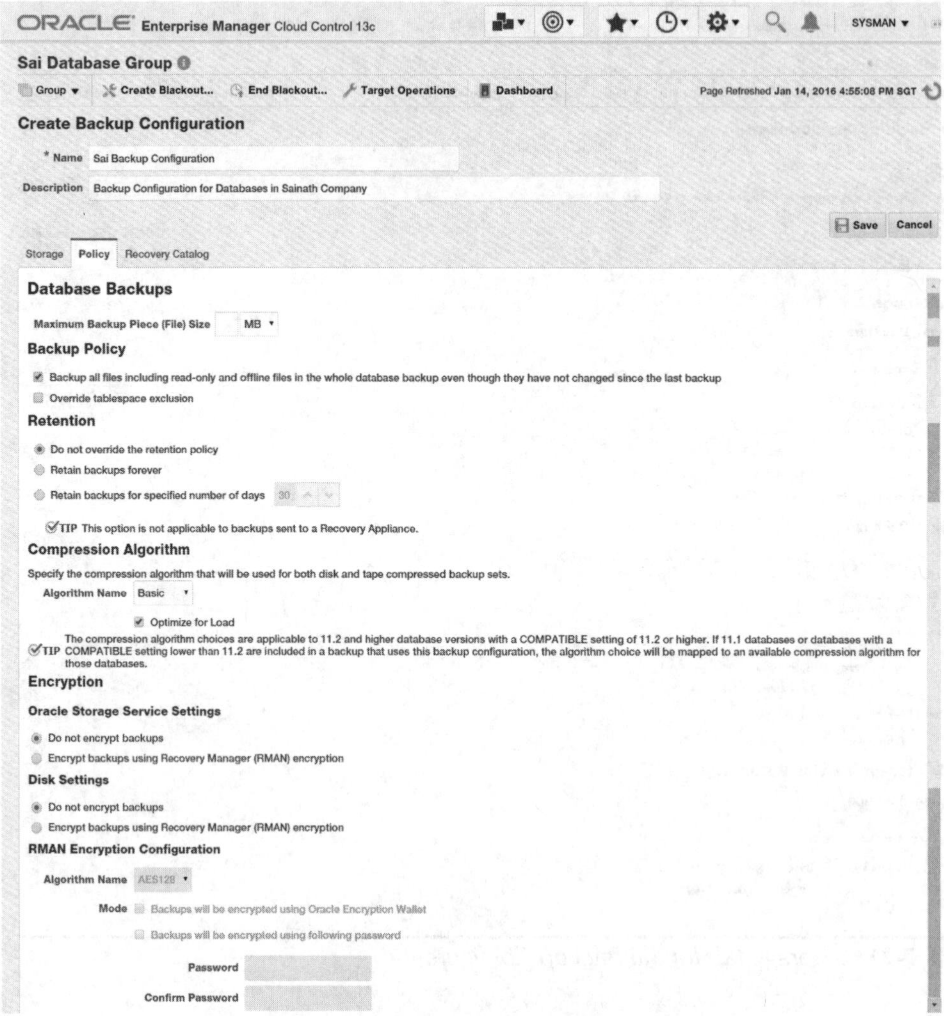

FIGURE 7-22. *Policy tab for Sai Backup Configuration*

On this tab, you can also set the Maximum Backup Piece (File) Size in MB and specify if you want to override the backup optimization and/or tablespace exclusion set at the database level. You can also set up the compression algorithm for all the databases that are to be backed up.

The lower half of the tab shows the Encryption options that you can choose for all the backups. You can encrypt the backups using RMAN encryption, with the default algorithm of AES 128-bit, using an Oracle encryption wallet and an optional password. We have decided not to encrypt the backups.

Move to the Recovery Catalog tab (Figure 7-23), where you can specify a common Recovery Catalog to be used for all the backups. In our case, we are using the Control File to record the backup for each database.

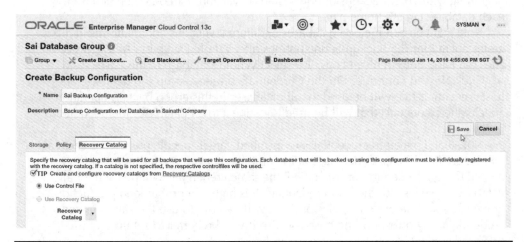

FIGURE 7-23. *Recovery Catalog tab*

Click Save. This will create the backup configuration.

Scheduling Group Backups

From the database Group menu, choose Schedule Backup. In the next screen, you can schedule a database backup for the entire group (Figure 7-24).

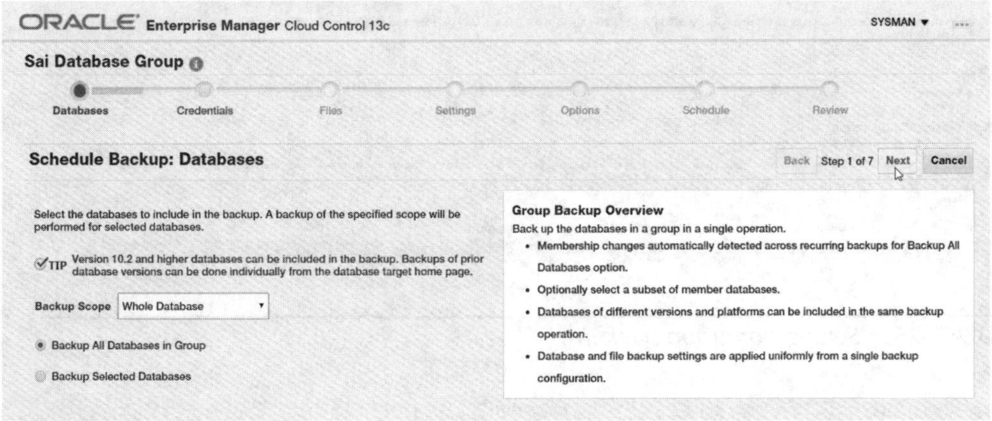

FIGURE 7-24. *Back up all databases in the group.*

When scheduling the group backup, you can decide whether to back up all the databases in the group or only selected databases from the same group.

This kind of group backup can be set up for any Oracle Database version beginning with 10.2. Backups of prior database versions can be scheduled from each database target's home page.

Note that you can include databases of different versions and platforms in a group operation. The Backup Scope options offer Whole Database, All Recovery Files On Disk, and Archived Logs. We select Whole Database in this case.

Click Next to continue. On the Credentials screen, set up the database and host credentials that will be used for all databases in this group backup operation. Specify the credentials that will be used to connect to all databases included in the backup operation.

Note that if preferred credentials are specified, target-specific preferred credentials will be obtained for each database at the time the backup operation executes. If named or new credentials are specified, the same credentials will be used for all databases. Likewise for the host credentials. It is highly improbable in production, however, that different databases or hosts will be able to use the same named credential and corresponding password, so it will be better to set up and use preferred credentials for each database and host.

Click Next. The Settings screen is shown in Figure 7-25.

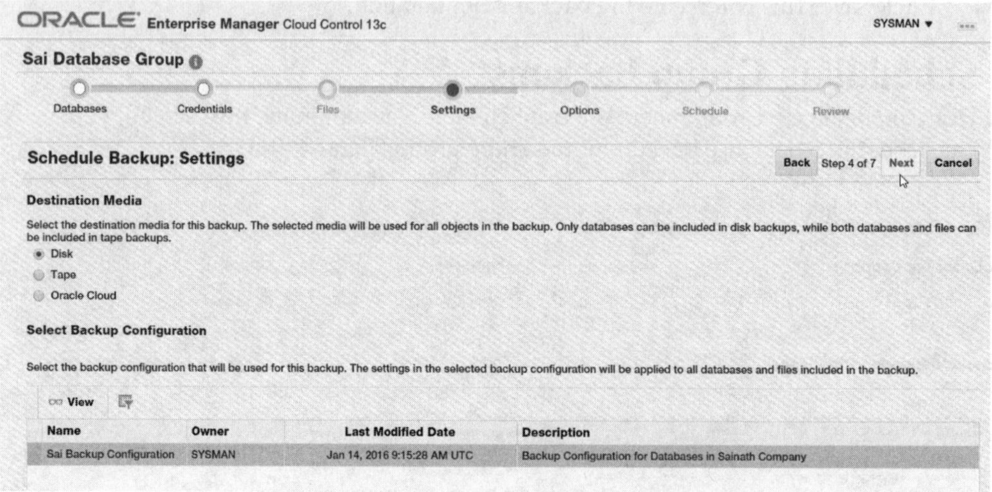

FIGURE 7-25. *Settings for group backup*

Specify whether Disk or Tape is to be used for the backup. You can also select Oracle Cloud at this step, provided it has been set up and RMAN configured to use the Oracle Cloud for backups, as explained previously. These settings will be applied to all the databases in the backup.

Select the Backup Configuration that was created previously and click Next to continue.

In the Options screen (Figure 7-26), specify whether you want a Full or Incremental database backup, Online or Offline, and other RMAN maintenance options similar to when setting up the backup for a single database.

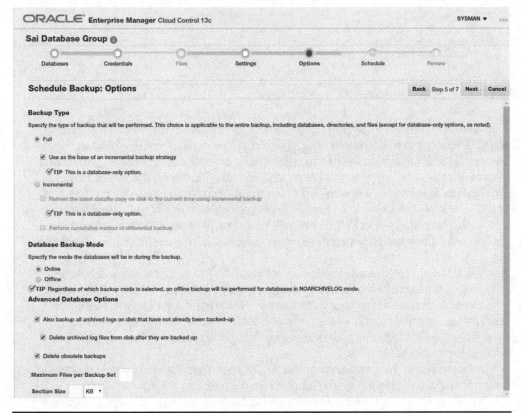

FIGURE 7-26. *Options screen for group backup*

Click the Next button. The Schedule screen is shown in Figure 7-27.

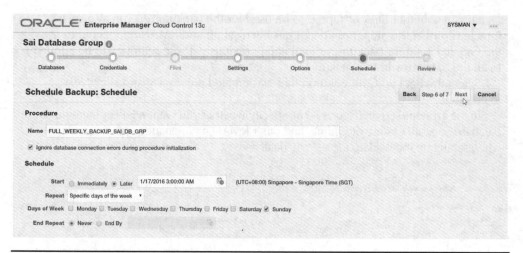

FIGURE 7-27. *Schedule screen for group backup*

Name the procedure appropriately. Select Ignore Database Connection Errors During Procedure Initialization. This is an important option, since by default the procedure will fail during the initialization step if an error is encountered connecting to any database in the group to be backed up, resulting in no databases being backed up. Selecting this option will cause the procedure to ignore such errors and continue, allowing all backups to run despite possible failure of individual backups.

In this screen, we specify that this Full backup will be executed on every Sunday at 3:00 A.M. Click Next to open the Review screen, where you can double-check the settings.

Click Submit to schedule this group backup. The job is submitted and initiates the RMAN backup of each database in the group, as shown in Figure 7-28, where the three databases in the group are shown. Note that if a database cannot be backed up for some reason—for example, if it is not in ARCHIVELOG Mode, and you have specified an online backup—then that particular database will be skipped during the group backup.

As we can see, the group backup is actually a sophisticated deployment procedure that iterates in parallel through the supplied list of databases and Oracle homes.

When working with a large number of databases, you can place all the databases in a group and start the group backup all at once, so that the actual backup of databases and archived logs will occur in parallel. Some companies may still want to space out the backups to avoid any potential network performance issues. However, currently, there is no way to throttle the group backup by forcing only a certain number of database backups to take place at any one time rather than all at once.

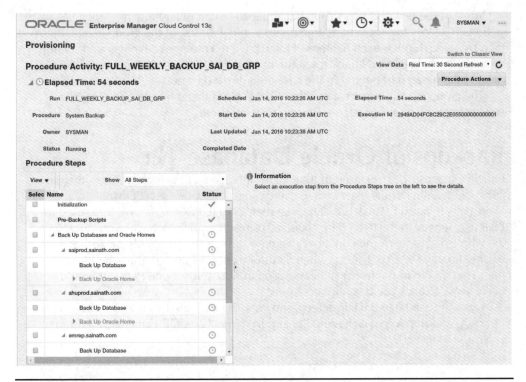

FIGURE 7-28.   *Checking the group backup procedure*

A workaround, however, could be to create smaller database groups, for testing, development, and production, and then do a group backup at different times to avoid all the backups running together. This would look something like this:

```
DB_Backup_Prod_Group_1
DB_Backup_Prod_Group_2
...
DB_Backup_UAT_Group_1
DB_Backup_UAT_Group_2
...
```

Coming back to our trial run, we can see that the deployment procedure has backed up the three databases, and this is followed by the archived logs being backed up for all databases.

You can select any of the steps and view the step details. You can also have a look at the output details for the group backup of any of the component database.

You can view the group backup jobs that are scheduled, running, or completed by selecting Enterprise | Provisioning and Patching | Procedure Activity from the Enterprise Manager menu. Group backups can also be viewed in the Manage Current Backups screen that was shown in Figure 7-16, earlier in the chapter.

You can see how the new group backup feature can potentially help the DBA in setting up RMAN backups for a large number of databases, at the group level rather than by going through each database Home page in Enterprise Manager and setting up and scheduling RMAN backups at the database level. If used carefully, this could save a lot of time, particularly in the case of large cloud sites.

The group backup feature also allows backup of Oracle homes and other file systems, provided Oracle Secure Backup is being used.

Backups of Oracle Database 12c

Oracle Database 12c (released in June 2013) included a new architecture—the concept of container databases (CDBs) and pluggable databases (PDBs).

If you are backing up a 12c Database such as AHUPROD (that we have used for PDB as a service in the preceding chapters) using Enterprise Manager, you can select the whole database, or the container database root, or the pluggable databases to be backed up in an RMAN backup when a customized backup is being scheduled. In the case of a cloud container database used to host self-service PDBs, it would make sense to back up the entire container.

Open the Schedule Backup screen, shown in Figure 7-29, by choosing Availability | Backup and Recovery | Schedule Backup from the 12c CDB Database menu in Enterprise Manager).

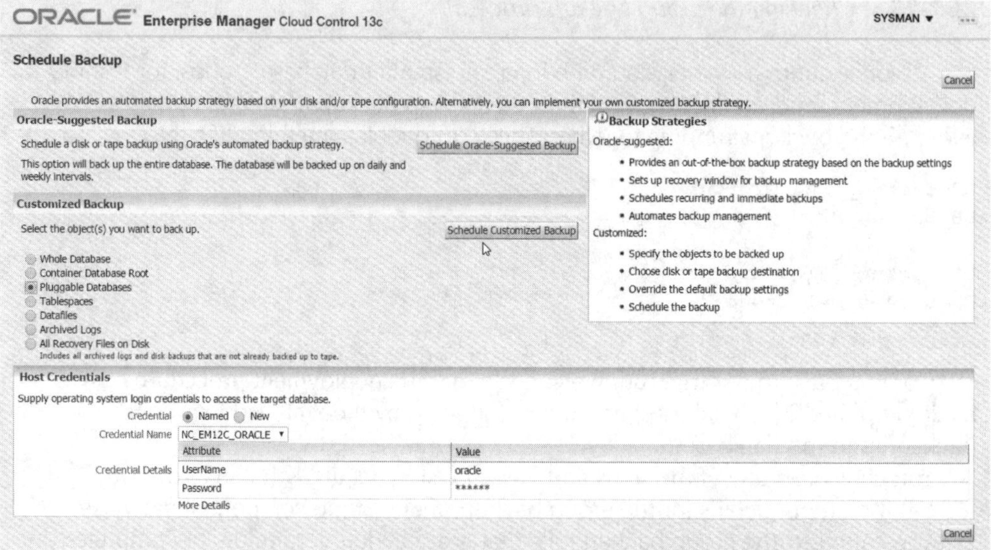

FIGURE 7-29.   *Customized Schedule Backup for Oracle Database 12c*

Select Pluggable Databases and click Schedule Customized Backup. In the next screen, you can see that only one PDB will be included in this customized backup (Figure 7-30), the SALES PDB. We can select multiple PDBs at this stage.

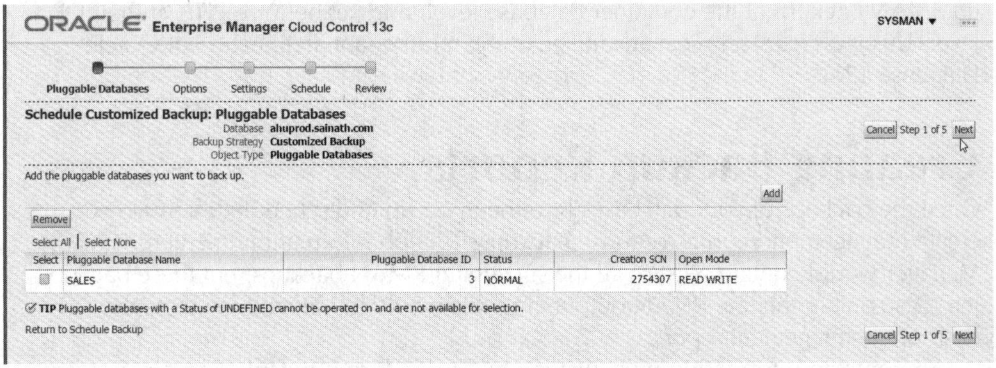

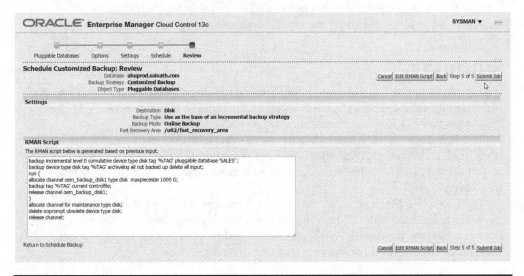

FIGURE 7-30. *Select PDBs to be included in customized backup.*

On the following pages, you can decide to perform either a full backup or an incremental backup of the selected PDBs, and then schedule the backup.

The RMAN script generated shows the pluggable database backup command (Figure 7-31). This demonstrates that RMAN understands the concept of CDBs and PDBs, in the case of Oracle Database 12*c*.

FIGURE 7-31. *RMAN script generated for a 12c CDB Database*

We have seen that RMAN cannot back up individual schemas, and it has always been difficult to perform point-in-time-recovery (PITR) at an individual schema level, since schemas can easily be distributed across multiple tablespaces.

The advantage in using PDBs in a container database is that you can easily set up RMAN backups at the container database level, and yet perform PITR at the PDB level. This is a clear technical advantage of the multitenant architecture of Oracle Database 12*c*.

Creating Backup Reports

Once the backups of your databases have been set up and scheduled, how do you create management reports for those backups? The job information in Enterprise Manager would contain a list of all the successful RMAN backups, but these backup job logs contain the raw RMAN output, and this would be difficult to use as the basis of a management report.

The backup information must instead be queried from outside Enterprise Manager. If a central RMAN recovery catalog is being used in the company, the catalog would have this information and could easily be queried. If a catalog is not being used, this backup information would be stored in the control file, and you would have to query each database's control file (using `V$ views`) to get the backup report.

Oracle BI Publisher, installed as an add-on to Enterprise Manager (out of the box from Release 4 onward) could be used for this purpose. However, note that if Oracle BI Publisher is used to query information from a source other than the Enterprise Manager repository database, a license would be payable for each database it accesses—so in this sense using a central recovery catalog would be preferable.

Summary

The Oracle Database has always required a solid backup strategy. The ability to set up and schedule database backups easily using all the modern techniques of RMAN has great importance, and this is done easily by Enterprise Manager.

This approach could potentially have more steps to follow than the traditional UNIX shell script and cron approach. But in the real world, these steps can be accomplished quickly using the wizards of Enterprise Manager, and all the scripts are autogenerated.

The Enterprise Manager Agent must first be installed on every database server you want to back up. But this task should not be included in time comparisons, since the Agent is the foundation of all Cloud Control activities for the server it is installed on, and RMAN backups are just one of its many uses.

Here is a summary of the numerous advantages for using the Cloud Control approach. If we consider only the time taken in the wizards, we can see that the use of Cloud Control will save a lot of time. Contrast this to the many hours required for the earlier manual approach of writing, setting up, and testing script files and running them via a cron.

As a result, expensive DBA time can be drastically reduced, which will be very helpful in a multiproject multidatabase provisioning environment. DBA time can be used in more productive ways rather than in mundane tasks such as shell script writing and setting up backups using the manual method for every new database that comes along.

The probability of human error is also reduced because of the RMAN wizard-driven backup setup. You can mistype almost nothing if you are merely selecting options.

The need to hire and retain skilled shell scripters is also largely eliminated, since Cloud Control generates its own RMAN scripts in Perl wrappers. No more tinkering with miles of shell scripts. At the most, you need to retain RMAN command expertise in case you need to add to the generated scripts. And RMAN is well known to most DBAs.

Debugging has also become a lot simpler because of less script lines to debug. In fact, you don't write any scripts! Enterprise Manager writes the RMAN scripts for you.

Maintenance and future enhancements are also a lot easier since a new backup job can be created using the Cloud Control console if any new backup requirements come up in the future or if the backup strategy needs to be changed. A previous job can be easily deleted from the job system.

When using the Enterprise Manager wizards, the latest advances in RMAN technology are available as options depending on the Database version in use. This immediately creates an awareness in the minds of the DBA of the new possibilities of RMAN, as the DBA starts using these new techniques—such as backup compression, encryption, block change tracking, and so on. Compare this to the scripted approach, where in many cases old 8*i* RMAN scripts are still being executed almost unchanged against new 9*i*, 10*g*, or 11*g* Databases, without using any of the RMAN enhancements.

Enterprise Manager enables centralized control of database backups. It is possible to set up and schedule RMAN backups for all the databases in a large company, use a consistent backup strategy, and refer to all past RMAN output logs at any time since they are stored in the Cloud Control repository. There is also no need to use a central RMAN catalog since information about the backups is centrally available from Cloud Control.

It seems likely that Enterprise Manager Cloud Control 13*c* will become increasingly popular with companies that are looking for an easy way to manage their ever-increasing databases. DBAs will understand that RMAN backups can be easily set up and scheduled for every new provisioned database and even those set up by self-service users—in a fraction of the time taken by the manual approach. And the group backup feature enables even faster RMAN backup setups for all the databases that are part of an Enterprise Manager group.

In the next chapter, we will examine how Enterprise Manager Cloud Control 13c aids in the setup and management of Oracle Standby Databases using Oracle Data Guard, another common DBA activity used for disaster recovery capability.

CHAPTER
8

Managing Standby Databases

Database and server downtime can be meticulously planned or totally unplanned, but as far as business dollars are concerned, any type of downtime is expensive. Planned downtime can be controlled and reduced by database technology features such as rolling upgrades or out-of-place patching. Unplanned downtime, however, means employees are idle during this time and corporate web sites are unreachable, which results in revenue loss as well as prestige loss.

High availability (HA) is the main strategy used by companies to protect themselves against server failures. For many years, this strategy has often been implemented as active-passive clusters, in which a storage unit, or logical unit number (LUN) is shared between two servers but accessed by only one primary server at a time. The database files are placed on the LUN, and the Oracle instance starts in memory on the primary server.

When the primary server goes down, the LUN is switched over to the secondary server, and the instance is restarted in the memory of that server. This active-passive technology was the HA norm in corporate computer centers for many years. The only complaint was that the cluster could automatically and unexpectedly switch over to the passive server, even for very trivial reasons, such as slow network access to the active server or database maintenance shutdowns by a naive DBA. In the latter case, the cluster-monitoring software had to be disabled before any maintenance work could be done on the database.

Oracle performed early experiments with active-active clusters, in which a single database had instances on multiple servers, and all accessed the same database storage. The first versions were known as Oracle Parallel Server (OPS), but at that time the clustering technology was primitive and used the shared storage itself to transfer blocks from node to node. This had performance limitations and was very complex to set up, and consequently implementations of OPS were rare; DBAs who were experienced in the workings of OPS could command large salaries.

The picture was decidedly and vastly improved when Oracle developed the new version of active-active clusters and called it Oracle Real Application Clusters (RAC) in Oracle 9*i*. This also introduced the latest Oracle technology of Cache Fusion where, in a technical breakthrough, the database used the memory (cache) of the nodes for the first time to transfer requested blocks across the interconnect.

The caches of the instances on the cluster nodes were "fused" together, in a manner of speaking. This technique improved cross-instance block-access performance dramatically and made Oracle Database 9*i* RAC a very practical and scalable alternative to the active-passive technology.

Oracle RAC afforded protection against server failures: if one of the nodes died, the database still stayed up since the other nodes kept on working. So it was a valid HA solution.

In addition, the other great advantage was that an optimum use of all the servers in the cluster could be achieved via intelligent load balancing. Because the load is shared across all nodes, the RAC cluster can scale out horizontally—which is impossible for an active-passive cluster to achieve, unless the application and database is broken up into pieces.

How long can you continue to slice and dice an application and a database? There is no need to do this in the RAC configuration so far as the majority of applications are concerned. And you can start with a small number of RAC nodes, rather than initially deploy a large server to accommodate future growth.

In late 2009, a new HA technology was introduced by Oracle: Oracle RAC One Node in Oracle 11g Release 2. This was RAC running on one node in a cluster with failover protection, the same as the active-passive scenario. The difference is that RAC One Node can easily be upgraded online to a full active-active RAC cluster. This is not possible with other third-party active-passive clusters.

The Old Days of Oracle Disaster Recovery

Suppose your entire computer site goes down, as in the case of an actual disaster, either natural or manmade. In such an event, HA technology will not be able to cope. All the active-passive or active-active RAC servers in the site hit by the disaster would be down. You would need a genuine disaster recovery (DR) solution, with servers ready to take over at a totally different site that was distant enough not to be affected by the disaster at the primary site.

The concept of DR was first applied to Oracle Database by the Oracle consulting team in response to client requests. A manual standby database was the main instrument, this being in the days before Oracle 7.3. The technique was very primitive, but it laid the groundwork for Oracle's ongoing concept of the standby database. The steps performed were basically as follows:

1. Install the Oracle Database software on the standby server.

2. Shut down the primary database, backup the database files, and FTP/SCP them across to the standby server.

3. Start recovery of the copied database.

4. Write UNIX shell scripts that keep transferring the archive logs from the primary database, as and when generated.

5. Write UNIX shell scripts that keep applying the archive logs on the standby database in a continuous recovery mode.

6.   Write UNIX shell scripts that monitor the primary and standby databases, making sure that logs are being applied and that no gaps exist in log application.

7.   Write UNIX shell scripts to failover to the standby database by stopping recovery and opening it up as a read-write database, in case the primary database was no longer workable due to a disaster.

There were issues with this process, however. Sometimes gaps arose in log applications—for example, if the archive logs were not transported to the standby server due to network failure. Or, even if they were transported, they were not applied on the standby because of some reason such as unauthorized deletion or perhaps hard disk corruption. The resulting gaps had to be resolved manually in all these cases.

Amazingly, there are some companies that even today deploy their standby databases using this manual scripted method. This is because they use the Oracle Database Server Standard Edition (SE) Database software—and only the Oracle Database Server Enterprise Edition (EE) provides the use of the latter-day advanced standby technology from Oracle. This is one of the many advantages of using EE instead of SE.

Oracle's official support for standby database mechanisms began with version 7.3 of the Database software. As each version was announced, this support was improved considerably. In Oracle Database 8.1.7, the logs were transported between the primary and the standby via the mechanism of Oracle SQL*Net, replacing the use of the FTP/SCP operating system utilities. The other new feature introduced at that time was managed database recovery, which automatically applied the transferred archive logs on the standby.

As a result of these new features, some of the manual scripts used previously in the standby setup were now unnecessary. This was a good first step toward automation.

But the big thing in version 8.1.7 was the Oracle Data Guard technology, a culmination and amalgamation of what came before. You had to download Oracle Data Guard separately from the Oracle Technical Network (OTN), and then unzip it in a subdirectory under your Oracle home.

Oracle Data Guard at that time was a collection of UNIX shell scripts, such as dgdeploy.sh, which deployed the Data Guard configuration of the primary and standby databases. It also had a command-line interface, Data Guard Control (dgdctl), which allowed you to perform a switchover or a failover to the standby database quite easily.

In Oracle 9i, Data Guard was promoted to become part of the Oracle kernel, resulting in better performance and memory management. A new Oracle background process, DMON, was now started specifically for the Data Guard broker, along with all the other background processes.

In versions 10g and 11g, Oracle Database continued the enhancements to the Data Guard technology. But the setup, configuration, and maintenance of Data Guard increased correspondingly in complexity, and human error became more likely in the entire process—especially if you had multiple primary databases and their corresponding standbys.

With the increasing complexity of Oracle Database 9i and later versions, a powerful tool was needed that would drive the setup and configuration of Data Guard. Oracle created just the right tool—Oracle Enterprise Manager 9i, with a wizard that allowed the setup of Data Guard standbys directly from the Enterprise Manager console. You could also perform a switchover or failover to the standby database from Enterprise Manager 9i itself, instead of doing it manually using the Data Guard command-line interface.

The next version of Enterprise Manager that handled standby databases was Grid Control 10g. This further enhanced the setup process of the Data Guard configuration and also included a monitoring interface for the entire configuration. Grid Control 11g, Cloud Control 12c, and Cloud Control 13c handle standby database creation and monitoring equally well, and in addition new features such as the snapshot standby database are also included.

In general, Enterprise Manager, with its new architecture and interface, has already proven to be of great help to the DBA. Cloud Control 13c excels at streamlining and automating many daily tasks of the DBA—tasks as varied as performance diagnosis, tuning, scheduling database and OS scripts, and setting up and scheduling database RMAN backups. Plus, it delivers and applies database patches and provides configuration management and monitoring of the application, database, OS, and the server. And of course, you can also easily set up Data Guard configurations, manage the configurations, switchover or failover the database, and monitor the primary and standby databases using Cloud Control 13c—an ideal way to set up disaster recovery capabilities in your company.

Oracle 9i, 10g, 11g, and 12c are all included in the Data Guard setup and management capabilities of Enterprise Manager Cloud Control 13c. Typically, a large company would have different versions of the database existing in their corporate environment.

The wizard for creating the standby database is a step-by-step, guided, error-free procedure to set up Oracle Data Guard. Using this procedure, you can set up the standby database on any server in your corporate space, provided the Cloud Control 13c agent is already installed and running on that server prior to the setup.

If a large company standardizes on the use of Enterprise Manager Cloud Control 13c, it could set up DR painlessly and seamlessly, for Oracle databases in the entire corporate complex. A lot of time can be saved, customized scripts can be eliminated, and human error greatly reduced.

Note that the base installation of Enterprise Manager Cloud Control 13*c* includes several features free of charge with the purchase of any Oracle software license or support contract. Configuring and viewing standby databases using Enterprise Manager is covered under the Base Database Management Features, as explained in the Oracle Enterprise Manager Licensing Information guide.

Initial Steps

On every host that you want to monitor and manage via Enterprise Manager Cloud Control 13*c*, the Enterprise Manager 13*c* Agent must be installed and running. This is a prerequisite because the agent is used to communicate between the targets on the host and the Oracle Management Service (OMS).

Presuming that the primary database is already managed by Cloud Control 13*c*, you can turn to the server that is to be used as the standby. As per Oracle Data Guard requirements, the primary and standby databases should have the same OS, but the OS patch set release may be different.

The requirement for the Oracle software is stricter. The Oracle software should be the same version—including the Oracle patch set release.

First, on the standby server, install the Enterprise Manager Cloud Control 13*c* agent, using a separate agent home located on the target server. Once the EM Agent starts communicating with the central OMS, all information about the standby server is available on the central Enterprise Manager site.

After the Agent installation is complete, the standby server has the agent home, but there is no Oracle home since the Oracle database software has not been installed on this server.

You can manually install the Oracle Enterprise Edition (EE) software from a CD or use the downloaded installation files from the Oracle Technology Network (OTN). Make sure that you do not install the Standard Edition (SE), which does not allow the use of Data Guard.

Another faster and better way to do this is to use the provisioning capabilities of Enterprise Manager Cloud Control 13*c*. From the Enterprise Manager console menu, choose Enterprise | Provisioning and Patching | Database Provisioning. Then select the Deployment Procedure Provision Oracle Database. This enables you to deploy the Oracle software from Enterprise Manager itself, from a pre-stored gold copy known as a Profile in the Software Library. This capability requires the license for the Enterprise Manager Database Lifecycle Management Pack (DBLM).

After the deployment procedure has completed, a new Oracle home exists on the standby server. It is now possible to proceed with the creation of the standby database.

Adding a Standby Database

On the Enterprise Manager Cloud Control 13c console, choose Targets | Databases, and select the ahuprod production database from the list of databases. This will be the primary database in the Data Guard configuration. It is a 12c container database and is being used in our Pluggable Database as a Service, as you have seen in an earlier chapter.

On the Database home page, select Availability | Add Standby Database, as shown in Figure 8-1.

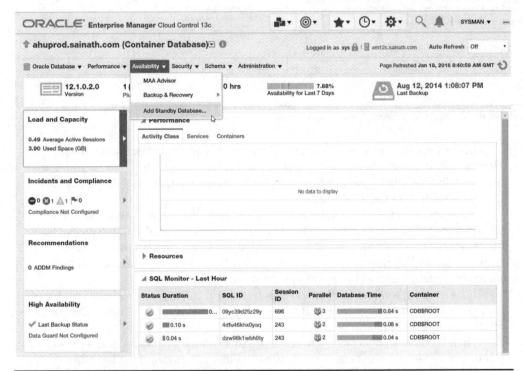

FIGURE 8-1. *Adding a standby database*

If you have not logged in to the ahuprod database, you will have to do so at this point from the login screen.

Connect with SYSDBA privileges. This is required for setting up and monitoring Oracle Data Guard in all databases up to version 11g. Oracle Database 12c includes a new privilege, SYSDG, which allows a user to perform Data Guard operations—in other words, you can now manage Data Guard without SYSDBA privileges. This is a popular enhancement request that has finally been fulfilled in the 12c database version.

The wizard displays the next screen (Figure 8-2), where you can select the type of standby database that is to be created.

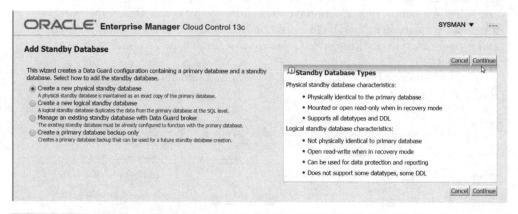

FIGURE 8-2. *Selecting the standby type*

You can create a new physical standby or a new logical standby database. However, if you have already set up a standby database manually, you can add it at this stage in the Data Guard configuration by choosing Manage An Existing Standby Database With Data Guard Broker.

Beginning with Oracle Database 12*c*, when you add a standby database, the wizard does not continue unless all the pluggable databases (PDBs) in the production container database (CDB) are open. If any PDB is closed, an error is displayed: "One or more pluggable databases are not open. The container database and the pluggable databases must be open to perform this operation."

The wizard is therefore CDB- and PDB-aware and can create a standby database from a container database. Note that the standby created is for the entire CDB and all PDBs contained in it.

When it comes to choosing between a physical standby database and a logical standby database, in most cases, a physical standby database is best because it offers better performance. The logical standby also has a number of restrictions as to the data types allowed.

Hence, select Create A New Physical Standby Database to use a physical standby. Click Continue. The wizard now starts, displaying the first step, as shown in Figure 8-3.

Choose the backup method that will be used to create the physical standby. The easiest option is to perform an online backup of the primary database, via Oracle RMAN. The backup files will be copied by RMAN to the standby server. This will provide the most recent copy of the primary database—the physical standby being an exact copy of the primary.

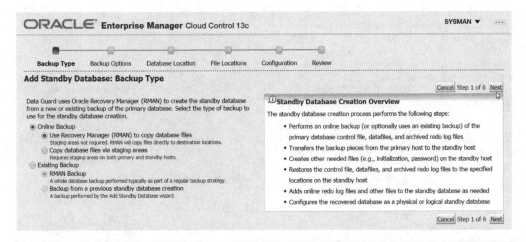

FIGURE 8-3. *Selecting the backup type*

It is also possible to use an RMAN database backup that has been created previously—perhaps your nightly backup. You can do this if the database is large and you do not want to take an online backup again at this time.

Select Online Backup and Use Recovery Manager (RMAN) To Copy Database Files. In this case, the files will be copied by RMAN to the standby server, so a staging area is not required. However, if you wish, you can select a staging area to be used—this must be on both the primary and standby servers.

Click Next to continue. The Add Standby Database: Backup Options screen is shown in Figure 8-4.

On this page, you can enter the number of concurrent file copy processes. These are the parallel channels to be used by RMAN to copy the database files to the standby. You can increase the number of processes (2, by default), but only if sufficient bandwidth is available. Using a higher number of processes can potentially speed up the creation of the standby.

A new section staging area is visible on this page only if you are creating the standby on a separate host (not the primary host) and you are not using RMAN to copy the database files in the case of an 11g or later database; in this case, you selected Copy Database Files Via Staging Areas under the Online Backup option shown in Figure 8-3.

In our case, however, we are using RMAN, so Figure 8-4 does not display this section—indicating the dynamic nature of the screens.

The wizards also display different options in different database versions, as per the technological advances in that version.

The Primary Host Login credentials can also be specified on this page. You can use existing Preferred or Named Credentials, or create a new credential.

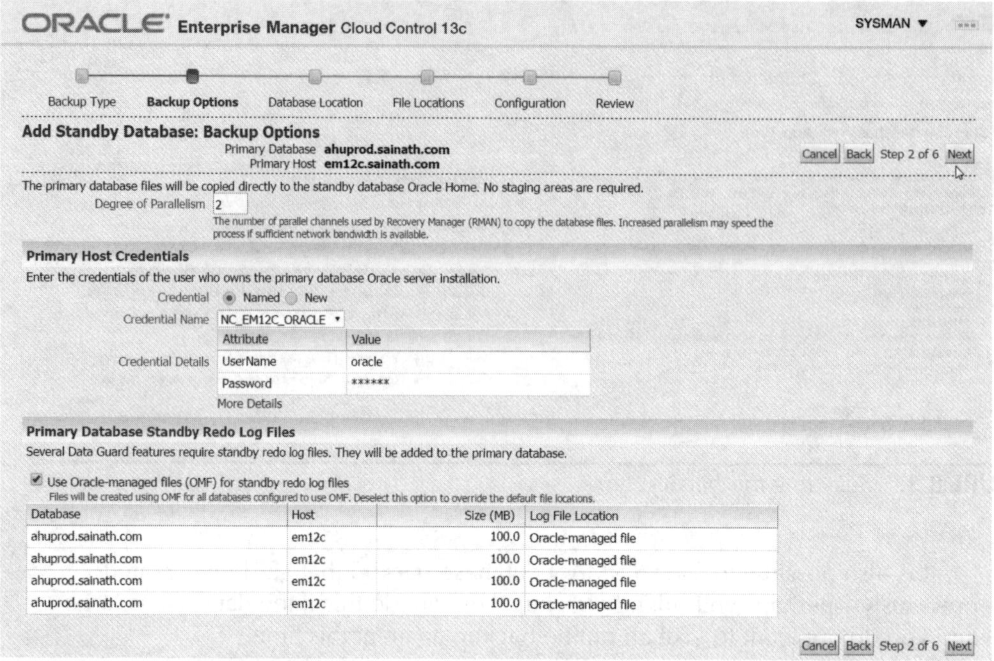

FIGURE 8-4. *Backup Options*

The section Primary Database Standby Redo Log Files indicates that standby redo log files will be added to the primary database automatically by the wizard.

Standby redo logs are very important for the functioning of Data Guard. Their main purpose is to enable real-time apply of redo data onto the standby by populating the standby logs with redo data almost simultaneously with populating the redo logs in the primary database. So you don't have to wait for the archive log to be shipped to the standby. This means that if there is a failover, the loss of data will be minimal in the case of real-time apply, since no redo data would have been lost.

Consequently, when either the synchronous or asynchronous redo transport modes are used, Standby redo logs are mandatory at the redo transport destination. They are also created at the primary database, because they enable the primary database to receive redo log data after it assumes the standby database role.

To simplify the setup, you can use Oracle-managed files (OMFs) for the standby redo files. Oracle will automatically name and place these files in the directory structure. If you don't use OMF files, you have to specify your own filenames and directory locations.

Click Next to continue. You can specify the Standby Database Attributes on the next screen (Figure 8-5).

FIGURE 8-5. *Standby Database Attributes*

The Instance Name must be unique on the standby host. In our case, we have named the standby database ahustby. Choose File System as the Database Storage type for the standby database. The other alternative is Oracle Automatic Storage Management (ASM). You can specify this as the standby database storage only if an ASM instance is operating on the standby server.

Under Standby Database Location, enter the hostname and the Oracle home location for the standby database you are creating. You can select this from a list of host targets in the Cloud Control 13c system. The list displays only hosts with the same operating system used by the primary, since this is a requirement of Oracle Data Guard, and Enterprise Manager Cloud Control 13c understands this. The Oracle home for the standby also needs to be of the same version as the Oracle home on the primary. Refer to My Oracle Support (MOS) Note 413484.1 for a list of Data Guard configurations that are supported.

Differences in Oracle home binaries may exist due to word sizes at the database or OS level, or due to different hardware, different operating systems, or even different Linux distributions. In such cases, you cannot create standby databases using the Data Guard standby creation wizard on such different primary and standby platforms, but you can create them manually and then start to manage them with the Data Guard broker (the option to manage existing standby databases is shown in Figure 8-2, earlier).

Remember that the new Oracle home has already been created on the standby host. In our case, for demonstration purposes, we are creating the standby database on the same host, but in real life it will be on a separate host in a different location in the same city or a different city, since that is the only way a true disaster recovery can be achieved—in other words the primary and standby should not both be on the same host.

Click Next to continue. As shown in Figure 8-6, you can specify the Standby Database File Locations in this screen.

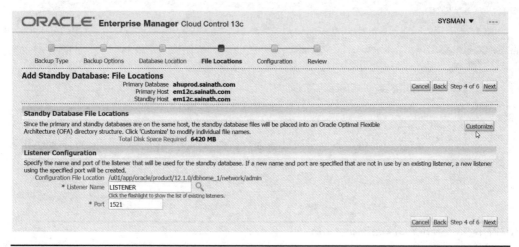

FIGURE 8-6. *Standby file locations*

You can accept the suggested Optimal Flexible Architecture (OFA) locations or change the file locations manually by clicking the Customize button.

In Figure 8-7, you can see the suggested file locations for the standby database. Based on OFA, the locations for datafiles and tempfiles are as follows:

- /u01/app/oracle/oradata/ahustby/system01.dbf

- /u01/app/oracle/oradata/ahustby/temp01.dbf

If you want to change these locations, you can do it for a group of files at a time—for all datafiles together or for tempfiles, log files, and control files that are shown throughout the page. Scroll down to the Log Files and Control Files sections shown in Figure 8-8.

You can set the location for all the different groups of files, a group at a time, to an appropriate directory. In the Log Files section, the standby redo logs recently added to the primary database are shown as Oracle-managed files.

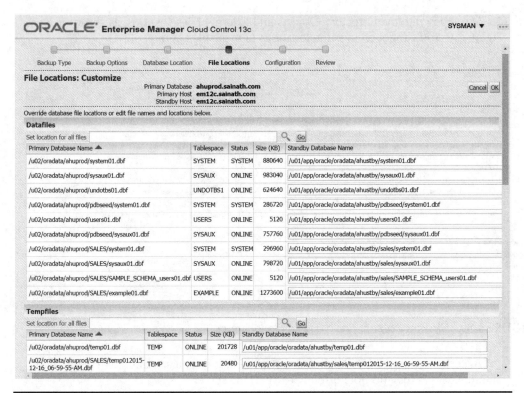

FIGURE 8-7.   *Customized file locations for datafiles and tempfiles*

Log Files

Set location for all files

Group ▲	Primary Database Member	Size (KB)	Standby Database Member
1	/u02/oradata/ahuprod/redo1.log	102400	/u01/app/oracle/oradata/ahustby/redo1.log
2	/u02/oradata/ahuprod/redo2.log	102400	/u01/app/oracle/oradata/ahustby/redo2.log
3	/u02/oradata/ahuprod/redo3.log	102400	/u01/app/oracle/oradata/ahustby/redo3.log
4	Oracle-managed file	102400	Oracle-managed file
5	Oracle-managed file	102400	Oracle-managed file
6	Oracle-managed file	102400	Oracle-managed file
7	Oracle-managed file	102400	Oracle-managed file

Control Files

Set location for all files

Primary Database Name ▲	Standby Database Name
/u02/oradata/ahuprod/control01.ctl	/u01/app/oracle/oradata/ahustby/control01.ctl
/u02/fast_recovery_area/ahuprod/control02.ctl	/u01/app/oracle/oradata/ahustby/control02.ctl

FIGURE 8-8.   *Log file and control file locations*

Scroll down to the Directory Objects and External Files sections, as shown in Figure 8-9. You cannot change the locations of these files here.

Directory Objects

Previous 1-10 of 14 ▼ Next 4

Directory Name ▲	Primary Directory Path	Standby Directory Path
ORACLE_BASE	/	/
DATA_FILE_DIR	/u01/app/oracle/product/12.1.0/dbhome_1/demo/schema/sales_history/	/u01/app/oracle/product/12.1.0/dbhome_1/demo/schema/sales_history/
OPATCH_LOG_DIR	/u01/app/oracle/product/12.1.0/dbhome_1/QOpatch	/u01/app/oracle/product/12.1.0/dbhome_1/QOpatch
DATA_PUMP_DIR	/ade/b/1281484529/oracle/admin/seeddata/dpdump/	/ade/b/1281484529/oracle/admin/seeddata/dpdump/
SS_OE_XMLDIR	/ade/b/1281484529/oracle/demo/schema/order_entry/	/ade/b/1281484529/oracle/demo/schema/order_entry/
ORACLE_HOME	/	/
OPATCH_INST_DIR	/u01/app/oracle/product/12.1.0/dbhome_1/OPatch	/u01/app/oracle/product/12.1.0/dbhome_1/OPatch
SUBDIR	/ade/b/1281484529/oracle/demo/schema/order_entry//2002/Sep	/ade/b/1281484529/oracle/demo/schema/order_entry//2002/Sep
XSDDIR	/u01/app/oracle/product/12.1.0/dbhome_1/rdbms/xml/schema	/u01/app/oracle/product/12.1.0/dbhome_1/rdbms/xml/schema
MEDIA_DIR	/u01/app/oracle/product/12.1.0/dbhome_1/demo/schema/product_media/	/u01/app/oracle/product/12.1.0/dbhome_1/demo/schema/product_media/

Previous 1-10 of 14 ▼ Next 4

External Files

Name ▲	Directory Name	Size (KB)
sale1v3.dat	DATA_FILE_DIR	1
qopiprep.bat	OPATCH_SCRIPT_DIR	2

Cancel OK

FIGURE 8-9. *Directory object and external file locations*

Accept the changes by clicking OK. The directories you specified will be created automatically if they do not currently exist on the server.

Next, you're returned to the File Locations screen. Click Next to continue to the Standby Database Configuration screen (Figure 8-10).

The parameters controlling the standby can be set here. You can add the Database Unique Name of the standby database via the DB_UNIQUE_NAME parameter. This is set to ahustby. No other database in the company should have the same name.

Next, set the Target Name of the standby database. This is used as the display name of the target on the Enterprise Manager Cloud Control 13*c* screens. This name can be the same as the unique name: ahustby.

You can also change the Standby Archive Location and configure it as the Fast Recovery Area (FRA). This is where Data Guard will place the archived redo logs that are received from the primary database. Normally, the size of the FRA should be set to twice the database size. However, this estimate is treated differently in different companies. In our case, we chose 7500MB.

The Enterprise Manager monitoring credentials for Data Guard are also specified on these screens. A SYSDBA login should be used if you intend to monitor a mounted physical standby database (only a SYSDBA can connect to a mounted database); otherwise, use ordinary credentials—for example, the dbsnmp user to satisfy the security requirements of your company.

Scroll down to the Data Guard Broker section, shown in Figure 8-11.

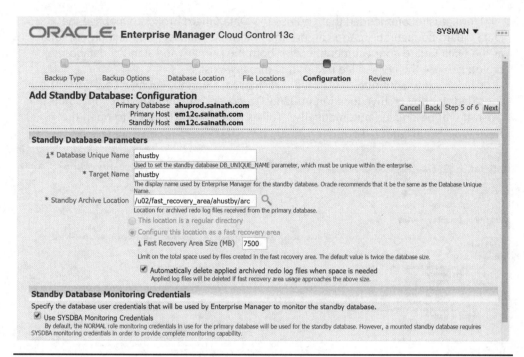

FIGURE 8-10.   *Configuring the standby database*

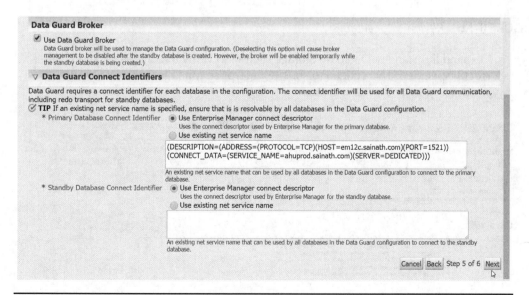

FIGURE 8-11.   *Data Guard Broker section*

Here, it is recommended that you use the Data Guard Broker to manage the Data Guard configuration. You can use the Enterprise Manager connect descriptors as the Data Guard connect identifiers for both the primary and standby databases, or you can use the net service names that already exist.

Click Next to continue. A warning is displayed: "Standby Archive Location - The specified standby archive location (/u02/fast_recovery_area/ahustby/arc) does not exist. It will be created automatically." This is fine. Click Continue to open the Review screen (Figure 8-12).

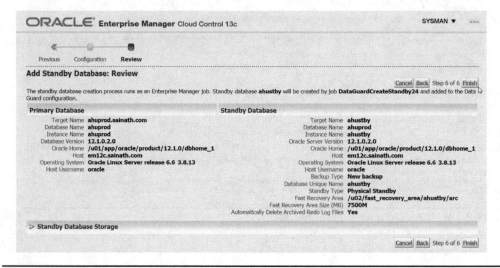

FIGURE 8-12. *Review your settings*

Expand the Standby Database Storage section to verify that all the locations are correctly specified. Then click Finish. The Enterprise Manager job system now submits the standby database creation job (Figure 8-13).

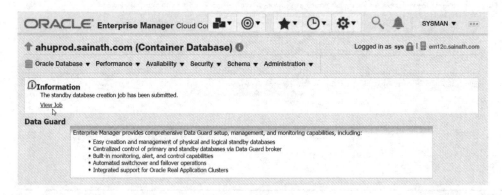

FIGURE 8-13. *The job has been submitted*

Using the techniques you selected in the Wizard screens, Enterprise Manager creates the standby database, using an RMAN backup and copy or the other methods.

You'll see the Data Guard home page (Figure 8-14) for this database. You'll use this screen later on to monitor the Data Guard operations. Choose View | Job if you want to monitor the progress of the standby creation job.

FIGURE 8-14. *Job completed successfully*

The standby creation job finally completes after a period of time that depends on the size of the primary database and the method chosen to create the standby database. At this point, choose Targets | Databases to see a list of Enterprise Manager Cloud Control 13c primary and standby databases, as shown in Figure 8-15.

You can see the Database Instance: Container, Primary and the Database Instance: Container, Physical Standby. The status of both databases are displayed as up. The PDB in the standby is down, and that's OK since the standby works at the CDB level.

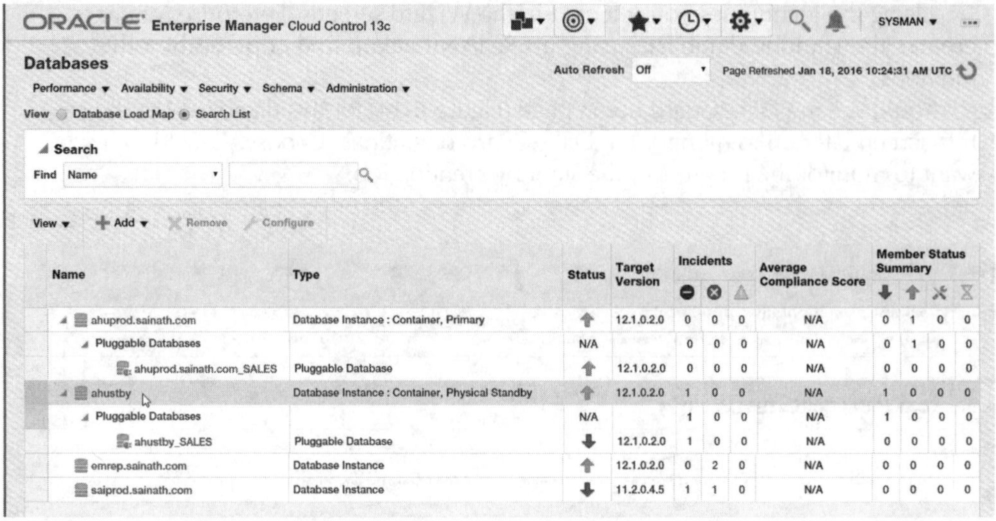

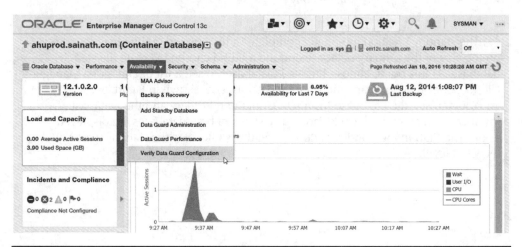

FIGURE 8-15. *Database target list*

Menu Options for Data Guard

Move to the primary database's home screen in Enterprise Manager Cloud Control 13*c*. Choose Availability to see options (Figure 8-16) that pertain to Data Guard. These options are shown because Enterprise Manager is aware there is a Data Guard configuration that is active for this primary database.

FIGURE 8-16. *Data Guard menu options*

You can choose from the options Data Guard Administration, Data Guard Performance, and Verify Data Guard Configuration. These options are in addition to Add Standby Database that was mentioned previously.

Select Verify Data Guard Configuration to go through scripted and automatic checks on the Data Guard configuration to make sure the machinery of log transport and application works as expected, without actually performing a failover or switchover.

Note that a "Data Guard Internal error" message may be displayed immediately after you select the verification for the first time. You can simply ignore the error and select Verify Data Guard Configuration again. This verification is recommended to be performed on initial setup as well as periodically. Various primary and standby database settings are verified by this step, as shown in Figure 8-17.

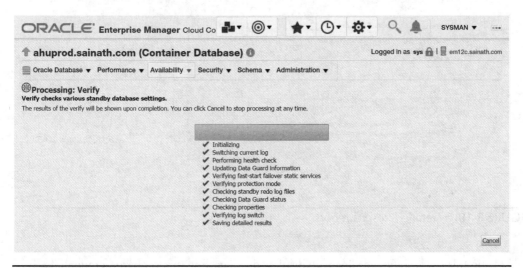

FIGURE 8-17. *Verification of standby database settings*

As a part of this process, the current log on the primary database is switched, followed by a verification of the fast-start failover services and a verification of the protection mode.

The standby redo log files are then checked. The log application on the standby is verified as successful, as shown in Figure 8-18.

The verify configuration process has produced a detailed report on the health of the Data Guard configuration, which helps in bringing any urgent issues to the attention of the DBA.

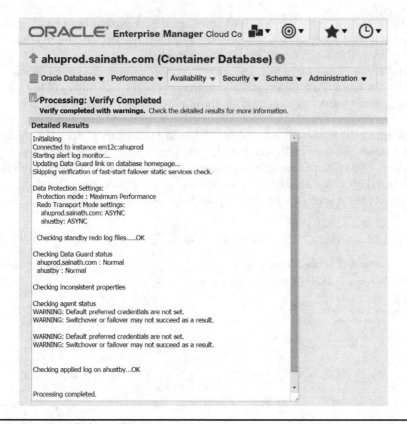

FIGURE 8-18.   *Detailed Results report*

In this case, some warnings are displayed, suggesting that preferred credentials should be set so that switchover or failover will succeed:

```
Checking agent status
WARNING: Default preferred credentials are not set.
WARNING: Switchover or failover may not succeed as a result.
```

You can set the preferred credentials as indicated. Do so for both the production and the standby database, by choosing Setup | Security | Preferred Credentials.

Choose Availability | Data Guard Performance to open the Data Guard
Performance screen shown in Figure 8-19.

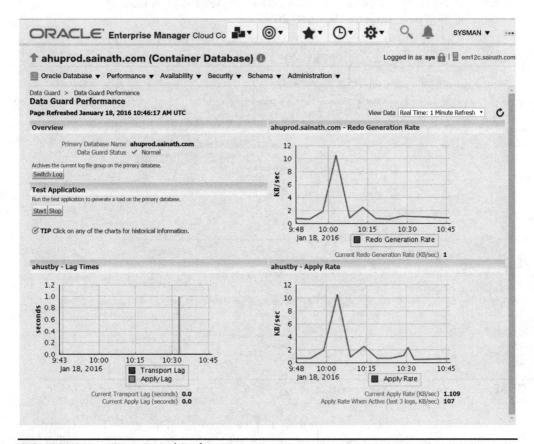

FIGURE 8-19. *Data Guard Performance screen*

Here you can monitor the redo generation rate in the primary database and the
apply rate and lag times in the standby database. In general, the redo generation and
apply rate graphs should appear approximately the same, as they do in this case.

You can click the Switch Log button to test the apply rate and lag time. This
archives the current log file group on the primary database.

Another useful option is the Test Application capability. Click the Start, Stop, or
Pause button to generate a load on the primary database and see how the Data
Guard configuration copes.

Data Guard Administration

Choose Availability | Data Guard Administration to see the Data Guard Administration page shown in Figure 8-20.

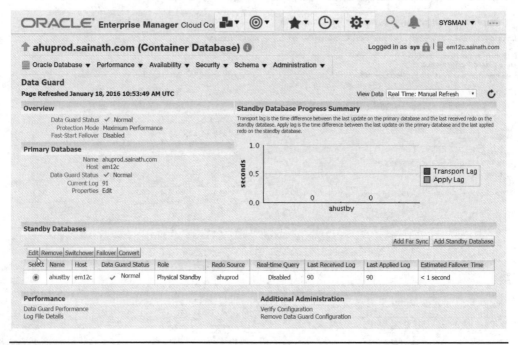

FIGURE 8-20.   *Data Guard administration overview*

Use this screen for the administration and management of the entire Data Guard configuration for this primary database and the standby databases associated with it. The screen shows the Data Guard Status, here shown as Normal. It also shows the Protection Mode used—by default, this is Maximum Performance.

You can also see if Fast-Start Failover is enabled or not. By default, this feature is disabled. Fast-Start Failover was introduced in Oracle Data Guard 10*g*. If this feature is enabled, the standby database is able to assume primary status—that is, a failover is performed without human intervention in case the primary database has failed for any reason.

Look at the Standby Database Progress Summary section, which displays the transport lag and apply lag in a bar chart. The transport lag is the time difference between the last update on the primary database and the last received redo on the standby. The apply lag pertains to the last applied redo on the standby. From these two lag calculations, the DBA can understand at a glance how far the standby is behind the primary, regarding both the transport of the logs and the application of the logs.

You can also see the status of both databases—Normal. This screen also displays the current log of the primary and the last received and last applied log on the standby. The estimated failover time is calculated as less than 1 second.

From here, you can also edit the Data Guard properties of the primary or standby. You can even add standby databases to this Data Guard configuration—up to 30 can be added with Oracle Data Guard versions 11.2 or 12.1.

The DBA can also elect to perform a switchover or a failover, directly from the screen, to the selected standby database. A disaster scenario resulting in unplanned downtime would necessitate a failover, whereas a switchover can be used for planned downtime, such as the installation of operating system patches or a machine upgrade.

Editing Standby Database Properties

From the Data Guard Administration page, you can edit the Data Guard properties of the primary or standby databases. In the Standby Databases section, click the radio button of the database you want to view, and then click Edit to view the Edit Standby Database Properties screen (Figure 8-21).

You'll see three tabs—General, Standby Role Properties, and Common Properties.

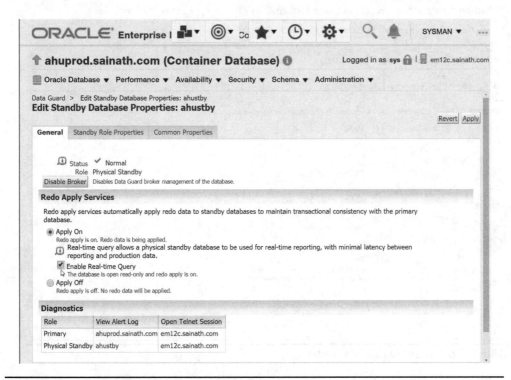

FIGURE 8-21. *Edit Standby Database Properties screen*

General Tab Settings

In the General tab, although it is not recommended, you can disable the Data Guard Broker management by clicking Disable Broker. Under Redo Apply Services, you can turn on or off the Redo Log Apply so that all application of redo logs to the standby database is either restarted or suspended.

You can also enable Real-Time Query on the Standby Database, which means that Redo Logs are being applied while the Database is open in the read-only mode. This is the Active Data Guard option and requires an additional license.

In the Diagnostics section, you can view the alert logs of the primary or standby databases or open a telnet session to either of the servers.

Enable Real-Time Query before moving to the Standby Role Properties tab.

Standby Role Properties Tab Settings

In the Standby Role Properties tab shown in Figure 8-22 you can modify the Redo Transport Mode to SYNC—the opposite of the default ASYNC.

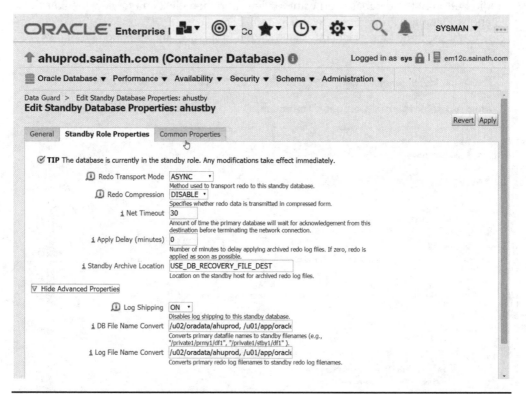

FIGURE 8-22. *Standby Role Properties tab*

You can also change the Net Timeout property in case it is a slower network, and change the Apply Delay to leave a specific time gap for applying logs between the standby and primary databases. If any manual errors are committed by users on the primary database, and if the DBA becomes aware of this in time, because of the time gap it may be possible to recover the data from the standby database or simply failover to the standby database.

These are important Data Guard properties and you must understand them and implement them carefully. Enterprise Manager Cloud Control 13c shows you all the properties at a glance, which helps you understand the possibilities.

Suppose, for example, that 15 minutes has been specified as the Apply Delay. This means that logs transported to the standby server will not be applied on the standby database until 15 minutes has passed. If a user now drops a table, and then makes the DBA aware of this immediately, the DBA can stop the application of logs on the standby and then make an effort to recover the dropped table from the standby, or failover to the standby if need be.

You can also enable Redo Compression on this tab, so that redo data is transmitted in compressed form.

Common Properties Tab Settings

Move to the Common Properties tab (Figure 8-23). This tab shows the Data Guard connect identifier in use and the number of log archive processes.

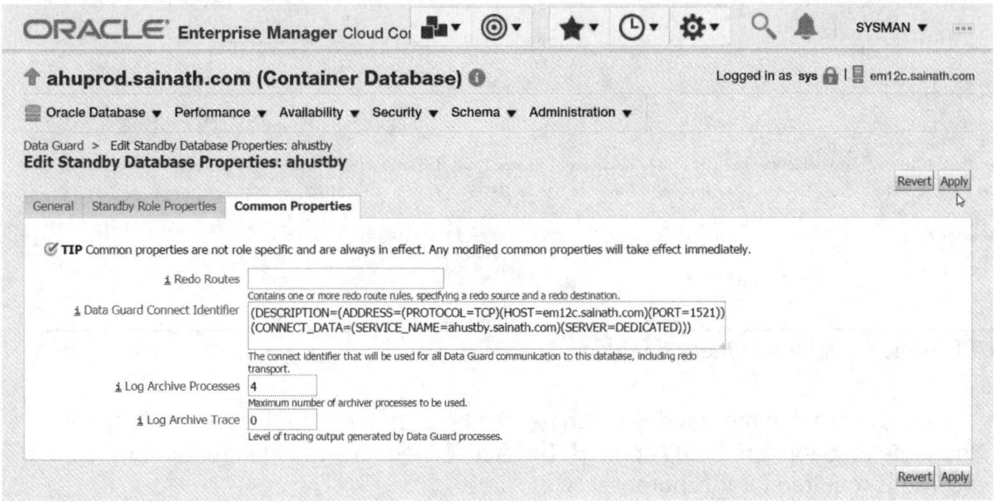

FIGURE 8-23. *Common Properties tab*

It also displays the Log Archive Trace level, which can be set to a higher value when debugging the Data Guard configuration.

A new feature in Database 12*c* enables you to add Redo Routes on this tab. These contain one or more redo route rules, where you can specify a redo source and a redo destination.

Saving and Checking Your Settings

After making your settings, click Apply. The properties are saved.

From the database home screen, choose Availability | Data Guard Administration. You can see that Real-time Query is now enabled on the standby database (Figure 8-24).

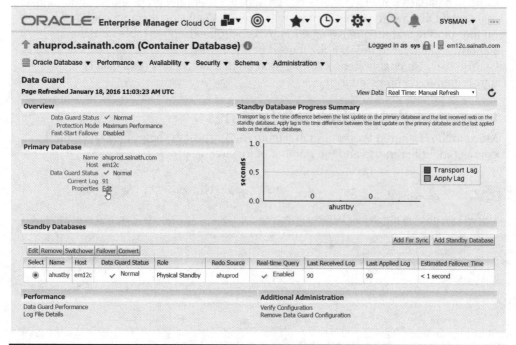

FIGURE 8-24. *Real-time Query enabled*

This means that the standby database can be used for reporting or other uses at the same time logs are being applied. The Active Data Guard database option license is required for this purpose.

Editing Primary Database Properties

From the Data Guard Administration page, you can edit the properties of the primary database by clicking the Edit link under Primary Database, as shown in Figure 8-24.

In the Edit Primary Database Properties screen (Figure 8-25), you'll see three tabs similar to those on the Standby Database Properties screen.

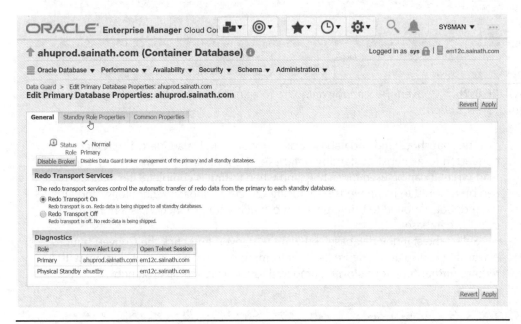

FIGURE 8-25. *Edit Primary Database Properties: General tab*

In the General tab, under Redo Transport Services, you can turn on or off the Redo Log Transport so that all transfer of redo logs to any of the standby databases is either restarted or suspended. You would do this in the case of a network outage or any similar event, when you know the logs cannot be sent to the standby database and it is pointless for the primary database to keep trying to send the logs across. Or, if the primary database was being brought down for maintenance work, turning the redo transport off would be a best practice.

The two other tabs, Standby Role Properties and Common Properties offer settings similar to those tabs in Standby Database Properties, discussed earlier.

Converting to Snapshot Standby

Move back to the Data Guard Administration page from the primary database home screen. Notice the Convert button in the Standby Databases section (Figure 8-26). You can click Convert to convert the standby database into a snapshot standby database.

Standby Databases

Add Far Sync   Add Standby Database

Edit | Remove | Switchover | Failover | Convert

Select	Name	Host	Data Guard Status	Role	Redo Source	Real-time Query	Last Received Log	Last Applied Log	Estimated Failover Time
◉	ahustby	em12c	✓ Normal	Physical Standby	ahuprod	✓ Enabled	90	90	< 1 second

FIGURE 8-26. *Convert the standby database to a snapshot standby database by clicking the Convert button.*

The snapshot standby database was introduced in Data Guard 11*g*. Once converted to a snapshot standby database, the database becomes open for read-write. It can be used for testing, and when testing is complete, the database can be restored to its previous state (using Oracle Flashback Technology) and all the redo logs applied to bring it back into synch with production as a normal standby database.

Select the standby database you want to convert and click the Convert button. A warning is displayed (Figure 8-27), informing you that a snapshot standby will require further time for failover, compared to a normal physical standby.

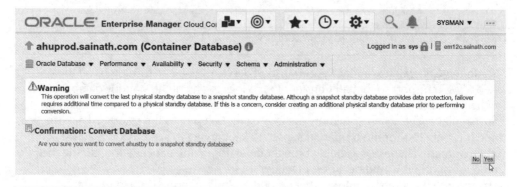

FIGURE 8-27. *Confirmation and warning for conversion*

Click the Yes button, and the database is converted to a snapshot standby database. After the conversion completes, the Data Guard configuration is automatically refreshed. The page will automatically forward to the overview page upon completion of the refresh. (If it does not do that, simply close the window and log back in to the Enterprise Manager console.)

The standby is now a snapshot standby, and this information is displayed in the Data Guard Administration page, shown in Figure 8-28.

Standby Databases

								Add Far Sync	Add Standby Database

Edit | Remove | Switchover | Failover | Convert

Select	Name	Host	Data Guard Status	Role	Redo Source	Real-time Query	Last Received Log	Last Applied Log	Estimated Failover Time
⦿	ahustby	em12c	✓ Normal	Snapshot Standby	ahuprod	N/A	91	90	48 seconds

FIGURE 8-28. *Current role of standby database: snapshot standby*

After your testing is completed, you can now convert the database back to the physical standby database by clicking the Convert button.

Switchover and Failover

Switchover and failover to the Standby Database are important features and the very purpose of using Oracle Data Guard. They are used in scheduled downtime (for switchovers) or unscheduled downtime (for failovers during a disaster situation).

With Oracle Database 12c, the standby is at the CDB level. It is not possible to switchover or failover to individual PDBs inside a CDB.

You have converted the database back to the physical standby, so the Data Guard Administration page (Figure 8-29) displays the database as a Physical Standby once again.

Standby Databases

								Add Far Sync	Add Standby Database

Edit | Remove | Switchover | Failover | Convert

Select	Name	Host	Data Guard Status	Role	Redo Source	Real-time Query	Last Received Log	Last Applied Log	Estimated Failover Time
⦿	ahustby	em12c	✓ Normal	Physical Standby	ahuprod	Disabled	94	93	82 seconds

FIGURE 8-29. *Beginning the switchover*

Performing a Switchover

It is easy to switch over to the standby database using Enterprise Manager. Click the Switchover button, and a message is displayed (Figure 8-30).

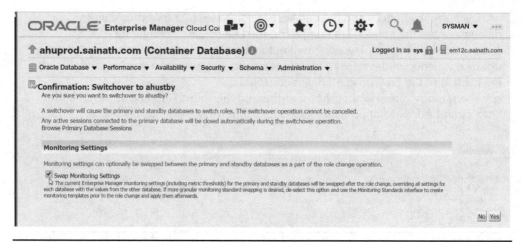

FIGURE 8-30. *Confirmation for switchover*

The switchover lets the primary database switch roles with the standby database. Since primary database sessions will be closed, you can browse them using the link on the page. Optionally, you can swap monitoring settings as well, including metric thresholds.

The Switchover process starts and displays the progress, as shown in Figure 8-31.

FIGURE 8-31. *Switchover Process*

When the switchover completes, the job and monitoring settings continue being transferred in the background when you click Return To Data Guard Overview.

On the Data Guard Administration page (Figure 8-32), you can see that the roles have reversed: the ahustby database is now the primary database and the ahuprod database is now the standby database.

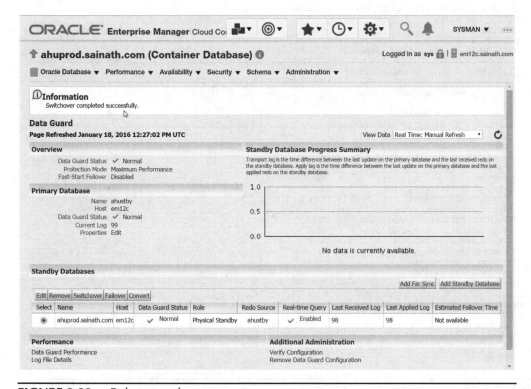

FIGURE 8-32. *Role reversal*

This can also be verified in the Data Guard command-line interface, `dgmgrl` (Figure 8-33).

The command-line interface of `dgmgrl` reflects the Enterprise Manager information and shows the reversed roles for the two databases. This is via the `show configuration verbose` command issued in `dgmgrl` after changing the Oracle environment to point to the ahuprod instance using the supplied oraenv script.

You can now perform the switchover again in Enterprise Manager to return the roles to their previous states.

```
[oracle@em12c ~]$ . oraenv
ORACLE_SID = [ahuprod] ? ahuprod
The Oracle base for ORACLE_HOME=/u01/app/oracle/product/12.1.0/dbhome_1 is /u01/app/oracle
[oracle@em12c ~]$
[oracle@em12c ~]$ dgmgrl
DGMGRL for Linux: Version 12.1.0.2.0 - 64bit Production

Copyright (c) 2000, 2013, Oracle. All rights reserved.

Welcome to DGMGRL, type "help" for information.
DGMGRL> connect sys
Password:
Connected as SYSDG.
DGMGRL>  show configuration verbose;

Configuration - ahuprod.sainath.com

  Protection Mode: MaxPerformance
  Members:
  ahustby - Primary database
    ahuprod - Physical standby database

  Properties:
    FastStartFailoverThreshold    = '30'
    OperationTimeout              = '30'
    TraceLevel                    = 'USER'
    FastStartFailoverLagLimit     = '30'
    CommunicationTimeout          = '180'
    ObserverReconnect             = '0'
    FastStartFailoverAutoReinstate = 'TRUE'
    FastStartFailoverPmyShutdown  = 'TRUE'
    BystandersFollowRoleChange    = 'ALL'
    ObserverOverride              = 'FALSE'
    ExternalDestination1          = ''
    ExternalDestination2          = ''
    PrimaryLostWriteAction        = 'CONTINUE'

Fast-Start Failover: DISABLED

Configuration Status:
SUCCESS

DGMGRL> █
```

FIGURE 8-33.   *Status of databases in dgmgrl*

Performing a Failover

A failover is used in disaster situations when the primary database has failed (for any reason) and is no longer available. In the failover process, the standby database must be opened as the primary database.

To perform a test, shut down the primary database ahuprod. Then choose Targets | Databases, and drill down to the home screen of the standby database ahustby. Select Availability | Data Guard Administration. Figure 8-34 shows the current state of the Data Guard configuration.

Since the primary database is down, the Data Guard Broker cannot reach it and the Data Guard status for this database shows the error "ORA-12514: TNS:listener does not currently know of service requested in connect descriptor."

Click the Failover button, and a confirmation screen is displayed (Figure 8-35).

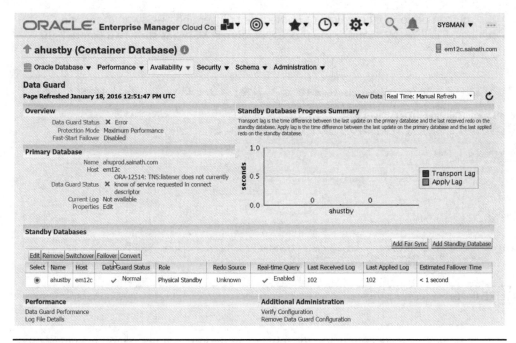

FIGURE 8-34. *State of the Data Guard configuration during failover*

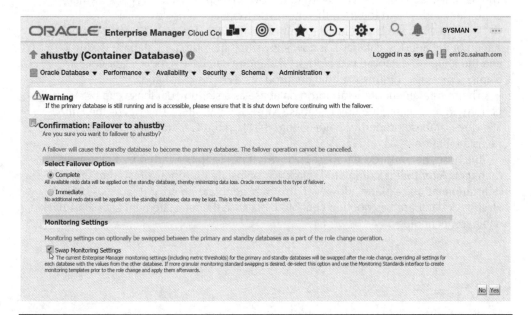

FIGURE 8-35. *Confirmation for failover to standby database*

You can perform a complete or immediate failover and also swap monitoring settings. Click Yes to confirm. The process of failover starts, as shown in Figure 8-36.

FIGURE 8-36.   *Failover process*

When the failover completes, the job and monitoring settings continue being transferred in the background when you click Return To Data Guard Overview. On completion of this process, the Data Guard configuration is automatically refreshed. The page will automatically forward to the overview page. If it does not do that, close the window and log in to the Enterprise Manager console.

Drill down to the Data Guard Administration page (Figure 8-37) from the home screen of the ahustby database. It now shows that the primary database is ahustby and the ahuprod database is the physical standby database. Under Data Guard Status, a message informs you that ahuprod needs to be reinstated.

The reinstatement of the ahuprod database as a standby database can be performed by clicking the link Database Must Be Reinstated. This opens the Edit Standby Database properties page (Figure 8-38). In the General tab, click the Reinstate button.

Because the ahuprod database is down, it needs to be started by Enterprise Manager. After that is completed, click the Reinstate button again so that the reinstatement takes place. However, this may generate an error (Figure 8-39) if Flashback database has not been enabled, because the reinstatement uses Flashback database technology.

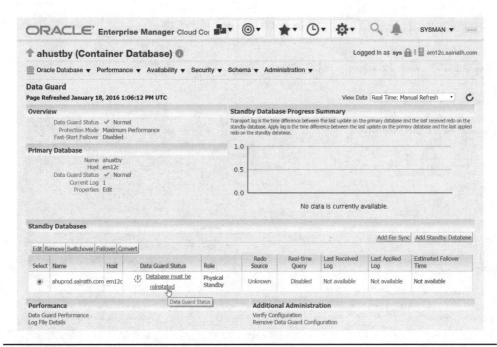

FIGURE 8-37. *Standby database needs to be reinstated.*

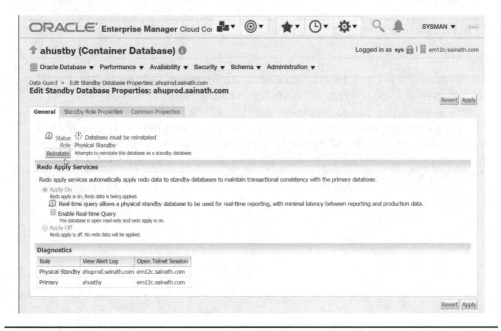

FIGURE 8-38. *Reinstating ahuprod as a standby database*

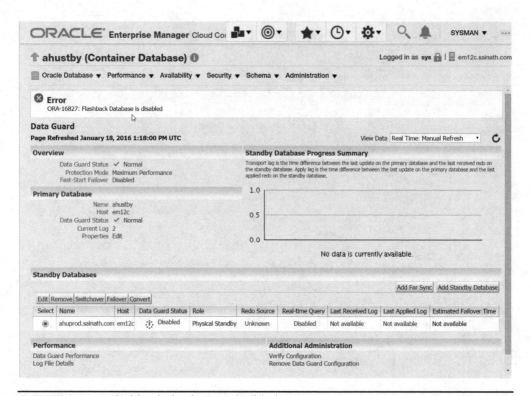

FIGURE 8-39. *Flashback database is disabled.*

Because of this error, the configuration status in dgmgrl changes to "the standby database needs to be re-created," as shown in Figure 8-40.

In this case, you can re-create the standby database as ahuprod, using the Enterprise Manager wizard that you used in earlier sections in this chapter. But this is a more tedious process. Alternatively, if Flashback database had been turned on in the ahuprod database initially, then the reinstatement of ahuprod as the standby database would have succeeded, as shown in Figure 8-41.

```
[oracle@em12c ~]$ . oraenv
ORACLE_SID = [ahustby] ? ahustby
The Oracle base for ORACLE_HOME=/u01/app/oracle/product/12.1.0/dbhome_1 is /u01/app/oracle
[oracle@em12c ~]$
[oracle@em12c ~]$ dgmgrl sys/welcome1
DGMGRL for Linux: Version 12.1.0.2.0 - 64bit Production

Copyright (c) 2000, 2013, Oracle. All rights reserved.

Welcome to DGMGRL, type "help" for information.
Connected as SYSDG.
DGMGRL>  show configuration verbose;

Configuration - ahuprod.sainath.com

  Protection Mode: MaxPerformance
  Members:
  ahustby - Primary database
    ahuprod - Physical standby database (disabled)
      ORA-16795: the standby database needs to be re-created

  Properties:
    FastStartFailoverThreshold      = '30'
    OperationTimeout                = '30'
    TraceLevel                      = 'USER'
    FastStartFailoverLagLimit       = '30'
    CommunicationTimeout            = '180'
    ObserverReconnect               = '0'
    FastStartFailoverAutoReinstate  = 'TRUE'
    FastStartFailoverPmyShutdown    = 'TRUE'
    BystandersFollowRoleChange      = 'ALL'
    ObserverOverride                = 'FALSE'
    ExternalDestination1            = ''
    ExternalDestination2            = ''
    PrimaryLostWriteAction          = 'CONTINUE'

Fast-Start Failover: DISABLED

Configuration Status:
SUCCESS

DGMGRL> █
```

FIGURE 8-40.   *Standby database needs to be re-created.*

As you can see, ahuprod is now the physical standby for the production database ahustby.

You can now failover back to ahuprod using the same procedure, so that ahuprod becomes the production database again, and ahustby becomes the standby again—as was the case previously.

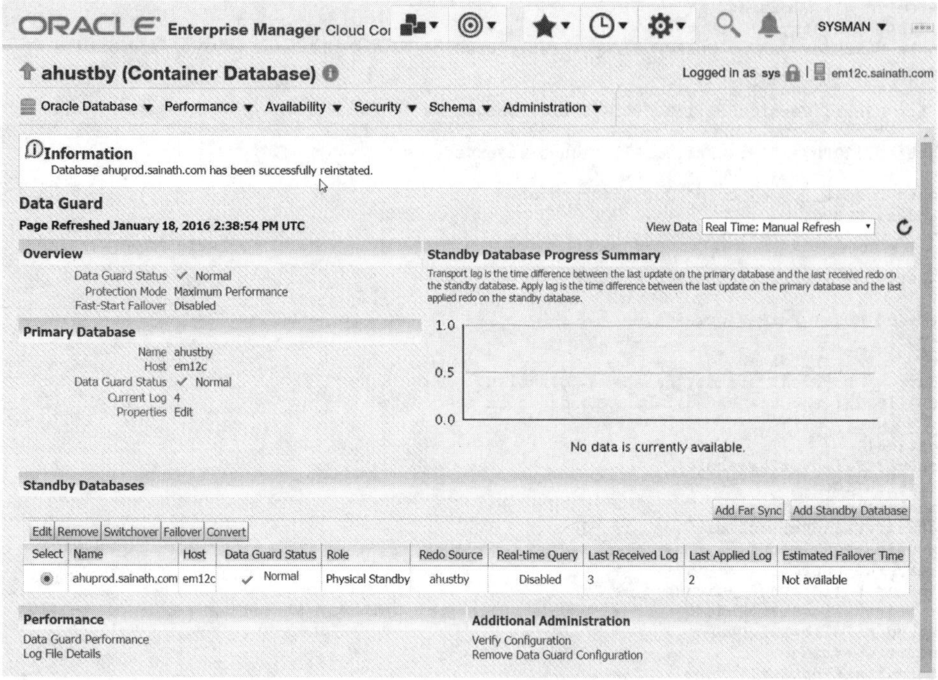

FIGURE 8-41. *Reinstatement of ahuprod as standby database succeeded*

Far Sync in Oracle Database 12*c*

Oracle Database 12*c* has a new kind of standby, *far sync*. An Oracle Data Guard far sync instance is actually a remote Oracle Data Guard destination that accepts redo from the primary database. The redo is then shipped to other members of the Oracle Data Guard configuration, such as other standby databases.

A far sync instance has a control file, receives redo into standby redo logs, and archives those logs to local archived redo logs. A far sync instance does not have user data files, so it cannot be opened for access, cannot run redo apply, and can never become a primary database (no switchover or failover) or any type of standby database.

Far sync instances are part of the Oracle Active Data Guard Far Sync feature, which requires an Oracle Active Data Guard license. The advantage is that you can have a far sync instance in close proximity (thus having low network latency) with the production instance, and it can therefore be kept in SYNC mode (achieving zero data loss) with the primary. The far sync instance can then ship redo data in ASYNC mode to a standby instance in a far-off disaster recovery location with high network latency. Using far sync achieves the benefits of maximum protection as well as performance.

Creation of far sync instances is supported in Enterprise Manager 13*c* Cloud Control. Also, externally created far sync instances will show up on the Data Guard Administration page.

On the Data Guard Administration page, you'll see a Add Far Sync button (Figure 8-42). Click that button.

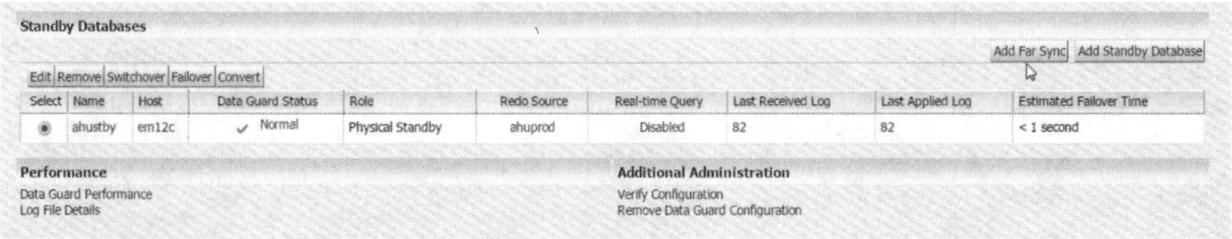

Standby Databases

Select	Name	Host	Data Guard Status	Role	Redo Source	Real-time Query	Last Received Log	Last Applied Log	Estimated Failover Time
⦿	ahustby	em12c	✓ Normal	Physical Standby	ahuprod	Disabled	82	82	< 1 second

Edit | Remove | Switchover | Failover | Convert

Add Far Sync | Add Standby Database

Performance
Data Guard Performance
Log File Details

Additional Administration
Verify Configuration
Remove Data Guard Configuration

FIGURE 8-42. *Click the Add Far Sync button.*

Note that the process of creating a new far sync instance should be done before you have run a failover test between the primary and the standby instance. If a bidirectional failover between the primary and the standby instance has been completed before you create the far sync instance, then the creation of the far sync may fail with a null configuration error from the Data Guard Broker. This will occur at the Add Far Sync to Data Guard Configuration step in the Enterprise Manager deployment procedure.

After you click the button, the Create Far Sync wizard starts. The first step is to specify the Host and Oracle Home locations (Figure 8-43).

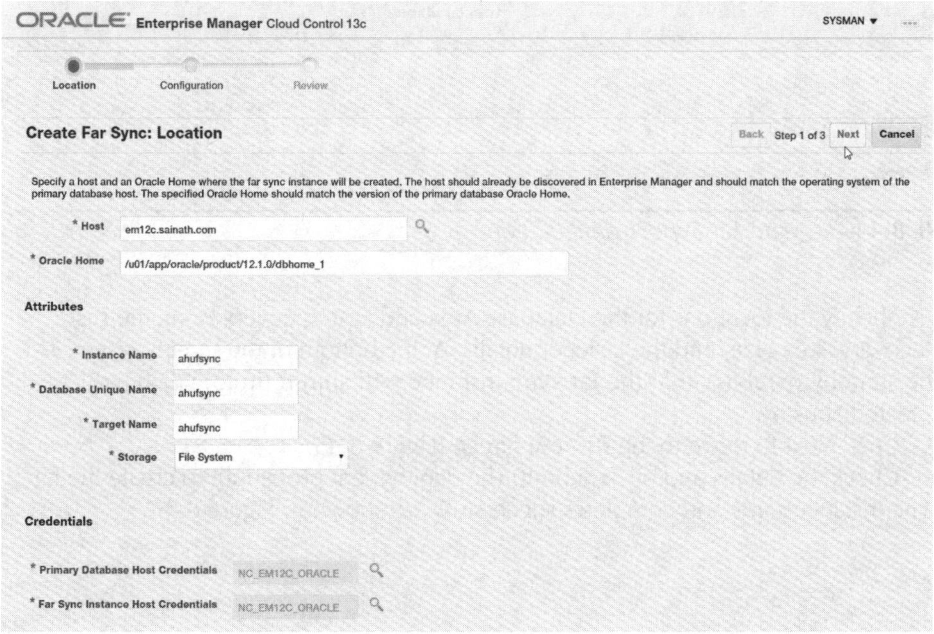

ORACLE Enterprise Manager Cloud Control 13c   SYSMAN ▼   ⋯

Location   Configuration   Review

Create Far Sync: Location   Back Step 1 of 3 Next Cancel

Specify a host and an Oracle Home where the far sync instance will be created. The host should already be discovered in Enterprise Manager and should match the operating system of the primary database host. The specified Oracle Home should match the version of the primary database Oracle Home.

* Host   em12c.sainath.com

* Oracle Home   /u01/app/oracle/product/12.1.0/dbhome_1

Attributes

* Instance Name   ahufsync

* Database Unique Name ahufsync

* Target Name   ahufsync

* Storage   File System

Credentials

* Primary Database Host Credentials   NC_EM12C_ORACLE

* Far Sync Instance Host Credentials   NC_EM12C_ORACLE

FIGURE 8-43. *Create Far Sync: Location*

In this step, we have named the far sync instance as ahufsync, specified the host and Oracle home, and the credentials for the primary database host and the far sync instance host. Click Next to start the Configuration step (Figure 8-44).

FIGURE 8-44. *Create Far Sync: Configuration*

Specify the locations for the Database Area and Fast Recovery Area, the Fast Recovery Area Size, and the Listener details. At the bottom of the screen, select the standby database that the far sync instance will ship redo to. We have selected ahustby.

Click Next to move to the Review screen (Figure 8-45).

Check the details and click Submit. The deployment procedure to create the far sync instance starts and completes successfully, as shown in Figure 8-46.

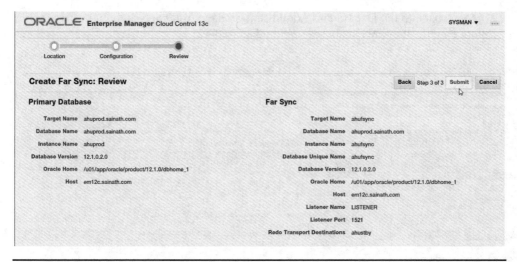

FIGURE 8-45.   *Create Far Sync: Review*

FIGURE 8-46.   *Successful creation of far sync*

Move back to the Data Guard Administration page. You can see the new far sync instance in the Standby Databases section (Figure 8-47).

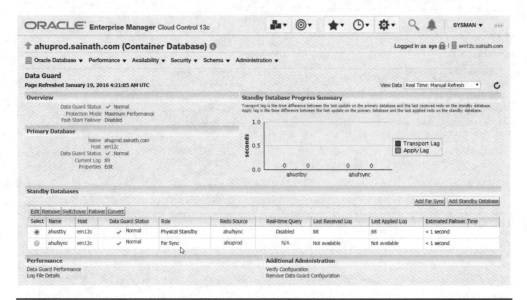

FIGURE 8-47. *Far Sync in Data Guard Administration*

The Redo Source of the far sync instance ahufsync is shown in the table as ahuprod, whereas the Redo Source of the physical standby instance ahustby is shown as ahufsync. This means redo data is sent from ahuprod to ahufsync, and then to ahustby. Enterprise Manager has set up the redo flow in the most appropriate manner for the far sync instance.

The transport lag and apply lag graphs also show the details for ahufsync as well as ahustby.

Move to the Data Guard Performance screen (Figure 8-48).

The Data Guard Performance screen shows the lag time and apply rate graphs for ahustby as well as ahufsync.

As mentioned, a far sync instance would normally use the Redo Transport Mode of SYNC to achieve maximum data protection. To change this property from ASYNC to SYNC, go to the Data Guard Administration page and edit the far sync instance properties. Change the Redo Transport Mode in the Standby Role Properties tab (Figure 8-49).

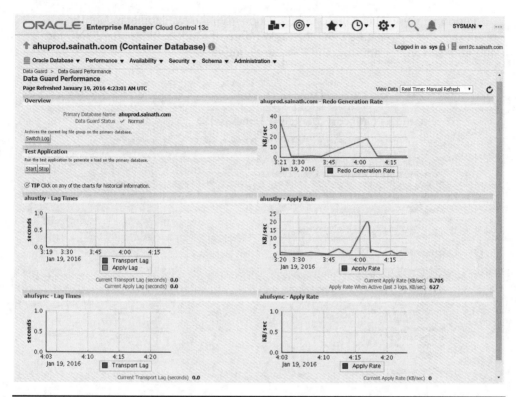

FIGURE 8-48. *Far Sync in Data Guard performance*

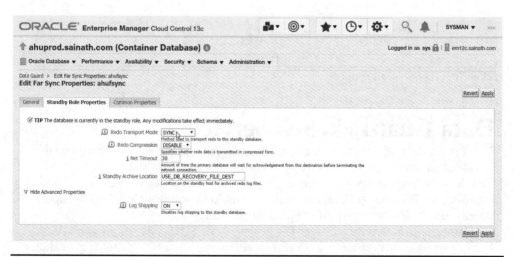

FIGURE 8-49. *Changing to SYNC Redo Transport Mode*

Perform a Verify Data Guard Configuration from the Availability menu. The results are shown in Figure 8-50: the Redo Transport Mode settings are ASYNC for ahuprod, ASYNC for ahustby, and SYNC for ahufsync.

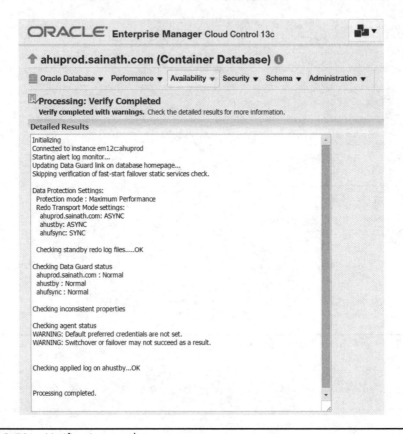

FIGURE 8-50. *Verification results*

Data Guard via Self Service

The standby database creation discussed so far in this chapter was performed by the private cloud administrator. This would mainly be for the 11*g* database pools used for schema self-service provisioning or the 12*c* CDB pools used for PDB self-service provisioning. The private cloud administrator would be responsible for setting up the standby databases for these pools behind the scenes.

Starting from Enterprise Manager 12*c* Release 4, the Self Service Application (SSA) user can include the creation of a standby database when requesting a service instance.

Beginning with Enterprise Manager 12*c* Release 5, the SSA user can also request a standby database from the Self Service Portal after the initial requested database has been created by clicking a button on the SSA user's database home page.

Summary

As demonstrated in this chapter, you can set up, manage, and monitor standby databases for any primary database using Oracle Enterprise Manager Cloud Control 13*c*. The web interface provided by Oracle for creating and managing Data Guard configurations is advanced in all aspects and extremely easy to use.

DBAs can use Enterprise Manager for the day-to-day monitoring and management of Data Guard configurations. They can also perform switchovers or failovers to the standby for planned or unplanned downtimes, and they can do all this from the Enterprise Manager Cloud Control 13*c* console or the `dgmgrl` interface.

Enterprise Manager Cloud Control 13*c* supplies a common, standard interface to set up and manage Oracle Data Guard for Oracle 9*i*, 10*g*, 11*g*, and Oracle Database 12*c*. Advanced features of Oracle Data Guard in different Database versions correspond to the version and are automatically offered to the DBA, thus reducing the learning curve.

Enterprise Manager Cloud Control 13*c* can be very useful in implementing Oracle Data Guard for the varied Oracle Database versions in a large company.

This concludes the book. We hope you have enjoyed reading it.

Index

Join the Largest Tech Community in the World

 Download the latest software, tools, and developer templates

 Get exclusive access to hands-on trainings and workshops

 Grow your professional network through the Oracle ACE Program

 Publish your technical articles – and get paid to share your expertise

Join the Oracle Technology Network
Membership is free. Visit community.oracle.com

🐦 @OracleOTN 📘 facebook.com/OracleTechnologyNetwork

Climb the Career Ladder

Think about it—97 percent of the Fortune 500 companies run Oracle solutions. Why wouldn't you choose Oracle certification to secure your future? With certification through Oracle, your resume gets noticed, your chances of landing your dream job improve, you become more marketable, and you earn more money. It's simple. Oracle certification helps you get hired and get paid for your skills.

93%
Hiring managers who say IT certifications are beneficial and provide value to the company[1]

7%
Salary growth for Oracle Certified professionals[5]

70%
Believe that Oracle certification improved their earning power[2]

90%
Say that Oracle certification gives them credibility when looking for a new job[2]

68%
Think that certification has made them more in demand[3]

6x
Increased LinkedIn profile views for people with certifications, boosting their visibility and career opportunities[4]

Take the next step
http://education.oracle.com/certification/press

[1] "Value of IT Certifications," CompTIA, October 14, 2014, [2] Oracle Certification Survey, [3] "Certification: It's a Journey Not a Destination," Certification Magazine 2015 Salary Edition, [4] "The Future Value of Certifications: Insights from LinkedIn's Data Trove," ATP 2015 Innovations in Testing, [5] Certification Magazine 2015 Annual Salary Survey

ORACLE®

Push a Button

Move Your Java Apps
to the Oracle Cloud

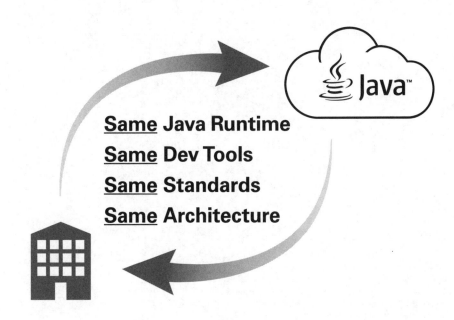

Same Java Runtime
Same Dev Tools
Same Standards
Same Architecture

... or Back to Your Data Center

Reach More than 640,000 Oracle Customers with Oracle Publishing Group

Connect with the Audience that Matters Most to Your Business

Oracle Magazine
The Largest IT Publication in the World
Circulation: 325,000
Audience: IT Managers, DBAs, Programmers, and Developers

Profit
Business Insight for Enterprise-Class Business Leaders to Help Them Build a Better Business Using Oracle Technology
Circulation: 90,000
Audience: Top Executives and Line of Business Managers

Java Magazine
The Essential Source on Java Technology, the Java Programming Language, and Java-Based Applications
Circulation: 225,00 and Growing Steady
Audience: Corporate and Independent Java Developers, Programmers, and Architects

For more information or to sign up for a FREE subscription: Scan the QR code to visit Oracle Publishing online.

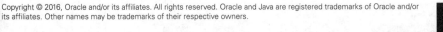

Beta Test
Oracle
Software

Get a first look at our newest products—and help perfect them. You must meet the following criteria:

- ✔ **Licensed Oracle customer or Oracle PartnerNetwork member**

- ✔ **Oracle software expert**

- ✔ **Early adopter of Oracle products**

Please apply at: pdpm.oracle.com/BPO/userprofile

If your interests match upcoming activities, we'll contact you. Profiles are kept on file for 12 months.